MODERN ART OF SOUTHEAST ASIA: INTRODUCTIONS FROM A TO Z

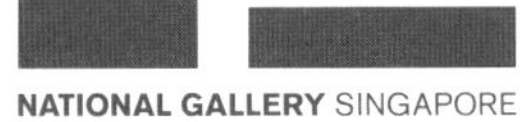

NATIONAL GALLERY SINGAPORE

Roger Nelson

What is "modern" about the modern art of Southeast Asia? What is "Southeast Asian" about this art? And what range of images, objects, activities and concepts can be encompassed by the word "art" in this context? What kinds of concerns does modern art engage with and illuminate, visually, as well as in its ideas and its relationship to society?

These are some of the questions which have animated me in writing this book. In it, I introduce many of the most significant ideas that have shaped the making of modern art that engages with Southeast Asia, as well as the terms that have framed the thinking, writing, and discussion about that art. These ideas and terms are often daring or even dangerous, sometimes beautiful, and frequently baffling. They are also profoundly exciting.

The pages that follow are filled with hundreds of stories about artists and artworks, texts and events, anecdotes and controversies. Taken together, the historical characters in these many accounts share a resolve to critically reappraise the art and ideas of the past, and to reimagine the possibilities of a modern art *in*, *from*, and *for* Southeast Asia. This book discusses more than 230 artists who are from Southeast Asia, or have a connection to the region: some of them are household names, and others are little known, even in specialist circles. The book also includes more than 250 illustrations, all in full colour, which include well-known and iconic artworks, as well as others which have been rarely seen.

ON THE EMERGENCE OF MODERN ART IN SOUTHEAST ASIA

Modern art — understood in the broadest sense as art which reassesses and, in some way, departs from the art of the past — emerged in Southeast Asia mostly during the 19th and 20th centuries. Part of what makes this art modern is its emphatic (indeed, often radical) concern with being new; it is also modern because it developed through its relationship to the modern world, which transformed through the formation of nation-states, the acceleration of industry and communications, the globalising of trade, and other dramatic upheavals.

Modern art came about through a multi-directional exchange of not just ideas, but also people and objects, within the region, as well as with other parts of Asia and the world beyond. This includes important exchanges with Europe and North America, which had been present in the region as colonising powers. Because of this, the history of modern art in Southeast Asia is inseparable from the history of colonialism in this region — yet it is also not reducible to this phenomenon alone. The role of colonialism in shaping modern art is best considered in relation to other crucial factors, especially both longstanding and newly emerging connections within Asia. References to colonial encounters — which always involved exchanges and negotiations, as well as domination — recur throughout what follows. One of the many values of studying modern art is its capacity to illuminate the historical nature and enduring legacies of colonialism in this region.

Southeast Asia is a vast, tropical territory of mountains and plains, archipelagos and peninsulas, which lies south of China, east of India, and north of Australia. The region is most often characterised by its extraordinary internal diversity, of all kinds. It is therefore unsurprising that the ideas, techniques, and institutions of modern art took very disparate forms in different places within Southeast Asia, and that these aspects of modern art emerged at quite different times throughout the region. In some places, aspects of modern art predate the 19th century, and various ideas about modern art also continue to unfold and develop today, alongside discussions about contemporary art.

Notwithstanding the great variety of forms that modern art has taken, and the differing times at which it has emerged, some aspects of this diverse history have been commonly shared across Southeast Asia. In most areas, the ideas, techniques, and institutions of modern art — including art schools — first emerged at least in part due to the involvement of colonial individuals or authorities. Moreover, in most areas, after this initial emergence, these ideas, techniques and institutions of modern art have been sharply challenged in various forms of debate. This pattern of emergence followed by contestation has recurred throughout the region, albeit in quite different ways, and not at the same time.

In the past, most studies of modern art in this region were focused on examples from a single nation; however, in recent years this has shifted, with more scholars choosing to compare modern art from different parts of the region, and to emphasise the importance of exchange and interaction among artists and other figures. One important effect of this shift has been to counter the influence of nationalisms in the researching and telling of art history. Nationalisms emerged in Southeast Asia in part as a challenge to colonialism—as an aspect of the struggle for independence—yet the phenomenon is also in some ways a product of the colonial encounter, since European powers also played important roles, alongside Southeast Asians, in inventing and articulating the identities and borders of modern nations. This is one reason why when we study the modern art of Southeast Asia, we also pay attention to art made by Europeans and others who visited or lived in the region, especially during colonial times, even while our primary focus is on art made by Southeast Asian people.

This book follows the intraregional (sometimes called "transnational") approach to narrating the histories of modern art in Southeast Asia, instead of focusing on any single nation. Artists and artworks from distant places and disparate times are frequently discussed in relation to each other. In this regard, the book is also transhistorical in approach. I repeatedly draw unconventional and perhaps unexpected connections between artists, artworks, and historical moments not usually discussed in relation to each other, and invite readers to observe the striking and—I hope—often illuminating effects of these juxtapositions and comparisons. As there is not a fixed, stable, or widely agreed-upon canon for the modern art of Southeast Asia, and as the study of modern art is continuing to take on new forms and functions within the region, I believe it is especially valuable to find novel paths through this history, rather than relying solely on more established or better-known narratives. At several points throughout the book, I also introduce more recent examples of contemporary art. While contemporary art is often thought of as distinct from modern art in the way it is produced and circulated, it nevertheless also emerges from and extends modern art in important ways. Discussing contemporary art alongside modern art reveals that the key ideas and terms relating to modern art continue to be vital today, and also continue to shift and transform.

ON THE FORMAT OF THE BOOK

This book is structured as a series of 60 entries which are arranged alphabetically. These texts may be read in any sequence: it is not necessary, and indeed not intended, that the book be read from front to back in the conventional manner. Rather, I hope that readers will be able to discover their own links and overlaps between ideas and terms. In each entry, related key terms are <u>underlined</u>, indicating that one can read more about those topics in other entries. Readers can flow from reading about one idea to another in any way they choose; the book does not impose any single overarching narrative. I have also deliberately avoided arranging the book according to areas or themes, as this would have unduly emphasised my own suggested connections between the assembled ideas, while obscuring other possible trajectories through the entries.

In deciding on which 60 ideas and terms to discuss in this book, my aim has been to gesture toward the inestimable breadth of thinking that has contributed to the making of and discourse on the modern art of Southeast Asia. Most of the entries deal with ideas and terms that have had a very broad impact across Southeast Asia throughout much of the 19th and 20th centuries, and continuing today. A great number of these ideas and terms, like <u>realism</u> and <u>abstraction</u>, have been hotly debated, and taken on quite different meanings in different places and at varying times. Terms such as these may originate in Western art historical contexts, but have often transformed through the process of transfer to and adoption within Southeast Asia. Many terms are used in quite different ways in this region. It can be exciting to observe the shifts and distinctions in ideas and terms which may be familiar from discussions of Western art, yet take on new meanings when used in relation to the modern art of Southeast Asia. Some entries in this book, like those dealing with <u>women</u> or the <u>nation</u>, make use of categories that are not typically discussed in relation to modern art. A smaller number of the entries in this book relate to developments in art that are specific to only a certain period, or only a limited range of places within Southeast Asia. For example, ideas about <u>conceptual</u>

and <u>contemporary</u> approaches in art only emerged during and after the 1970s, while <u>genocide</u> and <u>socialist realism</u> have directly affected the development of modern art in only some Southeast Asian countries.

I have also tried, wherever possible, to point to the multiplicity of ideas at play in the modern art of Southeast Asia: ideas that have at times been pitched sharply against one another, as well as ideas that have emerged in remarkably similar fashions among people in distant places, at different times. As an art historian, I am deeply committed to the value of history—which means the value of *histories*, or, put another way, the value of many stories about many pasts, involving many people and objects, in many places. Central to these stories are the histories of ideas, including about what modern art should be, and what Southeast Asia can be. Every artwork is also an idea, even while it may be many other things as well.

<table>
<tr><td>

ON THE SCOPE OF
THE BOOK

</td><td>

I have said that this book introduces many of the most significant ideas and terms that have shaped the making and discussion of the modern art of Southeast Asia. In explicating these ideas and terms, I have introduced many of the most widely cited examples of artists and artworks that have played a role in the emergence and development of the modern art of this region. Yet I have also sought to strike a balance, juxtaposing more famous names and images with figures that are lesser known. Even accepting that it is plainly impossible for any book to include everyone or everything, some readers may be surprised by my inclusions and omissions.

Two key factors have affected what has been included in this book. The first is my own interests and priorities, as an art historian, and as a student of and resident in Southeast Asia who is not Southeast Asian. These interests and priorities have necessarily shaped my reading and writing. For example, I have deliberately discussed many artists who are women, and have also considered many depictions of women in art, because I believe that these offer crucial insights which have too often been overlooked in accounts featuring (overwhelmingly, but usually unapologetically) mostly men. As a result of my efforts to include mention of as many historically significant women as possible, around one quarter of the artists discussed here are female. Although still low, this number is much higher than in most previous books on the modern art of this region.

The second factor affecting the book is the uneven nature of the available scholarship and resources on modern art of this region. Existing writings have not evenly distributed their attentions across the geographies of Southeast Asia, nor across different artistic media, or the decades and centuries in question. Perhaps regrettably, the artists discussed here do not constitute a representative indication of the countries or cultures of the region. Moreover, despite my interest in photography, sculpture, and other forms of visual culture, the book discusses paintings more than it does any other art form. In part, this reflects the privileged position of painting as the most celebrated medium for modern art. Yet instead of offering separate entries on this and various other media or art forms (like sculpture, or installation, or batik or lacquer, for example), throughout what follows, the book emphasises transmedial intersections between different kinds of artworks; I suggest that these intersections offer special insights into art and its reception.

It is my hope that readers will embark on further reading and research of their own, including to redress the inevitable imbalances in this book. Readers wishing to delve deeper into any of the topics introduced here may consult the list of works cited for some suggestions. Although I have occasionally drawn on my own original research (both published and unpublished), what follows relies chiefly on my reading of secondary materials. The asymmetries of this book are thus a result of my own preferences and shortcomings, and of the choices made by the writers whose work I have drawn on here.

</td></tr>
<tr><td>

ON QUESTIONS

</td><td>

In one of the earliest books to survey the arts of this region, first published in 1927, the art historian and curator Ananda Coomaraswamy affirms that the history of premodern architecture and artefacts in the area now called Southeast Asia "deserves in the general history of art a higher place than can be denoted by the term colonial...

</td></tr>
</table>

it derives its energy from indigenous sources." He also notes that "only within the last twenty years" has the art of this region "been seriously studied…only the broad outlines have been deciphered, and there remain to be investigated innumerable undescribed monuments, and unsolved problems of more than local interest."

While Coomaraswamy's book predates the popularisation of the term "Southeast Asia," it encompasses discussion of much of the same territories, including parts of the countries now known as Myanmar, Thailand, Cambodia, Vietnam, and Indonesia, as well as Sri Lanka, India, and other parts of what is now known as South Asia.

What has changed in the decades since Coomaraswamy was writing? What remains unchanged? What insights have been offered by the many scholars who have come after him, and who have chosen to study modern art, instead of premodern traditions—many of whom are cited throughout this book? And when considering the modern art of Southeast Asia, how might we also learn from discussions of premodern objects and cultures from this region? How might we be enriched by keeping in mind the premodern as one implicit point of comparison when looking to modern art?

Let us add these questions to those asked at the beginning of this introduction, about what is "modern," what is "Southeast Asian," and what is "art." The pages that follow do not offer easy answers to these questions. But they do offer some ways to consider the key ideas from which the modern art of this region (in Coomaraswamy's words) "derives its energy." I hope readers will find these "of more than local interest."

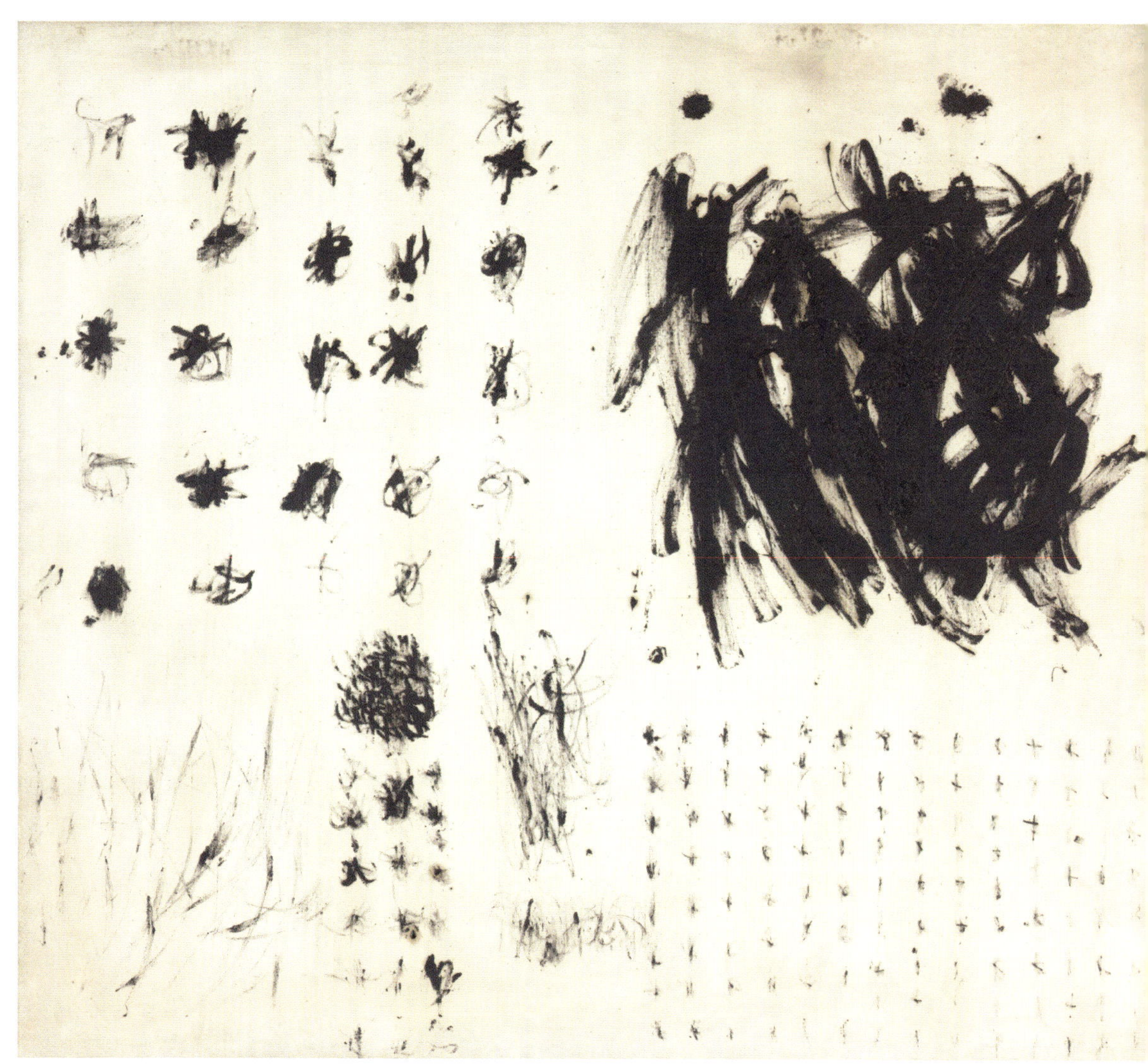

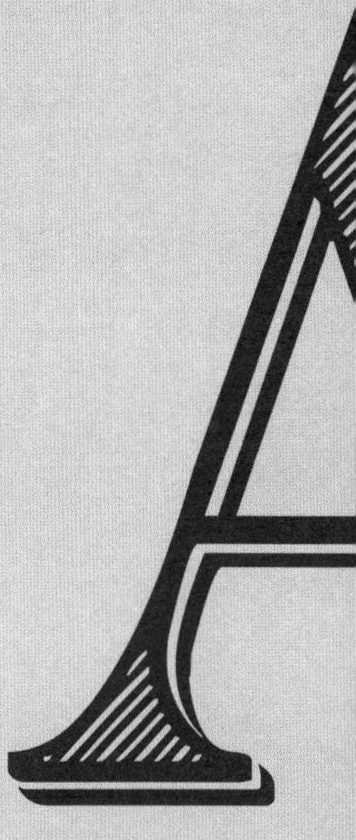

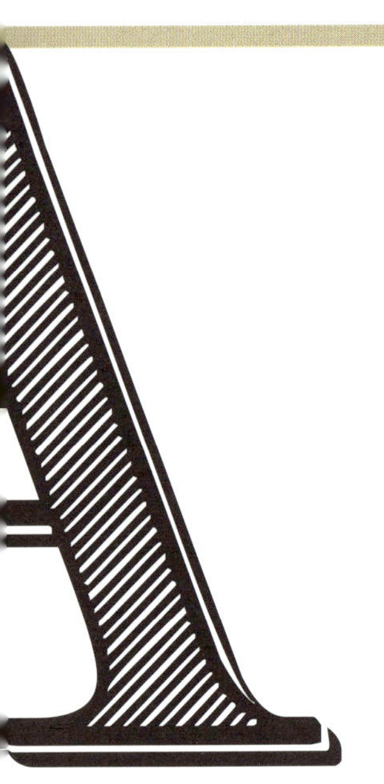

ABSTRACTION

Abstract art is art which does not attempt to depict a "real" scene, person, or object, or which deviates substantially from a realistic, representational approach. A complex and diverse notion, abstraction appears in modern art throughout most of Southeast Asia, yet in vastly divergent forms, and for many different reasons.

While abstraction is usually thought of internationally as a quintessentially modern phenomenon, many premodernsculptures and other objects may also be considered abstract—or "aniconic," a term more commonly used to describe religious artworks and objects. The *linga*, for example, is an abstract way of representing the Hindu deity Shiva. Appearing throughout Southeast Asia, the *linga* (also called *lingam* or *shivalinga*) is often worshipped in Buddhist and other contexts, as well as exhibited for its sculptural qualities.

The *linga* is usually understood to represent the phallus, and is commonly found resting on a *yoni*, which is usually understood to represent the vulva. In some cases, the resemblance to sex organs is sculpted quite explicitly, whereas in others, the form is much more stylised. Both the *linga* and *yoni* may nevertheless be considered abstract or aniconic, since they are worshipped as embodiments of deities or other <u>spiritual</u> forces.

The *yoni-linga* ensemble has been analysed in a dazzling variety of ways, demonstrating the ability of art—especially abstraction—to generate richly diverse philosophical interpretations. For example, art historians including Ashley Thompson have examined the *yoni* and *linga* in relation to the modern phenomenon of placing sculpture on a pedestal. We might conventionally think of sculpture as more important than its pedestal, but as Thompson reminds us, often "the artwork needs the pedestal in order to be the artwork that it is." So, too, a *linga* and *yoni* might mutually depend on one another to produce meaning. Thompson's analysis draws on the Algerian-French writer Jacques Derrida's notion of "parergon," a kind of formal and conceptual supplement or frame. This is an example of how abstract art can inspire diverse and challenging modes of analysis.

Like the *yoni* and *linga*—ancient forms still being produced today—modern abstract art also takes many forms, and can be approached in vastly different ways. In most areas of Southeast Asia, modern abstract art emerged during the mid-20th century. It is sometimes thought of in binary opposition to <u>realism</u>, and indeed some <u>social realist</u> and <u>socialist realist</u> artists argued against abstraction,

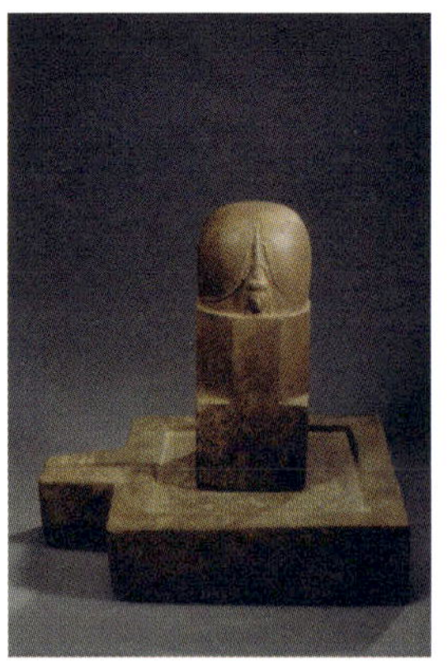

Shiva lingam and yoni. 9th century CE. Sandstone, 52 x 41 x 11 cm; 41 x 15.5 cm. Collection of the Asian Civilisations Museum, Singapore.

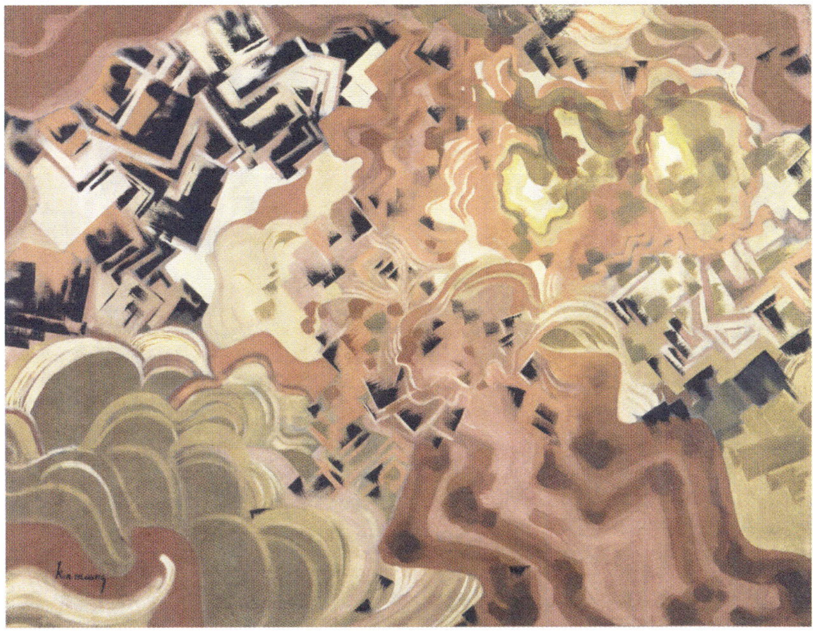

U King Maung (Bank). *Mandalay*. 1960s. Oil on canvas, 68.2 x 91.2 cm. Collection of Fukuoka Asian Art Museum.

considering it indulgent or foreign, in part because it was heavily promoted by the United States within the context of the Cold War. Yet despite this and other <u>debates</u> about what forms modern art should take, many other Southeast Asian artists have worked within a spectrum that encompasses both abstraction and representation. To view abstraction as totally opposed to figuration is overly simplistic.

Some early examples of modern abstract painting in Southeast Asia use straight lines and rectilinear block forms to convey a sense of urbanisation. Works by artists like Arturo Luz and Ahmad Sadali evoke in semi-abstract form the geometric appearance of modern cities, as well as their density, dynamism, dizzying energy, and perhaps also claustrophobic pressure. Works such as *Mandalay* by U King Maung (Bank) adopt a similar approach.

At around the same time, other artists like Ithipol Thangchalok, Sudjana Kerton, and Grace Selvanayagam were using abstraction to instead convey an impression of the experience of vegetation and natural <u>landscapes</u>. Selvanayagam combined the inherent flatness of batik and printmaking with a lively and radiant use of colour and composition. Ithipol, on the other hand, wrote of his "use of natural forms in silhouette and bands of color that reflect the concepts of time and change," and claimed that his "use of physical images was steadily reduced until they completely disappeared… in order to convey the 'abstract essence of

Arturo Luz
b. 1926, Philippines

Ahmad Sadali
b. 1924, Indonesia; d. 1987, Indonesia

U King Maung (Bank)
b. circa 1908, Myanmar; d. 1983, Myanmar

Ithipol Thangchalok
b. 1946, Thailand

Sudjana Kerton
b. 1922, Indonesia; d. 1994, Indonesia

Grace Selvanayagam
b. 1936, Malaysia

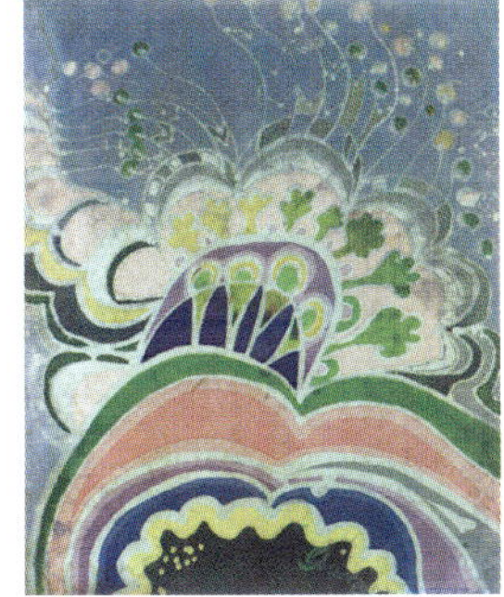

Grace Selvanayagam. Untitled. 1969. Batik, 102 x 83 cm. Collection of the Zain family.

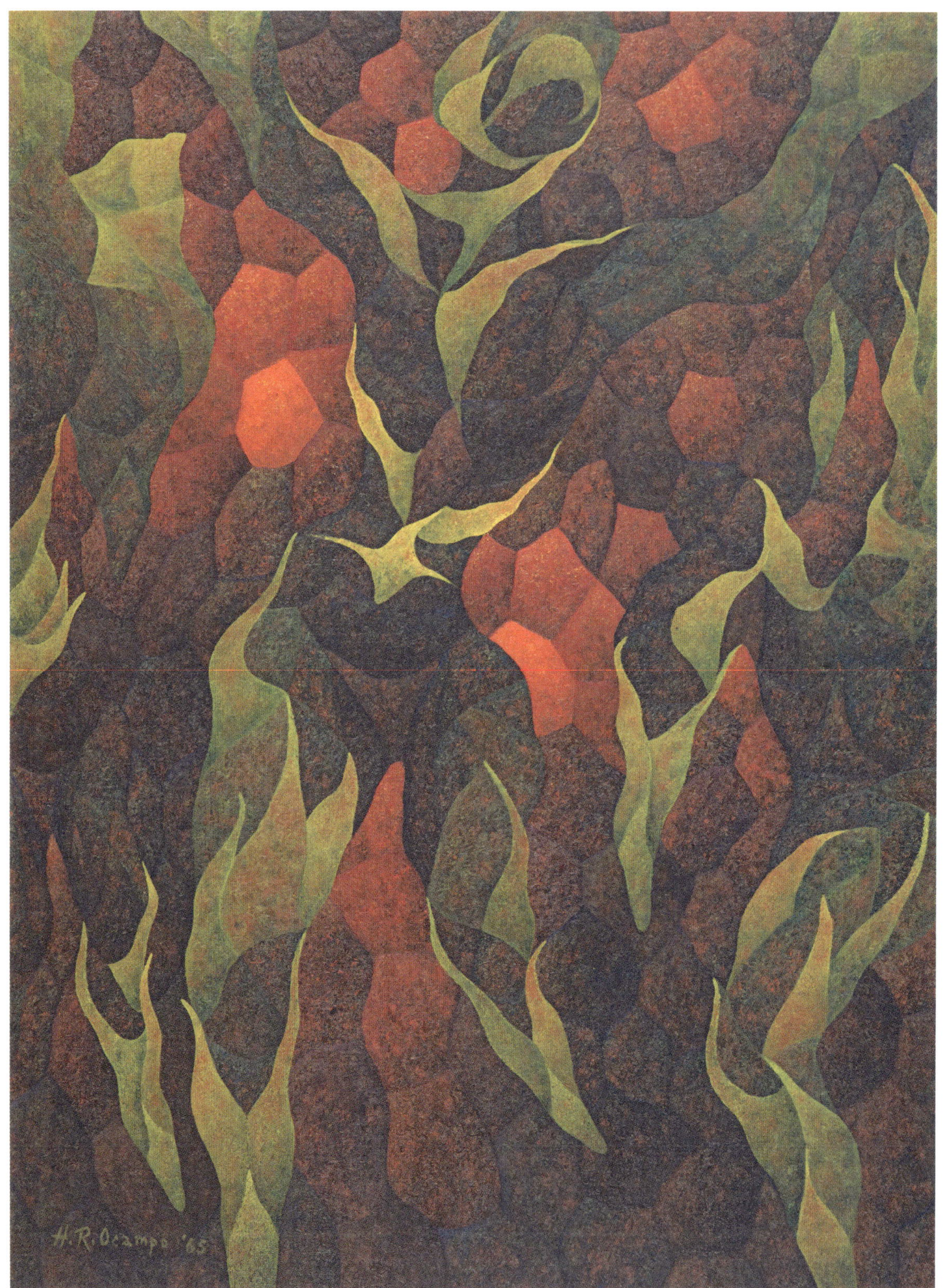

Hernando R. Ocampo. *Dancing Mutants*. 1965. Oil on canvas, 101.8 x 76 cm. Collection of National Gallery Singapore.

reality.'" Ithipol claimed that his use of abstraction "came about naturally 'by itself' as a result of the creative 'inner force.'" Also interested in the symbolic potential of organic phenomena, Hernando R. Ocampo is known for painting interlocking bulbous forms. These recall the shapes and lushness of tropical flora and fauna, as well as sometimes the more sinister suggestion of violence and disfigurement.

Hernando R. Ocampo
b. 1911, Philippines; d. 1978, Philippines

As well as using abstraction to explore a range of subjects, such as cities, nature, and landscapes, artists in Southeast Asia also had a wide variety of reasons for choosing to make abstract art—some personal, others relating to national or regional politics, and some connected to more globalised phenomena. During the Cold War, abstraction was closely associated with American modern art, and was covertly promoted in many places internationally by US government agencies in their attempt to challenge support for the communist bloc, which tended to favour socialist realism. Yet despite the importance of Southeast Asia in the Cold War, and the presence of American cultural diplomacy here, it appears that artists in the region largely adopted abstraction for their own reasons.

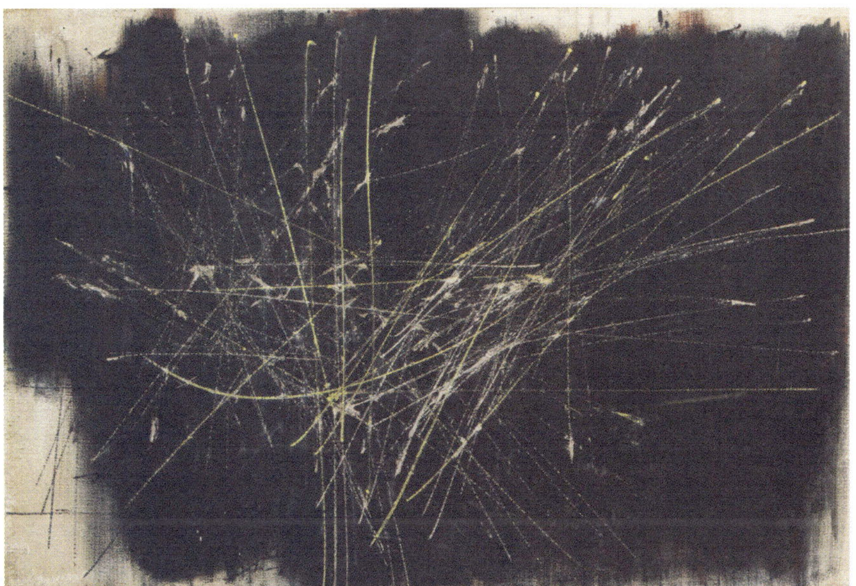

Fernando Zobel. *Saeta 44*. 1957. Oil on canvas, 62.5 x 93 cm. Collection of National Gallery Singapore. This acquisition was made possible through the generous support of Lam Soon Cannery Pte Ltd.

Some artists, like Fernando Zobel and Tang Chang, practised abstraction without formal training. Fernando Zobel came into contact with emotionally expressive abstract art while he was studying history and literature in the United States, having previously been informally trained

Fernando Zobel
(also known as Fernando Zobel de Ayala y Montojo and Fernando M. Zobel)
b. 1924, Philippines; d. 1984, Italy

Tang Chang
(also known as Chang Sae Tang)
b. 1934, Thailand; d. 1990, Thailand

Fernando Amorsolo
b. 1892, Philippines; d. 1972, Philippines

by Fernando Amorsolo, whose <u>oeuvre</u> varied in style and subject matter, but was never abstract. Zobel employed innovative and laborious techniques, famously applying lines of paint using a surgical syringe; despite the "athletic" and "well-rehearsed" manner of this technique, his works retain what art historian Rod Paras-Perez called "an air of freshness, of spontaneity." Zobel's use of abstraction might be considered a reflection of his cosmopolitan privilege, having been born into a wealthy Manila family and travelling widely in Europe and elsewhere. By contrast, Tang Chang was born into a relatively low-income Bangkok family. His paintings and drawings seem to demonstrate an awareness of forms of abstraction originating elsewhere, such as action painting (a genre usually associated with American artists) and concrete poetry (a term first used to describe a kind of writing in Brazil). Yet no evidence has been found of his contact with these outside forms, and Chang lived and worked mostly in reclusion.

Kim Lim
b. 1936, Singapore;
d. 1997, United Kingdom

Other artists adopted abstraction for more academic reasons. Best known for her sculptures, Kim Lim trained in the United Kingdom at a time when British abstraction and American minimalism were contending for primacy. Lim adopted the industrial materials and unornamented forms commonly used by British and American abstract artists at the time, yet travelled frequently through Asia, taking numerous photographs of temples and premodern artefacts, which may also be regarded as important references for her often serialised abstract forms. Many of Lim's works invite <u>poetic</u> reflection on internal spaces, including the gaps between repeated elements within her sculptures, as well as the architectural spaces that they occupy.

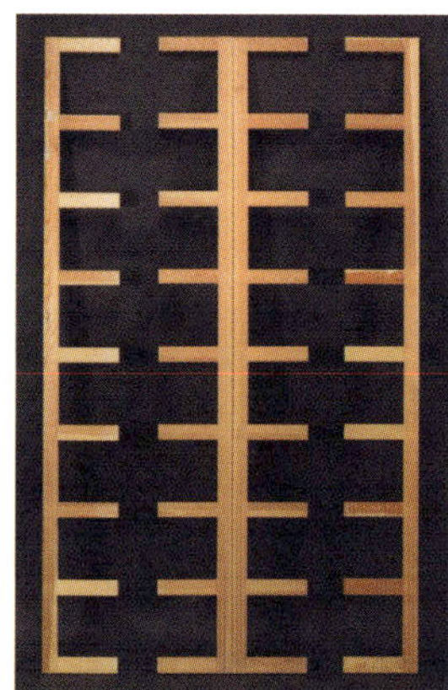

Kim Lim. *Intervals I plus II*. 1973. Pine, 182.8 x 22.2 x 2.1 cm each. Collection of National Gallery Singapore.

Eng Tow. *Shifting Plains*. 1985. Ink and pencil on canvas, 122 x 122.1 cm. Collection of Fukuoka Asian Art Museum.

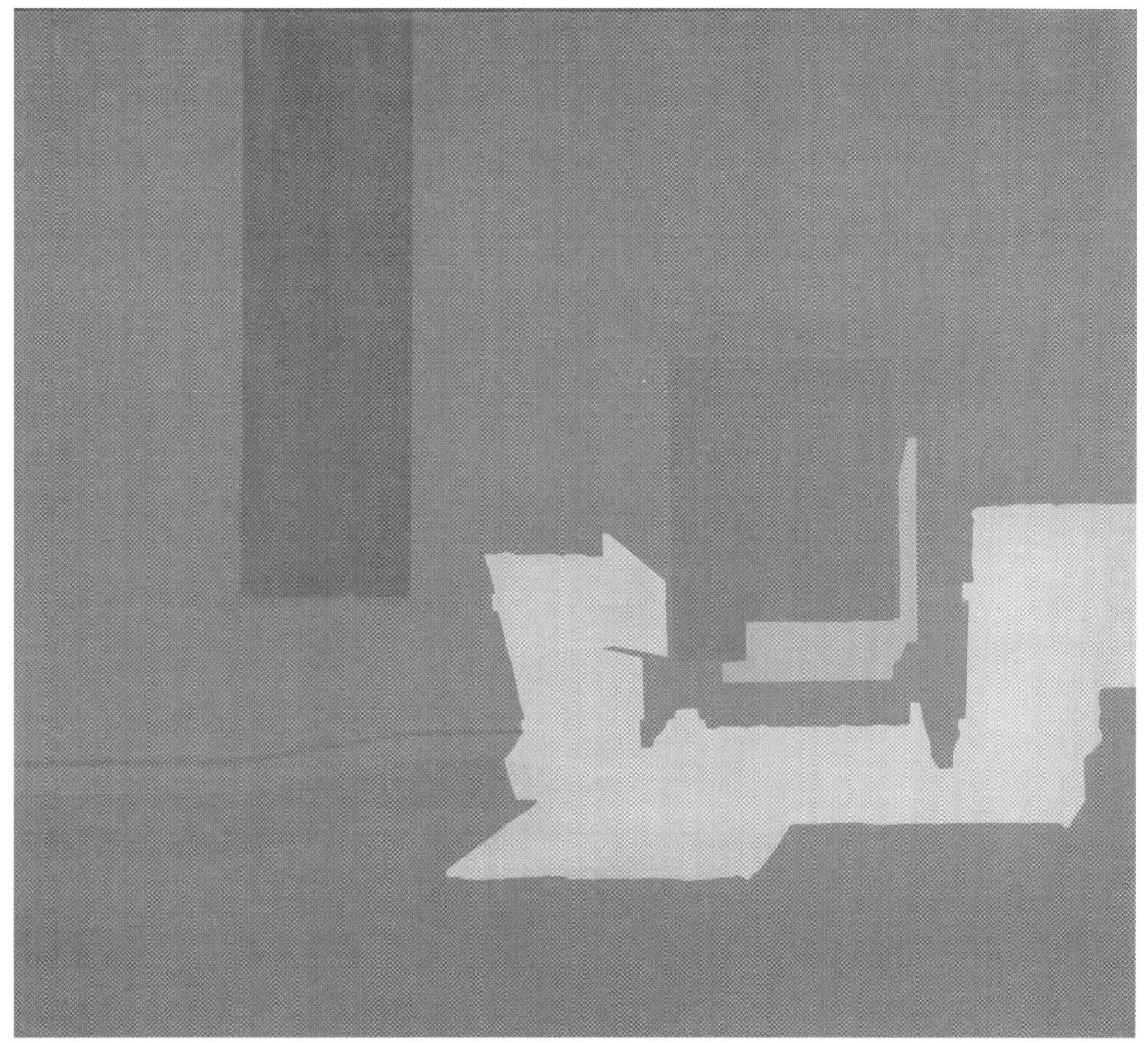

Preecha Thaothong. *Temple Interior*. 1975. Oil on canvas, 119.5 x 135 cm. Collection of National Gallery Singapore.

While many artists have shared Lim's interest in exploring spatial relationships, abstract art also often foregrounds colour. For example, Eng Tow explores tonal interactions between different hues in her textiles and prints, which have been described as "cloth reliefs" due to her sculptural treatment of their finely detailed surfaces. Abstract art often highlights formal questions about space, colour, line, and so on: these compositional, textural, and otherwise aesthetic and experiential elements of artworks can be brought to the fore in abstraction, in place of the subject matter which may often be more prominent in a representational artwork depicting a person, place, or thing.

Many Southeast Asian artists have combined an obvious interest in these formal qualities of abstraction with a desire to explore spiritual ideas. Some, like Preecha Thaothong, have done this through radically simplified and schematised depictions of the interiors of religious buildings, such as Buddhist temples. Others, such as Ismail Zain, have explored the ornamental forms that adorn Islamic architecture, finding in these a visual appeal which extends and also transcends their original contexts.

To say that there are as many kinds of abstraction in Southeast Asian modern art as there are artists would be a truism. There have certainly been recurrent tropes within the abstract art of this region. Yet there have also been many exceptional outliers. Abstract art has also often overlapped with many other ideas and approaches.

ARTIST

In most Southeast Asian vernaculars, as in English and many other languages, the term "artist" can refer to practitioners of any artistic medium. Yet in more recent usage—especially in the context of museums—an artist is often regarded as someone who works specifically in the visual arts. This is a somewhat ahistorical notion, as many significant modern artists in this region have worked across numerous disciplines: painting as well as writing, or designing buildings, acting or putting up other kinds of performance, and collaborating with musicians and filmmakers, for example.

Modern artists in Southeast Asia have commonly been portrayed as larger-than-life figures who transgress social norms, their art seen as a visceral expression of their individual personality and genius. In this stereotype, artists are also almost always male. Portraits of artists often exemplify this image through the use of exaggeration. Affandi's *Self-Portrait* is an evocative example of this trope. Heavy lines of yellow, red,

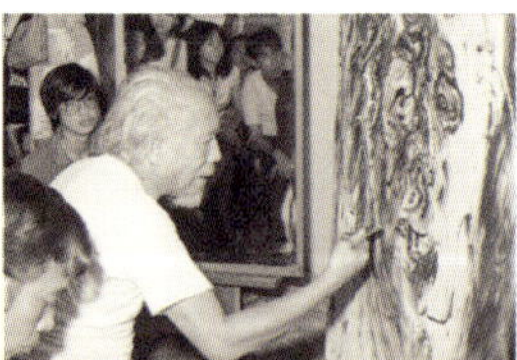

Affandi creating *Self-Portrait* at the National Museum, 1975.

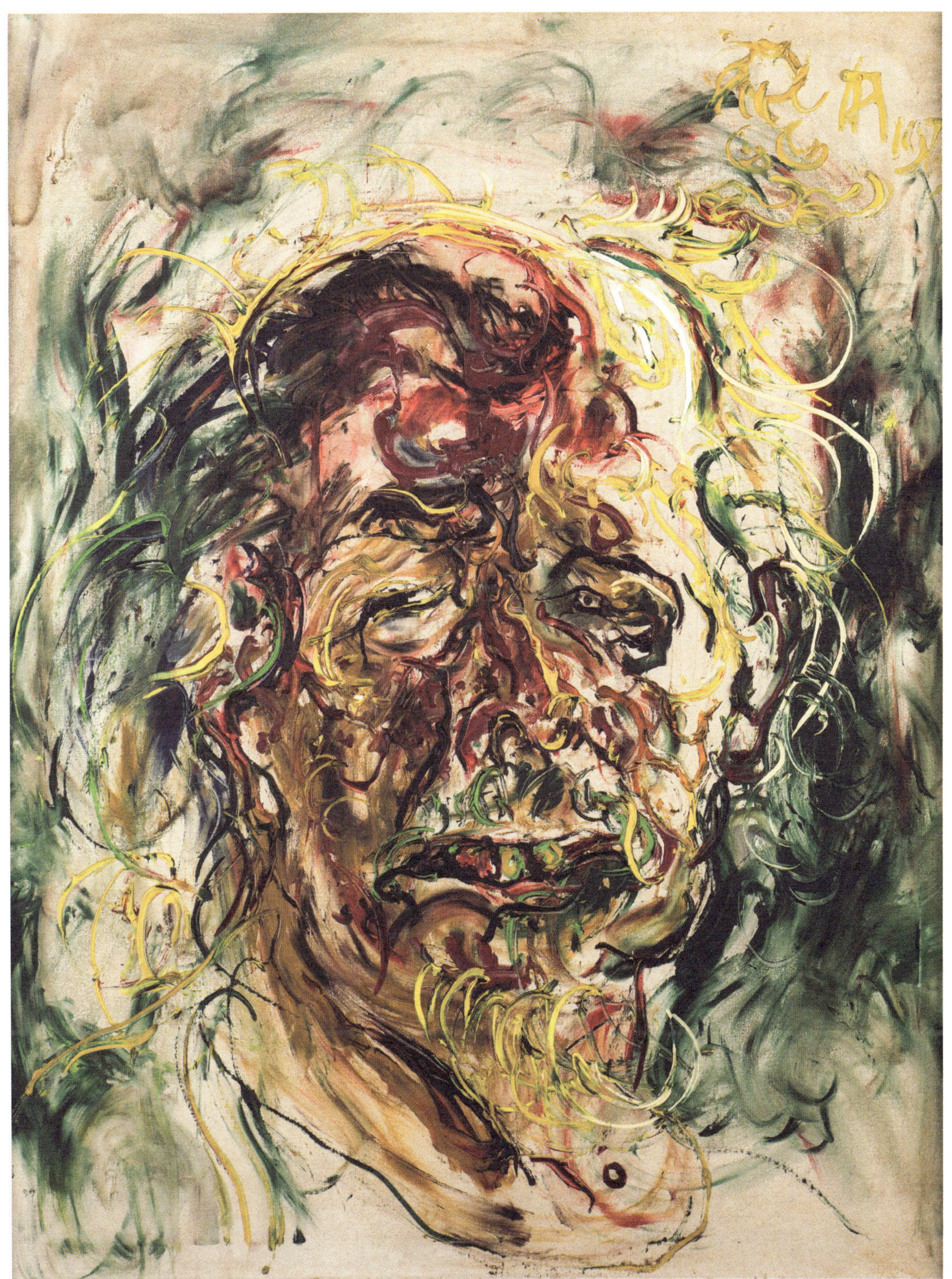

Affandi. *Self-Portrait*. 1975. Oil on canvas, 130 x 100.5 cm. Gift of the artist. Collection of National Gallery Singapore.

green and blue swirl from the artist's face; roughly applied in a wet-on-wet technique, these bold flourishes evoke the curls of the aging man's unkempt hair and beard. Yet these radiating daubs of impasto paint may also be interpreted as emanations of Affandi's genius, dynamism, and unruly individuality as an artist. The repeated swirling forms also recall Vincent van Gogh; admired by Affandi, the Dutch artist is also celebrated for self-portraits which depict an artist's personality as singularly irrepressible. Affandi's painting was made inside a gallery, where the audience could watch the "master" at work, further emphasising the idea, in this conception of what an artist should be like, that his special personality often rivals the artwork in appeal and importance.

An image like Affandi's, which celebrates his individuality, arises from a long historical process in which authors of artworks grew from being anonymous to being identified and named. This modern conception of an artist had developed in the West and been <u>transferred</u> to Southeast Asia through various processes including colonial institutions and the establishment of formal art <u>education</u>. While some artists were self-taught or adopted <u>naïve</u> approaches, nevertheless the notion that an artist should be professionally trained became widely accepted, and was part of what distinguished artists from practitioners of <u>craft</u>. The emergence of modern art in this region was, in part, signified by this invention of the idea of an artist: a named, unique, and professionalised individual. For example, we don't know the names of the people who designed and constructed most premodern temples, yet we do know the names of modern artists who depicted them in paintings, photographs, and films. In as early as 1849, Raden Saleh signed his name twice on his largest painting, *Boschbrand* (Forest Fire), carefully emphasising his identity as its artist.

Yet these examples represent just one of many types of modern artist. At another extreme, we may consider an untitled <u>propaganda</u> painting by Pech Song, made around 1984, to officially mark five years of Cambodia's occupation by Vietnamese forces. Here, artists are depicted as the equals of farmers, soldiers, and workers. Artists are not individual geniuses, as in Affandi's painting, but instead anonymous revolutionary comrades. It is significant that in Song's painting—which was probably mass-produced as a poster—artists are specifically depicted as contributors to the revolutionary struggle. By contrast, in many other communist regimes, the "masses" have been represented only by workers, peasants, and soldiers. It is also significant

Vincent van Gogh
b. 1853, Netherlands; d. 1890, France

Raden Saleh
b. circa 1811, Indonesia; d. 1880, Indonesia

Pech Song
b. 1947, Cambodia

that both male and female artists are depicted here, and that Song shows them working in multiple artistic forms.

More research is needed on artists who were women, many of whom practised as "amateurs" rather than trained "professionals." A 1959 art magazine in Myanmar features an article urging women to become artists, accompanied by an illustration of a woman painting a nude, thus doubly transgressing <u>taboos</u>. In the article, the artist Myat Kyaw exhorted women: "To be an artist, you don't need to be physically pretty like an actress; you don't need to be very stout, strong and healthy like a woman military officer. Plus, you won't lose your composure like a woman hawker or a woman traditional dancer."

Artists can also teach us about art and its histories. Art historian Nora A. Taylor has proposed, "Artists are the main source of information for Southeast Asian art history, and they are the persons for whom Southeast Asian art history matters, and about whom it is written." One risk of this view is that it privileges artists' interpretations of their own work over other possibilities for its <u>reception</u>. Yet since the late 20th century, many contemporary artists, such as Erika Tan and Ho Tzu Nyen, have also conducted research on other, historical artists as part of their practice.

Myat Kyaw
b. 1918, Myanmar; d. 1977, Myanmar

Erika Tan
b. 1967, Singapore

Ho Tzu Nyen
b. 1976, Singapore

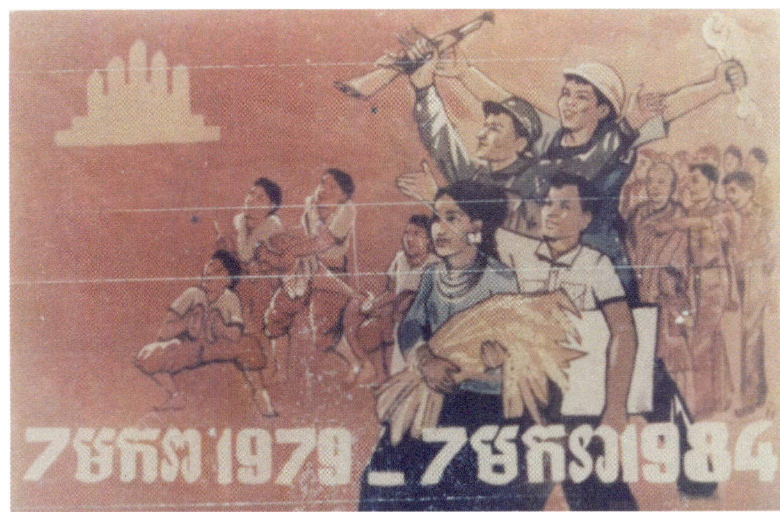

Pech Song. Untitled (*7 January 1979–7 January 1984*). Medium and dimensions unknown.

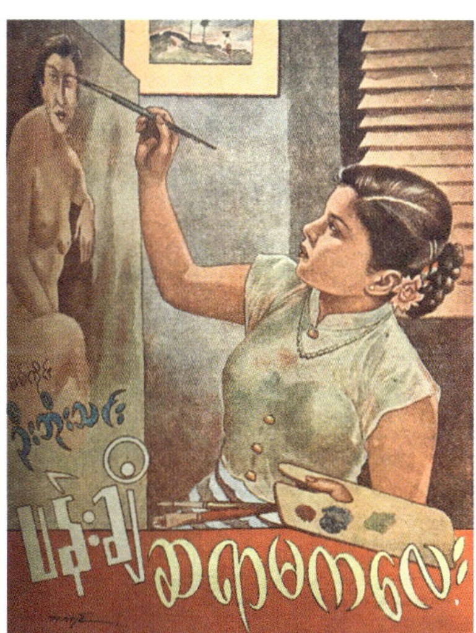

Artist unknown. Illustration accompanying an article by Myat Kyaw titled "Burmese Women, Make Art!" published in *Pangyi* [Art/Painting] magazine, 1959.

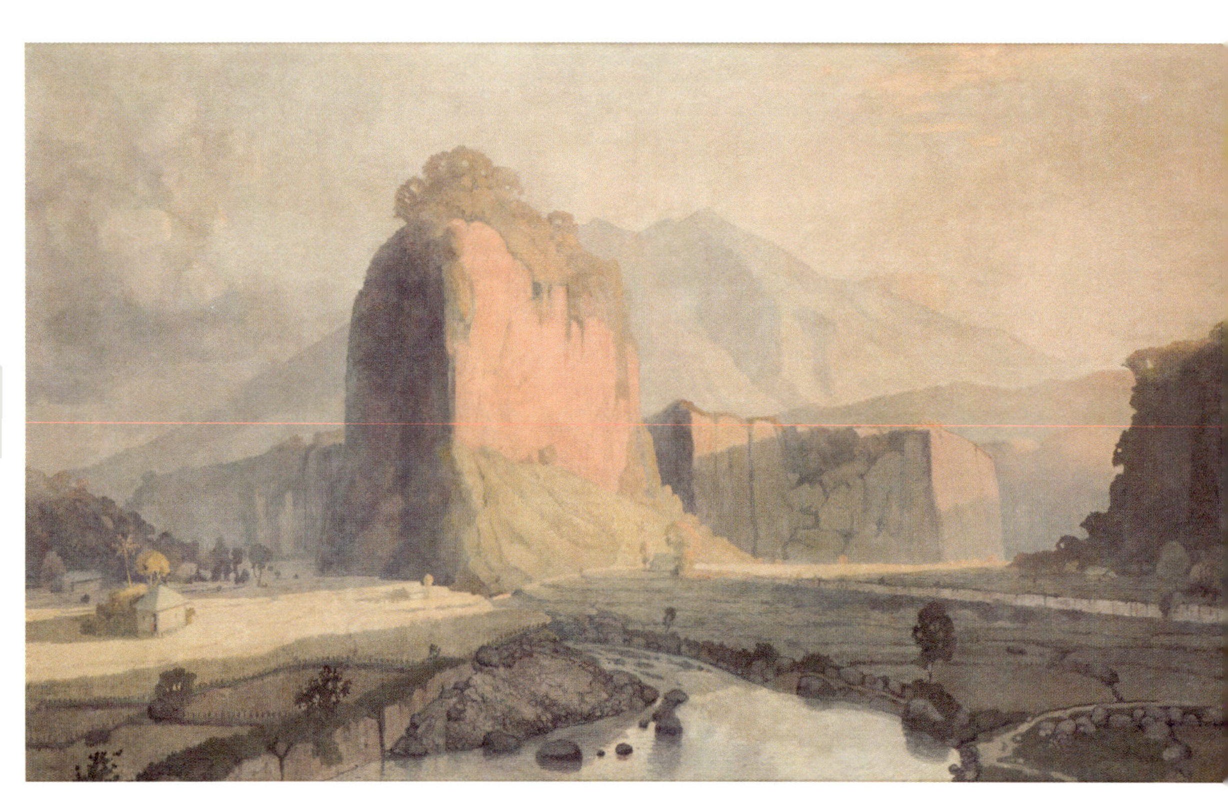

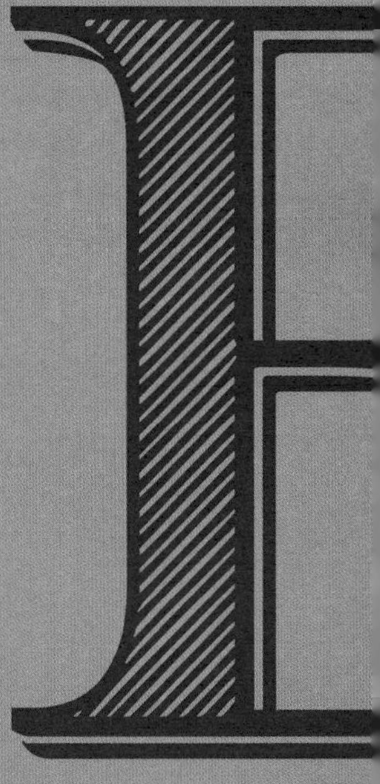

Wakidi. *Ngarai Sianok.* c. 1940s. Oil on canvas, 85 x 145 cm. Collection of National Gallery Singapore.

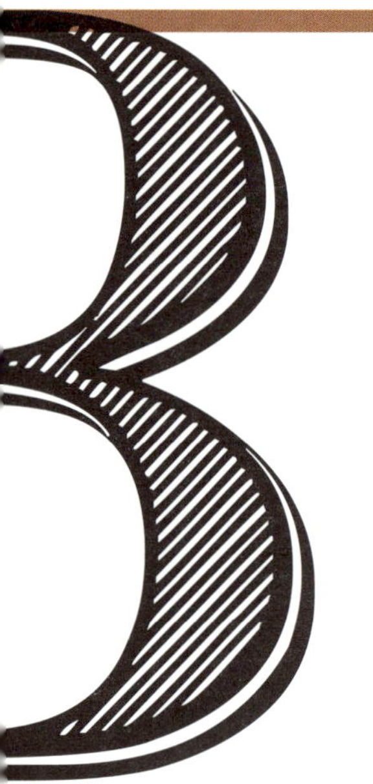

BIENNIAL

A biennial is an exhibition, usually of art, which recurs regularly or semi-regularly, usually every second year. The term is used interchangeably with "biennale," which is Italian; both words simply mean "every other year." Because they tend to be large in scale and bring together artists from disparate locations, biennials have often been important in providing artists and audiences with an opportunity to compare new art from different parts of the world. The significance of biennials has increased in recent decades, since the gradual shift from modern to contemporary art. Today, biennials are usually overseen by a curator, who often selects artists and artworks because of their engagement with a chosen theme or idea, usually in an attempt to express the <u>zeitgeist</u>, or spirit of the times. Biennials are also closely affiliated with the art market, including art fairs, which differ from biennials in that the artworks they exhibit are publicly offered for sale.

Since the 1990s, participation in biennials of <u>contemporary</u> art has been a significant milestone for many Southeast Asian artists, and some Southeast Asian curators. It has become a mark of prestige—as well as often a financially lucrative achievement—for a Southeast Asian contemporary artist to be included in a biennial. Moreover, in recent decades, several biennials which are mostly or exclusively focused on Asian and Pacific art have been established, including in Brisbane, Jakarta, Singapore, and Gwangju, as well as in several Chinese cities, and most recently in Southeast Asian cities like Bangkok, Krabi, Kuala Lumpur, and Manila. Biennials have become a key forum for discussion of ideas in contemporary art.

This is a significant expansion in the role of biennials prior to the 1990s. Before this, biennials appear to have not been so important for modern artists in this region, compared to artists from other parts of the world. However, there were nevertheless numerous cases of artists from Southeast Asia appearing in international biennials throughout the second half of the 20th century.

The first biennial was established in Venice in 1895—the use of the Italian term "biennale" dates to this event—and Thai King Chulalongkorn visited the 1897 and 1907 editions, but it would be more than half a century before a Southeast Asian artist exhibited in Venice. Several Cambodian and Vietnamese artists participated in the first Biennale de Paris, in 1959, yet no evidence has come to light of the event having had much impact. Several other Cambodian and

Chulalongkorn (Rama V)
r. 1868–1910

Vietnamese artists appeared in some editions of *Intergrafik*, a recurring exhibition of "graphic arts" (chiefly prints) held in then-communist East Germany during the 1960s. Yet for these artists and their peers, it was perhaps the relationships and <u>connections</u> formed while organising participation in these events that were most significant, possibly more so than the actual exhibitions. *Intergrafik*, as well as the *First International Exhibition* held in Saigon in 1962—considered a kind of proto-biennial—are examples of exhibitions organised within the context of the Cold War. According to art historian Boitran Huynh-Beattie, during this period the <u>patronage</u> of Americans living in South Vietnam was considerable. More research is needed on how the format of large-scale, international exhibitions like biennials were used as a form of cultural diplomacy in Vietnam and elsewhere, with art serving as a kind of <u>propaganda</u>.

Affandi was the first Southeast Asian artist to appear in numerous biennials internationally, some of which were <u>canonical</u> events in the emerging history of <u>exhibitions</u>. The Indonesia-based artist, known for his expressive, gestural style, appeared in important biennials in Brazil (1952), Venice (1954), Sao Paulo (1956), and Sydney (1973), among others. These events introduced him—and, by extension, Southeast Asian modern art—to many new audiences. Affandi's repeated appearance is indicative of the often self-legitimising nature of biennials: because organisers tend to select artists they have seen in other biennials, being included in one such exhibition tends to lead to subsequent opportunities. Several other Southeast Asian artists appeared in the *Sao Paulo Biennial* from the 1950s to the 1970s, including Fernando Zobel and Jose Joya, and more research is needed on the effects of this participation on their practices, and on establishing links between the region and other parts of the world.

Although biennials are usually large and spectacular exhibitions, some recurring art events in Southeast Asia since the 1990s have been smaller in scale, and more oriented to ephemeral events and local communities. Examples include the *Chiang Mai Social Installation*, which occurred for several years in the early 1990s, *Viva Excon*, which has taken place semi-regularly in the Philippines since 1990, and *Womanifesto*, held in Thailand since 1995. Such biennial events are now thought to have marked a turning point in the emergence of contemporary art in this region.

BIOGRAPHY

How can we think about the relationship between an artist's biography and their artwork? How important is it to know about an artist's life in order to appreciate their <u>oeuvre</u>? While most accounts of Southeast Asian modern art employ biography as a tool for understanding art, these questions are open to debate. Often, the way biography is used to help narrate and interpret artworks helps us to see how modern art is related to <u>history</u>.

An artist's biography is often an important part of the larger context that helps illuminate their artwork. Various biographical details are usually taken into account in discussions of artworks, from the places artists travelled to, to the people they met, and the environments they lived and worked in. This is an approach taken in early art historical writings on art, such as Giorgio Vasari's influential 16th-century account of Italian Renaissance artists titled *The Lives of the Most Excellent Painters, Sculptors, and Architects*, or simply, *The Lives*.

Working in the Southeast Asian context, art writers Claire Holt and Marco Hsu, writing in the 1960s, often provided details such as where and with whom artists were <u>educated</u>, and how the places they lived in or travelled to appeared in their artworks. Holt, for example, explained the predominance of <u>landscapes</u> in Wakidi's <u>oeuvre</u> by noting that the artist lived "in West Sumatra, where he paints the gorges, mountains, streams, and fields of the area around Bukit Tinggi." Similarly, Hsu contended that even though many of the <u>diasporic</u> artists he wrote about were "ethnic Chinese" or born in China, "because they grew up in Malaya, they have innate feelings and ideas for the land and life here, which differentiate them naturally from the foreign artists." Biographical context is also used to explain artists' political leanings. Holt notes that S. Sudjojono had been "raised in an atmosphere of mounting nationalism, with a general socialist outlook." As Holt recounts, Sudjojono famously railed against the aesthetic of Wakidi's work, launching a major <u>debate</u> about what he called "beautiful Indies" paintings.

Sometimes, biographical details that are unrelated to an artist's work are also invoked. This is apparent in descriptions of artists who are <u>women</u>, which are often quite different from those about their male counterparts. For example, Sun Yee is described in a 1948 essay by her peer, Liu Kang, as "a woman who possesses both beauty and intelligence... a lively lady with an elegant manner, gentle of voice, lofty of spirit." Male artists are rarely described in such terms.

Wakidi
b. 1889, Indonesia; d. 1979, Indonesia

Sindudarsono Sudjojono
b. 1913, Indonesia; d. 1986, Indonesia

Sun Yee
(also known as Sunyee and Shen Yan)
b. 1919, China; d. 2009, Singapore

Liu Kang
b. 1911, China; d. 2004, Singapore

These are typical examples of art historians using facts about an artist's life to illuminate their artwork; sometimes, however, the interpretation of artworks can in turn enhance our understanding of an artist's life.

For example, art historian Ambeth R. Ocampo's study of a group of family <u>portraits</u> made by Juan Luna leads him to speculate that the artist "must have thought that he would not return to the Philippines" when he travelled to Spain in 1897. Ocampo's evidence for this claim about Luna's likely state of mind is that the family portraits painted before the artist's 1897 departure appear especially "quick" in their execution. Indeed, as curator Clarissa Chikiamco notes, Luna's anecdotally reported ability to paint as many as five or six family portraits in a day has "become part of Luna's legend" and "attests to his prodigious skill." Despite their speedy execution, Luna's 1897 family portraits convey extraordinary emotional depth through the artist's deft handling of light, expression, and detail. More than mere technical ability, Luna's mastery over portraits and <u>history</u> paintings was celebrated since his own lifetime as demonstrating the possibility and necessity for reform in the Philippines; he has been consistently celebrated as a national hero in the struggle against colonialism.

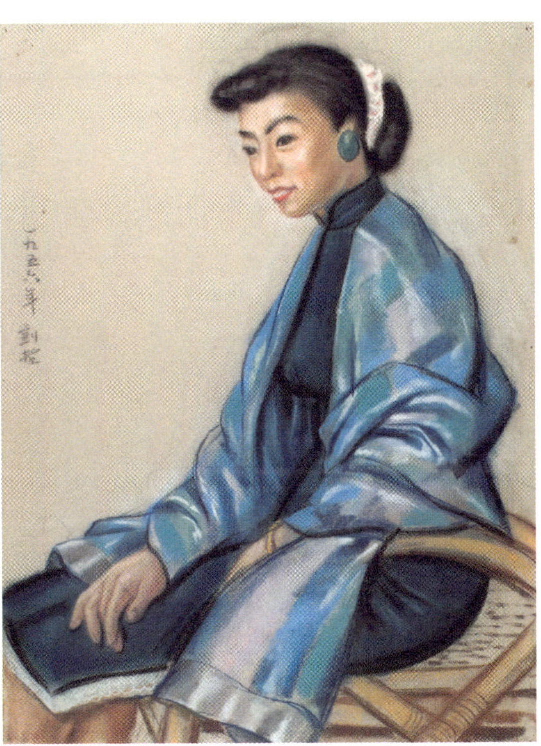

Liu Kang. *Lady in Blue Dress (Artist—Shen Yan)*. 1956. Pastel on paper. 64 x 48 cm. Gift of the artist's family. Collection of National Gallery Singapore.

Yet this championing of Luna overlooks or downplays a significant episode in the artist's life: his murdering of Maria Paz Pardo de Tavera, his wife, as well as her mother, Juliana Gorricho, in a jealous rage in 1892. How can the perpetrator of such violence (and, arguably, misogyny) still be celebrated as a national (and, more recently, regional) hero? And how might his subsequent portraits of women—including his own female relatives, as painted in 1897—be interpreted in light of this biographical fact?

There aren't easy answers to such questions; they underscore that the relationship between an artist's biography and artwork is never simple or fixed, and indeed that it is possible to analyse artworks even without any reference to an artist's biography at all. Exploring overlaps and tensions between an artist's life and oeuvre can enrich our understanding of both, and of the <u>zeitgeist</u>, or spirit of the times, that they may embody.

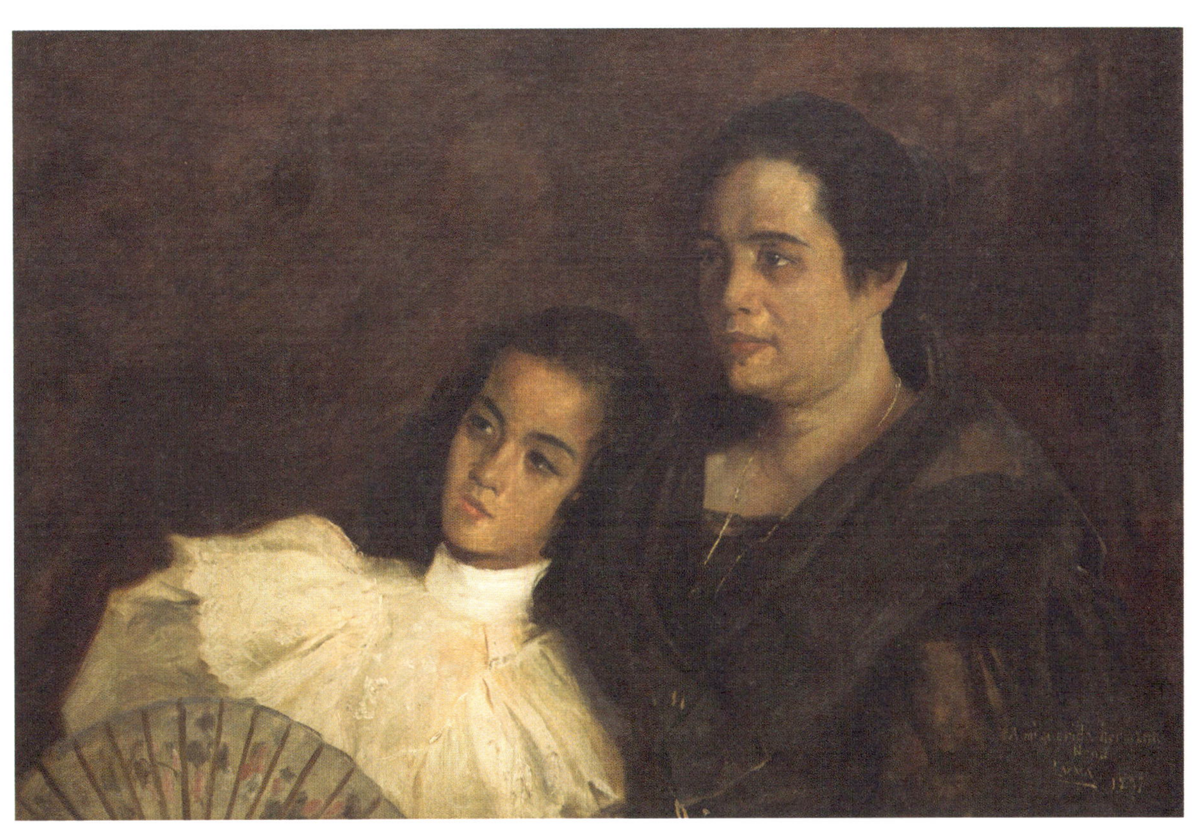

Juan Luna. *Nena y Tinita* (Nena and Tinita). 1897. Oil on canvasboard, 78 x 104 cm. Collection of Paulino and Hetty Que.

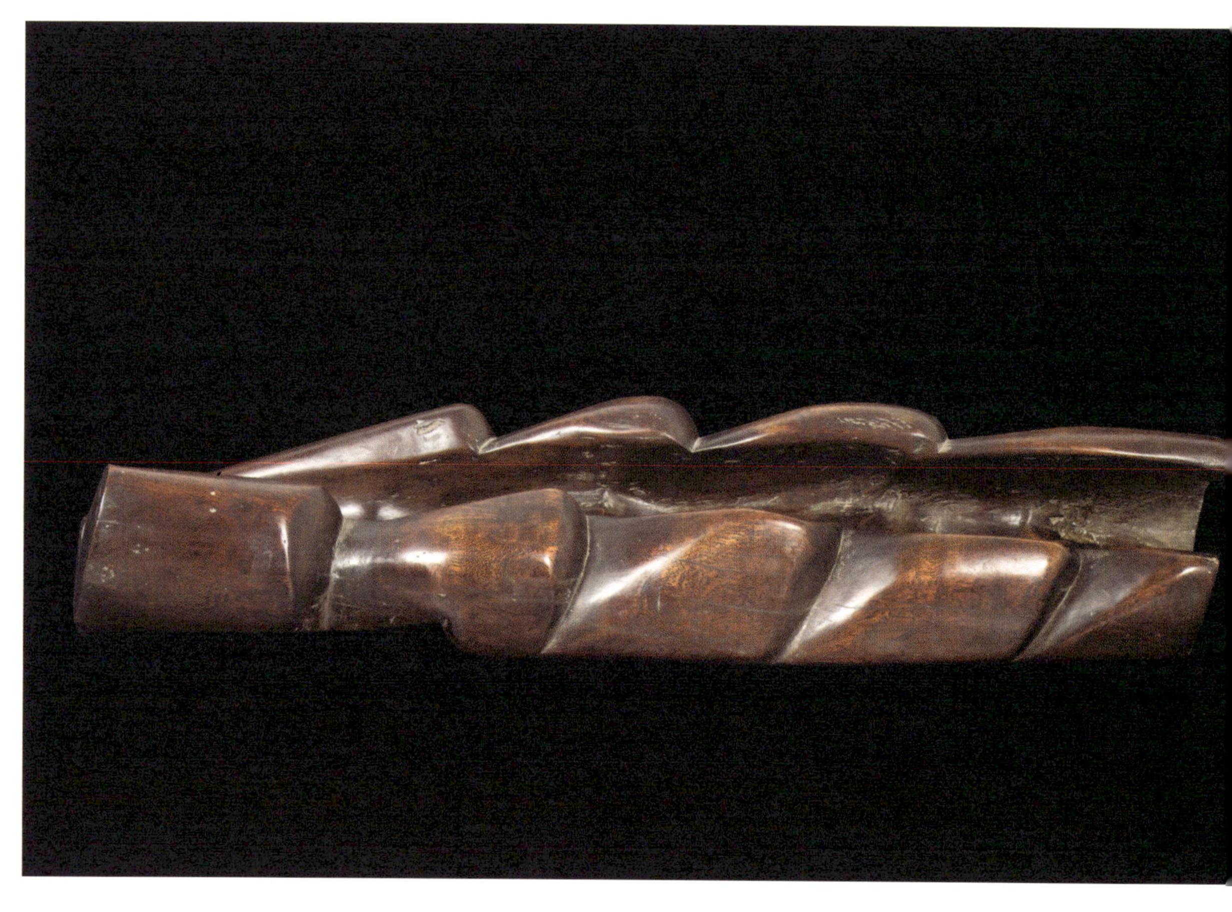

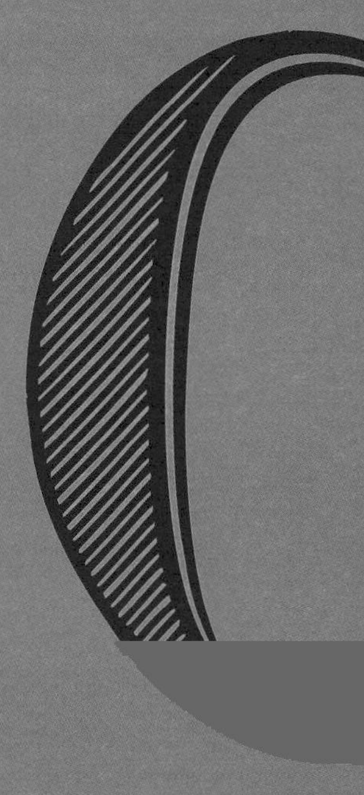

Inson Wongsam. *Wise People Wake Up Early*. 1974. Teak, 40 x 40 x 122 cm. Collection of the artist.

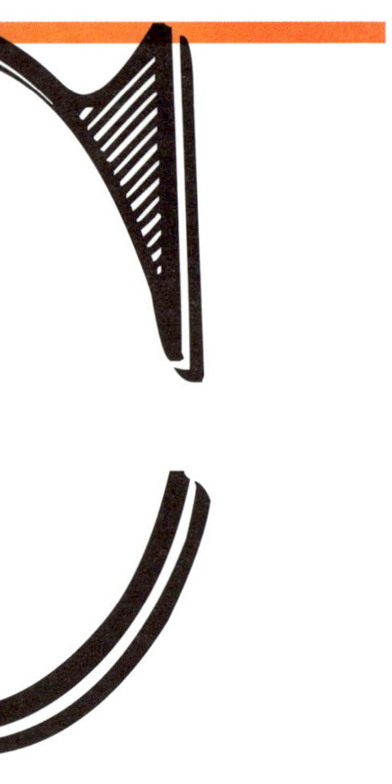

CANON

In discussions of art and culture, a canon is a body of artworks and texts generally accepted as foundationally important. Inclusions and exclusions from the canon are always contested, as is the relative significance of canonical works. These contestations have increased exponentially in recent decades, with the rise of feminist art historians and others specialised in kinds of practice which had previously been overlooked and excluded from the canon. Some scholars have challenged the whole idea of the canon itself, while others have instead worked to expand the canon to include more artists and artworks.

Despite these debates and challenges, the canon in many parts of the world has become relatively stable, at least in referring to a group of artists and artworks which are most widely known, and considered foundational before further specialisation. A few examples of canonical artists from elsewhere in the world demonstrate this. To study East Asian art without knowing the work of Katsushika Hokusai would be impossible. Pablo Picasso is similarly canonical in European art. In Australian art, Arthur Streeton has a certain place in the canon, as does Jackson Pollock in North America. Of course, debates continue about these artists, but they are nevertheless taught to all students and are widely known outside of specialist art circles.

However, there is no canon of modern art in Southeast Asia. That is, there is no group of artists who specialists agree to be important and who are also household names across the region. While there are strong and well-developed national canons in many Southeast Asian nations, there is nevertheless no canon that encompasses the entire region. To be sure, the importance of a few key figures has in recent years become quite widely agreed upon. These include early pioneers like Raden Saleh, hailed as the first Southeast Asian artist to achieve prominence in Europe, and more recent firebrands such as Redza Piyadasa, who is valued for being among the earliest to adopt conceptual and contemporary approaches in his practice. Moreover, some institutions—mostly museums, but also some university departments—are beginning to settle on a few names which recur more prominently within the narratives of Southeast Asia's modern art history, although necessarily to the exclusion of other artists.

Yet many of the names which may be seen as canonical in one nation's modern art history remain almost unknown elsewhere, both in the region and further afield. Some

Katsushika Hokusai
b. 1760, Japan; d. 1849, Japan

Pablo Picasso
b. 1881, Spain; d. 1973, France

Arthur Streeton
b. 1867, Australia; d. 1943, Australia

Jackson Pollock
b. 1912, United States; d. 1956, United States

Raden Saleh
b. circa 1811, Indonesia; d. 1880, Indonesia

Redza Piyadasa
b. 1939, Malaysia; d. 2007, Malaysia

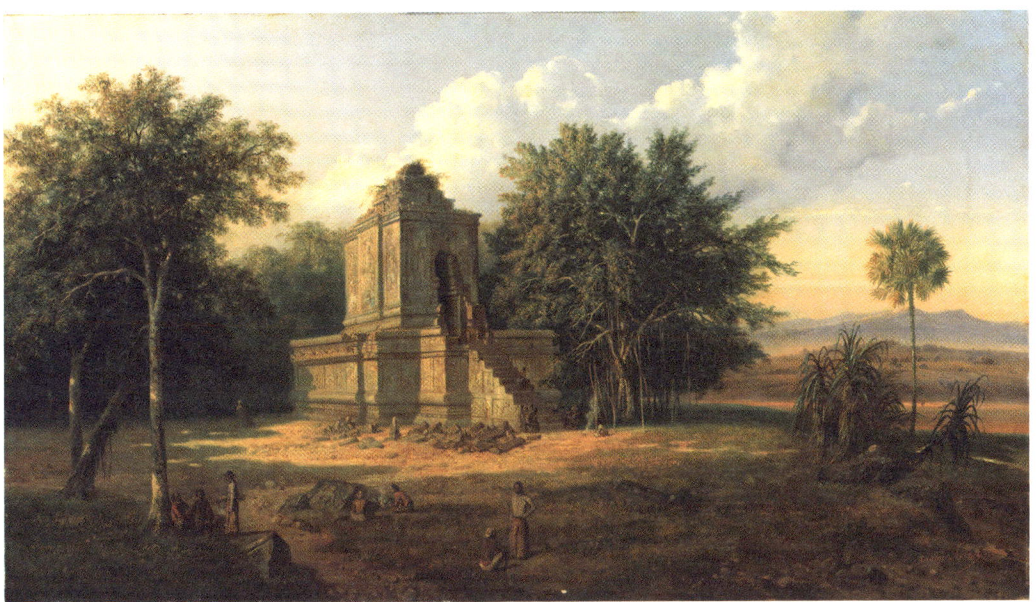

Raden Saleh. *Javanese Temple in Ruins*. 1860. Oil on canvas mounted on fibreboard, 105.4 x 187 cm. Gift of Mrs Sally Burbank Swart. Collection of Smithsonian American Art Museum.

examples include: Georgette Chen and Tang Da Wu, both until recently little-recognised outside of Singapore despite being widely loved within that country; or Nhek Dim, invisible outside of Cambodia, but famous within the nation and among its diaspora; or Inson Wongsam, who is largely unknown except in Thailand, where he is lauded by both official and independent commentators.

This phenomenon reflects the dominance of the idea of the nation as a structuring frame, within which much of the history of modern art in Southeast Asia has been written. Efforts to understand modern art from across the entire region, or comparatively within it, have been rare, and most have appeared only recently. This has been a significant barrier to the construction of a canon of modern art in Southeast Asia.

Another obstacle to the development of a regional canon has been the scarcity of art history curricula in schools and universities. Much art historical research and writing in the region has instead been occasioned by exhibitions, which are usually temporary in nature. It may be that a canon of Southeast Asian contemporary art from the late 20th and early 21st centuries could be more readily accepted than a canon of modern art of the 19th and 20th centuries.

In recent years, institutions including the Fukuoka Asian Art Museum and National Gallery Singapore have collected artworks from all across Southeast Asia and conducted extensive research on them. This is perhaps beginning to stabilise a canon of modern art in this region, even if these institutions are actively trying to resist and reflexively challenge this seemingly inevitable effect of their working across the entire region.

These processes of canon-making and contestation should generate further debate about inclusions and exclusions, as well as about the significance not only of canonical artists and artworks, but also about the very notion of the canon itself.

CINEMA

Since emerging in the late 19th and early 20th centuries, cinema has been energetically entwined with other kinds of modern art. Intersections between movies and other modern arts have been especially pronounced and significant in Southeast Asia. Even though cinema is often thought of as different from and perhaps less serious than other modern art <u>media</u> due to its popular entertainment appeal, it is especially rich ground for exploring transmediality—that is, the links that exist between it and other modern art forms.

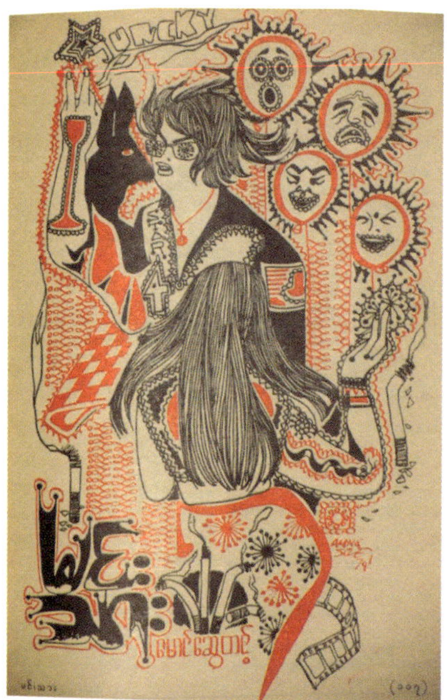

Bagyi Aung Soe. Illustration accompanying an article titled "The Actor," published in *Shumawa*, March 1974.

<u>Biographical</u> intersections between movies and other media abound: many artists have worked with cinema. Bagyi Aung Soe, for instance, was a successful actor in many feature films produced in Myanmar during the 1970s.

Bagyi Aung Soe
b. 1924, Myanmar; d. 1990, Myanmar

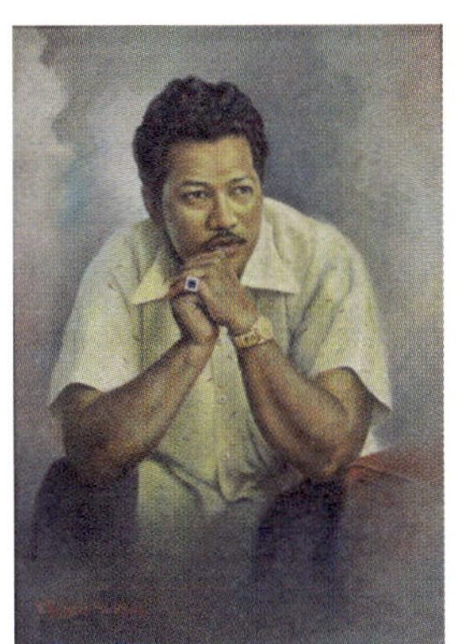

Aris Aziz. *Portrait of P. Ramlee*. 1983. Oil on canvas, 100 x 71 cm. Collection of Penang State Art Gallery.

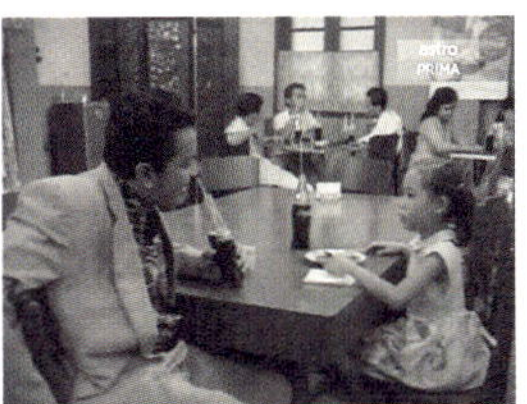

P. Ramlee, director. *Pendekar Bujang Lapok* (Worn Out Bachelor). 1959. Scene features P. Ramlee, who also starred in the film.

The relationship between these movies and Aung Soe's paintings and illustrations has yet to be fully explored. Another example is Vann Nath who, while acclaimed for his paintings depicting the horrors of the Cambodian <u>genocide</u> of the 1970s, had also made movie posters during the 1960s. Several other well-known artists, such as Affandi, also painted movie posters. Other artists have made works celebrating cinema as a source of inspiration, as in Aris Aziz's glamorised portrait of P. Ramlee, a prominent filmmaker who enjoyed unrivalled popularity in the Malay world. The mise-en-scene (or aesthetic elements) of Ramlee's films has also been described as being painterly in atmosphere.

Early movie theatres often boasted daring architectural designs, as in Manila's Capitol Theater, which was built in 1935. The theatre also housed a mural by artists Victorio Edades, Carlos Francisco and Galo Ocampo, which generated extensive <u>debates</u> about art's function, due to its use of a style that deviated radically from predominating romantic modes of <u>realism</u>. Francisco also worked extensively in cinema, including as a designer of <u>fashionable</u> costumes and sets, having earlier worked in layout for newspapers and periodicals.

These and other intersections between film and other artistic media are instructive, and warrant further study. The ways in which research has been conducted about cinema, and the terms in which films are discussed, often vary quite significantly from those used by art historians, curators, and others concentrating on visual art. There has been little sustained dialogue between these two fields. Yet it is exciting to consider whether cinema scholarship might further enlighten and enliven our understanding of visual art.

One concept popular in studies of cinema but less prevalent in discussions of other art forms is that of intertexuality, or the resonances between different works. Although some scholars still choose to focus on the <u>oeuvres</u> of individual film directors—an approach sometimes called "auteur theory"—many instead concentrate on the collaborative nature of filmmaking. This approach also takes into account the contributions made by actors, cinematographers, distributors, locations, and so on, and their effect on how people experience films. For example, because people often choose to see a film based on the actors starring in it, viewers may be intertextually reminded of other films, and this may shape their understanding of and engagement with these films. Cinema researchers have articulated a "star theory" to investigate this and related phenomena, often focusing not only on filmmakers' intentions, but also audiences' subjective reception of movies.

Similar kinds of intertextuality may also arise with painting, sculpture, and other modern art forms, such as when different artworks depict similar scenes or use similar materials or techniques. However, the effects of intertextuality have been under-explored in visual art. The _artist_ is often given attention over other people and factors contributing to the production and distribution of artworks, such as models (often _women_), _patrons_, _exhibitions_, and so on.

Another concept prominent in cinema-related discourse in Southeast Asia that is less developed in relation to visual art, is _independence_. Described as "a vitalizing if vague signpost" by moving image theorist May Adadol Ingawanij, independence often refers to the absence of state intervention in a cinematic production. More than this, though, Ingawanij also asserts "the fallacy of describing a film funded by international investors through various co-production deals as the product of a single national territory." In other words, films rarely come from a single country. The way films are produced and received is therefore, in a sense, independent of any single territory: it transcends national boundaries. Visual artworks also often result from complex and transnational _connections_ between patrons, curators, and institutions, yet because we tend to focus on artists rather than other contributors to specific artworks, discussions of visual art remain largely bounded to particular _nations_, more than is the case for cinema.

CONCEPTUAL

Cheo Chai-Hiang
b. 1946, Singapore

In 1972, Cheo Chai-Hiang wrote instructions for a conceptual artwork titled _5' x 5' (Singapore River)_, which has been remade in several versions, such as _5' x 5' (Inched Deep)_. It consists of nothing more than four lines on the wall and floor, together making the shape of a square.

Modern Art Society
Active since 1963; based Singapore

Georgette Chen
b. 1906, China; d. 1993, Singapore

Cheo's piece was conceived as a submission to an exhibition run by the Modern Art Society, one of at least ten groups which dominated Singapore's art scene during the decades following World War II. The stark work cut a naked contrast to prevailing depictions of the Singapore River by artists including Georgette Chen, which idealised the appearance of the _landscape_. Although pleasing to look at, these paintings, it was argued, lacked critical engagement with more complex realities, such as _quotidian_ daily life and _urbanisation_. In creating this work, Cheo perhaps felt that the critical spirit underlying the _social realism_ of previous decades had, by the 1970s, been subsumed into a sentimental

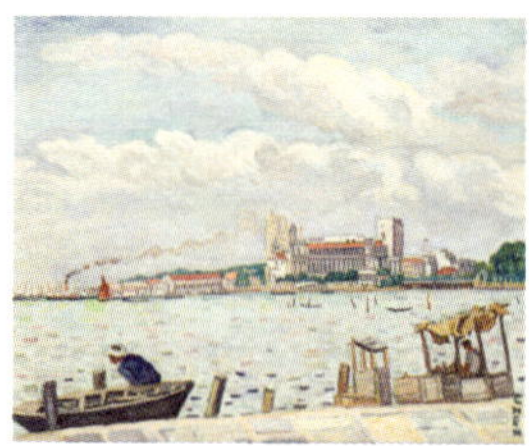

Georgette Chen. _Singapore Waterfront._ 1963. Oil on canvas, 50 x 61 cm. Gift of Lee Foundation. Collection of National Gallery Singapore.

nostalgia, one which he turned on its head with a work that was decidedly uninterested in having an appealing appearance.

5' x 5' is a typical example of conceptual art, and is considered one of the earliest and most influential instances of this kind of practice in Southeast Asia. In conceptual art, the artist's idea is the most significant part of the work—more than technical skill, aesthetic appearance, or emotional engagement. The main elements of conceptual art are decided by the artist before making the work; execution is secondary.

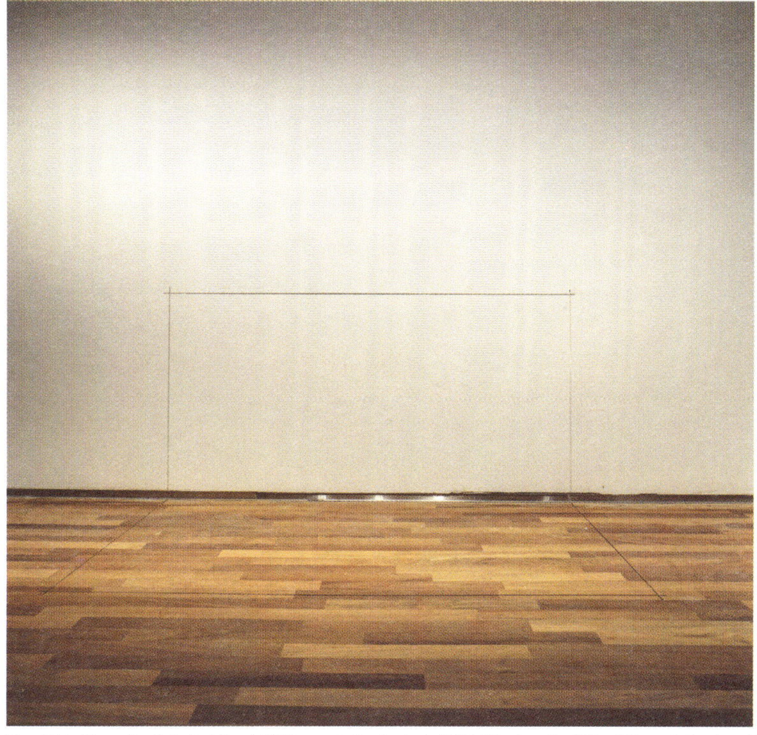

Cheo Chai-Hiang. 5' x 5' (Inched Deep). 1972, remade for display in 2015. Mixed media, 150 x 150 cm. Collection of National Gallery Singapore.

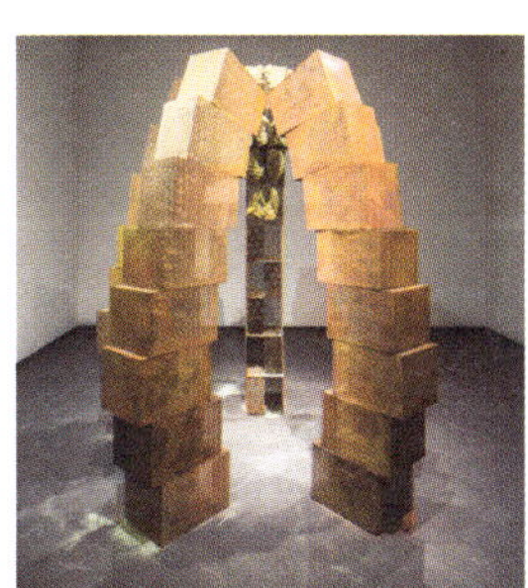

Montien Boonma. *Nature's Breath: Arokhayasala*. 1995. Metal, terracotta and herbs, 256 x 215 x 215 cm. Collection of Disaphol Chansiri. Installation view at *The Collectors Show: Weight of History*, Singapore Art Museum, 2013.

Conceptual practices in Southeast Asia take a variety of forms. Many widely cited figures, including Roberto Chabet and the spiritually focused Montien Boonma, are known for installations which engage viewers' movement through space. Others, such as Imelda Cajipe Endaya, work across diverse media, and combine artistic experimentation with a commitment to feminist politics. Some, like Apinan Poshyananda, combine artistic practice with academic and curatorial research and writing. In all of their work, aesthetics do still remain important. The textured surfaces in Montien's sculptural installations and the trace of the artist's hand in Endaya's collages and prints, for example, make this especially apparent.

Roberto Chabet
b. 1937, Philippines; d. 2013, Philippines

Montien Boonma
b. 1953, Thailand; d. 2000, Thailand

Imelda Cajipe Endaya
b. 1949, Philippines

Apinan Poshyananda
b. 1956, Thailand

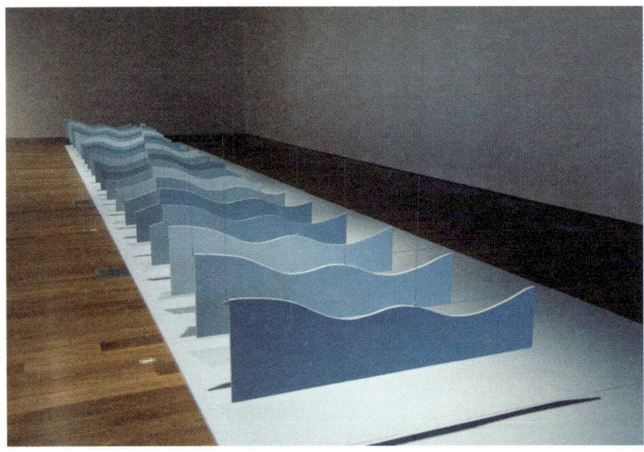

Roberto Chabet. *The Waves*. 1975. Plywood and synthetic polymer paint, dimensions variable. Collection of Carmen Mesina. Installation view at *The 9th Asia Pacific Triennial of Contemporary Art (APT9)*, Queensland Art Gallery | Gallery of Modern Art, Brisbane, 2018.

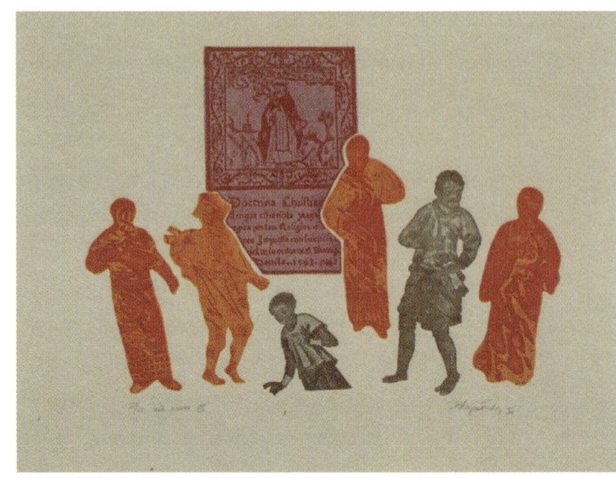

Imelda Cajipe Endaya. *Mga Ninunong Tagalog* (Tagalog Ancestors). Edition of 25. 1979. Collage and photoengraving, 38 x 51 cm. Collection of National Gallery Singapore.

Yet what unites such disparate approaches is the centrality of (often complex and challenging) *ideas*—over and above appearances—in art. As painter Ho Ho Ying wrote in 1972, regarding Cheo's *5' x 5'* proposal, "this new type of art requires a statement in order to communicate efficiently." Cheo himself wrote in 1974 that his practice aimed "to suggest something which is capable of provoking the awareness of beholders if they think really hard."

Of course, ideas are important in all art, and most artists make important choices before they begin making artworks. Raden Saleh, for example, would have carefully planned his compositions before picking up a paintbrush, and debates about how to interpret Raden Saleh's ideas, as expressed in his paintings, have shaped the <u>reception</u> of his work.

Nevertheless, Raden Saleh's paintings are primarily understood as aesthetic objects: what distinguishes conceptual art is that its aesthetics are secondary to its ideas. As Ho wrote in his 1972 response to Cheo's proposal, "Viewers will not get any satisfaction even if they look at it for a whole day." That Cheo chose to write instructions for *5' x 5'* instead of actually producing the artwork by hand emphasises this. Many conceptual artists employ similar strategies to foreground the centrality of their concept. Redza Piyadasa, for example, often integrated text into his artworks, to emphasise the <u>value</u> of the ideas behind them. Whereas the main way to appreciate Raden Saleh's paintings is to look at their appearance, the main way to appreciate conceptual artworks is to read and think about them. This is the case even for works like Montien's and Endaya's, which also reward more straightforwardly visual and spatial investigation.

Ho Ho Ying
b. 1936, Singapore

Raden Saleh
b. circa 1811, Indonesia; d. 1880, Indonesia

Redza Piyadasa
b. 1939, Malaysia; d. 2007, Malaysia

Considering the ideas behind these artists' works greatly enriches our experience of their <u>oeuvres</u>.

Despite this, aesthetics are not discounted completely in conceptual art—and perhaps remain especially important in Southeast Asian examples. The shape of Cheo's 5' x 5', for instance, clearly refers to the conventional shape of a painting. The lines extending from the wall onto the floor draw our eyes down, revealing that the space in which it is exhibited is also part of the artwork. This reference to painting, and to the immediate context of the work, is made through its aesthetic form, while also contributing to its conceptual underpinning.

In this way, conceptual art revises our understanding of the conventions and genres that precede it, and transforms the possibilities for <u>contemporary</u> artists working in its wake.

CONNECTIONS

Modern art has been shaped by many different kinds of connections between artists, just as modern life is characterised by countless new forms of social interaction. Thinking about both of these kinds of interpersonal links can electrify and enlarge our understanding of the modern art of Southeast Asia.

Modern art—including modern literature and other cultural forms—is uniquely able to communicate the manifold and often unexpected intersections and bonds between people with quite different backgrounds, brought together by the circumstances of <u>urbanisation</u> and modern life.

Indeed, modern cities have forged unprecedented and intimate connections between people of different cultures and classes by placing them in close, neighbourly proximity to one another, and by speeding up the experience of <u>time</u>. A passage from *Noli Me Tangere*, an 1887 novel by Jose Rizal regarded as a Philippine nationalist classic, evokes this: "The hustle and bustle everywhere, so many carriages and cabs at a dash, Europeans, Chinese, and natives, each dressed after their own fashion, fruit pedlars, messengers, porters stripped to the waist." Similar descriptions of the interpersonal affinities of modern life can be found from across Southeast Asia, with <u>modernities</u> being pictured through metaphors of interaction. For example, 19th-century artists depicted scenes of social mixing on trams; 20th-century artists evoked the energy of riots; and many popular films took relationships between neighbours as their subject.

A key example of art conveying unexpected links between people is a painting by Rizal's friend and political ally, Juan Luna, which depicts a working-class funeral in France. Through his rendering of the hunched posture of the anonymous mourners, Luna reveals their sorrow: a suffering which seems to transcend their immediate loss, and extend into a larger disaffection with their <u>quotidian</u> lives of hardship. Luna's capturing of the scene also intimates his feeling of empathic connection with these faceless strangers.

Connections among artists from diverse backgrounds and locations, as well as between the communities they belong to, have been an important factor driving developments and innovations in modern art. These links have often been established when Southeast Asian artists travelled in pursuit of an <u>education</u> abroad or to participate in international <u>exhibitions,</u> when artists from elsewhere visited the region, and in other more idiosyncratic ways.

During the 19th century, perhaps the most prominent bond for Southeast Asian modern artists was with Europe, especially the then-colonial powers of Britain, France, and the Netherlands. In Thailand, which was never formally colonised, Italian artists were commissioned to help develop art institutions and depict changing <u>fashions</u>. Ideas were also exchanged between Southeast Asian artists and European artists who spent time in Southeast Asia, such as Alix Ayme (who lived and taught in Vietnam, helping to popularise the use of the <u>craft</u> technique of lacquer in art, and also painted in Laos), and early photographers who established studios in the region.

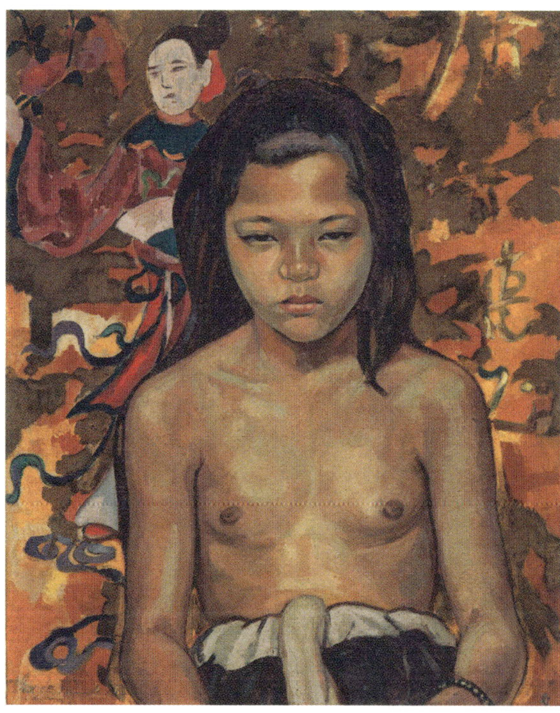

Alix Ayme. *Portrait of a Girl.* c. 1938. Oil on canvas, 56 x 38 cm. Private collection, Singapore.

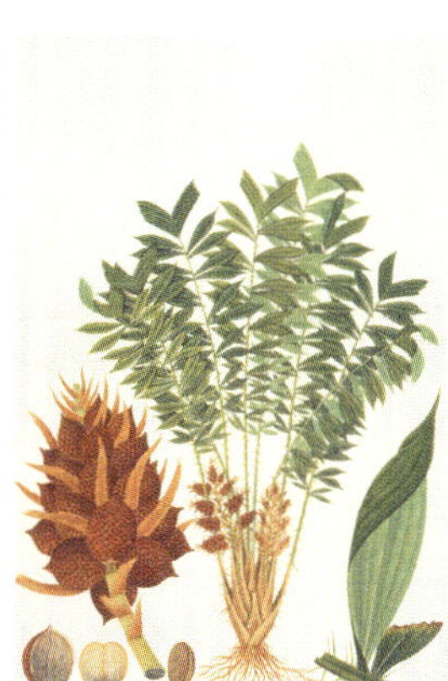

Artist unknown. *Salak*, from the William Farquhar Collection of Natural History Drawings. 1803–1818. Watercolour on paper, 55 x 38 cm. Gift of Mr G.K. Koh. Collection of National Museum of Singapore.

Alongside ties to Europe, links with Chinese artists were also vital to the emergence of modern art in Southeast Asia. Some of the earliest depictions of the region to deploy new visual technologies like single-point linear perspective were made by Chinese artists. Early Southeast Asian modern artists like Damian Domingo also used techniques, such as painting on ivory, which were popular among Chinese artists, especially those producing paintings for trade and circulation. Colonial bureaucrats also employed anonymous Chinese artists; for example, scholars believe that the 400-odd drawings of the Malay peninsula's flora and fauna produced under the direction of William Farquhar, the first colonial Resident and Commandant of Singapore, were by Chinese artists. Furthermore, according to art historian Apinan Poshyananda, Chinese art was used to introduce realism into Siamese painting in the early and mid-19th century, and "art works of this period show an amalgamation of Chinese and Siamese styles."

After World War II, artists' connections with the United States and the Soviet-backed communist bloc became increasingly prominent. Both the United States and the communist bloc used art as propaganda during the Cold War decades, organising exhibitions and performances in Southeast Asia and sponsoring the region's artists to study abroad, thus establishing new ties. For example, Latiff Mohidin recounts that he met Damrong Wong-Uparaj, A.D. Pirous, and several other Southeast Asian artists while they were all in New York in 1969 with American funding support. Cold War-era connections with the United States have been studied more substantially than those with the communist bloc.

Alongside these and other links shaped by colonialism and geopolitical circumstances, modern art has also been enriched by less well-known connections between individuals and communities from varied geographies and cultures. For example, the most prominent and successful photographers in Yangon during the late 19th and early 20th century worked at the Ahuja studios, founded by a family from present-day Pakistan. At that time, Yangon was among the most culturally diverse cities in the world, attracting more migrants than New York City during the 1920s and 1930s, and most of its residents were migrants from South Asia. Contact between Indian and other South Asian artists with those in Myanmar (until 1930, a part of India) has yet to be fully explored.

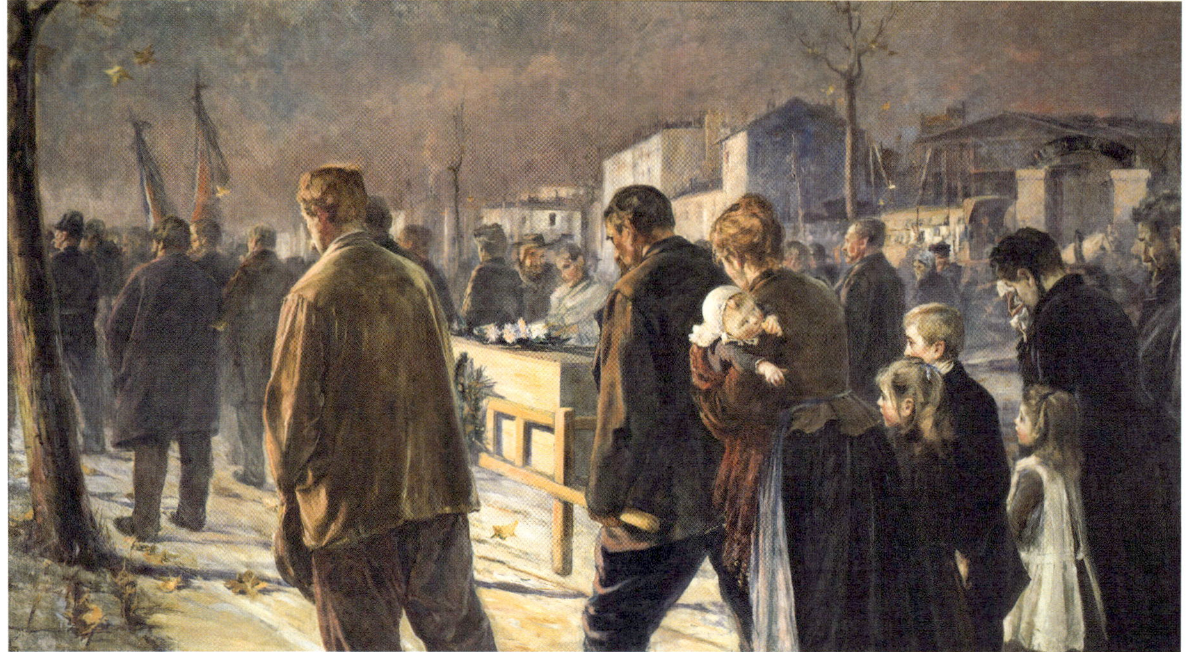

Juan Luna. *Les Ignores* (The Unknown Ones), also known as *Heroes Anonimos* (Anonymous Heroes). 1890–1891. Oil on canvas, 195 x 358 cm. Collection of Biblioteca Museu Victor Balaguer, Vilanova I la Geltru, Spain.

Connections with Africa, Latin America, Oceania, Australia, and other areas have also been studied much less than artistic intersections with Europe, the United States, and Asia. It is known that Ahmad Sadali, for example, exhibited in Rio de Janeiro in 1964, yet the nature and extent of the personal, intellectual or aesthetic links he may have established there have yet to be fully explored. Given that Sadali is celebrated for his use of <u>abstraction</u>, especially in his depictions of cities, it may be fruitful to consider his work in relation to his Latin American artist peers, some of whom (such as Lygia Clark) were also working with abstraction. Yet to date most attention has focused on the (limited) effects of Sadali's American-sponsored connections to the United States in the context of the Cold War.

The possibility for comparison is one obvious benefit of paying attention to connections between different artists and locations. A comparative method can sometimes yield insights that may not be possible to reach when focusing on a single subject. Moreover, scholars have often embraced comparison as a means to demonstrate experiences that are shared across <u>national</u> boundaries, thereby counteracting the effects of nationalism which have dominated many studies of <u>Southeast Asian</u> modern art. The nationally delimited nature of much art history writing has meant that many artists

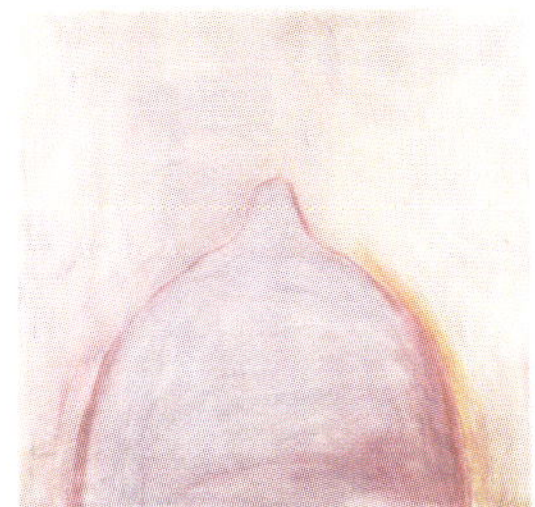

Pinaree Sanpitak. *Pink Breast*. 1994.
Acrylic and pastel, 105.5 x 106.5 cm.
Private collection.

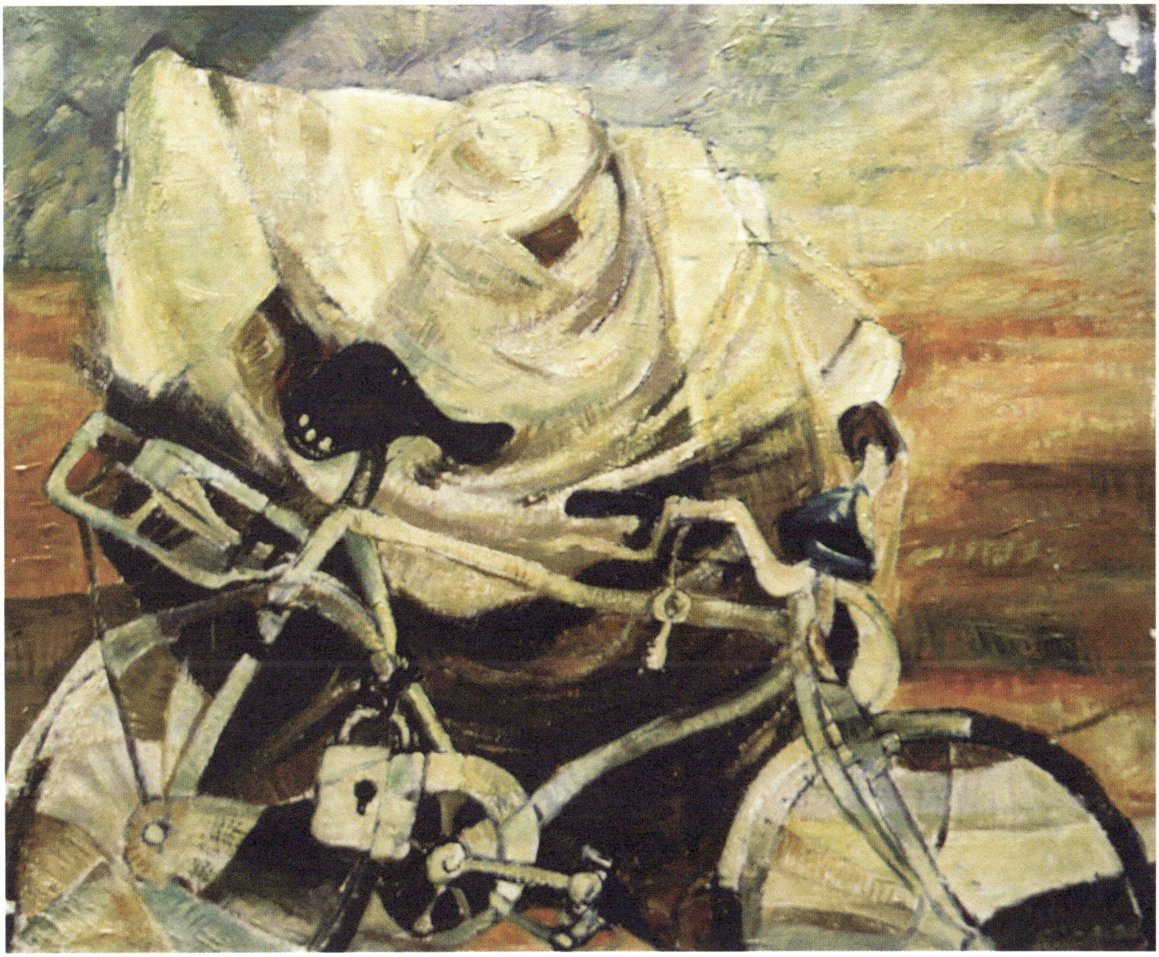

are <u>canonical</u> in their own country, but largely unknown elsewhere in the region.

With <u>globalisation</u> continually expanding and intensifying in recent decades, many artists have travelled farther and more frequently than ever before, and unexpected, individual connections have been increasingly important in their practices. For instance, the elegant simplicity of Pinaree Sanpitak's work, and her repeated revisiting of organic forms, may be attributed in part to her studies in Japan. Another example is You Khin, who relocated from Cambodia to France in 1973, escaping civil <u>war</u> and <u>genocide</u>, and who later worked for many years in North and West Africa and the Middle East, painting <u>quotidian</u> scenes which were at once <u>exotic</u> and familiar. In several paintings, You Khin focused his attention on other migrants he encountered who were also working in these locations, such as Pakistani merchants in Qatar.

You Khin. Untitled (*The Pakistani Man and His Bike*). 1989. Oil on canvas, 65 x 81 cm. Private collection.

In recent years, many scholars have emphasised the significance of <u>diaspora</u> artists and transnational connections in their accounts of Southeast Asian modern and contemporary art. Examples of artists displaying such cosmopolitan affinities include Latiff Mohidin, who travelled extensively within Southeast Asia and took shared visual forms in the region as his subject matter, as well as Chen Cheng Mei, who also travelled extensively within and beyond the region, often exploring a seemingly harmonious interdependence between <u>tradition</u> and modernity.

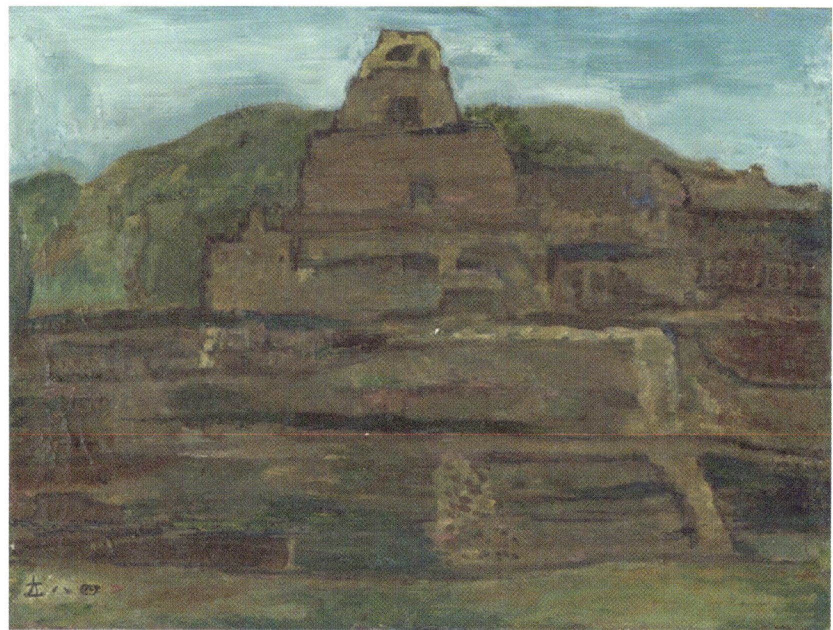

Chen Cheng Mei. *Sun Tower, Mexico*. 1984. Oil on canvas, 60.5 x 85 cm. Gift of the artist. Collection of National Gallery Singapore.

Indeed, there is room to focus more on connections within and between countries inside Southeast Asia. Art historian Kevin Chua observes that when teaching Southeast Asian modern art, "The (seeming) dominance of the West-Southeast Asia axis can produce peculiar anxieties… there is a strong, almost compensatory need to stress the interactions between Southeast Asian countries." Even if compensatory, focusing on what Chua calls "interactions between Southeast Asian countries" could also help redress the over-emphasis on the region's links with India and China in accounts by pioneering historians of premodern Southeast Asian cultures, such as George Coedes and Ananda Coomaraswamy. In considering the region's multiple and global connections, it is worth bearing in mind that most accounts of premodern Southeast Asian cultures have emphasised older historical links with China and India, and that this approach has shaped many understandings of the region's place in the world even today.

Just as modern cities like Rizal's Manila forged new affinities between people hailing from distant places, differing cultures, and diverse social positions, so too modern art has been shaped by countless overlapping and omnidirectional connections.

CONTEMPORARY

"If Picasso were an art student today, he'd probably flunk the course... Nowadays, it isn't enough to just sit there sketching nudes. You have to think deep. You have to have a 'concept.' So my friends [at art school] were all into concepts. All they did each day was wander beyond the school walls to scavenge for concepts."

This anecdote is from a parodic short story by Prabda Yoon, published in Thai in 2000. It captures two key tenets of contemporary art, which emerged between the 1970s and 2000s in Southeast Asia. Contemporary art exists alongside modern art; they are imprecise categories which overlap. Nevertheless, the ideas encompassed in Prabda's account help to distinguish contemporary from modern art.

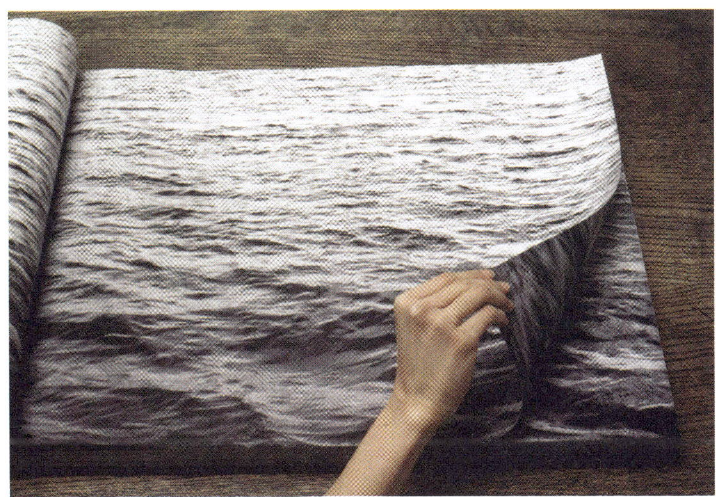

Lani Maestro. *a book thick of ocean* (detail). 1993. Installation with oak table, hardbound book with duotone printed pages of same photo image, cameo dull paper, embossed silver-stamped title on black linen-cloth cover, 500 pages, dimensions variable. Installation view, Galerie Optica, Montreal.

First, as Prabda suggests, contemporary art stresses the centrality of concept: ideas are of equal importance as technical skill or formal innovation. Of course, ideas have always been important, but aesthetic appearance was usually the most crucial dimension in modern artworks, until

<u>conceptual</u> art practices emerged from the 1970s onwards in Southeast Asia. Contemporary art exists in the aftermath of conceptual art, which shifted away from the aesthetic and toward the idea. With contemporary art, however, artists do not focus exclusively on concepts. They also bring in other concerns, importantly including emotional or affective responses, experienced bodily rather than apprehended intellectually. This situation, which Prabda light-heartedly caricatures, has been theorised by scholar Peter Osborne, who claims that contemporary art is "post-conceptual" in nature. Lani Maestro's *a book thick of ocean* is an example. It suggests ideas about <u>diaspora</u>—the artist lives in self-imposed exile from the ocean-bound archipelago of her birth—while also <u>poetically</u> invoking *feelings* of awe and longing, like the sea it represents.

Second, Prabda's anecdote also indicates the decreased importance of skills developed in a <u>studio</u>, which in contemporary art are displaced by engagement with the world outside the studio, or "beyond the school walls." The concepts underpinning much contemporary art often relate to social, environmental, and cultural changes, including those heralded by <u>globalisation</u>; hence, contemporary artworks often draw on community engagement or invite audience participation. For example, Rirkrit Tiravanija often makes art by preparing and sharing food, thus facilitating sociable conviviality. Although contemporary art can take any form—and artists increasingly work in more than one <u>medium</u>—some types of artwork are especially prevalent. Installation—which takes ordinary objects and transforms them into art by placing them in an exhibition or other art context—as well as performance, video and photography are among the most prominent types of contemporary art, in part because they rely less on technical skill, and instead point to the world outside the artist's studio. Examples include Melati Suryodarmo's performance using sticks of household butter, and Suzann Victor's installation made with eggplants attached to the wall of a contemporary art space run by the 5th Passage Artists, located in a Singapore shopping mall corridor.

As well as being "post-conceptual" and "post-studio," contemporary art is also characterised by its enmeshment in various kinds of networks linking artists and audiences from different locations. For example, <u>biennials</u> have proliferated since the emergence of contemporary art, and are increasingly significant sites for exchanging ideas, as are commercially oriented art fairs. More informal, self-organised <u>connections</u> including artist-run spaces, residencies,

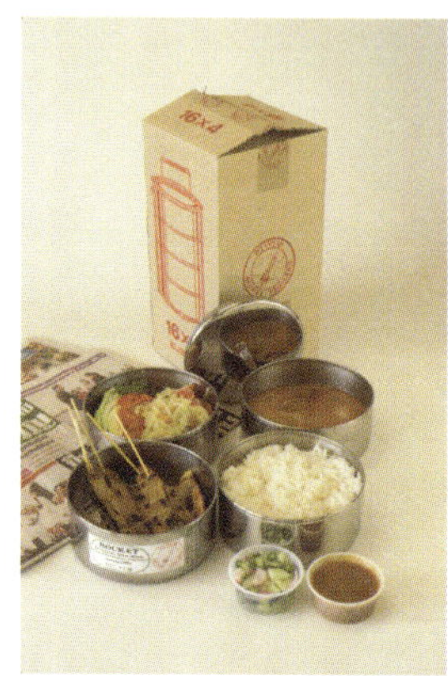

Rirkrit Tiravanija. *Untitled (Lunch Box)*. 1996. Multiple of stainless steel container, Thai newspaper, and Thai meal.

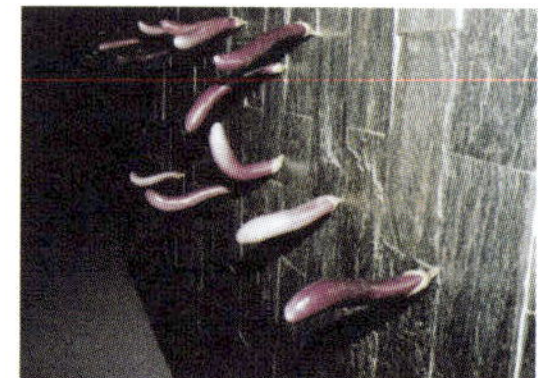

Suzann Victor. *Still Life*. 1992. Eggplants, clips, dimensions variable. Installation view, 5th Passage, Singapore.

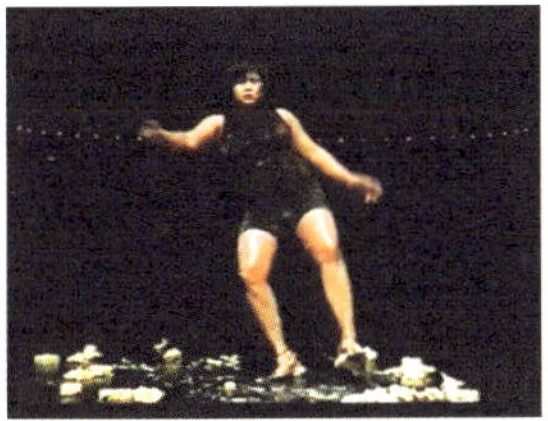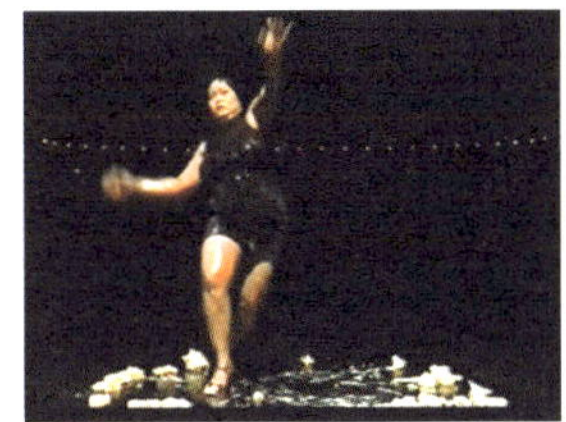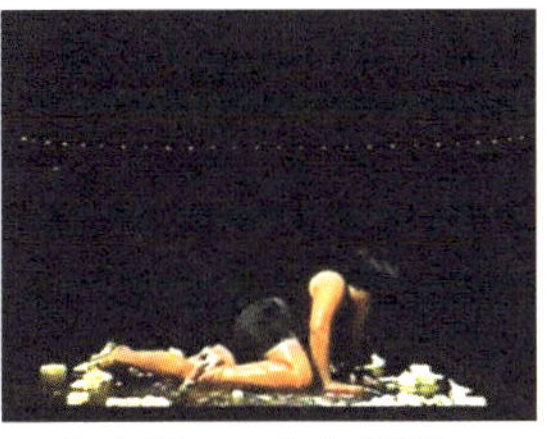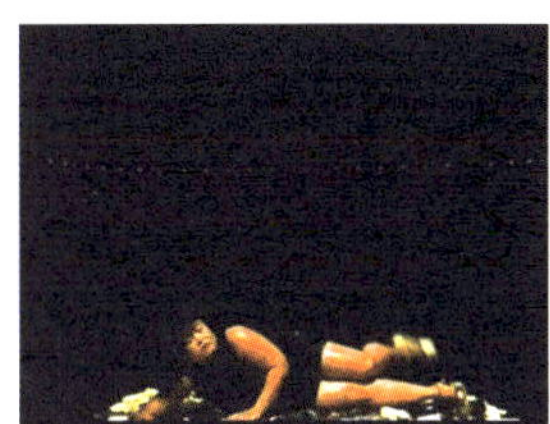

Melati Suryodarmo. *Exergie—Butter Dance*. 2000. Stills from footage of first public performance, at Hebbel Theatre, Berlin, 2000.

and festivals are also crucial, and contemporary artists often work collaboratively in groups or collectives.

A final aspect of contemporary art which sets it apart from modern art is its foregrounding of art's multiple and complex relationships to <u>time</u>. The English word "contemporary" derives from "together with the times," and many equivalent terms in Southeast Asian <u>vernacular</u> languages have similar etymologies. As this naming suggests, the contemporary registers different under-standings of <u>history</u>, emphasising shared experiences of the present. In contrast, modernities and modern art are often future-oriented and imagine time as linear progress. This complicated idea is perhaps best understood through artwork. Modern time is imagined as linear: it goes in one direction. Contemporary attitudes to time, on the other hand, imagine many different directions overlapping all at once. These multiple ways of conceiving of contemporary time are suggested by the multiple routes for navigating Maestro's *a book thick of ocean*, as well as an installation comprising a maze-like arrangement of mosquito nets that she first exhibited alongside it, under the title *Cradle*. Such works can be "read" in any sequence, entered at any point; perhaps like time, they flow in every direction.

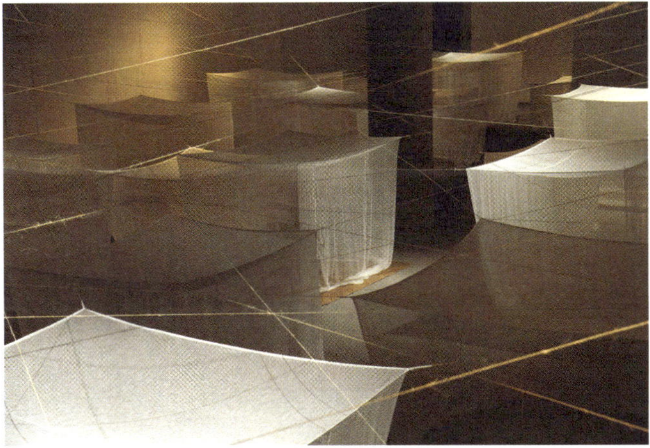

Lani Maestro. *Cradle*. 1996. Installation with hand-sewn mosquito netting, gauze fabric, sisal strings, handwoven Philippine hemp mats, dimensions variable. Installation view, *Art in General*, New York.

Craft is often considered to have a lesser <u>value</u> than art. Yet this idea seems to have no historical basis within Southeast Asia, and is derived from European traditions which were <u>transferred</u> to this region. The distinction between art and craft is arbitrary and blurred, and craft frequently appears in modern art. Craft techniques have often been used to assert a Southeast Asian identity for art, based on critical adaptations of <u>tradition</u>, and related to <u>quotidian</u> life.

Crafted objects generally have a more practical function than artworks (although sometimes art can be functional, and not all craft is useful). For example, weaving and other textiles are often considered craft, whereas paintings made on easels are usually considered art. Craft is also generally believed to require mostly technical (rather than compositional or <u>conceptual</u>) skill, which is why sometimes artists—including painters—maybe praised for their "craft," meaning their ability to render well. Craft is commonly associated with <u>women</u>, or regarded as a "feminine" practice. Identifying and differentiating between individual makers is often less important in craft than in art, where the modern concept of an <u>artist</u> rests on a singular style and persona. These understandings of craft, and its alterity to art, are modern inventions, emerging chiefly since the 19th century, and largely arising from contact with colonial and other systems of knowledge.

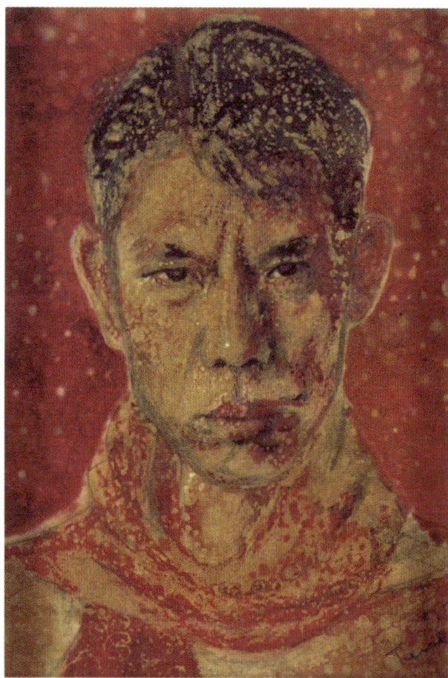

Chuah Thean Teng. *Self-Portrait*. c. 1950s. Batik, 31 x 21 cm. Gift of the Loke Wan Tho Collection. Collection of National Gallery Singapore.

The most prominent uses of craft techniques in Southeast Asia's art in the 20th century are paintings made with batik and lacquer, by professionally trained artists who would have seen themselves as quite distinct from artisans and makers of purely decorative or functional objects. For example, pioneer batik painters like Chuah Thean Teng adapted the technique of wax-resist fabric dyeing—used for intricate patterns in sarongs and other textiles—and redeployed it for figurative compositions, applying wax and pigment through various unorthodox methods, including sometimes with paint brushes. Some batik paintings, like Chuah's *Self-Portrait*, are <u>realist</u> in style and natural in appearance. More typically, batik paintings feature exaggerated depictions, conveying exotic impressions of kampong (village) daily life. One particularly large example by Seah Kim Joo was commissioned for the entrance to the Hotel Malaysia in Singapore, reflecting a new kind of <u>patronage</u>. Some batik paintings are more abstract, like Fatimah Chik's compositions that evoke <u>spiritual</u> geometries. Chik's teacher, Sivam Selvaratnam, painted batik designs on paper and canvas, and even made <u>fashionable</u> batik high-heeled shoes.

Chuah Thean Teng
b. 1914, China; d. 2008, Malaysia

Seah Kim Joo
b. 1939, Singapore

Fatimah Chik
b. 1947, Malaysia

Sivam Selvaratnam
b. 1937, Malaysia

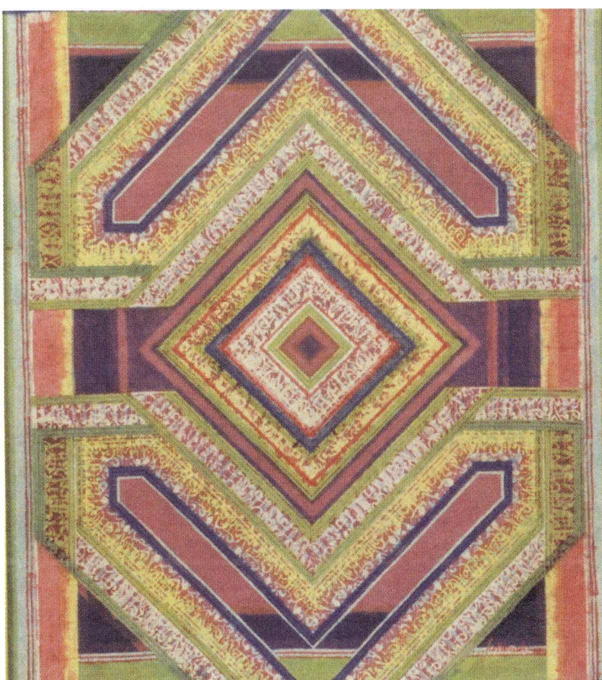

Fatimah Chik. *Meditation 1*. 1985. Batik, 96 x 85 cm. Collection of National Gallery Singapore.

Like batik textiles, batik paintings are found across the Malay archipelago and beyond; historian Farish A. Noor proposes that "batik was truly the lingua franca of the peoples of <u>Southeast Asia</u>."

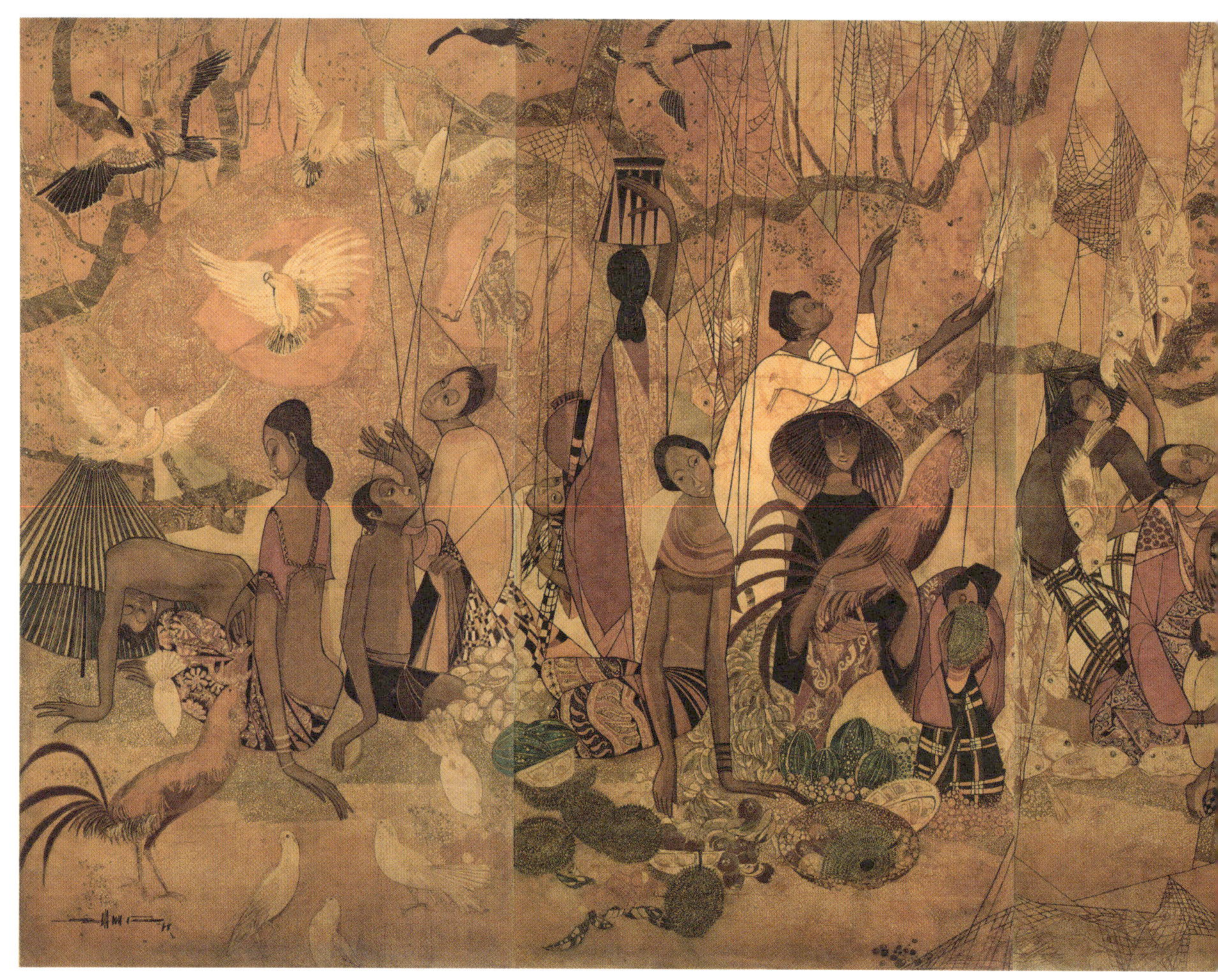

Seah Kim Joo. Untitled (*Malayan Life*). 1968. Batik, 256 x 294 cm. LASALLE College of the Arts Collection, Institute of Contemporary Arts Singapore.

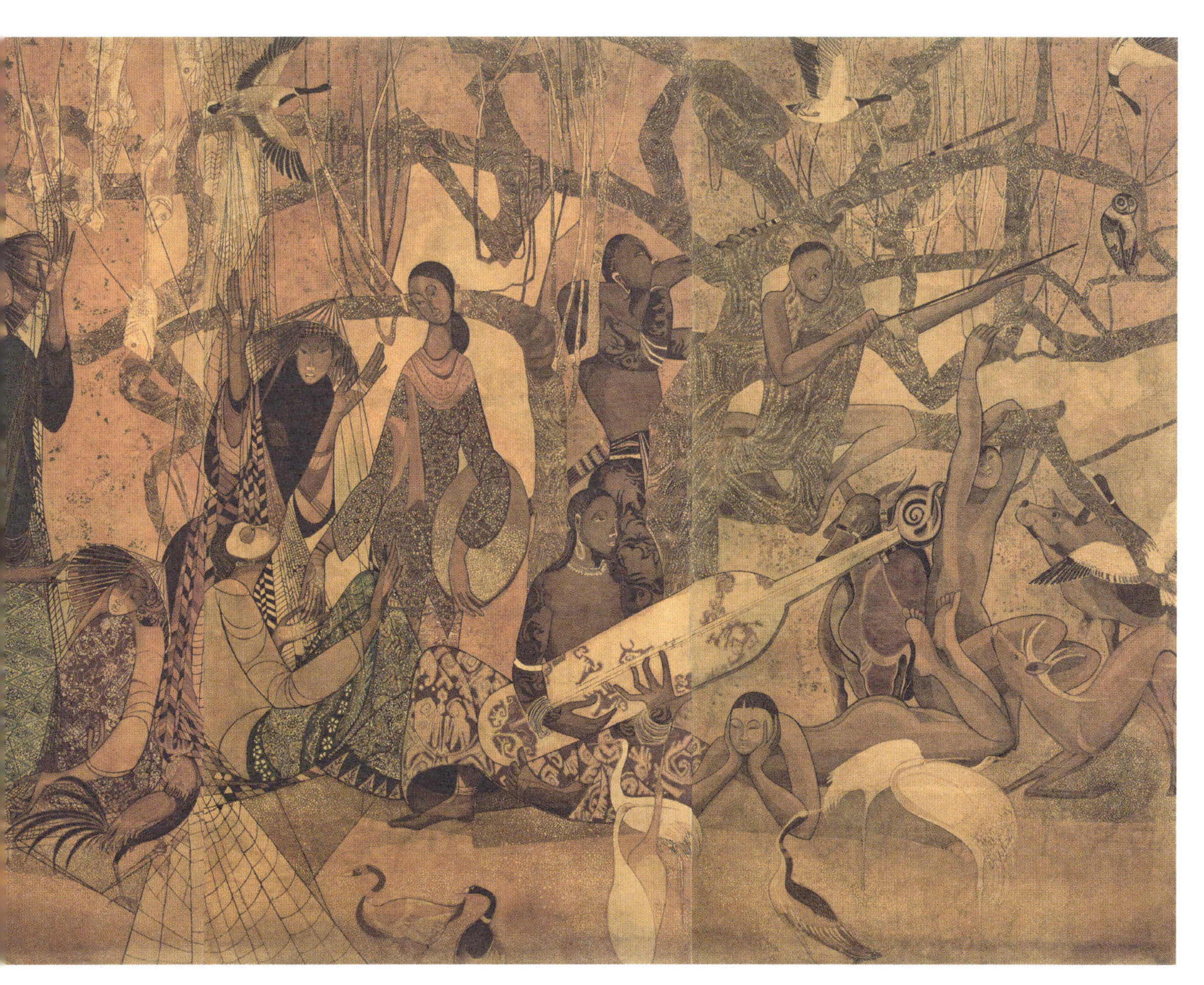

By contrast, lacquer is primarily linked to a single <u>nation</u>: Vietnam. Nguyen Gia Tri, one of the earlier generation of students to be educated at the newly established art school in Hanoi, was an especially celebrated figure popularising the use of lacquer (or *son mai*) in paintings, which were considered art, and thus quite distinct from craft. The material is typically used on functional household items like bowls, vases and jewellery boxes, where it is laboriously applied in many layers. Gia Tri combined use of the highly specialised lacquer technique with elements of composition derived from European-style <u>landscape</u> conventions, occasionally (as in *Landscape of Vietnam*) also drawing on some features of Chinese landscape composition. Because lacquer paintings are considered distinctively Vietnamese, they have even been used for <u>propaganda</u>, by artists like Nguyen Khang. However, modern artists from elsewhere in the region, like Chen Wen Hsi, have also experimented with lacquer.

As the most prominent craft materials used in 20th-century art, batik, and lacquer figure in many works of art. Other kinds of modern craft have, in contrast, been less well-studied. For example, the use of Japanese coloured glass to adorn temples in Luang Prabang may also be considered a distinctly modern innovation. So too are paintings on lanterns, known as *damar kurung*, by Sriwati Masmundari. According to art historians Carla Bianpoen, Farah Wardani and Wulan Dirgantoro, the decoration of paper lanterns is a longstanding tradition in Gresik, the cosmopolitan port-town where Sriwati was born. Taught by her parents to make *damar kurung*, Sriwati began decorating these lanterns when she was ten, but only held her first exhibition decades later, in 1987. Originally working with food dyes on oil paper, she later used permanent markers on sturdier tracing paper, also making paintings for display on a wall, rather than attached to a lantern.

Today, <u>contemporary</u> artists in Southeast Asia are increasingly adopting craft techniques, in part to critique modern art's privileging of some media, materials and ideas above others. Craft may be best understood as continuous with art, rather than distinct from it.

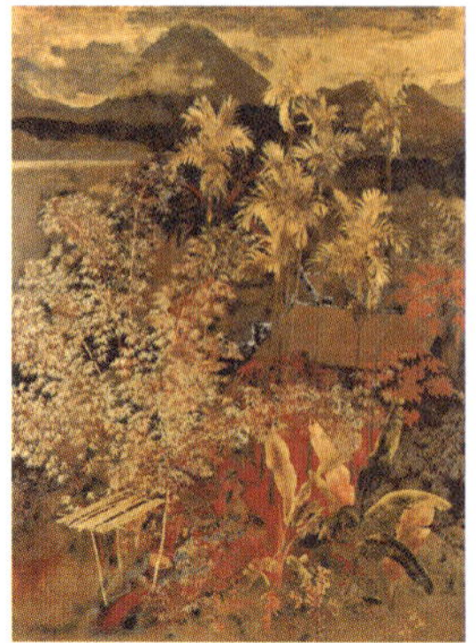

Nguyen Gia Tri. *Landscape of Vietnam*. c. 1940. Lacquer on board, 159 x 119 cm. Collection of National Gallery Singapore.

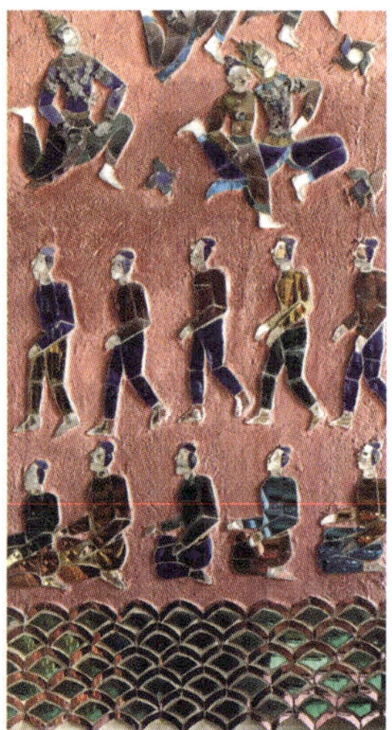

Mosaic made with Japanese coloured glass in Wat Xieng Thong, Luang Prabang, Laos. 1940s. Artist unknown.

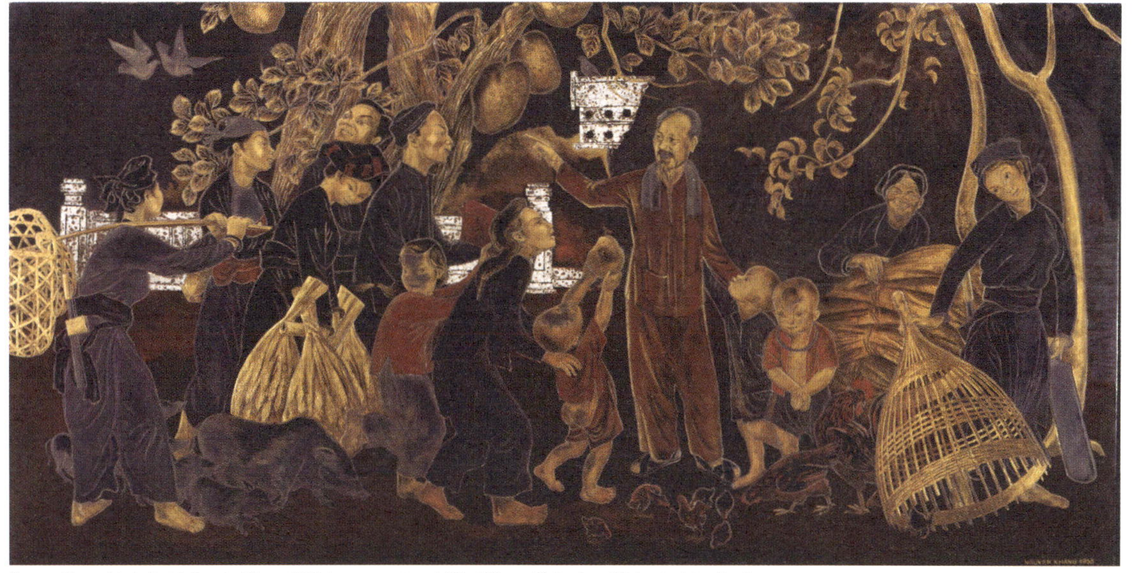

Nguyen Khang. *Uncle Ho Visiting the Village*. 1958. Lacquer on board, 92 x 190 cm. Collection of Fukuoka Asian Art Museum.

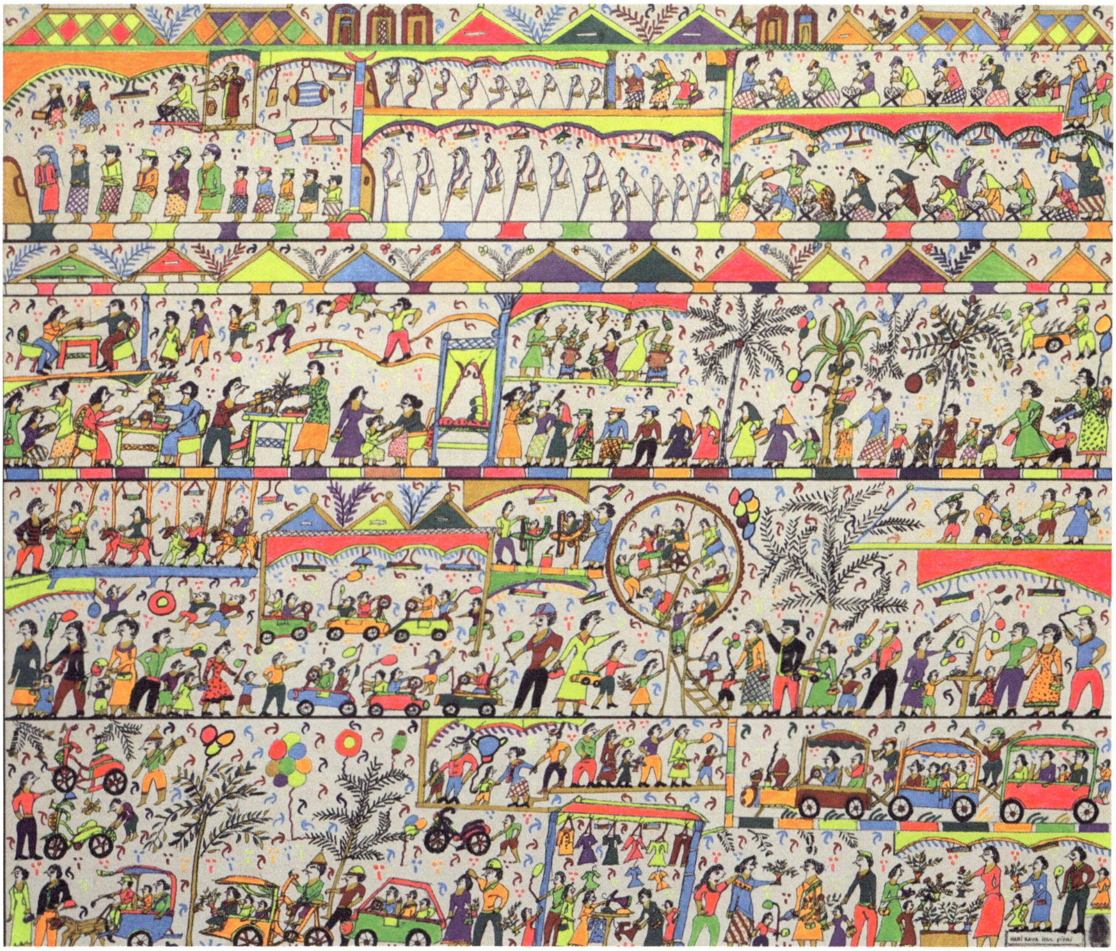

Sriwati Masmundari. *Hari Raya Idul Fitri*. 2002. Pen, watercolour and acrylic on canvas, 110 x 90 cm. Collection of Melani Setiawan.

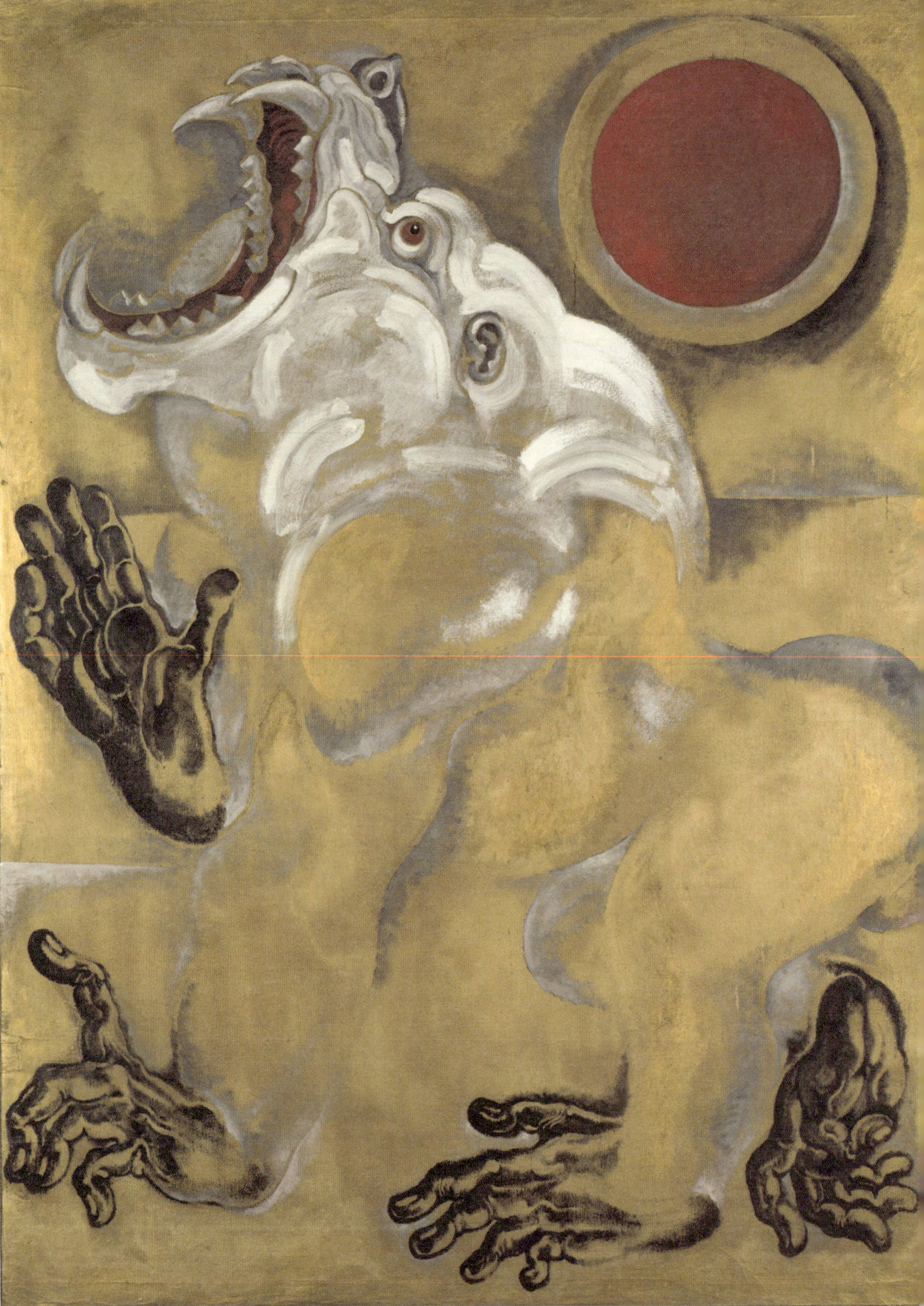

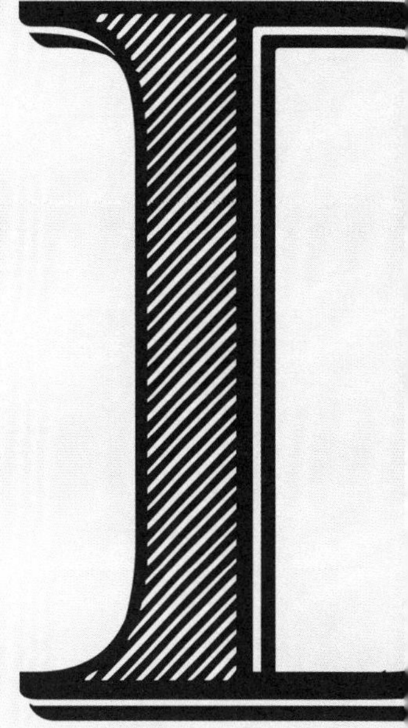

As ferocious as thunder, as gentle as morning clouds.

—Thawan Duchanee

Thawan Duchanee. *Hanuman*. 1973. Oil on canvas, 220 x 150 cm. Collection of National Gallery Singapore.

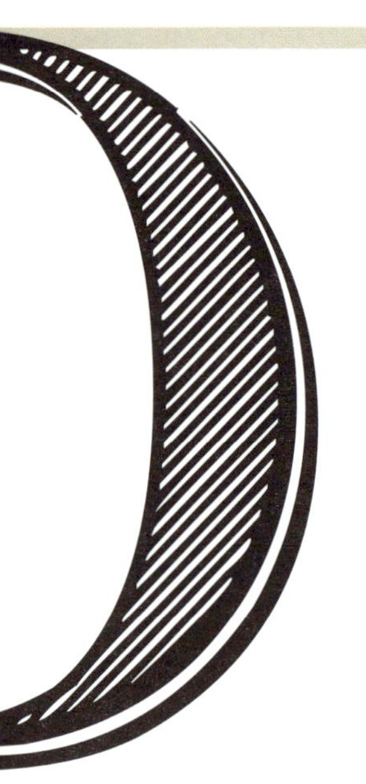

"The development of modern art in Indonesia, as a facet of cultural change," art historian Claire Holt wrote in her 1967 book, "is, of course, a part of the broader question about the future direction in which Indonesian culture would develop. This question has been passionately debated by the country's leading intellectuals for more than three decades." Describing this broad-ranging cultural discussion as "The Great Debate," Holt proposed that "the roots of the debate is the confrontation of the 'East' with the 'West.'" She identified the most contentious questions as including, "Is modernization equivalent to Westernization?"

Impassioned debates, like that which Holt wrote about, have occurred not only in Indonesia but throughout Southeast Asia. Modern art in the region has emerged and developed as a carnival of debates. Competing visions have appeared in manifestos and other statements by of individual artists and groups, and also in artworks themselves, and in the actions of governments, including those of genocide and war. While debates have raged about a wide variety of topics, in general, artistic and cultural disagreements have been about what forms of modernities are appropriate for Southeast Asian contexts. The modern is often synonymous with the new, and change has often been resisted or contested in various ways.

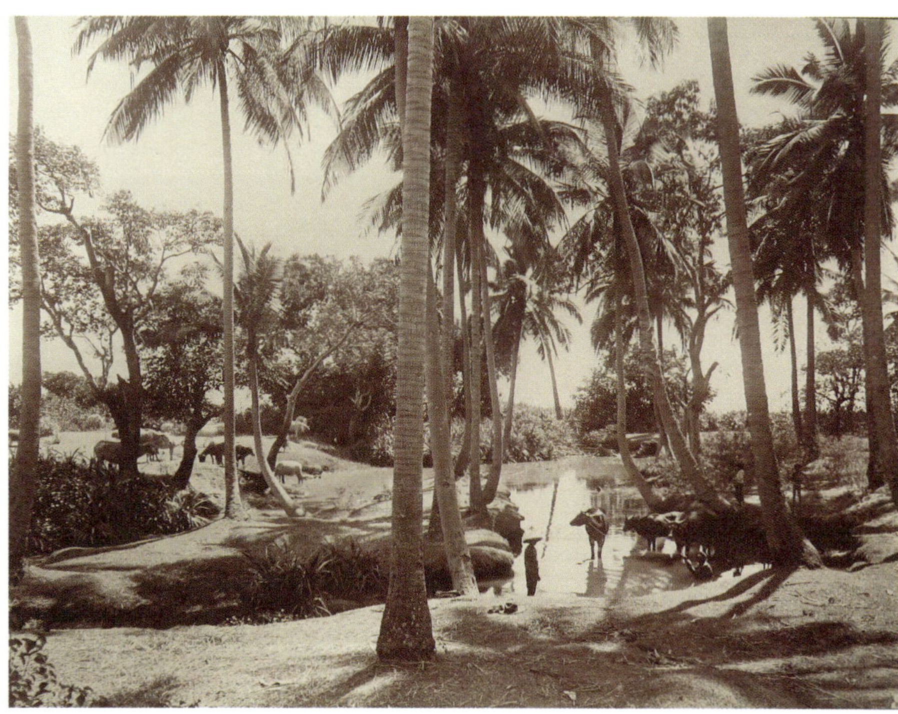

Thilly Weissenborn. *North Coast of Bali*. c. 1920s–1930s. Silver gelatin print, 20 x 25 cm. Collection of National Gallery Singapore.

While debates have recurred throughout the history of modern art, the years between the end of World War I and the beginning of World War II—referred to as the interwar period—were an especially heated cultural moment in many parts of Southeast Asia. In Indonesia during the 1930s, S. Sudjojono launched a vision for a new kind of <u>realism</u>, in opposition to what he saw as overly romanticised depictions of <u>landscape</u> by artists whose work was known as *Mooi Indie* ("Beautiful Indies"). Sudjojono charged that this aesthetic was overly interested in making the region seem exotic, and catered to foreign tastes. Artists associated with the *Mooi Indie* genre include painters like Wakidi, as well as photographers including Thilly Weissenborn, one of few women to run a professional photography studio at the time.

A similar debate took place around the same time in the Philippines, enacted both in artworks and in texts. When Victorio Edades painted *The Builders* in 1928, soon after his return to Manila from being educated in the United States, the proto-<u>social realist</u> composition was widely perceived as a riposte to popular, idealised depictions of <u>women</u> and <u>landscapes</u>, which dominated the work of Fernando Amorsolo and Fabian de la Rosa. After the early emergence of modern art <u>education</u> in the Philippines, the forms that modern art should take were now being contested, in a controversy that would continue for quite some time. Two decades later, in a written exchange with Guillermo Tolentino, Edades—who is commonly regarded as a forerunner of a new kind of modern art in the Philippines—accused his peer of backwardness. "The entire world has felt the impact of Modern Art," Edades wrote, "and though the conservatives, the academic painters and teachers, try to stave it off, the new art comes inevitably, for it expresses the present age."

Fabian de la Rosa. *In the Rice Field*. 1919. Oil on canvas, 55 x 80 cm. Private collection.

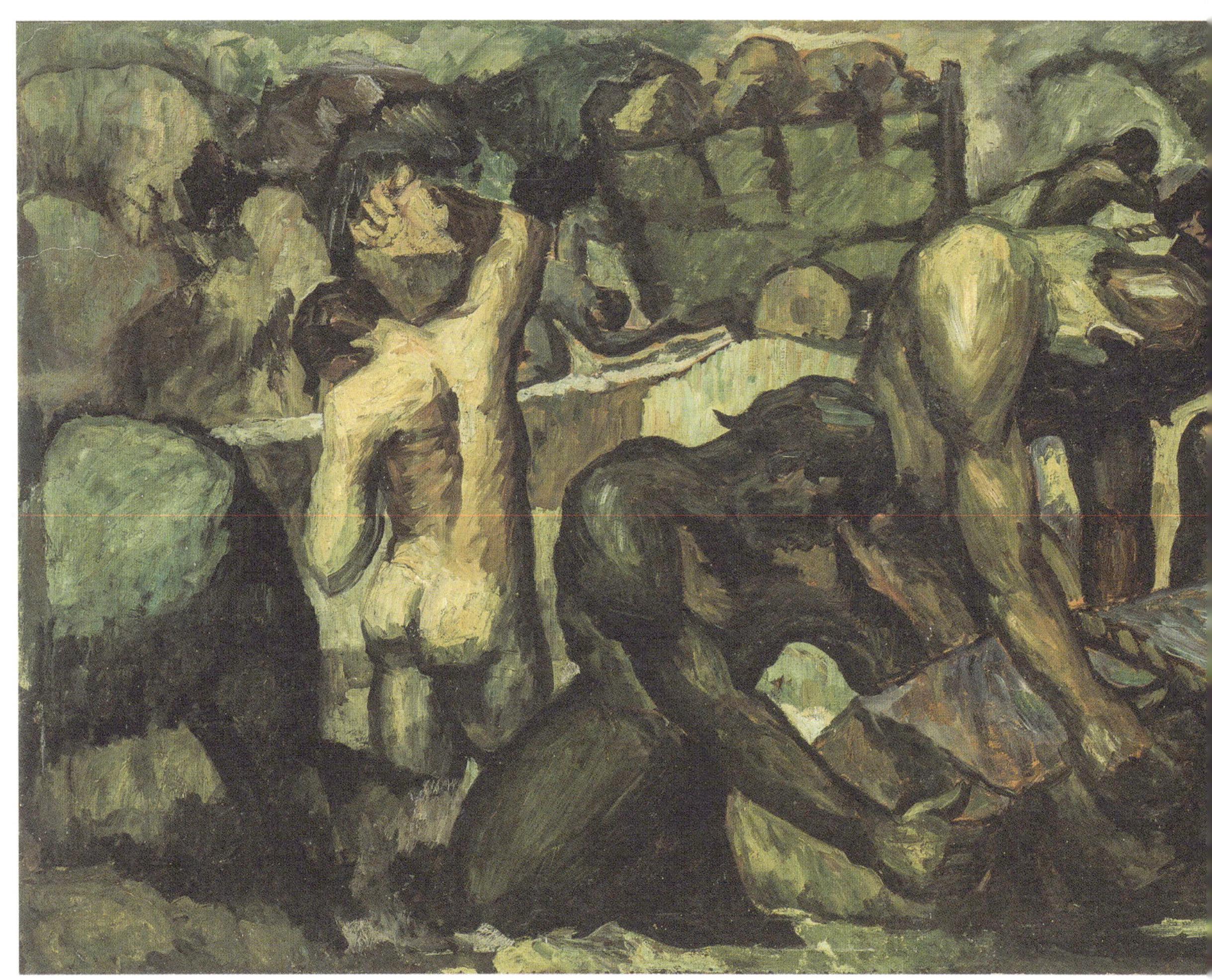

Victorio Edades. *The Builders*. 1928. Oil on plywood, 128 x 321 cm. Collection of Cultural Center of the Philippines.

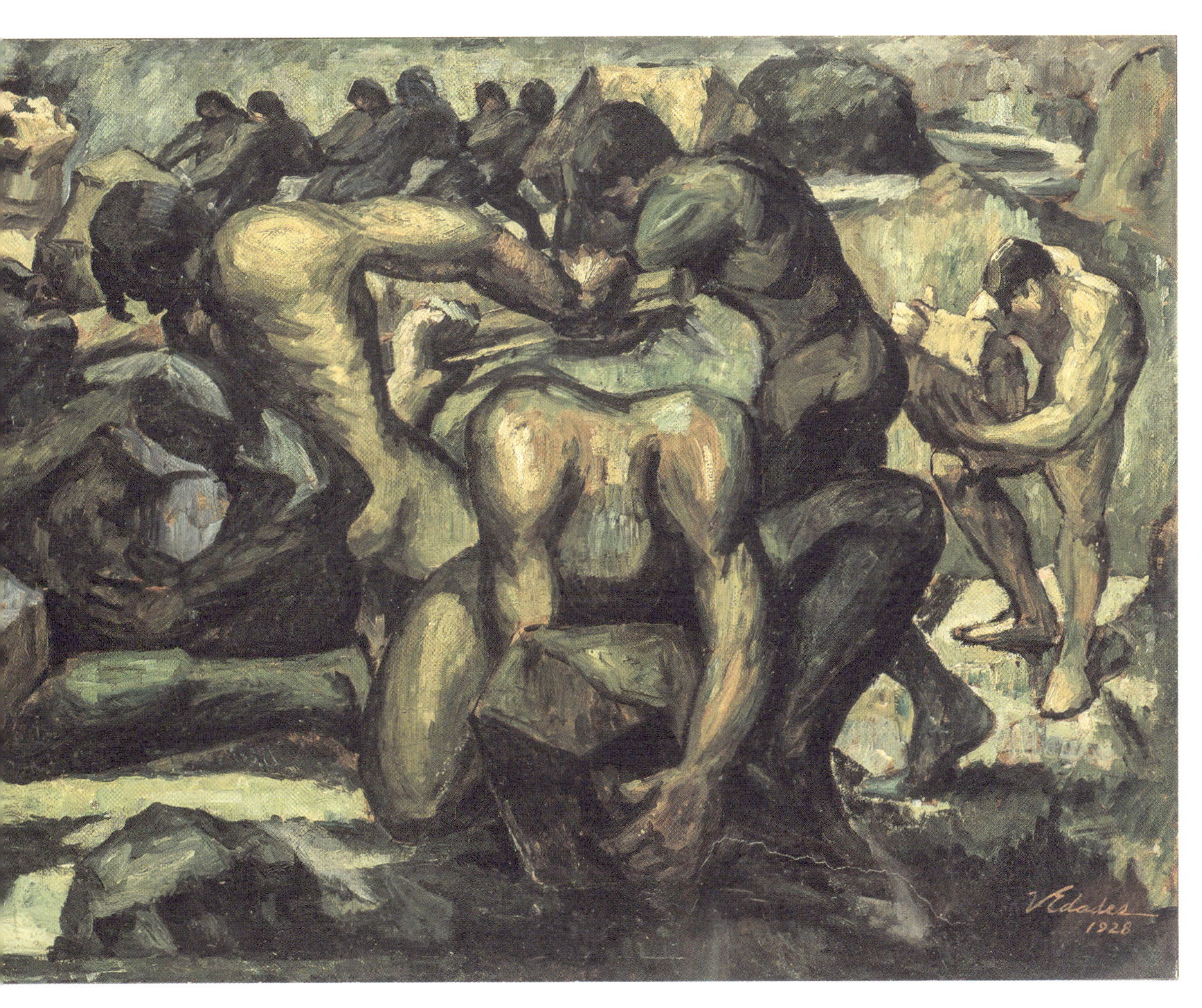

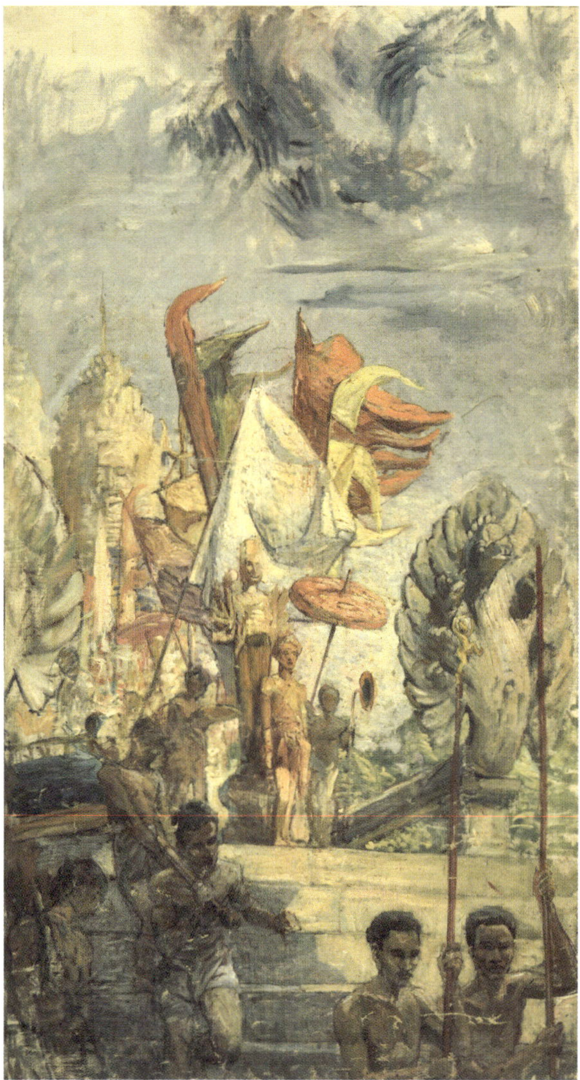

George Groslier. *Buddhism, Procession in Front of One of the Face Towers of the Bayon.* c. 1914. Oil on canvas, 176 x 97 cm. Collection of National Gallery Singapore.

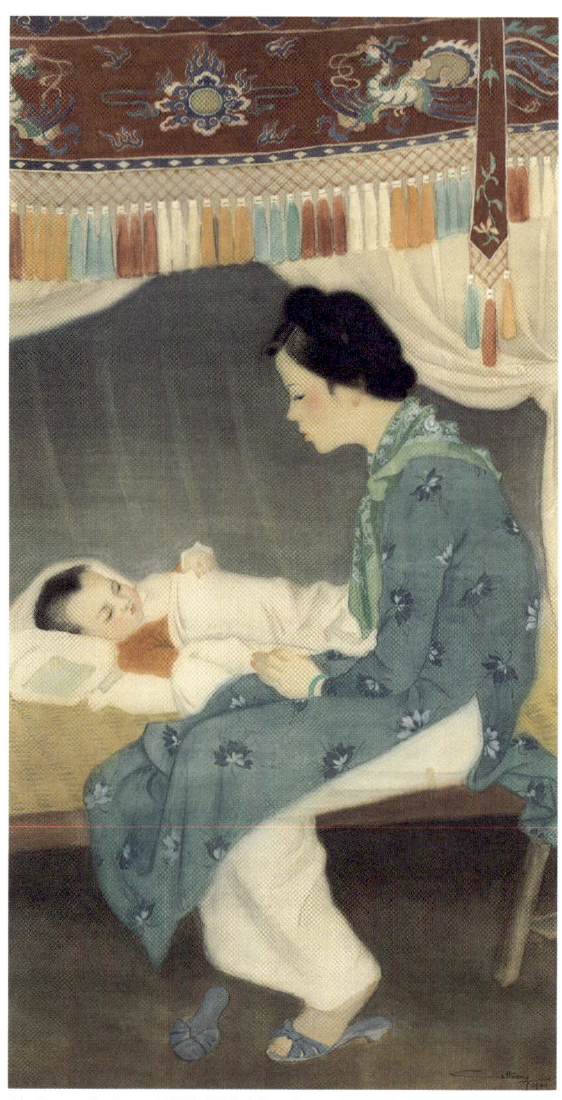

Cat Tuong. *Mother and Child.* 1940. Ink and gouache on silk, 75 x 39 cm. Del Monte Collection.

Meanwhile in Vietnam, interwar debates in art were closely informed by broader social transformations. In 1930s Hanoi, modern art and culture was linked to and inspired by changes in the way modern women were imagined. *Dumb Luck*, a novel by Vu Trong Phung published in Vietnamese in 1936, humorously satirises debates over modernisation and shifting gender roles, with one character even exclaiming, in reference to a new kind of risque <u>fashion</u> accessory, "Long live Europeanization! Long live rubber breasts!" Around the same time, Cat Tuong invented a new design for the *ao dai* dress, which was considerably more figure-hugging than previous versions. One of few known paintings by Tuong

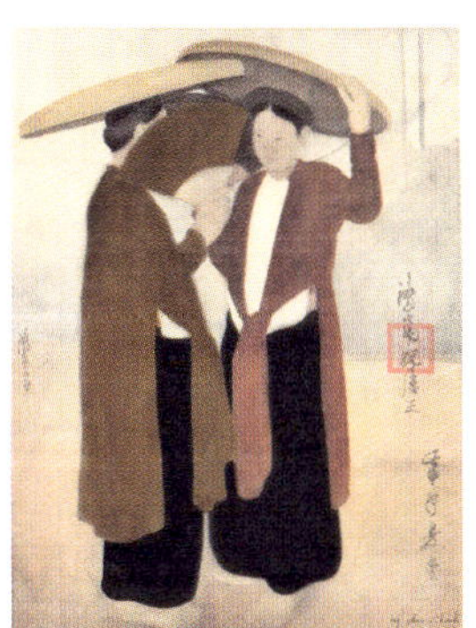

Nguyen Phan Chanh. *The Singers in the Countryside*. 1932. Watercolour and ink on silk, 65.4 x 49.4 cm. Collection of National Gallery Singapore.

depicts a woman in a conventional, maternal role, dressed in a modern *ao dai*.

However, contemporaneous works by artists such as Nguyen Phan Chanh indicate that such new fashions were certainly not universally adopted; Phan Chanh's silk painting —a new medium popularised at the newly established fine art school in Hanoi and considered to be distinctly Vietnamese—depicts rural women dressed in simpler, older styles of dress.

In Cambodia, a debate about modernisation exploded in 1940, when a Cambodian entrepreneur named Say developed a stamping machine which could make "patterned embossed silver boxes, buckles, and earrings," according to art historian Ingrid Muan. This machine innovated the manufacture of <u>craft</u> objects, which were being produced in large quantities at the School of Cambodian Arts, where the education system privileged "tradition" over new artistic styles and techniques. The school's founding director, George Groslier, was so enraged by Say's machine that he declared, "this machine should be thrown away and its inventor shot." The machine has since been lost, as has Say's <u>oeuvre</u>. Paintings by Groslier demonstrate his fascination with <u>spirituality</u> and <u>tradition</u> in Cambodia, which he saw as threatened by modernisation.

Later in the 20th century, ideas about what modern art and culture should be like have often continued to take the form of a polemic, almost always explicitly or implicitly addressed to a real or imagined opponent. For example, architect and cultural policymaker Vann Molyvann declared in the early 1960s that "Modernity should not be inspired superficially by Western ideas that destroy all traces of the past. New building should bring tradition and heritage back to life." As a concrete manifestation of his polemical yet nuanced position, Molyvann's design for the National Sports Complex in Phnom Penh synthesises modern engineering and aesthetics with ancient technologies and design principles, of the kind found in Khmer temples like Angkor Wat. The vast structure of Molyvann's stadium thus asserts a sense of Cambodian identity, which was seen as important in the context of regional sports competitions during the Cold War. The architecture insinuates the possibility of cultural continuity alongside modernisation and <u>urbanisation</u>, while also staking a neutralist position in the contest between communist and capitalist blocs.

Just as Molyvann's vision for a <u>hybrid</u> fusing of old and new forms seemed to be addressed to unspecified

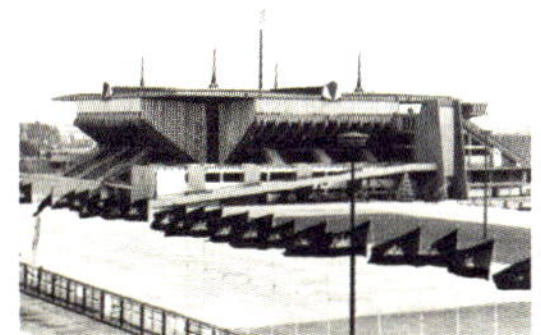

Vann Molyvann, architect. National Sports Complex, Phnom Penh. Completed 1964. Photographer unknown. c. 1964. Private collection of the late Vann Molyvann.

opponents, so too was the <u>manifesto</u> of the Gerakan Seni Rupa Baru in Indonesia. The group's vision for "new arts" also sounds directed against unnamed antagonists: "We reject as far away as possible the vision of 'art' that has thus far been recognized (we consider it 'old art'), i.e. art that is limited to only painting, sculpture, and drawing (prints)," the manifesto declares. Some works in the <u>exhibition</u>, such as *Paling Top* (Top Most) by F.X. Harsono, make this apparent in their formal composition. The artist's assemblage resembles a framed painting both in its proportions, and especially in its inclusion of a heavy and tiered wooden casing around its perimeter. The work has often been considered a contribution to debates about the militarisation of Indonesia under President Suharto's New Order regime. Yet in its aesthetic references to—yet defiant deviation from—the convention of framed easel painting, Harsono's work is also a visual manifestation of the GSRB manifesto's call for "new arts" to replace "old art." It therefore also speaks to debates about modern art, too.

More recently, many <u>contemporary</u> artists continue to articulate polemical positions. Anida Yoeu Ali, whose work often engages with <u>urbanisation</u> and the experience of <u>diaspora</u>, proudly describes herself as a "global agitator." Similarly, Hanh Thi Pham identifies as an "activist artist," and affirms that she intends for her work to be "inflammatory when need be, and all the more blatant to bring about change."

Art can reveal controversies so effectively because artworks can hold multiple ideas and seemingly opposing viewpoints together at once. Take, for example, the statement by Thawan Duchanee that his pictures are "packed with feelings for all kinds of man's and animal's emotions… As ferocious as thunder, as gentle as morning clouds." Thawan's artworks were violently slashed in 1971, by students angered by what they perceived as his disrespect of Buddhism. Yet while he tested the limits of <u>taboo</u>, Thawan remained a devout Buddhist. Just as he endeavoured to fill his artworks with the seemingly contradictory qualities of ferocity and gentleness—like thunder and morning clouds—so too he navigated a middle path, in his life and work. He was later celebrated, and awarded the title of National Artist.

Thawan's example demonstrates how tightly wound debates about modern art can be with debates about modern life and culture. Through these debates, we learn not just about art but about the hotly contested and often thrillingly contradictory nature of modern life and culture; they capture the <u>zeitgeist</u>, or spirit of the times.

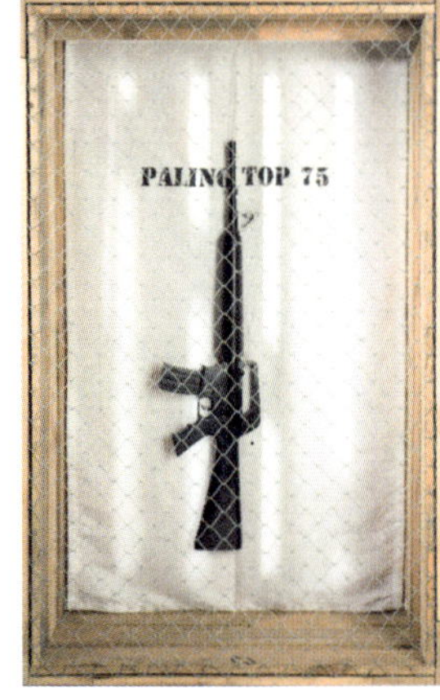

F.X. Harsono. *Paling Top* (Top Most). 1975, remade 2006. Plastic rifle, textile, wooden crate, wire mesh and LED tube, 156.7 x 99.5 x 50 cm. Collection of National Gallery Singapore.

The term "diaspora" can refer to any population who have been dispersed from their homeland. Diasporas are usually characterised by <u>connections</u> between a people and their original or ancestral homeland, which can manifest in many ways. For example, some people might have an active wish to return home, while others—including the descendants of migrants—may have emotional and social ties to their homeland while also seeing themselves as part of the places they now live in.

Many Southeast Asian people describe themselves as diasporic, and key developments in modern art have often been driven by diaspora populations who migrated to Southeast Asia. Some bring with them influences and learnings from their homeland, while others use their art to comment on the diasporic experience.

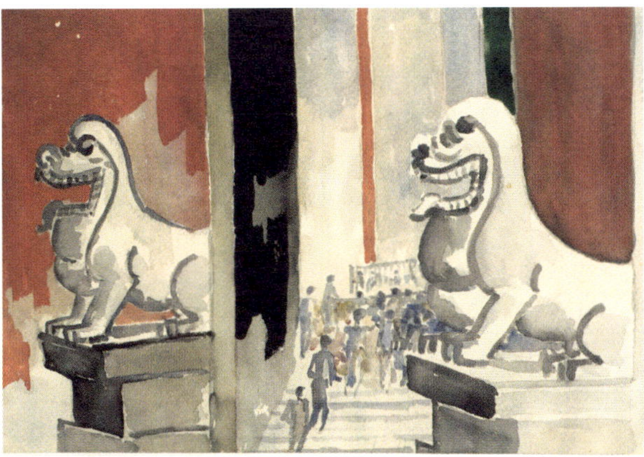

Yong Mun Sen. *Bank of China*. 1950. Watercolour on paper, 36.5 x 54.3 cm. Collection of National Gallery Singapore.

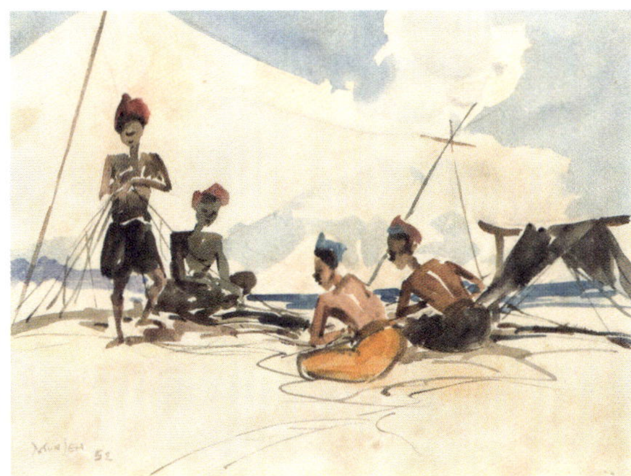

Yong Mun Sen. *Beach Scene with Four Fishermen*. 1952. Watercolour on paper, 27 x 38 cm. Gift of the Loke Wan Tho Collection. Collection of National Gallery Singapore.

Much attention has been paid to contributions made by Chinese diaspora to the development of modern art in Southeast Asia. An example is that of Yong Mun Sen, an early proponent of modern art techniques including <u>realism</u> in former Malaya. Although Yong was a fourth-generation Malayan, his diasporic Chinese identity remained strong, and he helped establish the Penang Chinese Art Club in 1935, and the Nanyang Academy of Fine Arts (NAFA) in Singapore in 1938. Many of his peers from China, including NAFA's first principal, Lim Hak Tai, were equally involved in developing art locally. Yong worked in several <u>media</u>, including photography, oil, and watercolour; his familiarity with Chinese ink techniques is reflected in his deft brushwork. Many early depictions of <u>urbanisation</u> are also attributed to

Yong Mun Sen
b. 1896, Malaysia; d. 1962, Malaysia

Lim Hak Tai
b. 1893, China; d. 1963, Singapore

19th-century Chinese artists, and the founder of Asia's first modern art school, Damian Domingo, was also identified by researcher Luciano Santiago as a Filipino-Chinese mestizo. These and countless other examples demonstrate the many overlaps and intersections between Chinese diaspora and other Southeast Asian artists.

Other diasporas in the region include the populations today referred to as "Malay," who have their origins in diasporic communities of Javanese, Bugis, and others throughout Southeast Asia's archipelagos. Through the movement of these diasporas, architectural styles from far-flung islands are <u>transferred</u> and synthesised in complex <u>hybrid</u> forms that reflect the strong connections within and across the Malay world. These forms can be seen in the mosques and other civic buildings commissioned by sultans; like art that is sponsored by <u>kings</u>, they exhibit a range of influences brought, in part, by dispersed populations, revealing the prominent role of diasporas in shaping the development of modern culture.

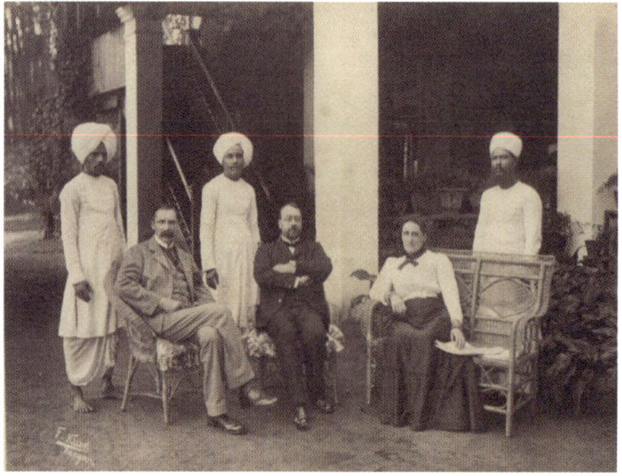

Philip Adolphe Klier. Title unknown. c. 1890s. Silver gelatin print. Collection de Flogny.

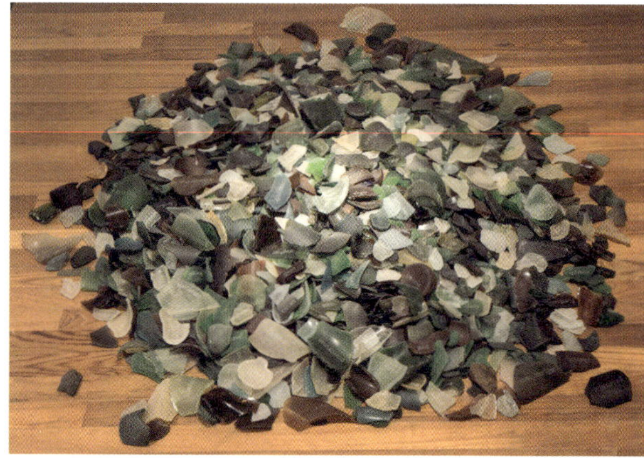

Simryn Gill. *Washed Up.* 1993–1995. Glass, dimensions variable. Collection of Singapore Art Museum.

Large numbers of Indians and South Asians have also been resident in Southeast Asia. By the end of the 19th century, the population of Indians in Yangon was so large that British colonial officials were required to master Hindustani as a language of communication, rather than the <u>vernacular</u>, Burmese. A <u>portrait</u> by Philip Adolphe Klier, who operated a photography studio in Yangon at the time, depicts Burmese Indians working as servants for Europeans. As this image demonstrates, diaspora populations have often been tied to distinct social classes.

During the second half of the 20th century, the more prominent Southeast Asian diasporas were those displaced by the Second Indochina War and related conflicts—chiefly hailing from Vietnam, Laos, and Cambodia—as well as people pursuing <u>education</u> abroad. Many artists have made works exploring these experiences. Nirmala Dutt Shanmughalingam, for example, combines news images and headlines with expressive brushstrokes to convey empathy for the suffering of displaced Vietnamese refugees. Many artists, like Asian-American performance group I Was Born With Two Tongues, express multiple senses of belonging: to the place in which they were born, and also to the places in which they were raised, educated, or lived.

Nirmala Dutt Shanmughalingam
b. 1941, Malaysia; d. 2016, Malaysia

I Was Born With Two Tongues
Active 1998–2003;
based Chicago, United States of America

In the 21st century, diasporas based on labour have emerged more prominently: that is, people employed abroad as domestic and childcare workers, or in construction and other lowly-paid industries. Many <u>contemporary</u> artists, who often engage with social issues including <u>globalisation</u>, have explored the experience of domestic workers; the issue has also been prominent in Southeast Asian <u>cinema</u> and literature. Artists including Brenda V. Fajardo have illuminated how domestic workers experience <u>urbanisation</u>.

Brenda V. Fajardo
b. 1940, Philippines

Diaspora appears in art not only in literal representations, but also as more open-ended, abstract suggestions of movement and displacement. "Life's a net, made up so many roads. Dirt roads, asphalt roads, virtual roads," says a character in the film *Night Passage* (2004), directed by Trinh T. Minh-ha and Jean-Paul Bourdier. "Sometimes you go in a straight line, sometimes you just go round and around in circles." A similar sense is evoked in *Washed Up* by Simryn Gill, which consists of a pile of glass shards, seemingly softened by the ocean, each inscribed with a different word in English. As art historian T.K. Sabapathy suggests, the work invites questions about dislocation. "Where have these shards come from? What were they part of and used for in their original forms?"

Trinh T. Minh-ha
b. 1952, Vietnam

Jean-Paul Bourdier
b. 1950, France

Simryn Gill
b. 1959, Singapore

Journeys and relocations can be inspiring experiences, offering fertile metaphors. As Minh-ha, who is also a scholar of diasporic theory, writes: "In the process of going, one is constantly in a state of transition." Yet, while some migrate by choice, others—especially refugees and displaced populations—are diasporic by necessity. Not everyone enjoys the liberty of flight. *Khleng Ek*, by Yim Maline—who grew up in the aftermath of <u>war</u> and <u>genocide</u>—is a kite made from heavy and fragile ceramic, instead of the usual paper or cloth. The work reminds us that conflicts not only create diasporic populations, but also restrict feelings of freedom.

Yim Maline
b. 1982, Cambodia

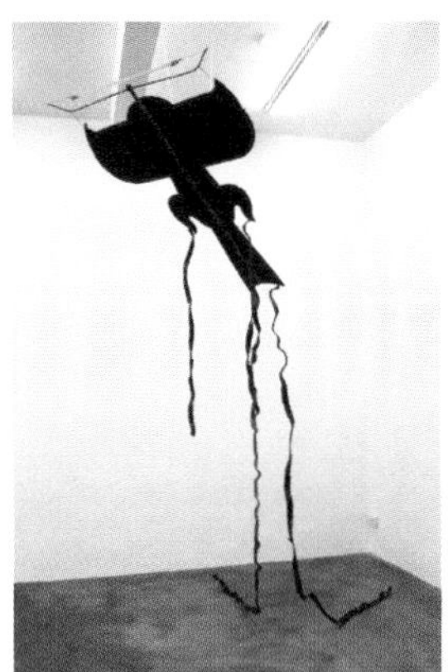

Yim Maline. *Hope*. 2010. Ceramic, bamboo, rattan, string, 460 × 100 × 6 cm. Installation view, Sa Sa Bassac, Phnom Penh. Collection of the artist.

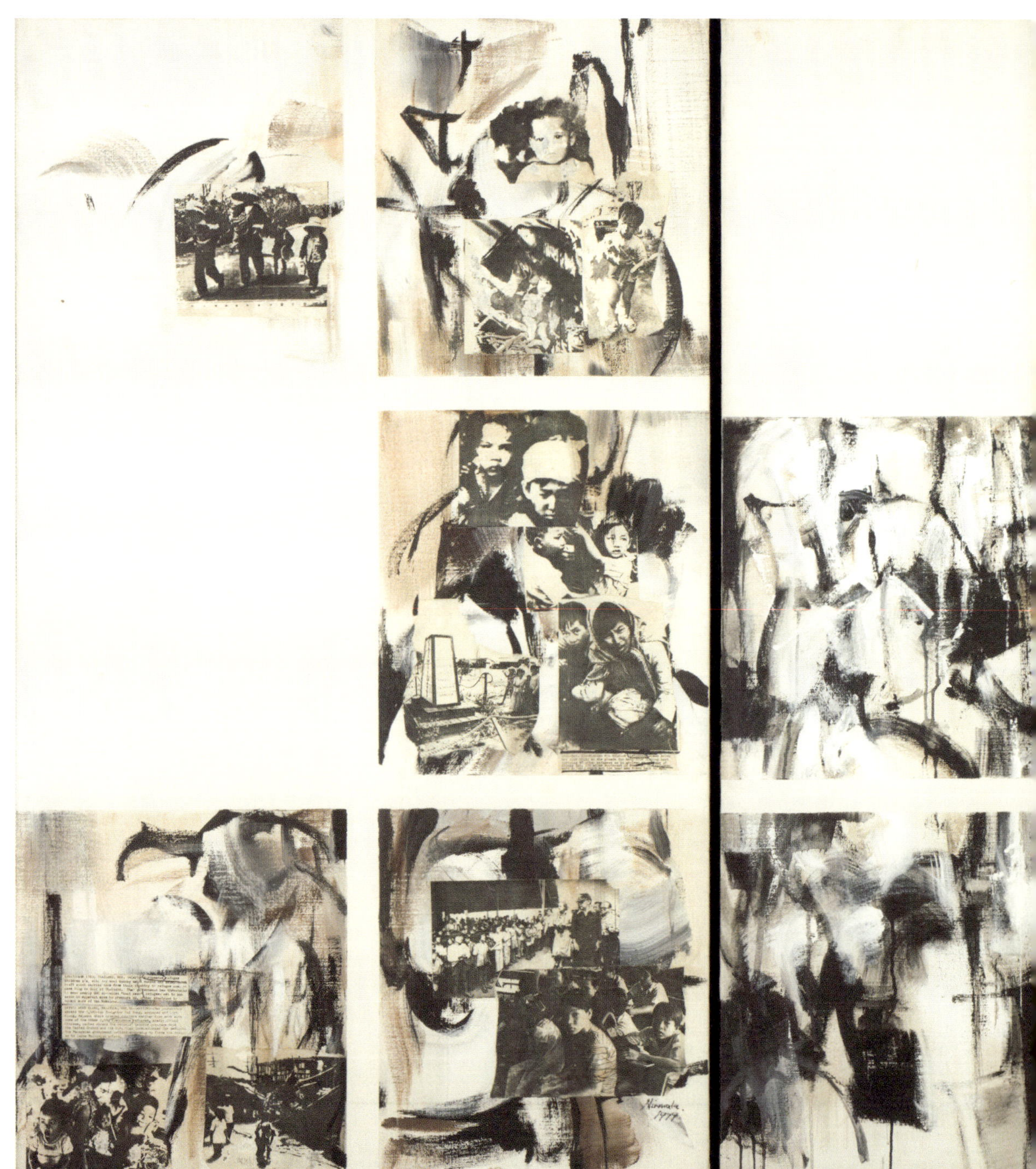

Nirmala Dutt Shanmughalingam. *Vietnamese Refugees, Cycle I*. 1979. Collage and acrylic on board, 132 x 81.5 cm. Collection of National Gallery Singapore.

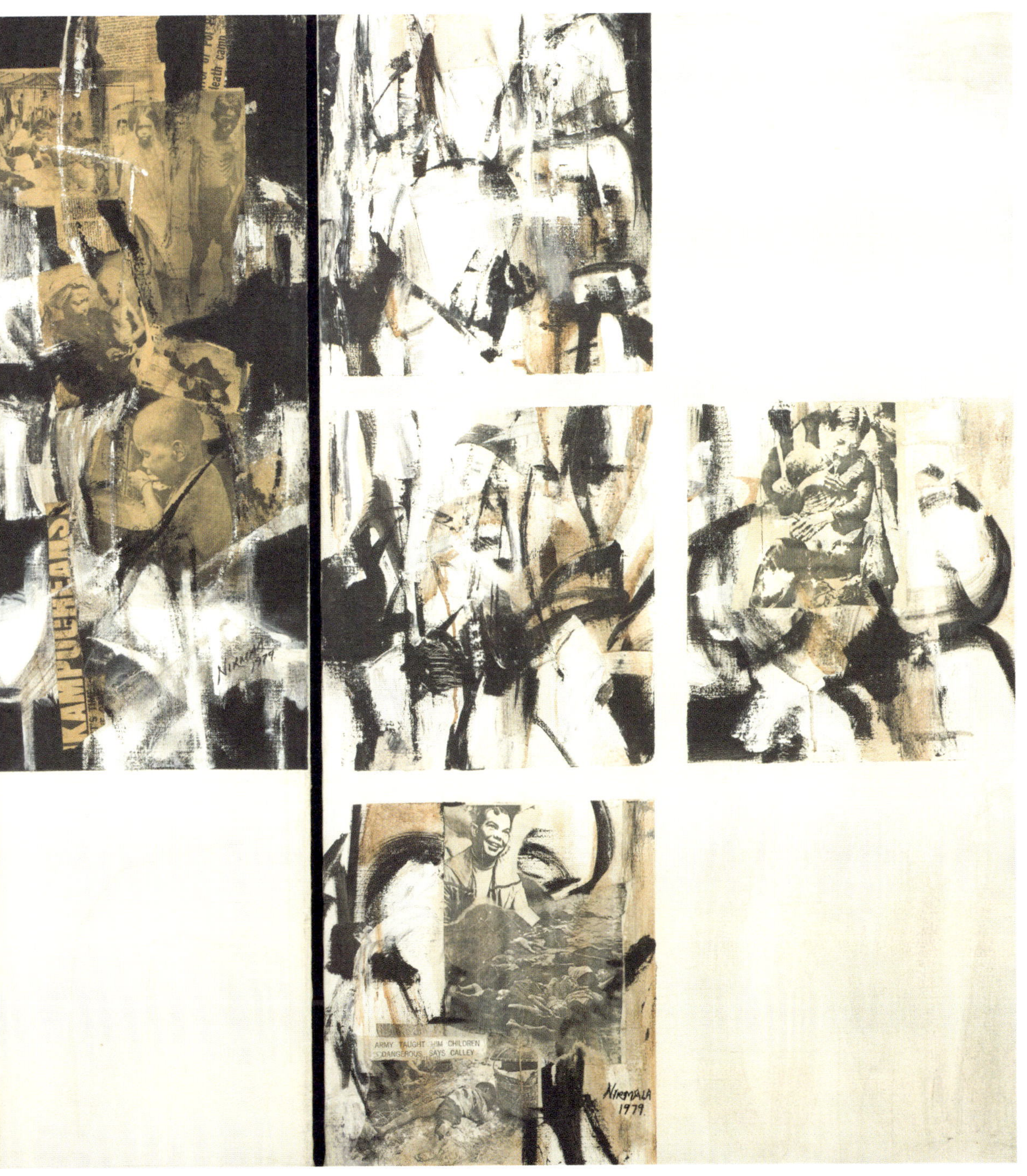

KAMPUCHEA
NIRMALA
1979
ARMY TAUGHT HIM CHILDREN
DANGEROUS SAYS CALLEY
NIRMALA
1979.

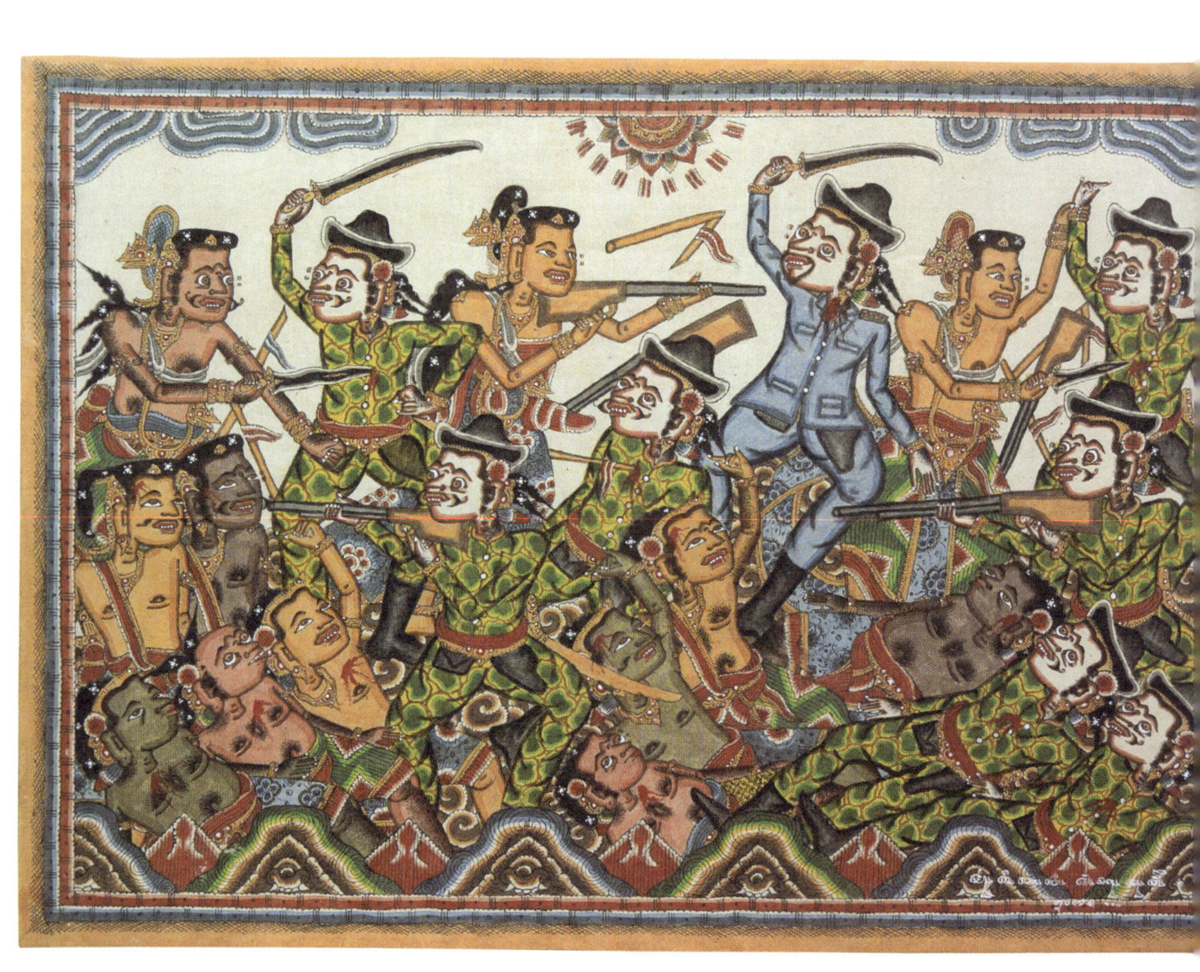

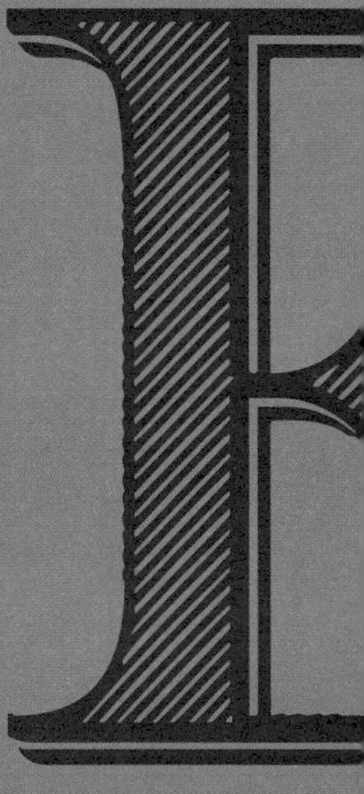

Mangku Muriati. *Perang Kusamba* (The Battle of Kusamba). 2015. Acrylic and natural pigment on cotton cloth, 53 x 83 cm.

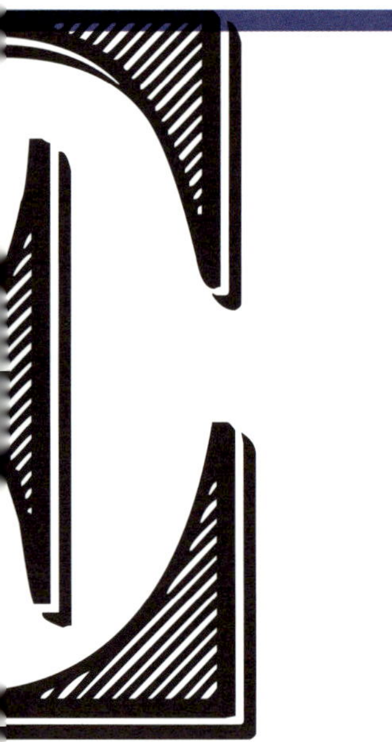

EDUCATION

Education abroad profoundly affected many Southeast Asian artists. Several influential 19th-century artists, like Raden Saleh and Juan Luna, studied in Europe. Later, many Southeast Asian artists studied in Paris, especially in the first half of the 20th century, and dozens more were educated in the United States, especially during the Cold War period. After communist regimes took power in 1975 in Vietnam, Laos, and Cambodia, many artists from these countries studied in formerly Soviet countries. Several artists—most famously Bagyi Aung Soe, but also Fua Haribhitak, Rusli, and Affandi—also studied at Santiniketan, a unique university established in India by Rabindranath Tagore. Artists also travelled within Southeast Asia to study in neighbouring countries. These various experiences abroad helped transfer modern art techniques and ideas from elsewhere to locations throughout the region. Alongside all this, some artists—especially women—have continued to be self-taught, some adopting naïve styles, and others developing very sophisticated practices.

The establishment of secular educational institutions within Southeast Asia was also extremely significant in shaping modern art. Asia's first modern art school was established in Manila in 1821, by Damian Domingo. This was succeeded by a drawing and painting academy in Manila, established in 1846 and operative from 1855. Art schools were established in India and China during the 1850s. In 1889, again in Manila, the University of the Philippines established Southeast Asia's first art school attached to a university. In 1918, a fine art school was established in Phnom Penh under George Groslier's direction, followed in 1925 by another in Hanoi, founded by Victor Tardieu with support from Nguyen Nam Son. In Laos, the first art school emerged during the 1930s, founded by French-born artist Marc Leguay, but this was established without official French colonial oversight. Art schools appeared in many places across the region: in Bangkok in 1933 (headed by Silpa Bhirasri), in Singapore around 1938 (founded by Lim Hak Tai), in Bandung in 1948, in Yogyakarta in 1950, in Kuala Lumpur in between 1966 and 1967, and in Jakarta in 1968, to name a few. Since their establishment, many of these schools have changed—for instance, the School of Fine Arts in Bangkok later became Silpakorn University in 1943—and many others have also emerged.

Although all these Southeast Asian art schools were established with principles based in part on European fine arts academic training, through the process of transferring that tradition to Southeast Asian contexts, the curricula at these schools have varied widely. Most have privileged drawing and painting, and to a lesser extent sculpture, over other fine arts <u>media</u>, although many have placed art students in the same setting as students of architecture, archaeology, craft, and other proximate disciplines. Art histories of Southeast Asia have rarely been taught in the region. In other contexts, such as Kamasan village in Bali, education happens outside of formal institutions. Mangku Muriati is typical of artists there: she was educated both at an art school in Denpasar, and in an apprenticeship with her artist father.

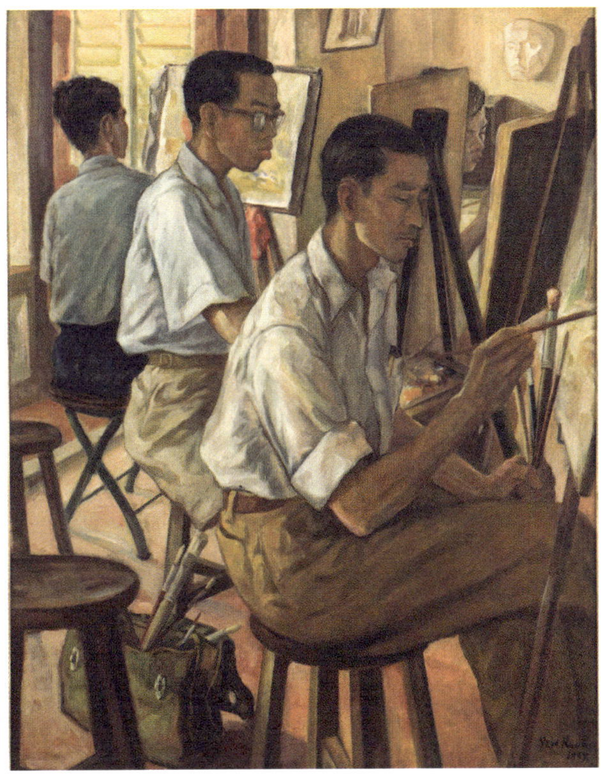

Lim Yew Kuan. *Painting Class*. 1957. Oil on canvas, 83 x 65 cm. Collection of National Gallery Singapore.

Lim Yew Kuan also followed in the footsteps of his father, and went on to make one of the most iconic representations of art education. Lim studied at Singapore's Nanyang Academy of Fine Art, where his father, Lim Hak Tai, was founding principal. In 1952, Lim Yew Kuan began teaching at the Academy, and in 1956 also co-established the social realist-dominated Equator Art Society, one of many artists' groups which proliferated after World War II. His *Painting Class*—made one year after the Society's founding—

emphasises the comradely experience of study, in keeping with his leftist politics and collectivist activities at the time.

The lasting impact of study is evoked in Bagyi Aung Soe's account of his time at Santiniketan. He was enrolled there in 1951, and described a formidable wealth of educational activities and resources, including a research department; classes in Chinese language and literature, Islam, Hinduism, and Sanskrit; books and periodicals published regularly; and frequent conferences. "The university's pedagogy is unlike anything in the West," Aung Soe affirmed. "It is based on the methods of ancient Hindu and Buddhist universities… Young students with beards and moustaches holding very heavy books reflect rather than drink." He enthused that "Santiniketan is well known in the world because it is where we can observe and study oriental culture." Aung Soe's later illustrations often deployed Buddhist concepts and symbols, and usually appeared in literary publications; according to art historian Yin Ker, "More than 30 years after leaving Santiniketan, Aung Soe continued to draw guidance and inspiration from his experiences there." In these and other ways, his studies helped shape his practice.

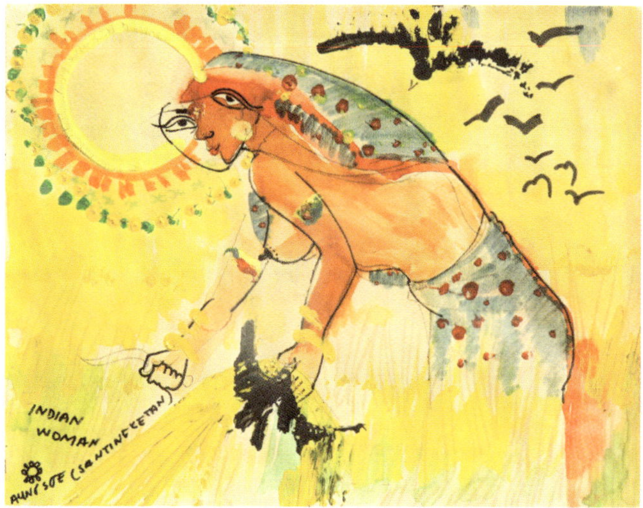

Bagyi Aung Soe. *Indian Woman*. c. 1985. Pencil, gouache and felt-tip pen on paper, 23 x 29.5 cm. Collection of Gajah Gallery.

EXHIBITION

An exhibition "is more than a physical room with pictures on the walls," proposes writer Yeo Wei Wei. An exhibition also makes "visually apparent" that "the history of art is also a history of ideas."

Exhibitions are important because they are usually how artworks reach audiences. Exhibitions also place artworks in conversation with one another, and with the texts and other events which often accompany their display. Exhibitions featuring more than one artist may propose <u>connections</u> or comparisons between their works, or propose a narrative about them. An exhibition can shape our encounter with art, creating an experience that may transcend that of any single work.

Some exhibitions have an especially strong impact on how we understand the history of art. Early exhibitions introducing Southeast Asian audiences to modern art from elsewhere have been seen as having catalysed changes in artistic practice through the <u>transfer</u> of ideas. Examples include the exhibition of European modern art in Java in 1929, or the exhibition of American modern art in the Philippines in 1957. Exhibitions which have attempted to survey the art of the region as a whole—rather than focusing on single artists or nations—have also attracted special attention for the way they imagine <u>Southeast Asia</u> and facilitate dialogues within the region. Early examples are the *First Southeast Asian Art Conference and Competition* in Manila in 1957, and the first exhibition of modern art from the five founding members of ASEAN (Indonesia, Malaysia, the Philippines, Singapore, and Thailand), held in Singapore in 1972.

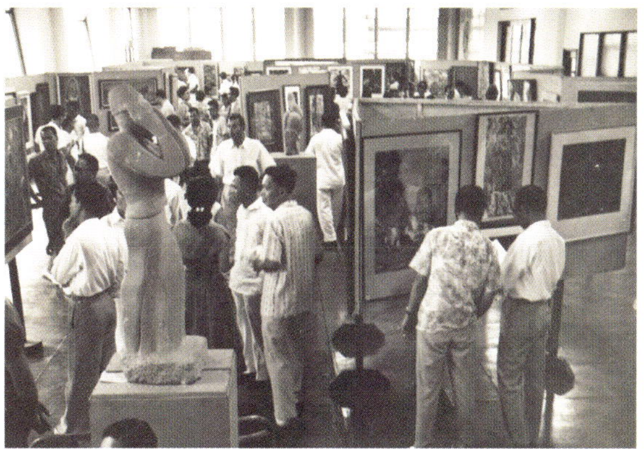

The first Southeast Asia Art Competition Exhibition, Manila, 12 May 1957. Photographer unknown. Collection of the Museum of Modern Art.

Some exhibitions in Southeast Asia have taken on unconventional forms. During the Second Indochina War, many exhibitions were held not in galleries but in villages and military bases, with Vietnamese communist artists' works (chiefly drawings and watercolours) displayed on fences, trees, and other improvised spaces for public critique. In Thailand, from the Cold War period onwards, many film screenings were held not in <u>cinemas</u> but in Buddhist temples, organised not only for human audiences but also as offerings to spirits. Since the early 1990s, artists have staged exhibitions, performances, and other events in a variety of spaces away from conventional galleries, such as in private homes, housing estates, streets, and religious sites. Examples include events organised by a group called The Artists Village in Singapore, semi-<u>biennial</u> events in Chiang Mai like the Chiang Mai Social Installation, and the biennial *Viva Excon* exhibition in Bacolod. In Southeast Asia as elsewhere, the history of exhibitions has only recently become recognised as an important part of the history of art. More research needs to be done on the exhibitionary contexts in which artworks have appeared and circulated, and on ways of interpreting this information which remain attentive to regional histories and contexts.

Some possibilities have been advanced. In 1981, Filipino artist and curator Raymundo Albano argued that the modern form of an art installation resonates with the older phenomenon of community "fiestas" involving the hanging of decorations, as well as what he calls "folk rituals." Albano's analysis suggests a way to understand installation art, as well as methods of installing and exhibiting artwork, as being perhaps closer to what he calls "our authentic selves" than the "borrowed" medium of painting. In a recent study of Cambodia's Tang Tok festival and exhibition—which featured artworks alongside other displays, and was held semi-annually from the 1890s to 1970 in Phnom Penh's Royal Palace—curator Erin Gleeson has proposed that the origins of the event may lie in Khmer temples and rituals.

Art historian Eileen Legaspi-Ramirez has researched the people behind the scenes whose invisible labour makes exhibitions possible. Usually <u>women</u>, these figures have been overlooked by history's usual focus on the singular figure of the <u>artist</u>. More attention to exhibitions may help bring into view the complex networks which have made modern Southeast Asian art public.

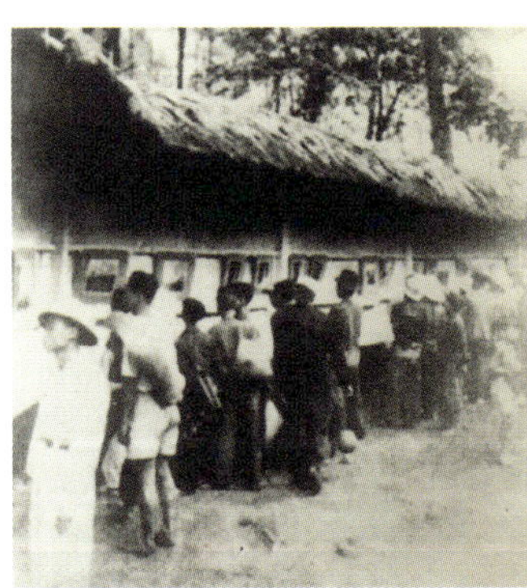

Exhibition of paintings at Tuyen Quang, 1 July 1951. Photographer unknown.

EXOTIC

In the 1930s, comedian Charlie Chaplin declared that "Anyone who has not been to Bali has not really visited Southeast Asia." This is how artist Liu Kang tells the story, in a 1953 essay, about his own trip to Bali with a group of fellow artists. Liu and his peers had migrated from China to Malaya in the decade prior to their Bali trip, and were deliberately immersing themselves in unfamiliar environments. For them, as for many other artists, Bali exemplified the supposedly exotic charms of Southeast Asia. Noting that Chaplin was one of many luminaries to be "smitten by the charm of the island," Liu describes Bali as a "paradise" in which "one is surrounded by such wonders that it is difficult to know where to begin."

Liu's account of Bali typifies the way in which modern art has drawn on an idea of the exotic—the perceived quality of being foreign or unusual—in Southeast Asia. Studying how artists saw the region as exotic is important as it reveals how artists—including those born here, as well as diasporic residents, and some travellers or educators—came to embrace Southeast Asia itself as subject matter and source of inspiration in their works. Exoticism is always subjective: Bali appeared bizarre and authentic only because Liu and his companions were not from there. Yet the entire region has also often been considered exotic, especially due to its tropical climate, and this has been a cause of attraction for artists from Europe and elsewhere, as well as a trope, or recurring theme, that is traversed by artists from here.

To explore the many implicit connotations of the exotic as it has appeared in the modern art of Southeast Asia, it is useful to observe in detail Liu Kang's description of his beloved Bali. Like many other artists who regarded Bali or other parts of the region as exotic, Liu took emphatic note of its landscape, art and craft, spirituality, and women. According to Liu, Bali's appeals included its "enchanting landscape" of "thick, lush forests," as well as the "Balinese people," who are "artistic" and "excel in music, dance and the art of carving" with a "distinctive style." Liu praises Balinese temple design, which "gives the impression that a connection exists between man and the gods," since "to the Balinese art is a form of spiritual cultivation with a religious purpose." Perhaps the most important of Bali's charms, for Liu, are Balinese women. "Anyone who has been to Bali will never forget the half-naked women," he rhapsodises, praising their "firm and eye-catching breasts," skill in

Charlie Chaplin
b. 1889, United Kingdom; d. 1977, Switzerland

Liu Kang
b. 1911, China; d. 2004, Singapore

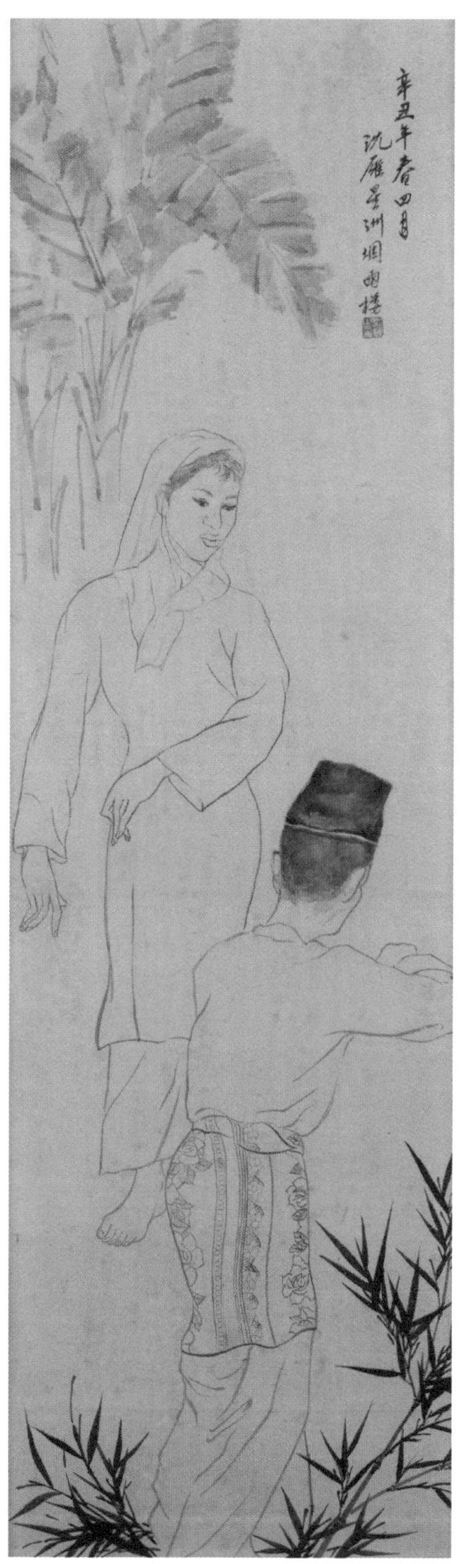

Sun Yee. *Malay Dance (Ronggeng)*. 1961. Ink on paper, 104 x 31.9 cm.
Collection of National Gallery Singapore.

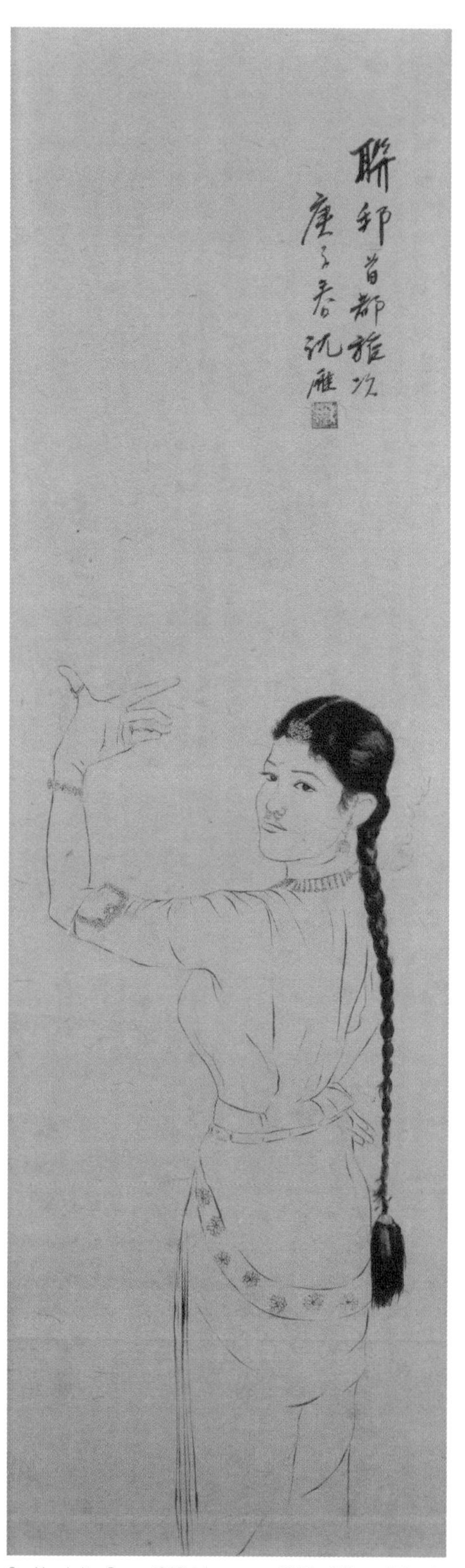

Sun Yee. *Indian Dance*. 1960. Ink on paper, 104.5 x 31.9 cm. Collection
of National Gallery Singapore.

"delicate handicrafts," and reputation for being "gentle and tender towards their husbands."

Most of these elements are evident in Liu's *Artist and Model*, which depicts the artist's peer, Chen Wen Hsi, painting a bare-chested (and unnamed) Balinese woman. Bright colours painted in flat blocks emphasise the exotically tropical landscape and foliage; the woman's exotically exposed breast is carefully rendered in silhouette; and her intricately decorated batik skirt is exotically contrasted with the artist's plain-coloured clothing. The use of white outlines may also be Liu's homage to the craft of batik.

We have seen that Liu particularly prizes the landscape, crafts, spirituality, and women of Bali as emblems of exoticism. Images of dancers have often recurred in conveying a sense of the region as an exotic inspiration, since dancers tend to be women, are often adorned with finely crafted <u>fashions</u>, and serve as representatives of religious and cultural difference. For example, Liu's peer, Sun Yee, made a series of studies of dancers from different cultural backgrounds. Several of these works are ink paintings, employing a style of outlining called *baimiao* which she would have learned while studying in Shanghai, before moving to Singapore. These works form part of Sun's effort to localise her practice, combining a pictorial language from elsewhere with subject matter from her adopted home and region. Other artists to have been entranced by dancers they saw as exotic include George Groslier and Auguste Rodin, who both depicted Khmer dancers during the early 20th century. Early photographs made in Southeast Asia—by Europeans, as well as by local photographers such as Kassian Cephas, thought to be the first Indonesian trained in photography— also concentrated on subjects that were foreign to Western eyes. Thus Cephas' photograph formed the basis for an exoticising poster by Albert Hahn Sr.

More recently, some artists have subverted the prevailing vision of Southeast Asia as exotic. Arahmaiani's outlandish costume worn while performing *Handle Without Care*, for example, juxtaposes symbols of clashing cultures, weaponising exoticism as a tool to raise questions about spirituality and consumerism. And Han Sai Por, in her use of semi-<u>abstraction</u>, emphasises the ambiguous appearance of organic tropical forms. Nature, in Han's art, is universal rather than exotic.

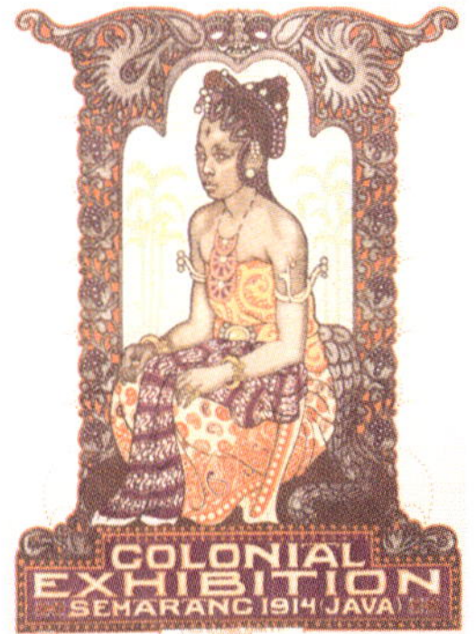

Albert Hahn, Sr. Poster for Colonial Exhibition, Semarang, 1914. 1912. Lithograph on paper mounted on linen, 82.5 x 108.5 cm. Collection of National Gallery Singapore.

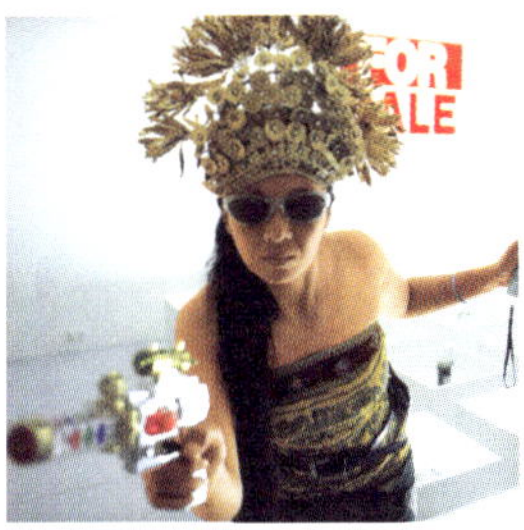

Arahmaiani. *Handle Without Care*. 1996. Performance. Photo by Manit Sriwanichpoom. Collection of the artist.

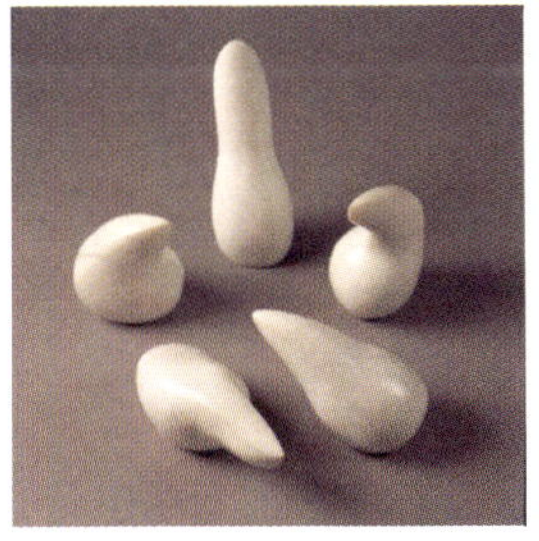

Han Sai Por. *Growth*. 1985. Marble, dimensions variable, approximately 40 cm high. Collection of National Gallery Singapore.

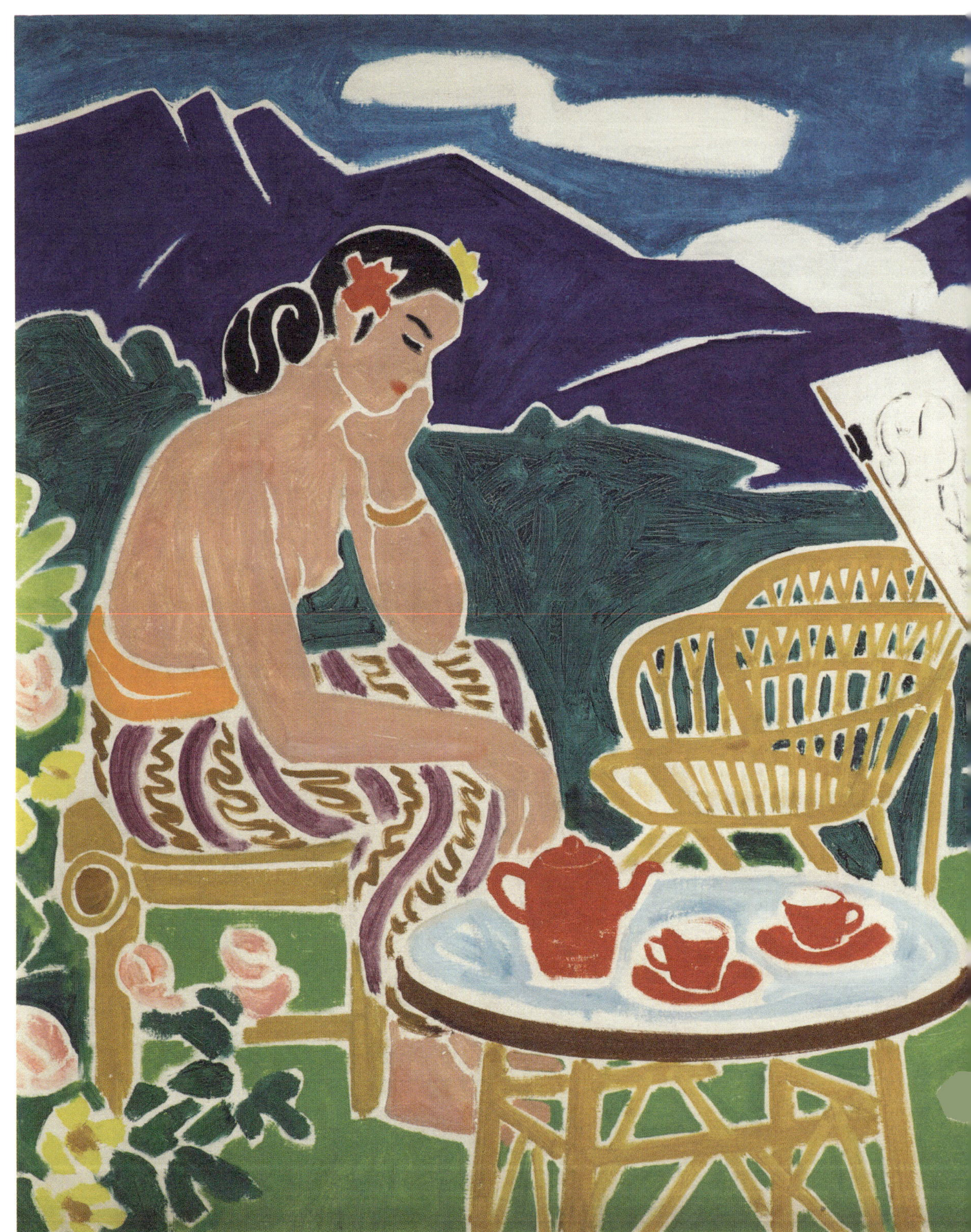

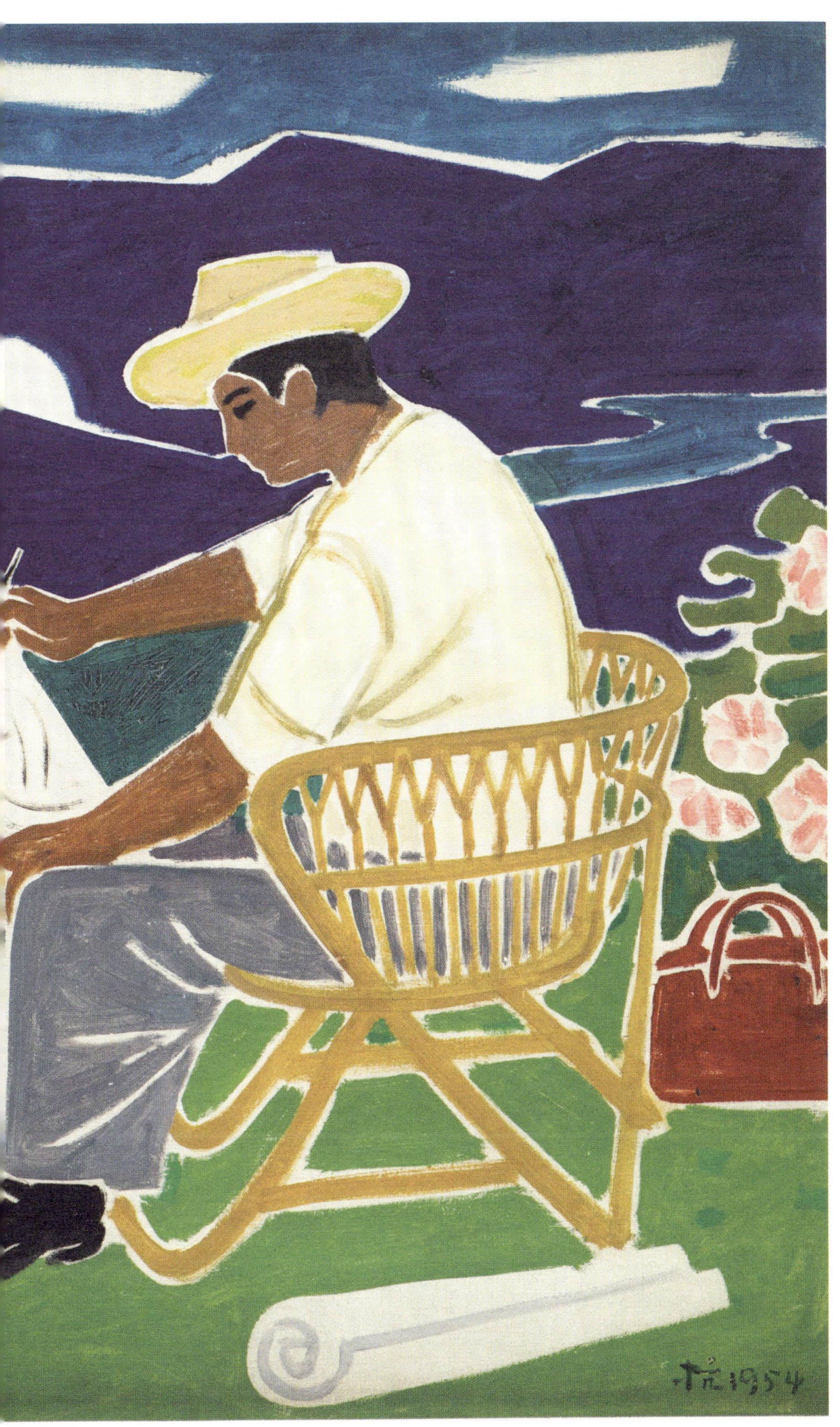

Liu Kang. *Artist and Model.* 1954. Oil on canvas, 84 x 124 cm. Gift of Shell Companies, Singapore. Collection of National Gallery Singapore.

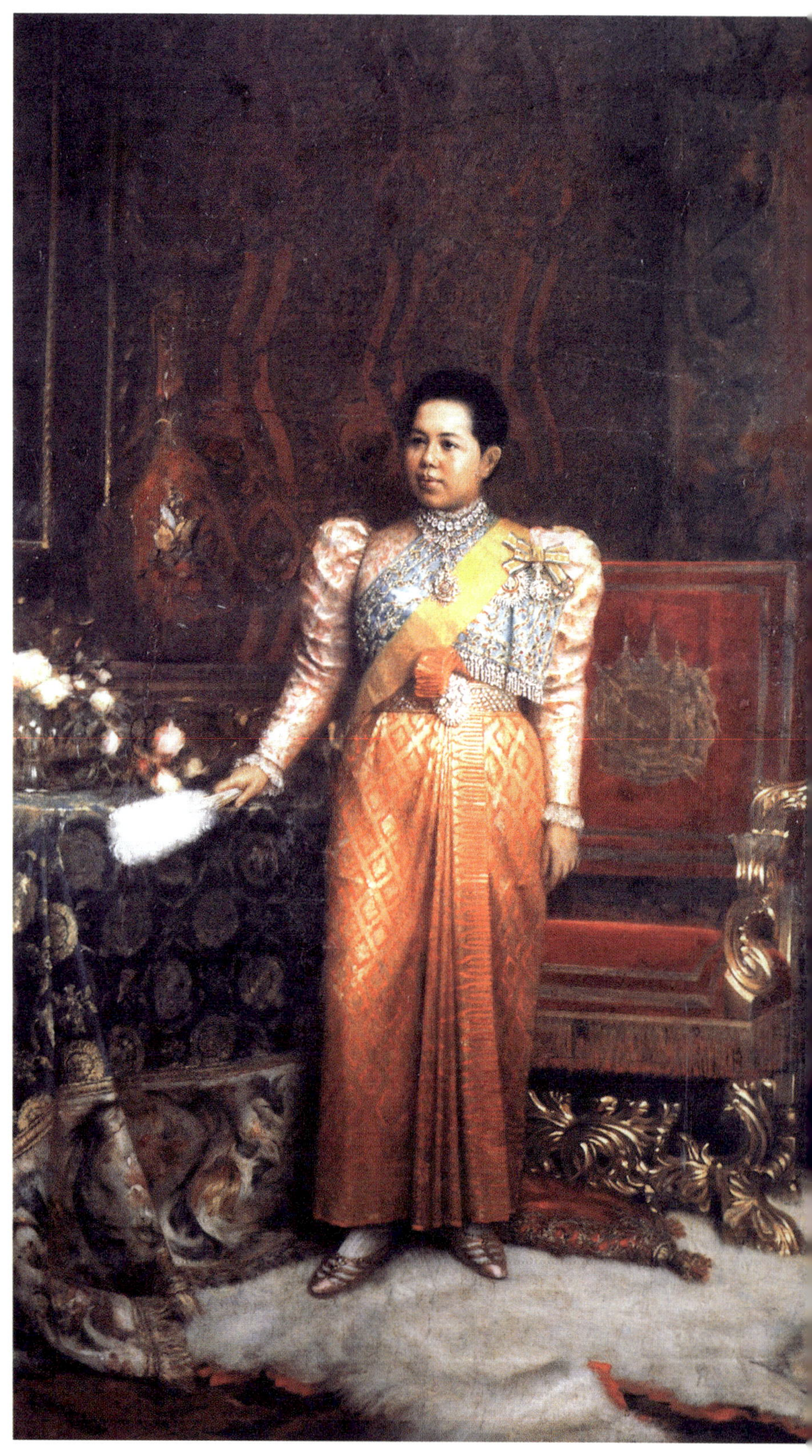

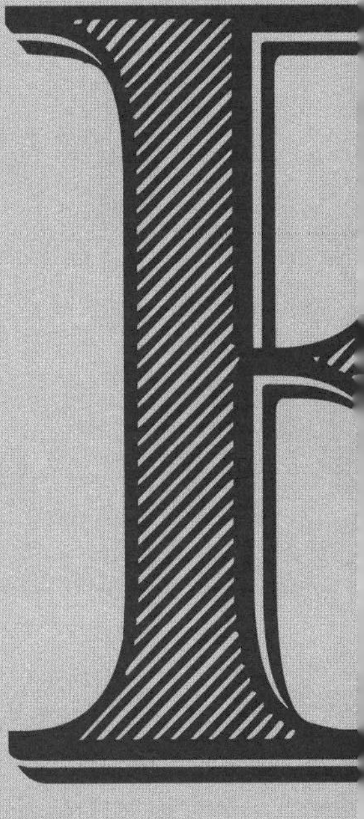

Michele Gordigiani. *Queen Saovabha Phongsiri*. 1896–1898. Oil on canvas. 257 x 153 cm. Collection of Uthayan Phumisathian Mansion, Bang Pa-In Palace, Ayutthaya Province.

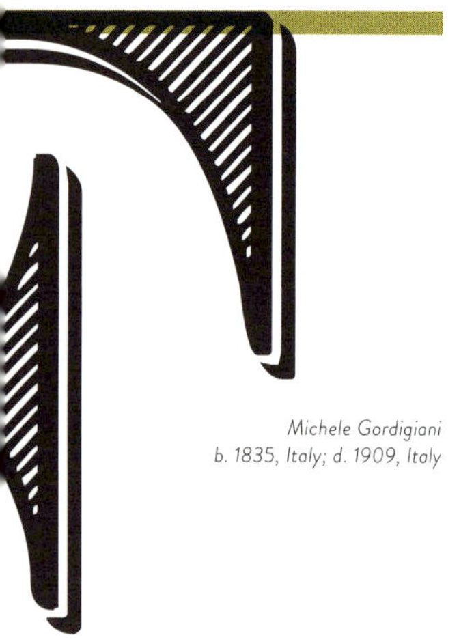

Chulalongkorn (Rama V)
r. 1868–1910

Mongkut (Rama IV)
r. 1851–1868

FASHION

It's often thought that we can gain insight into people from the way they choose to dress. The same can be true for clothes appearing in artworks, which speak not just about their wearers, but also of larger developments in society, from the political to the spiritual.

Queen Saovabha Phongsri is a notable example in this regard. Painted by Florentine artist Michele Gordigiani in the late 19th century, the portrait shows Queen Saovabha of Thailand in a fascinating combination of fashions. While her long skirt is Thai in style, her upper body is dressed following European high society fashions of the day, such as the striking "leg o' mutton" sleeves which are flamboyantly puffed at the shoulders and tapered at the wrists. As art historian Eksuda Singhalampong has observed, this style was usually worn in Europe with a corseted waist and voluminous skirt, but Queen Saovabha combined it instead with a long and elaborately pleated silk skirt.

In drawing on both European fashions and Siamese conventions, the queen epitomised a <u>hybrid</u> negotiation between the two, as Eksuda also argues. This reflects broader processes of modernisation at the time that were aimed in part at managing Siam's relationships with European powers and avoiding official <u>colonisation</u>. For instance, just a few years prior, King Chulalongkorn had implemented changes to official court attire: the *chong kraben*, which had been mocked by earlier European visitors for resembling men's breeches, was replaced by the long pleated skirt, which while recognisably Thai also appealed to Western tastes. Also replaced was the fashion for a partially shaved head for royal Siamese women, which Europeans decried for appearing androgynous. Queen Saovabha's hair, while short, is styled to appear distinctively feminine: manifest differentiation between <u>women</u> and men was deemed necessary for the process of modernisation.

Such symbolic changes were captured in royal <u>portraits</u> —including this one of Queen Saovabha—that were commissioned by King Chulalongkorn. Like his father King Mongkut, Chulalongkorn used portraits for diplomatic purposes, including to advertise Siam's modernisation. Thus, it was important that fashions were both aesthetically appealing and symbolically appropriate. Before Mongkut, it had been taboo to depict royalty in Siam.

Artistic depictions of fashion from the 19th century often reflect the <u>transfer</u> of modern ideas and aesthetics. Another key example is the genre known as *tipos del pais*, a style of watercolour painting popular in the Philippines in the 19th century which demonstrates a synthesis of various new artistic techniques and compositional styles, as practised by artists from Europe, China, and elsewhere. Literally meaning "types of the country," *tipos del pais* featured people of various ethnic groups, social classes and regions, each differentiated by their minutely detailed outfits. The fashions depicted in these artworks combine diverse styles, some of which (especially those from rural and regional areas) were likely perceived as <u>exotic</u> by the mostly urban-dwelling artists who portrayed them. Artists who worked in this genre include Damian Domingo, a pioneer in arts <u>education</u>, Justiniano Asuncion and Jose Honorato Lozano.

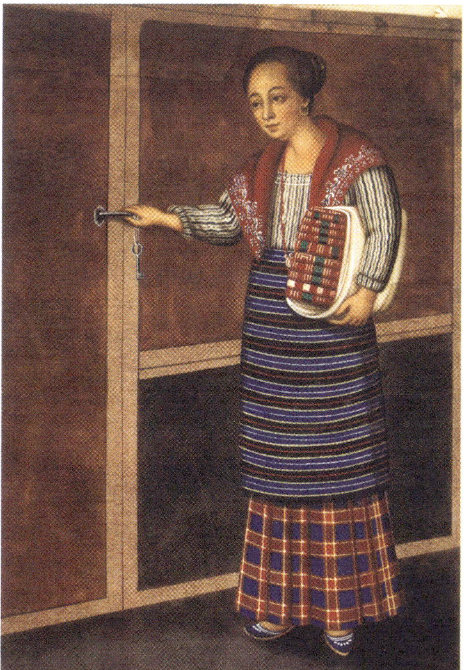

After Damian Domingo. *Una Mestiza Mercadera de Manila* (A Mestiza Merchant from Manila). c. 1820s–1830s. Watercolour on paper, 20.8 x 13.7 cm. Private collection.

Fashion is also used by some artists to communicate <u>ideological</u> affiliation. In a print by Sam Yoeun, farmers harvesting rice are identically dressed in plain, dark clothes and chequered scarves known in Cambodia as *krama*. This indicates they are rural peasants, and culturally Khmer, rather than being Vietnamese or members of another minority. This attire was also favoured by the Khmer Rouge, a communist group Yoeun was affiliated with, which later presided over a <u>genocide</u>, with forced agricultural labour contributing greatly to the number of deaths.

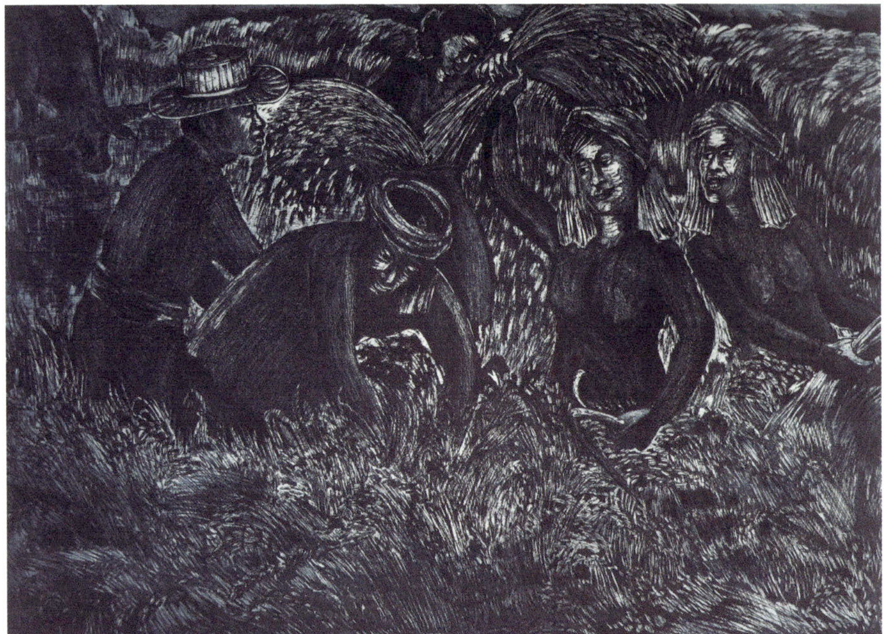

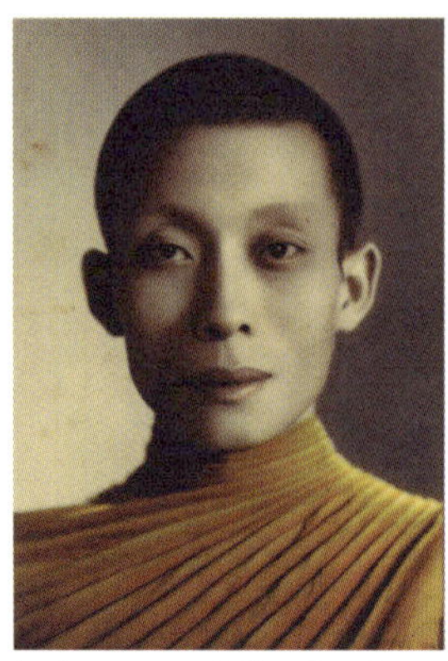

Studio portrait of Pha Oun Huean Hasapanya Maha Thela (1928–1982), a monk and photographer from Vat Nong Si Khun Mueang, Luang Prabang. 1956. Hand painted silver gelatin print, 25.3 x 17 cm. Given as a gift to Pha Khamchan, a monk at Vat Saen Sukharam, Luang Prabang. Collection of Vat Saen Sukharam/ Buddhist Archive of Photography.

Sam Yoeun. Not titled (*Harvesting Rice*). c. 1963–1965. Etching on paper, 29.2 x 40.3 cm. Gift of Dr Maria Heiner, Dresden, Germany. Collection of National Gallery Singapore.

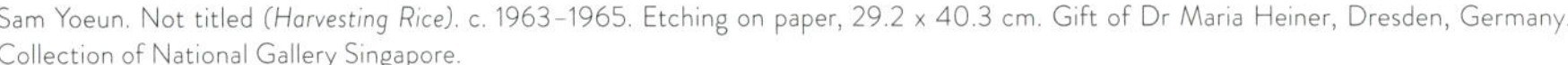

The dynamism of <u>spiritual</u> practice is conveyed in choices of attire among Buddhist monks, and in depictions of these in photographic portraits which Theravada monks exchanged as gifts since at least the early 20th century. Many of these images were collected by Lao monks in Luang Prabang, as souvenirs and educational objects. Variations in the way monks' robes are folded, as well as in the composition and presentation of these photographs, aesthetically indicates the changing nature of the Buddhist *sangha* (monkhood) and reveals Lao monks' active interest and proficiency in photography as a technology and an art.

FLATNESS

In discussions on modern art, flatness usually refers to un-modulated fields of flat painted colour, which allow abstract paintings to avoid creating any illusion of spatial depth. Less commonly, flatness may also refer to painted or photo-graphed depictions of flat surfaces as seen in nature. Both kinds of flatness have appeared in the modern art of Southeast Asia, and it can be fascinating to compare these two quite different types of flatness, even though flatness has not been a central concern in this region.

In the West, the first kind of flatness became a key topic for many modern artists during the 1960s and 1970s, and an important way to talk about modern painting more generally, due largely to influential American critic Clement Greenberg. He asserted: "Flatness, two-dimensionality, was the only condition painting shared with no other art." Greenberg argued that it was the "ineluctable flatness of the support that remained most fundamental in the processes by which pictorial art criticized and defined itself under Modernism." That is, for modern abstract artists in the West, exploring the flat nature of painting was a key strategy for making their work modern, and different from the art of the past. Greenberg's obsession with the flatness of modern abstract painting emerged as a reaction to the centuries-long tradition of Western artists using linear perspective to create the illusion of spatial depth in representational images.

In Southeast Asian modern art, flatness appears in surprising ways, including in both <u>abstract</u> paintings and depictions of landscape in various media. Yet while many artists have painted unmodulated fields of colour, and portrayed flat surfaces in the landscape, the idiosyncratic ways that they have engaged with flatness makes it clear that this has not been a key concern in discourses of modern art in this region, unlike in the West. Significantly, this demonstrates that despite their many <u>connections</u> with other <u>globalised</u> art worlds, Southeast Asian modern artists have also had quite different concerns from their peers elsewhere. Since the modern compositional technique of using linear perspective to create illusory depth had emerged in most of Southeast Asia only during the 19th century, it was less entrenched as a convention here. Therefore, artists in the region may have felt less drawn to rejecting it, in the way that artists in the West had done, as led by Greenberg.

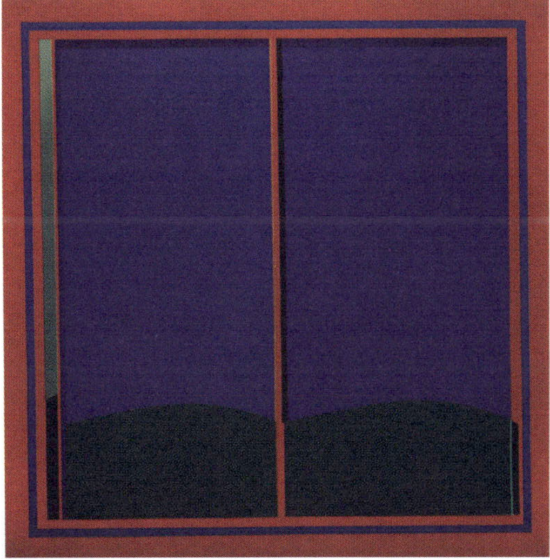

Lee Aguinaldo. *Linear No. 95.* 1969. Acrylic on marine plywood, 120 x 121 cm. Collection of Cultural Center of the Philippines.

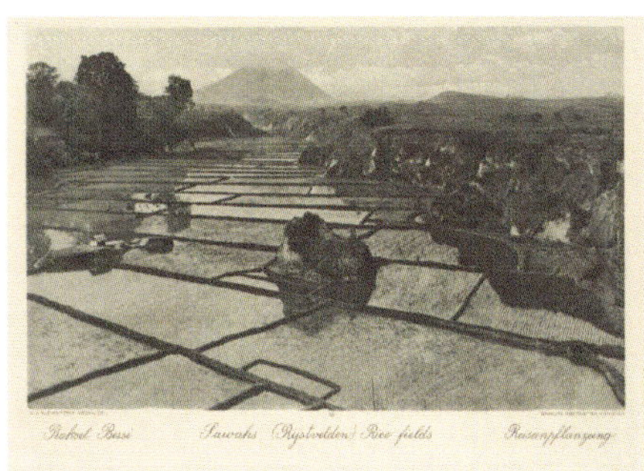

C.J. Kleingrothe. *A View of Rice Fields*. c. 1900–1915. Collotype print, 22.3 x 34.9 cm. Collection of National Museum of Singapore.

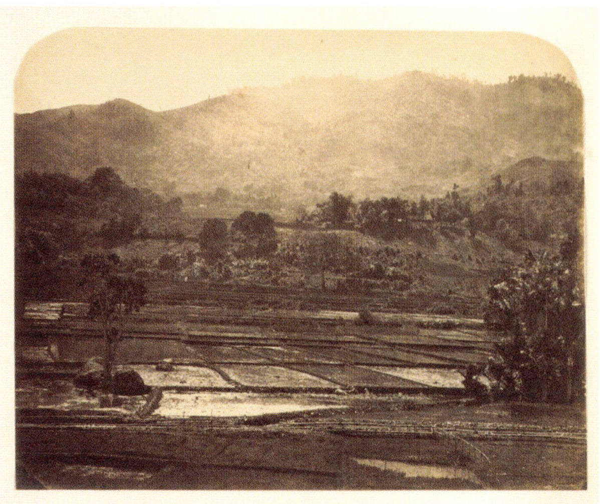

Isidore van Kinsbergen. *Rice Field at Buitenzorg (Bogor)*. c. 1870. Albumen print, 25.8 x 29.5 cm. Collection of National Museum of Singapore.

*Lee Aguinaldo
b. 1933, United States of America;
d. 2007, Philippines*

This is not to say that abstract artists in Southeast Asia never explored the possibilities of painting unmodulated fields of colour. For example, the surface of Lee Aguinaldo's *Linear No. 95* is completely flat and devoid of painterly texture: pigment has been carefully applied on a high-grade, mass-produced industrial material, without trace of the <u>artist</u>'s hand. Moreover, the painting consists entirely of unvarying blocks of colour, with no use of shading to suggest volume—unlike many of Aguinaldo's works from the same period (such as *Linear No. 6*), which tend to juxtapose planes of tonal gradation with bands of evenly applied, flat colour. Together with the smooth surface of the painting, the uniform areas of colour in *Linear No. 95* present an emphatic, double flatness; however, there is yet an illusion of depth that is implied by Aguinaldo's positioning of the large area of blue over the smaller, undulating mass of green, a scheme that resembles a conventional depiction of landscape. Critics at the time compared Aguinaldo's abstraction to new types of construction in <u>urbanising</u> Manila; perhaps the artist was reaching for radically simplified compositions to represent the environment as the architects of his time did, such as Leandro Locsin, whose quest for streamlined shapes in buildings earned him the nickname, "the <u>poet</u> of space."

*Leandro Locsin
b. 1928, Philippines; d. 1994, Philippines*

*Basoeki Abdullah
b. 1915, Indonesia; d. 1993, Indonesia*

Whereas Aguinaldo played with representational possibilities in abstraction, Basoeki Abdullah's *Sunset* and other similar <u>landscape</u> paintings emphasise almost abstract-looking forms in otherwise naturalistic, realist depictions of rural scenes. Intensely pink skies as seen in many of Basoeki's paintings are typical of the trope of depicting the tropics;

the glassy-flat surfaces of the terraced rice paddies, however, are more unusual. The depiction of such features in landscape painting seems to have been predated by images by photographers such as Isidore van Kinsbergen and C.J. Kleingrothe. Kinsbergen had arrived in Java with the intention of working in theatre, but later became a professional photographer when he was invited to capture "all peculiarities" in film—the flat surfaces of the flooded rice fields presumably among them. Kleingrothe's dramatic compositions were considered early examples of fine art photography presenting the region to a <u>xenophilic</u> Western market. These and other careful renderings of the reflective surface of flooded rice paddies recall contemporaneous depictions of bizarre geological phenomena in New Zealand by Charles Blomfield. All of these artists use familiar aesthetic conventions for depicting landscapes to highlight the exotic features of the scenes being depicted. Flatness is a rare sight in nature, and thus an effective device for underscoring the rich diversity of the tropical environment.

Beyond registering the ways flatness has figured in Southeast Asian modern art, making it quite different from art in the West, more research is needed on the connotations of flatness in the modern art of this and other parts of the world. For example, art historian Chika Okeke-Agulu posits that areas of flat colour in paintings by Demas Nwoko function primarily to communicate political ideas about white domination over "the destiny of independent black Africa." The multiple uses of flatness in modern art may be a rich site for further inquiry.

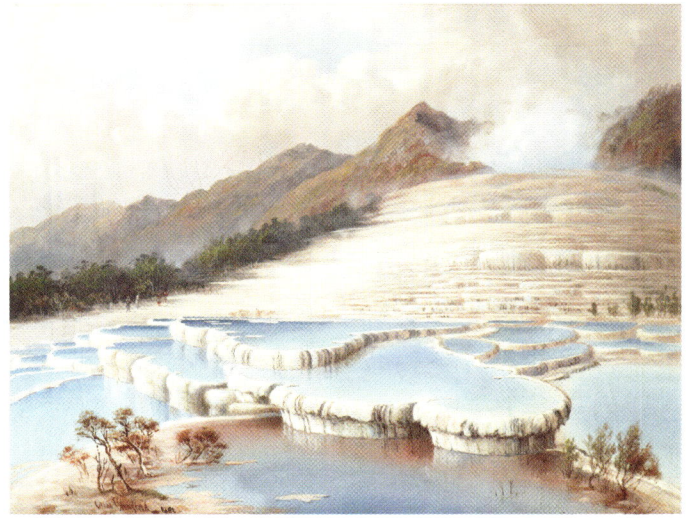

Charles Blomfield. *White Terraces*. 1882. Oil on canvas, 60.8 x 45.4 cm. Gift of Sir Guy Berry, South Africa, 1960. Collection of Museum of New Zealand Te Papa Tongarewa.

THERE IS A LIMIT
TO THE WORDS
OF HUMANS…
WE CANNOT
SPEAK AT ALL, WE
CANNOT DESCRIBE
A SUFFERING
THAT HAS NO
BOUNDARY, THAT
IS LIMITLESS.

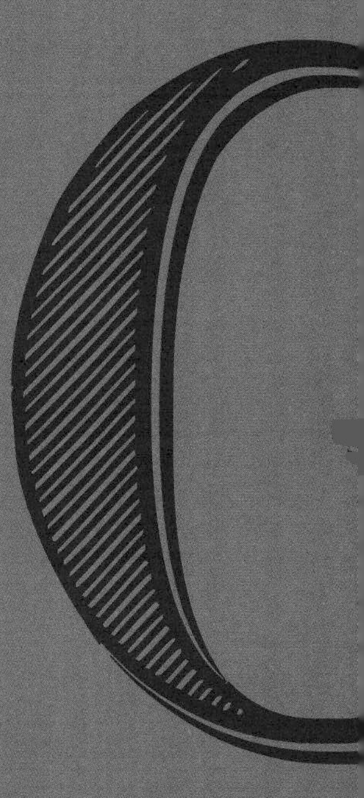

—Chheng Phon, 1983

GENOCIDE

"What of the progressive and modern ideas of the world; have not all the artists in the world loved freedom…? What do you think of the bitter suffering of our artists in Cambodia? This is the power of genocide… Who will take responsibility for the weakness, the feebleness and emaciation of the four million people who have survived?"

These impassioned words were written by choreographer and researcher Chheng Phon in 1983, about the Khmer Rouge atrocities in Cambodia during the 1970s, which took the lives of some two million people. Phon's desperation and disbelief at the scale of suffering and cruelty is palpable. "A heavy rock will weigh us down for many hundreds of years to come," he despaired.

The genocide in Cambodia is one of several in modern Southeast Asia. The intentional killing of a mass of people has become much more frequent, and been carried out with much greater efficiency, since the emergence of <u>modernities</u> all over the world, even though genocide also far predates the modern age.

In Indonesia between 1965 and 1966, approximately half a million communists and people accused of being communists were killed—many of them from Chinese families. This state-sponsored rampage of violence is often described as genocide. Many scholars and activists have also claimed that the Indonesian government perpetrated genocide against West Papuans after taking control over the region in 1963. It is estimated that over 100,000 Papuans died as a result of Indonesia's actions. Nearby in Timor-Leste, official records claim that there were over 102,000 deaths resulting from Indonesian occupation between 1975 and 1999, most infamously in the massacre of more than 250 pro-independence demonstrators in Dili in 1991. In Cambodia, between 1975 and 1979, approximately two million people—about one quarter of the population at that time—died under the Khmer Rouge regime ruled by Pol Pot. Chheng Phon claimed that artists were specifically targeted; other historians have also chronicled the organised killing of intellectuals and educated people, as well as political opponents of the Khmer Rouge, cultural and religious groups including Cham Muslims and Vietnamese, and other minority communities. More recently, attacks on the Rohingya people in Myanmar since 2012, which have massively intensified since 2016, have also been described as genocide by many commentators, including United Nations officials and specialist scholars such as Ben Kiernan. Approximately

700,000 Rohingya fled their homes in northern Myanmar within just a few months in late 2017 and early 2018. There are numerous reports—from the United Nations and other organisations—of mass rapes, destruction of villages, and mass killings, carried out by the Myanmar armed forces.

Genocide is often omitted from discussions of art and culture, as it is seen to be a political or moral topic. But genocide is also significant for understanding modern art, in Southeast Asia as elsewhere. Why do so few modern art-works from Cambodia from the years before 1975 survive? Why did LEKRA—a large communist-affiliated group of artists in Indonesia, which advocated realism in the arts—suddenly disappear during the mid-1960s, despite its great influence in the preceding decade? And why will art historians, curators and museums in the future all struggle to understand the arts of today's minority ethnic and religious groups in Myanmar?

LEKRA
Lembaga Kebudayaan Rakyat
(Institute for the People's Culture)
Active 1950-1965; based Indonesia

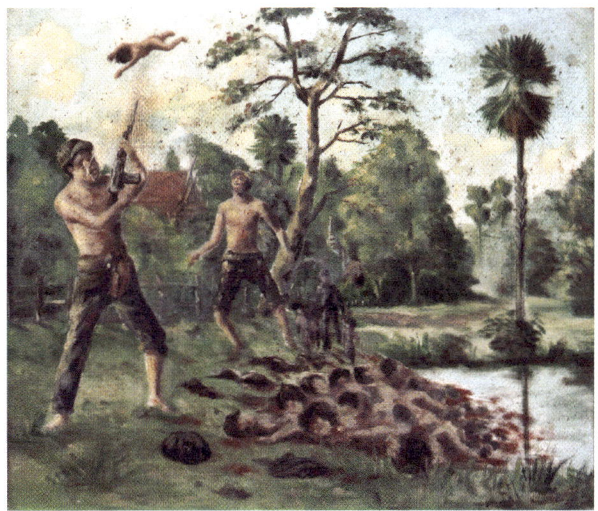

Vann Nath. *In the Province*. 1982. Acrylic on canvas, 50 x 60 cm. Collection of Tuol Sleng Museum.

The short answer to these questions is: because of genocide.

Genocide has had three significant effects on histories of modern art in Southeast Asia.

First is the killing and exiling of artists, audiences, and other figures from various art worlds. Between 80 and 90 per cent of all artists in Cambodia were killed or exiled by the Khmer Rouge, according to Phon, who wrote that "the summits of wisdom and creative genius... reached zero in the genocidal regime. All artists, all poets suffered greatly, terribly despondent at the evil misfortune that had befall-en the nation's cultural foundations." Phon was referring to artists of all kinds, working in diverse media. Artists regarded as "modern" seem to have fared especially badly. Almost all of the biggest names in Cambodian modern arts were killed, including painter Nhek Dim, popular musicians Sinn Sisamouth and Ros Sereysothea, and many more. Vann Nath, who had been a <u>cinema</u> sign-painter before the Khmer Rouge took power, only survived because of his ability to paint <u>portraits</u> of Pol Pot, as <u>propaganda</u>. "To simply read the names of the students who had entered the School of Cambodian Arts… during the 1950s and 1960s and then compare these lists to the living today is to provoke a haunting liturgy to the dead," wrote art historian Ingrid Muan in 2001. An entire generation had been nearly wiped out.

How many of those killed in Indonesia between 1965 and 1966, as well as in Timor-Leste, West Papua, and Myanmar were also artists, audiences, <u>patrons</u>, or otherwise involved in their local art worlds? It is impossible to know for sure. Historical accounts and studies of these atrocities usually focus on political rather than artistic or cultural effects of the violence. But it is certain that killing on such a scale changed the course of art history.

A second, related effect of genocide is the loss and dispersal of artworks. This has especially significant implications in Southeast Asia, where much (perhaps most) of the research and writing on modern art histories has been occasioned by <u>exhibitions</u>, or conducted by museums and other institutions of display. Art historian T.K. Sabapathy has also observed that "Exhibitions are dominant sites for the production of discourse on contemporary art in Southeast Asia." Therefore, it is rare that research or writing focuses on artists whose <u>oeuvres</u> include very few surviving works available for study or potential exhibition.

A third effect of genocide on the modern art of Southeast Asia is the trauma that it has caused. Some artists have attempted to depict their own experience of witnessing the horror of mass killings. A large series of densely composed drawings by Bun Heang Ung combines pictorial narrative devices from political cartoons and Khmer bas-relief murals. Paintings by Vann Nath, depicting his memories of life in a prison camp, are displayed in Phnom Penh's Tuol Sleng Genocide Museum, functioning both as art and evidence. But many others have found it impossible to make art addressing such violence, having been muted by the experience of surviving genocide. Phon described this phenomenon, writing that "There is a limit to the words of humans… We cannot speak at all, we cannot describe a suffering that has no boundary, that is limitless." Art historian Wulan

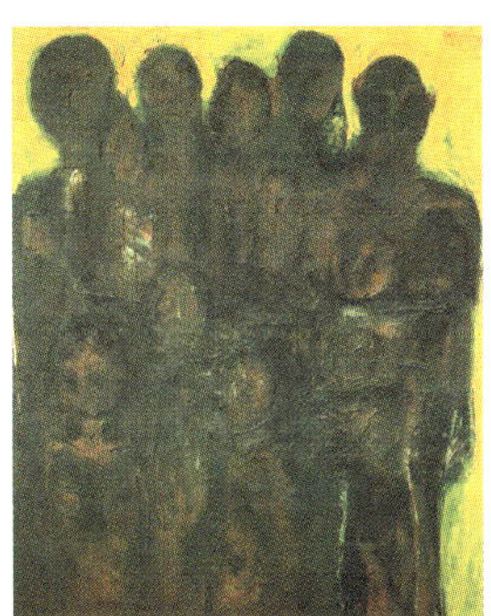

Srihadi Sudarsono, *Manusia Lapar II* (Hungry Men II), 1967. Oil on canvas, 100 x 120 cm. Private collection.

Dirgantoro has proposed that some <u>abstract</u> paintings made in Indonesia after the atrocities of 1965 and 1966 can be interpreted as reflecting artists' inability to directly address the mass killings. For example, she contends that elements in Srihadi Sudarsono's *Manusia Lapar II* (Hungry Men II) "might be read as symbols of absence and as an index of witnessing the historical trauma of 1965-66."

This interpretation is at odds with most accounts of modern art in Indonesia following the anti-communist purges, which don't consider trauma. Artist and writer Jim Supangkat claimed that the events of 1965 and 1966 were followed by a decade of "depoliticised art." Art historian Aminudin T.H. Siregar describes this period as "marked by the victory of universal humanism" and "a strong tendency to explore new things."

These differing opinions reflect changes in <u>reception</u> and the subjective nature of <u>history</u>. Yet they all also affirm that genocide has had a profound and significant effect on the development of modern art in Southeast Asia.

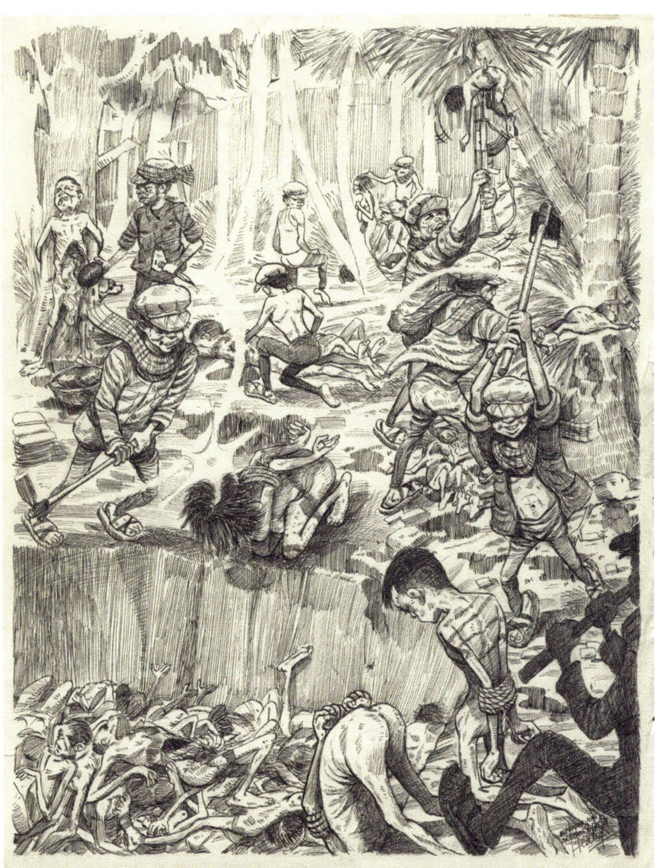

Bun Heang Ung. *No. 77 Massacres at the District Hospital.* 1981. Indian ink on paper, 34 x 39 cm. Collection of Australian National University.

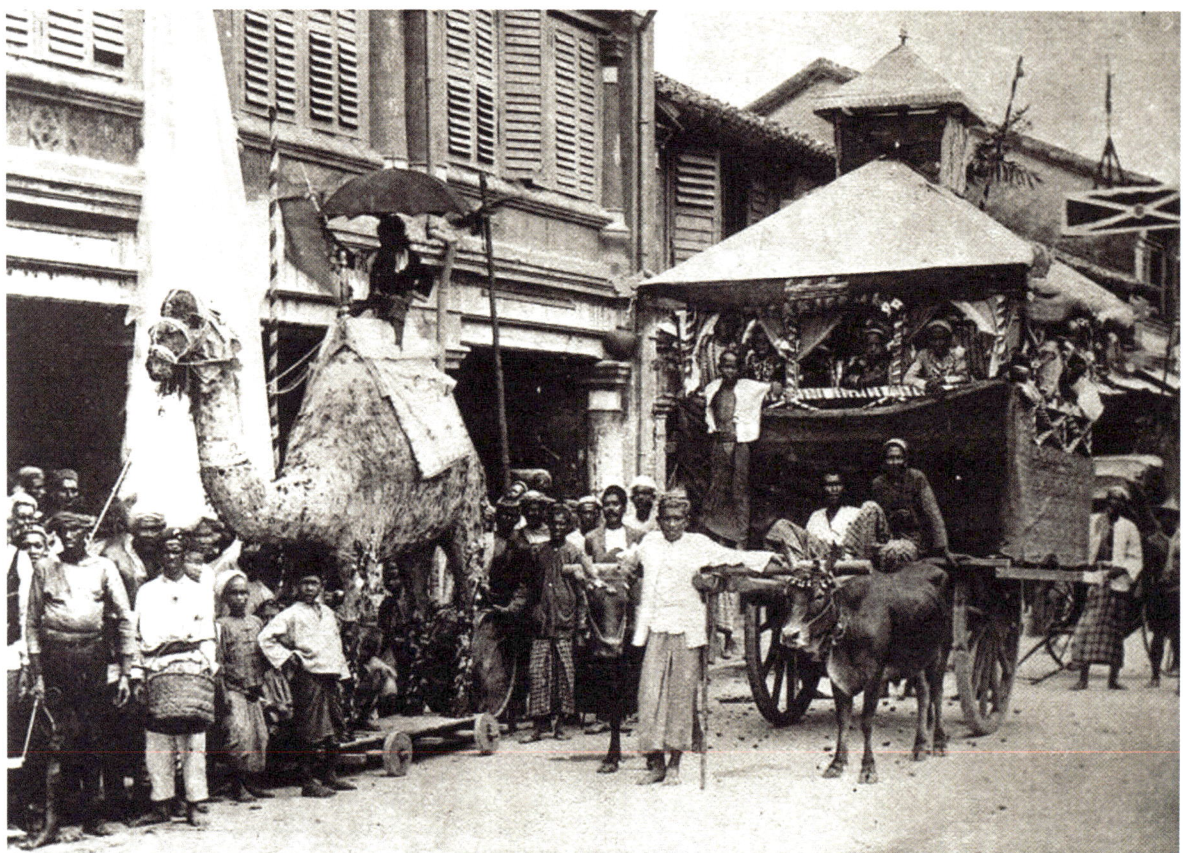

Procession during Diamond Jubilee Celebration, Beach Street, Penang, 1897.

A camel—on wheels!—is paraded along a busy street in Penang, Malaysia. It is 1897, the year of Queen Victoria's Diamond Jubilee, and the accompanying celebrations take the form of *boria*, a theatrical performance consisting of song, dance and sketches.

This surprising spectacle—as captured in a carefully composed photograph—bespeaks a range of origins: it is an emblematic artistic and cultural manifestation of globalisation. While *boria* is considered to be a Malay form, it is of Indian origin. The *boria* performers in this parade were likely Tamil, and they attest to the presence of Tamil speakers from the southern regions of India in Penang since the late 18th century. Camels, on the other hand, are endemic to northern India, but not originally found in the Tamil-speaking south, nor anywhere in Southeast Asia. As for photography, the technology made its way to Penang soon after its invention, and through the 19th and early 20th centuries, many photography <u>studios</u> there were run by Chinese, European, and other <u>diasporic</u> communities.

Worldwide interaction and interconnection between people and places, such as those in this single scene, are often understood as a key feature of globalisation. Globalisation manifests in various ways, and has often been fueled by trade, the spread of religions and <u>spirituality</u>, and colonialism. Yet it cannot be reduced to any one of these factors.

Although the term "globalisation" took on its current meaning only in the 1970s, the phenomenon started happening long before this. Many scholars have described premodern examples, as seen in the proliferation of Chinese ceramics throughout Southeast Asia, or the dispersal of Sanskrit and Malay words and <u>abstract</u> depictions of Hindu deities across vast territories. Globalisation increased in speed, reach, and intensity with the spread of modernity. Once again, camels figure in this history; specifically, the 3,500 camels which were used to build the Suez Canal. Completed in 1869, the Suez Canal cut the distance for maritime travel between Asia and Europe by over 10,000 kilometres. Trade in Southeast Asia exploded, with the volume of goods passing through Singapore alone almost doubling between 1869 and 1870. This meant huge profits, as well as an sharp rise in <u>connections</u> within the region, and between the region and the world beyond.

The implications of globalisation for modern art can hardly be overstated. The photograph of the cosmopolitan *boria* celebrations in 1897 Penang typifies how Southeast Asian artists and others embraced globalisation's exciting potential to enrich cultural forms. Globalisation facilitated the spread of ideas, styles, and techniques of art, along with the movement of people, goods, and capital. Some artists pursued an <u>education</u> in places far from home. Many others depicted local effects of global trade in their works, which explains the prominence of ports in early depictions of <u>urbanisation</u> in the region.

With distances between far-flung places collapsing, globalisation has also accelerated many people's experience of <u>time</u>. "Time's passing so quickly," says Nopphon, the protagonist of *Behind the Painting*, a Thai novel by Siburapha, written in the late 1930s. This feeling comes after Nopphon is told by another character, "You're my Columbus. You've brought me to a new world." Artists have captured a similar sense of time speeding up by juxtaposing new and old technologies and formations within a single scene.

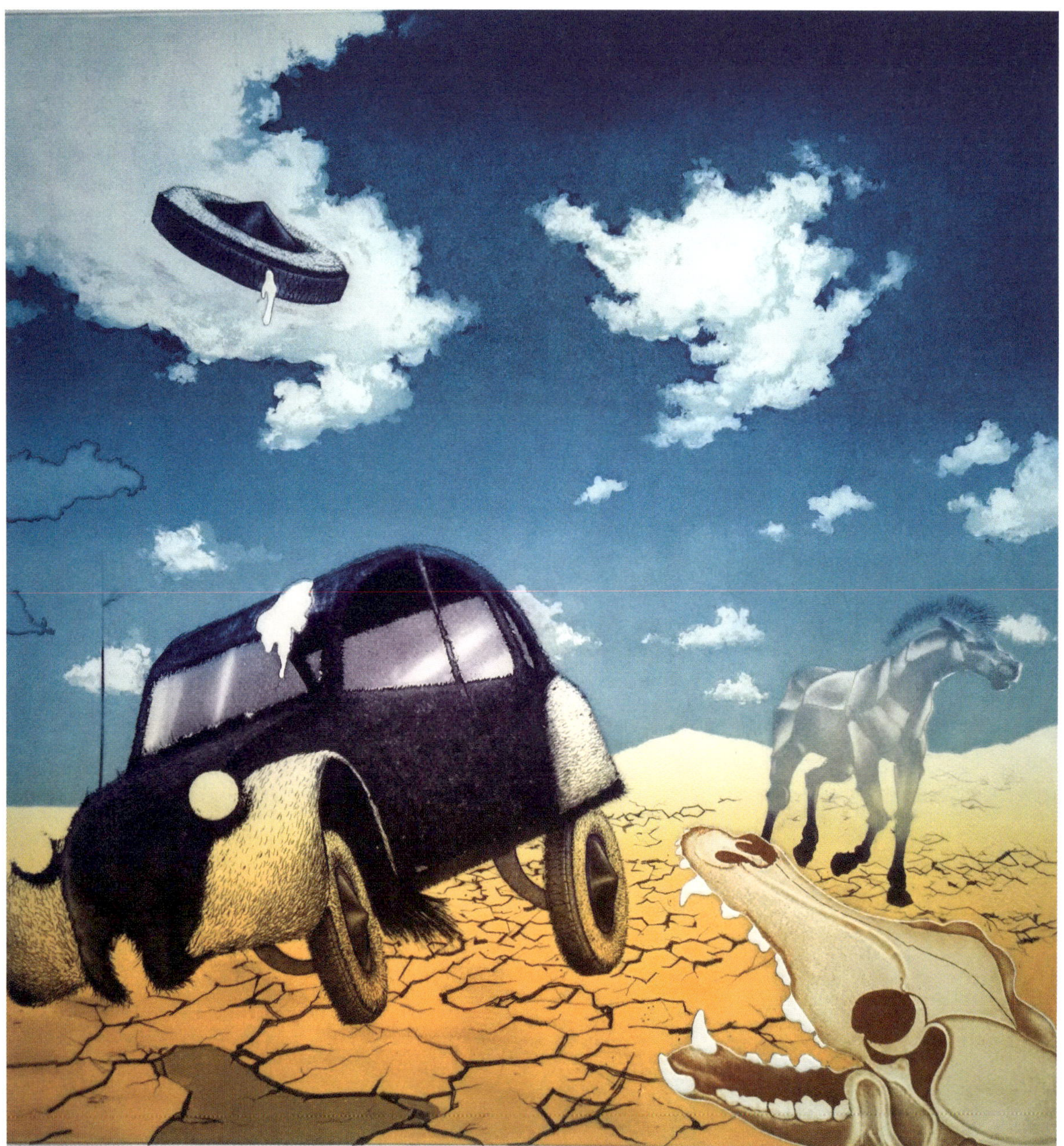

Long Thien Shih. *Dead Souls Are Laughing at Us*. 1974. Etching aquatint, 48 x 48 cm. Collection of the artist.

More recent commentaries include *Dead Souls Are
Laughing at Us*, an etching by Long Thien Shih. In this work,
vehicles again figure as emblems of globalisation—it is not
camels, however, that inhabit the desert in this work, but a Cit-
roen car and a flying saucer overhead. As the artist explained,
"The piece was done in Paris during the Arab-Israeli conflict
in 1973. Arab members of the Organisation of the Petroleum
Exporting Countries (OPEC) imposed an embargo against
the West. There was rationing for petrol and I practically
didn't have any use for my car... because I couldn't get petrol."

That a Malaysian-born artist would make work in Paris
commenting on a political and economic crisis originating
in the Middle East is typical of globalisation. Examples like
these signify also the intensification of globalisation later in the 20th century due to increased intersections between large, transnational corporations and postcolonial
states. The expanding role of <u>biennials</u> and the tendency for
<u>contemporary</u> art to engage with global issues are some
examples of how accelerated globalisation manifested in art.

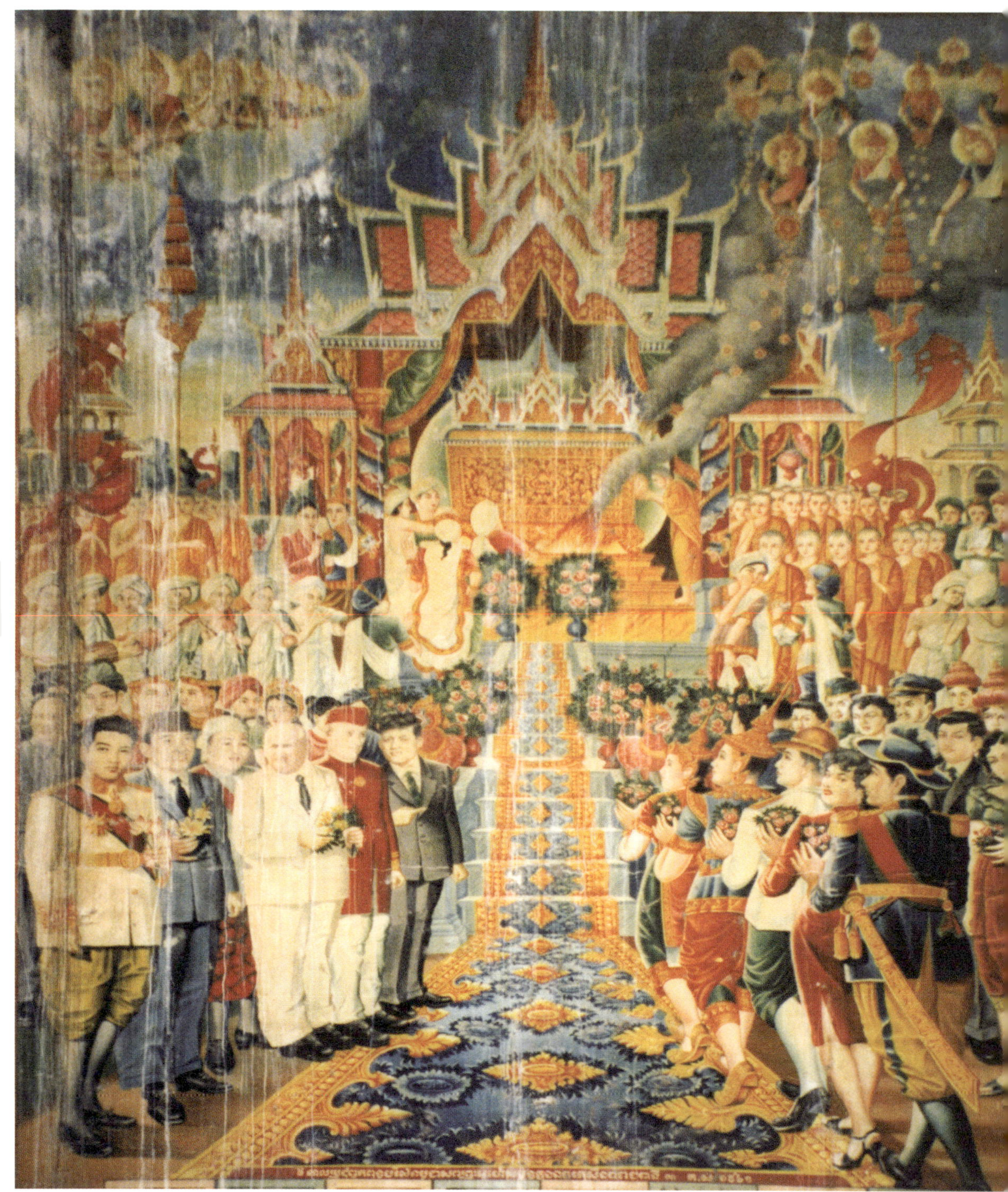

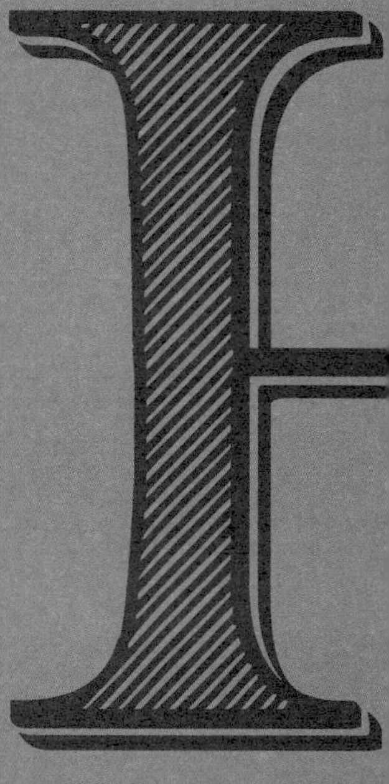

HISTORY

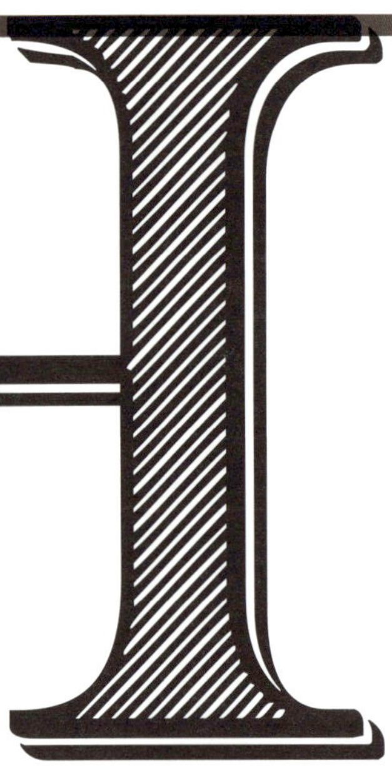

In modern usage, the word history refers to narratives about the past, and to the past itself. While history is nowadays generally understood to be a truthful, universal account of past events which really occurred, every historical account is always subjective and shaped by the ideas and opinions of its author. In fact, in early English, "history" and "story" could both be used to describe any tale of events, either imaginary or true: there was essentially no difference between a history and a story. The concept of history itself is also formed by cultural, religious, and political contexts.

There are many links between history and modern art. Artists engage with history in many ways, from depicting past events, people, and places, to asking larger questions about the nature of history, such as how it is unstable, and the ways in which it changes according to the times and the way it is told.

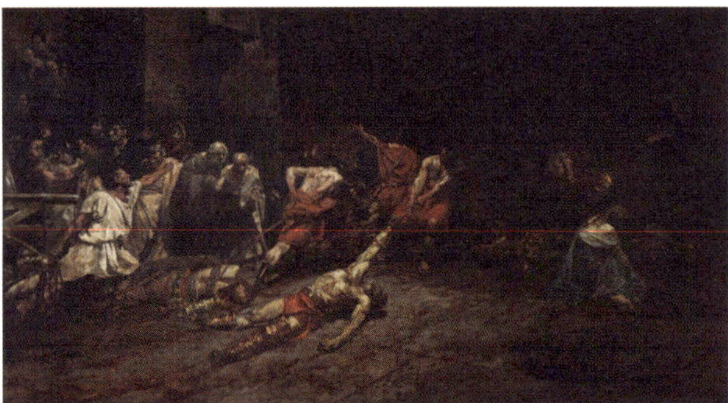

Juan Luna. *Spoliarium.* 1884. Oil on canvas, 422 x 766 cm. Collection of National Museum of Fine Arts, Manila.

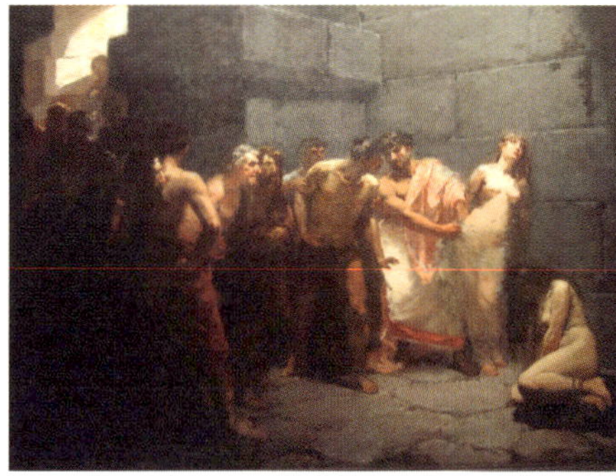

Felix Hidalgo. *Las Virgenes Cristianas Expuestas al Populacho* (Christian Virgins Exposed to the Populace). 1884. Oil on canvas, 115 x 157 cm. Collection of Bangko Sentral ng Pilipinas.

Juan Luna
b. 1857, Philippines; d. 1899, Hong Kong

Felix Hidalgo
b. 1855, Philippines; d. 1913, Spain

The intertwining of art and history can be seen in the example of *Spoliarium* by Juan Luna and *Las Virgenes Cristianas Expuestas al Populacho* (Christian Virgins Exposed to the Populace) by Felix Hidalgo. While these works do not portray actually identifiable historical events, they are clearly set in ancient times, and are an example of "history painting." This is a genre that was once regarded as the most prestigious form of composition in Western art; history paintings generally capture a group of figures in an instant of dynamic, narrative action, in a recognisably historical setting. For their paintings, Luna and Hidalgo won a prestigious gold and silver medal, respectively, in an 1884 exhibition in Madrid. They were celebrated as the first Southeast Asians to win awards in European competitions. This honour, which was much applauded in the Philippines, was further woven with other histories, including the Philippines' anti-colonial struggle for national independence.

In an 1884 speech celebrating Luna and Hidalgo, the writer and anti-colonial campaigner Jose Rizal enthused, "In *Spoliarium*—on that canvas which is not mute—is heard the tumult of the throng, the cry of slaves, the metallic rattle of the armor on the corpses." He similarly affirmed that "in Hidalgo's work there are revealed feelings of the purest kind; ideal expression of melancholy, beauty, and weakness— victims of brute force," continuing that "in Hidalgo we find all is light, color, harmony, feeling, clearness; like the Philippines on moonlit nights, with her horizons that invite to meditation and suggest infinity." These descriptions of the paintings assume extra metaphorical force alongside Rizal's declaration that "The Philippines' patriarchal era is passing... that [Philippine] race, lethargic during the night of history while the sun was illuminating other continents, begins to wake, urged by the electric shock produced by contact with the occidental peoples, and begs for light, life, and... progress." With these poetically allegorical terms, Rizal linked Luna's and Hidalgo's history paintings depicting imagined scenes two millennia prior with the Philippines' anti-colonial struggle at the time.

More recently, many artists have challenged the idea of history as factual and true, suggesting that objectivity in historical accounts is not only impossible, but undesirable. An example is Nguyen Trinh Thi's combination of fiction with documentary in her films, which juxtapose carefully framed interviews, often about history, with dreamlike footage of landscapes, ruins, and archival images. Thi thus proposes that history is formed through many tales and multiple perspectives, which can only ever be partially grasped.

More research is needed on <u>vernacular</u> conceptions of history in Southeast Asia, and their relationship to modern artistic forms. Different languages and cultures give rise to divergent ways of defining and understanding history. For example, historian Theara Thun argues that in Cambodia, there had been a longstanding, pre-colonial literary genre of royal court chronicles which recounted myth as history; this was gradually accompanied and even superseded by a new historiographical genre which arose through contact between Cambodian and French intellectuals. Thus, he proposes, "new ways of mapping the national past emerged during the first decades of the 20th century, in conflict with the traditional ways."

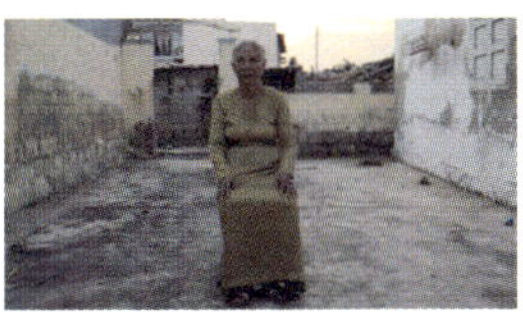

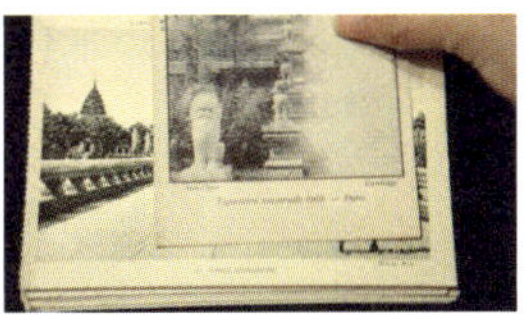

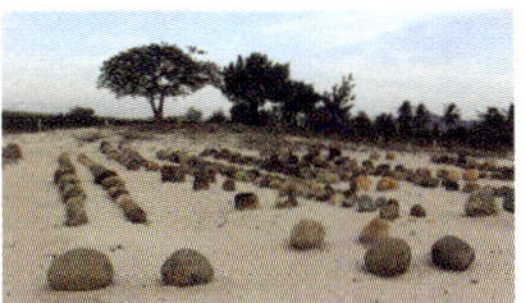

Nguyen Trinh Thi. Stills and production shot from *Letters from Panduranga*. 2015. Single-channel video, colour and black and white, sound, 35 mins. Collection of the artist.

Perhaps we also see this conflict between different conceptions of history manifesting in Buddhist mural paintings in Cambodia, in which recognisable, historically living politicians and <u>kings</u> appear alongside mythical characters from Buddhist tales and Indic epics. These paintings do not depict the past or the present, but instead visually imagine the <u>contemporaneous</u> coexistence of multiple historical <u>times</u>. This reveals the shifting nature of history, and also emphasises the aesthetic choices that go into the telling of any story about the past.

HYBRID

"He does not know which custom he should conform to," reads the caption for a 1941 cartoon from Laos. "He is caught between two things."

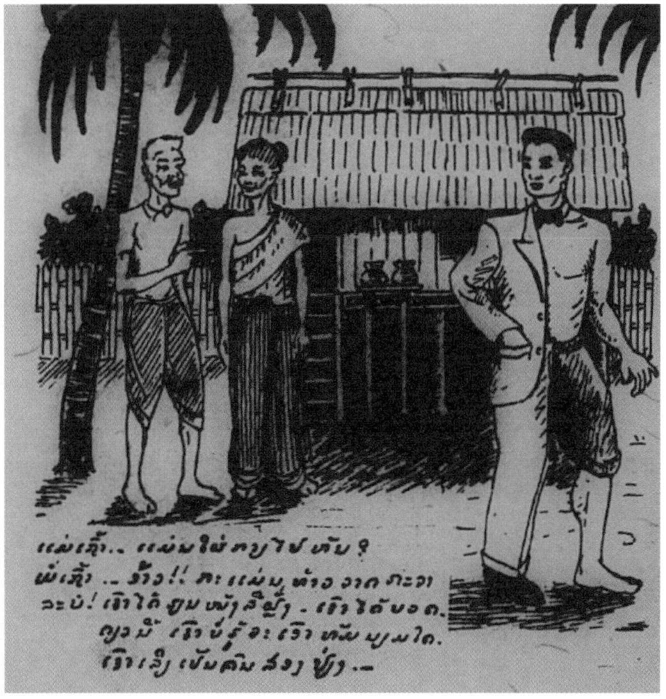

Cartoon from an early edition of *Lao Nhay*, the first Lao periodical, 14 February 1941. Author unknown. Translation by Chairat Polmuk.

The caption accompanies an image of a man whose appearance is stylised to emphasise his seemingly hybrid identity: one half modern and European, and the other half "traditional" and Lao. He is dressed in a European-style modern suit and bowtie on one side of his body, and in typical Lao dress of the time on the other side, including a bare torso and tied *sampot*. The caption explains that the man had ordained as a monk, as was customary for Lao Buddhist males, while also having "studied with the French." The strangeness of his visage is emphasised by contrast with a conventionally dressed older Lao man and woman standing next to a typical wooden hut, who signify the "<u>traditional</u>," rural way of life in Laos. This older couple is made to appear normal, whole, and pure in contradistinction to the man whose identity and aesthetic presentation is split, mixed, and perhaps impure: that is, hybrid.

Images of hybridity appear in modern art throughout Southeast Asia. As in the Lao cartoon, these are often expressions not only of cultural intermixing — typically between Western and Southeast Asian ways — but also of times commingling, between the "traditional" and the modern, or the old and new. One celebrated example is *Ken Dedes* by Jim Supangkat, in which a replica of a 13th-century Javanese image of the deity Prajnaparamita, resplendent with sculptural detail, has been placed atop an unornamented white plinth. On this pedestal, Supangkat has drawn the torso and legs of a bare-breasted modern woman, dressed only in tight jeans, which are unbuttoned to reveal her pubic hair. The resulting image is a hybrid of sacred and profane, graceful and lascivious, Javanese and Western: an expression, among other things, of the complex and multiple nature of modern subjectivity.

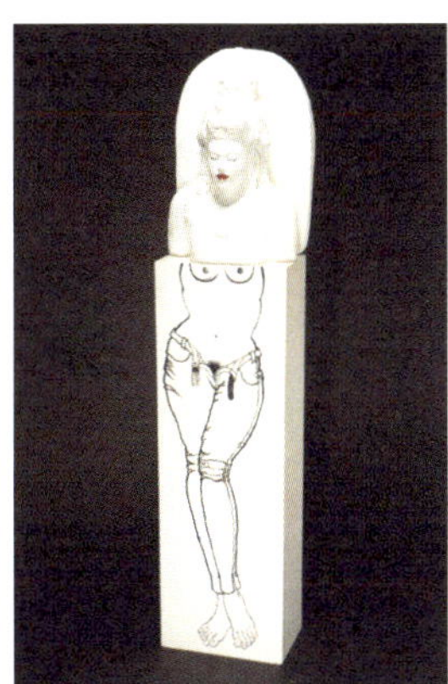

Jim Supangkat. *Ken Dedes*. 1975, remade 1996. Plaster, wood, marker pen and paint, dimensions variable. Collection of National Gallery Singapore.

Jim Supangkat
b. 1948, Indonesia

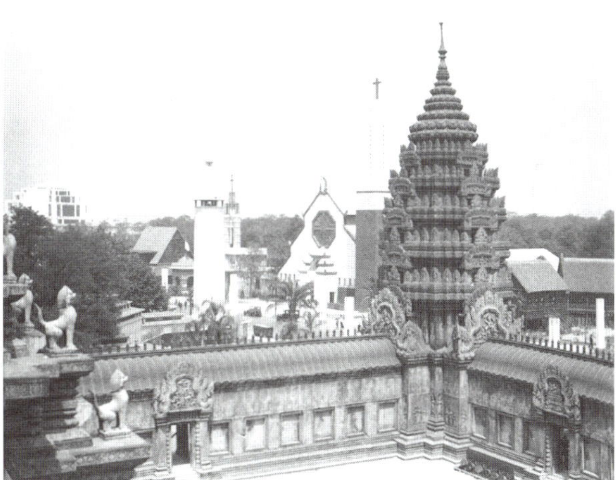

"Reconstruction" of Angkor Wat at the 1931 Colonial Exposition, Paris. Photographer unknown.

Colonial authorities and artists also employed hybrid constructions to articulate their possessive vision of Southeast Asia. The reconstruction of Angkor Wat in France at colonial expositions during the 1920s and 1930s was a hybrid, combining the outward appearance of the 12th-century Khmer temple with modern construction techniques and secular <u>exhibitionary</u> functions, in a demonstration of imperial mastery.

Latiff Mohidin
b. 1941, Malaysia

The *Pago-Pago* series by Latiff Mohidin, begun in the 1960s, represents a less cynical kind of hybridity. These paintings and drawings syncretise architectural and ornamental forms from different religions, suggesting the <u>spiritual</u> and cultural intermixing found throughout Southeast Asia, and combining this also with shapes derived from nature, such as bamboo shoots.

Perhaps the many mythological creatures familiar in Southeast Asia, which combine elements of several existing animals, might be considered older manifestations of hybridity. Some consideration of the cultural connotations behind these creatures may reveal understandings of hybridity not tied to Western systems of knowledge.

While it has a broad range of uses and connotations, hybridity is a contested concept. The term first emerged in Europe in the early 17th century, in the field of biology. In its original meaning, a hybrid is defined as the offspring of two animals or plants of different species. Some synonymous terms include "half-breed" and "mongrel," indicating the often pejorative or denigrating function of the word. To be described as a hybrid of two things is often to be thought of as lesser than either of them.

Despite this, however, in modern discussions of culture, hybridity has been a popular notion for theorising identities, as well as cultural formations, such as artworks. Postcolonial scholars like Homi Bhabha have adopted hybridity not as a descriptive tool but rather as an interpretive mode: a way of thinking, including about art. In Southeast Asia, this approach has also been taken up by many writers, including Supangkat.

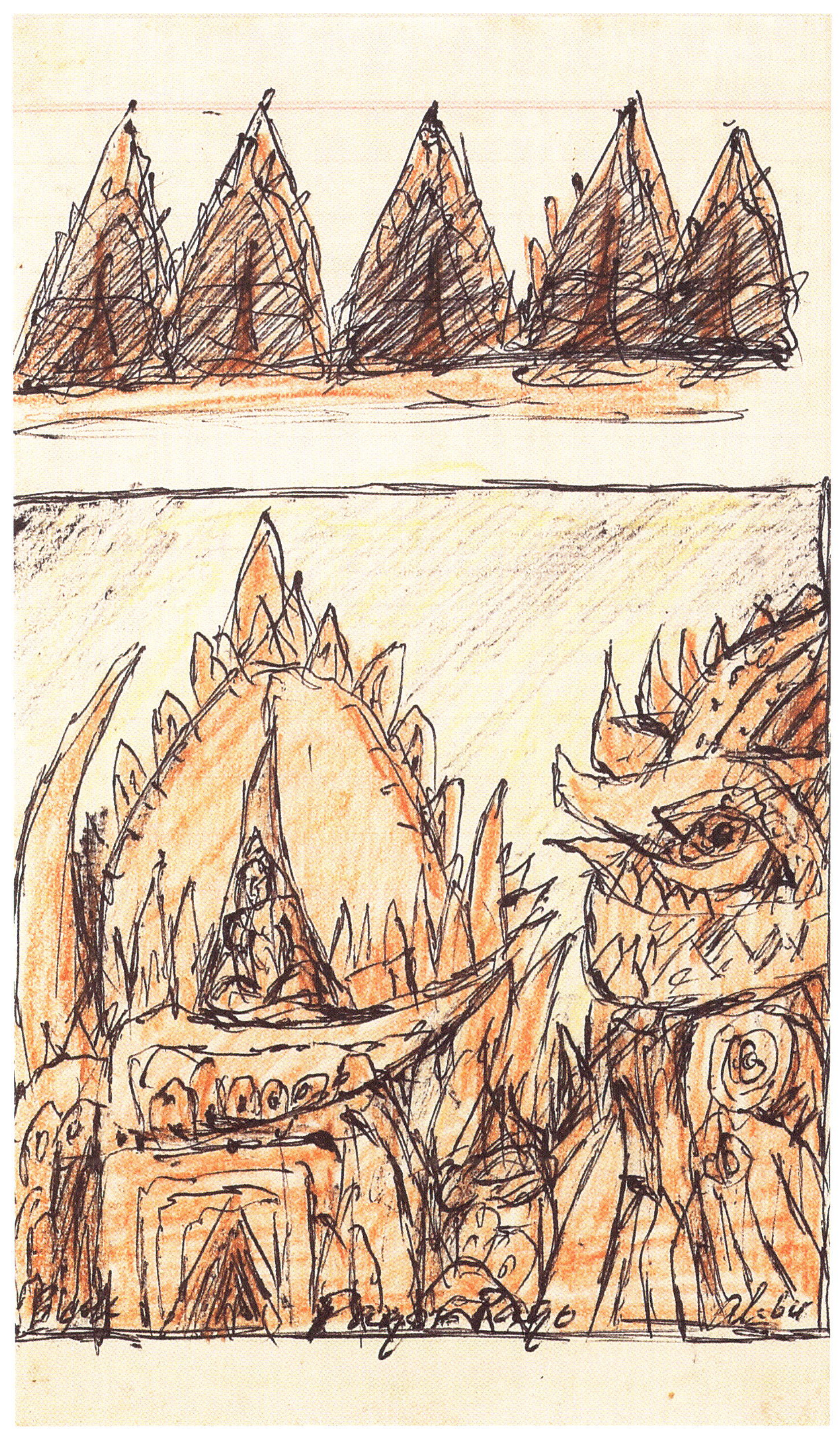

Latiff Mohidin. *Pago-Pago*. 1964. Ink wash on paper, 14.5 x 9 cm. Collection of the artist.

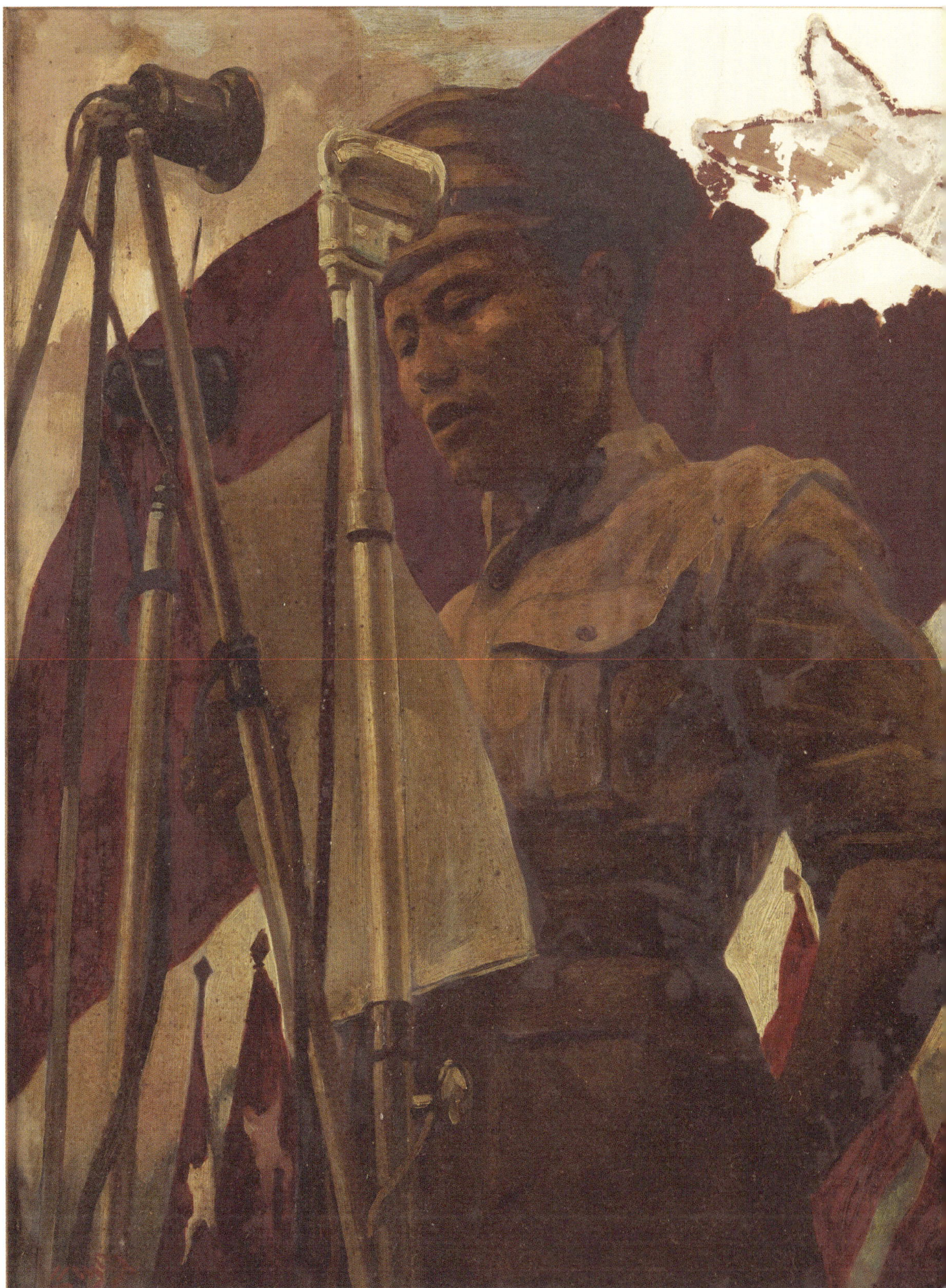

U Ngwe Gaing. *Portrait of General Aung San*. c. 1950–1967. Oil on cardboard support lined on pre-primed cotton fabric, 50 x 39.5 cm. Collection of National Gallery Singapore.

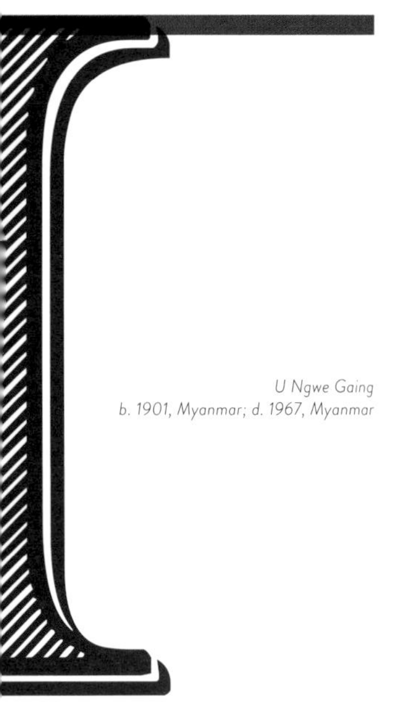

INDEPENDENCE

Winning independence from colonial rule was a decisive moment in the modern political history of most Southeast Asian states, and is a fertile symbol of <u>national</u> identity in the region. Independence offers a rich well of inspiration for modern art in Southeast Asia. Many artworks celebrate independence, and studying them illuminates the processes of decolonisation, emphasising their nuances and variations.

Artistic expressions of independence adopt many different approaches and perspectives. For example, U Ngwe Gaing's portrayal of Bogyoke Aung San, the general widely considered to be the chief architect of Myanmar's independence from British rule, articulates a modern, forward-looking vision. In this portrait, which is likely based on a photograph from the 1940s, Aung San stands proudly in military uniform as he delivers a speech, appearing at once human and heroic. Behind him are flags of either the Anti-Fascist Organisation, a Myanmar resistance movement during World War II, or its successor, the Anti-Fascist People's Freedom League, a major political coalition active from 1945 to 1958. It is difficult to identify the flags due to damage to the painted star, but it is certain that they represent an organisation of central importance in Myanmar's anti-colonial campaign.

Aung San was assassinated in 1947, shortly before the declaration of Myanmar's freedom from colonial authority in 1948. He is synonymous with independence, and a potent symbol of the struggle against colonial rule. The sense of optimism that would have accompanied this hard-earned independence can be felt in Ngwe Gaing's portrayal: the <u>realist</u> technique of representation, as well as the pristine uniform and gleaming microphones, all signal an optimistic sense of newness, which is claimed for Myanmar. The artist captures Aung San from an unusual vantage point, and renders details and tonal shifts softly yet precisely, securing his reputation as one of Myanmar's leading artists of the post-World War II period.

Whereas Ngwe Gaing's painting of Aung San characterises independence as defined solely by novelty and innovation, in Vientiane and in Phnom Penh, monuments that were commissioned to celebrate decolonisation drew instead on old as well as new forms. Phnom Penh's Independence Monument, commissioned by patron of the arts Prince Norodom Sihanouk, and designed by architect Vann Molyvann, combines the geometric proportions devised by Le Corbusier—which are distinctly modern,

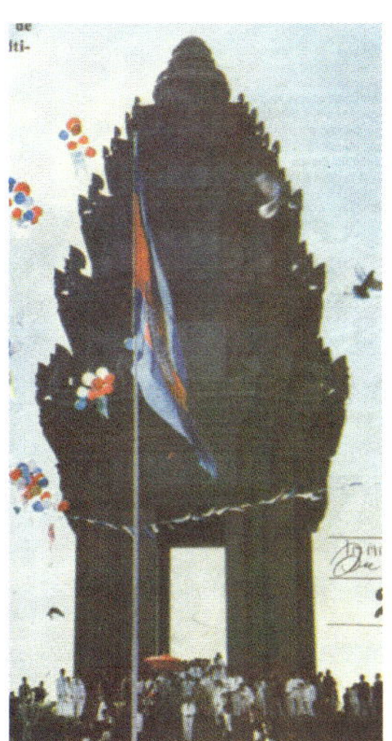

Vann Molyvann, architect. Independence Monument, Phnom Penh, completed c. 1957. Photographer unknown.

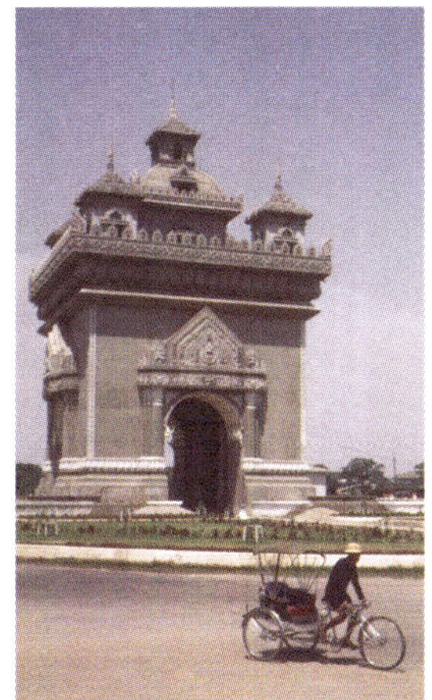

Tham Sayasithsena, designer. Patuxai, Vientiane. Commissioned 1957, completed c. 1968.

but also French—with the recognisably Khmer, but also ancient, decorative style found in the 10th-century temple of Banteay Srei. The design thus symbolises Cambodian independence by synthesising diverse cosmopolitan architectural traditions, combining both new and old aesthetic visions.

Similarly, in Vientiane, the Patuxai monument—originally called the Tomb to the Unknown Soldier—combines the arched profile of the Arc de Triomphe in Paris with decorative elements commonly perceived as distinctly Lao. This simultaneous reference to French and Lao traditions (among others) is striking given that the monument was intended to celebrate national independence. As the historian Grant Evans remarks, "for post-colonial nationalists it became *de rigeur* to de-emphasize connections between their project and the colonial state." Yet Patuxai, like Molyvann's monument in Phnom Penh, instead suggests considerable cultural continuities, by adopting stylistic elements that remained popular before, during, and after independence.

Although usually referring to freedom from colonial rule, independence may also denote other significant moments in Southeast Asia's history. In Vietnam, for example, French rule ended in 1954, yet the "reunification" of North and South Vietnam in 1975 brought another kind of independence after decades of <u>war</u>, in the eyes of many (although this is debated among some Vietnamese). So too did the opening of the country to international trade and exchange after the Doi Moi reforms of 1986, and the fall of the Soviet Union in 1989. Filmmaker and scholar Trinh T. Minh-ha explores these layered processes of decolonisation in *Surname Viet Given Name Nam*, a film comprised largely of archival footage, blurred with age, as well as interviews. "When I first met the women of the South," one woman explains in the film, "we looked at each other with distrust, if not with hostility. Slowly we started talking to each other. From distrust we have come to dialogue." Independence makes possible new kinds of freedom and discourse, and art makes manifest this shift.

*Trinh T. Minh-ha
b. 1952, Vietnam*

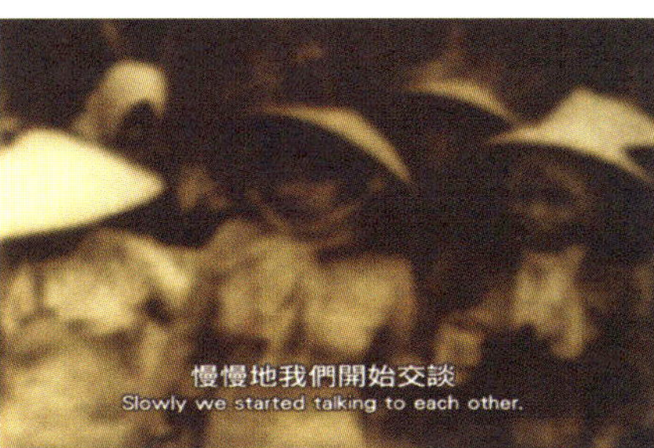

Trinh T. Minh-ha, writer and director. *Surname Viet Given Name Nam*. 1989. 6mm film, 108 min.

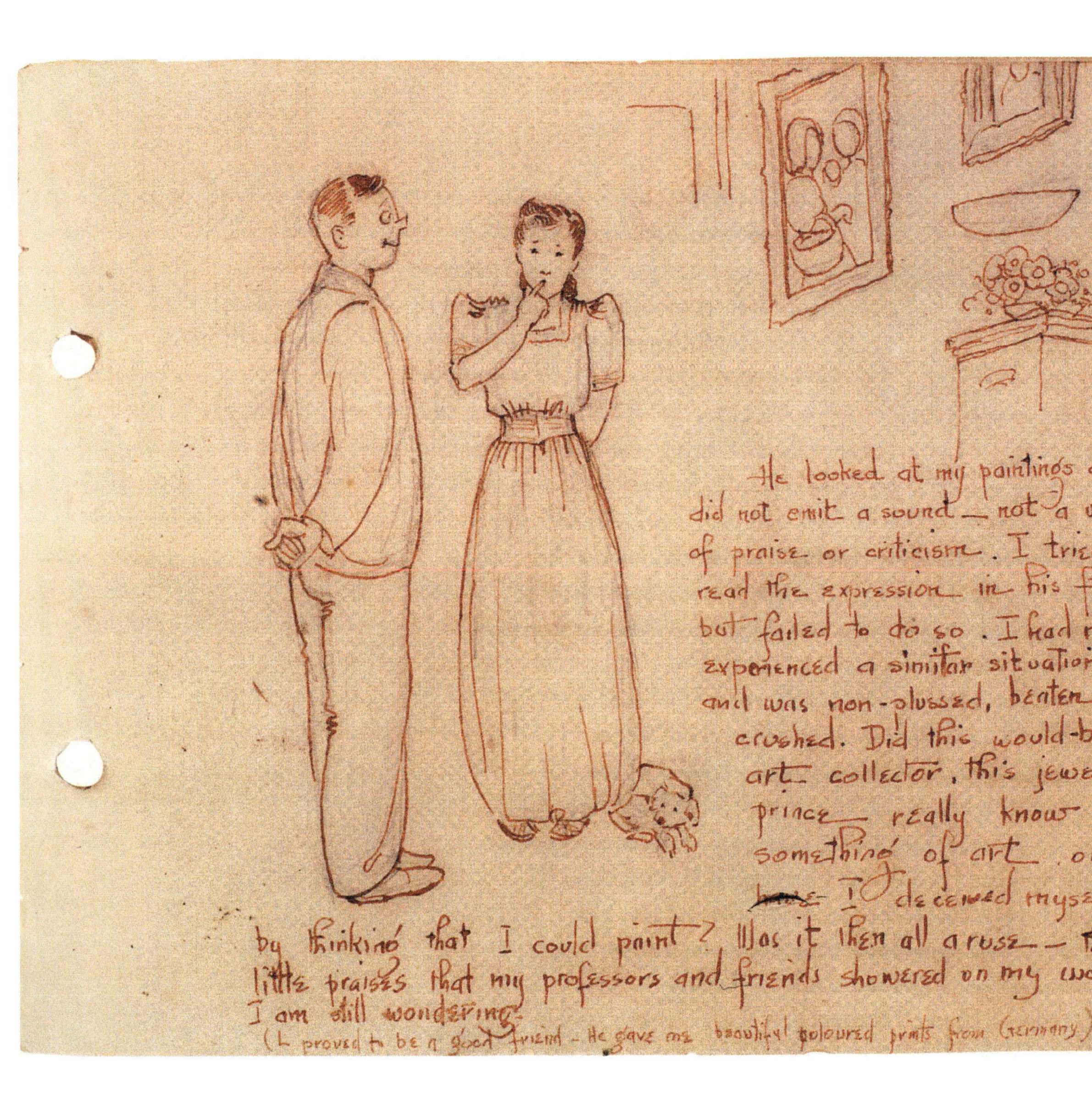

He looked at my paintings and
did not emit a sound — not a word
of praise or criticism. I tried to
read the expression in his face
but failed to do so. I had never
experienced a similar situation
and was non-plussed, beaten,
crushed. Did this would-be
art collector, this jewel
prince — really know
something of art . or
~~have~~ ! I deceived myself
by thinking that I could paint? Was it then all a ruse — the
little praises that my professors and friends showered on my work.
I am still wondering.
(L proved to be a good friend — He gave me beautiful coloured prints from (Germany)

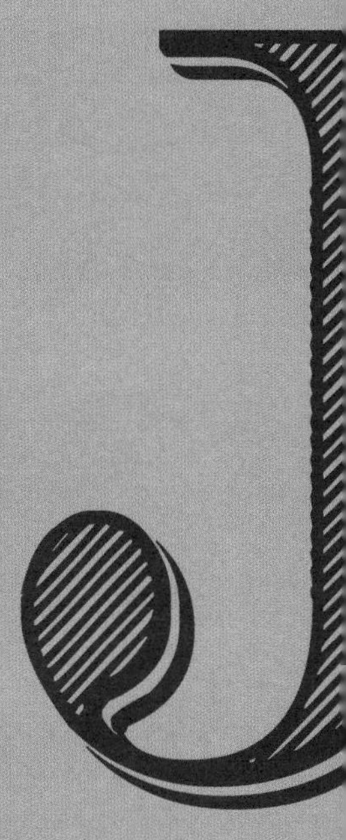

Artists' journals—as well as memoirs, letters, and other personal writings—can be a rich resource for understanding and appreciating artworks, and situating them in historical contexts. An example from Vietnam demonstrates the potential of these private writings to illuminate artworks.

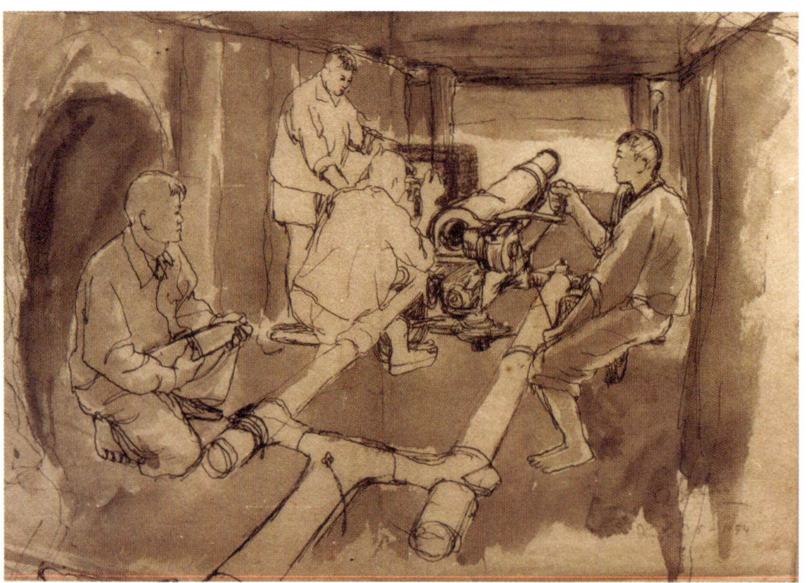

Pham Thanh Tam. *In a Bunker, Gunners Prepare to Open Fire*. 1954. Ink on paper, 20 x 27 cm. Collection of Ho Chi Minh City Museum of Fine Arts.

Pham Thanh Tam
b. 1933, Vietnam

Like most sketches made by artists engaged in <u>war</u>, Pham Thanh Tam's *In a Bunker, Gunners Prepare to Open Fire* has been quickly drawn. It was made at Dien Bien Phu, a major battle in the First Indochina War in which French military forces were devastatingly defeated. In Tam's drawing, only schematic outlines of the soldiers' faces are given, yet the artist has indicated with just a few lines the great care with which the soldier kneeling at the left of the image is handling his munitions.

The artist's diary, written while at battle, offers an illuminating and unexpected anecdote which brings this small detail in the artwork alive.

"Taking to heart [an order] to economise on munitions, [soldiers] The and Phuc are banging old shells back into shape. Dang tried fitting one of the shells back into the cannon, it worked. Thang, the company deputy commander, told him to make a note in his report of how many shells were fixed."

This entry, dated 3 April 1954, suggests that perhaps the soldier seen in the artwork is aware of a shortage of munition

—perhaps even that the shell he is carefully holding might be an old one that has painstakingly beaten "back into shape." The diary entry continues: "As for Tao, he has been composing poems. As I write, close by, artilleryman number 8 is admiring the blue and green reflections of the French flares on the polished steel surface of the cannon, like a fanciful dance of fireflies."

With these words in mind, looking again to the artist's monochromatic sketch, can we imagine these brilliantly hued effects of light? This entry from Tam's diary confirms his later reflection that "there is an aesthetic in war. Because the events you are witnessing are too dreadful, it is up to the artist to use his art to reaffirm life itself and to communicate his belief in a better future." This statement reveals that, like most Vietnamese war artists, Tam sketched with a commitment to supporting the war effort, and the ideology he served; his art was also a kind of propaganda. Thus, his artworks never contain images of horror as violent or confronting as those recounted in his diary. Moreover, the diary describes sensory and emotional experiences which cannot be captured in visual form alone, as in Tam's mention of "young soldiers [who] stunk of perfume they had found in the French parachuted supplies."

Sometimes, journals may be created with an audience or readership in mind, but even if they aren't made exclusively for the self, they can provide special insights into otherwise private moments in an artist's life. Anita Magsaysay-Ho recorded formative artistic and personal events in a handmade diary during World War II. One entry recalls the first time that a "would-be art collector" came to view her paintings. Magsaysay-Ho's professional nervousness is conveyed in both the image and accompanying text, describing her feeling as "non-plussed, beaten and crushed." The artist would later join the Thirteen Moderns, a loose grouping who employed social realism and abstraction to foster debate about art in the Philippines.

In some cases, as with Mia Bustam, written accounts by artists can be used to explore their historical significance, when very few of their artworks are known to have survived. Although Bustam had exhibited alongside her more famous husband, S. Sudjojono, and other members of LEKRA, a communist-affiliated group of artists, before the genocide in Indonesia between 1965 and 1966, only a few of her paintings, as well as some works of embroidery, have survived. Thus, her memoirs are more illuminating than her oeuvre.

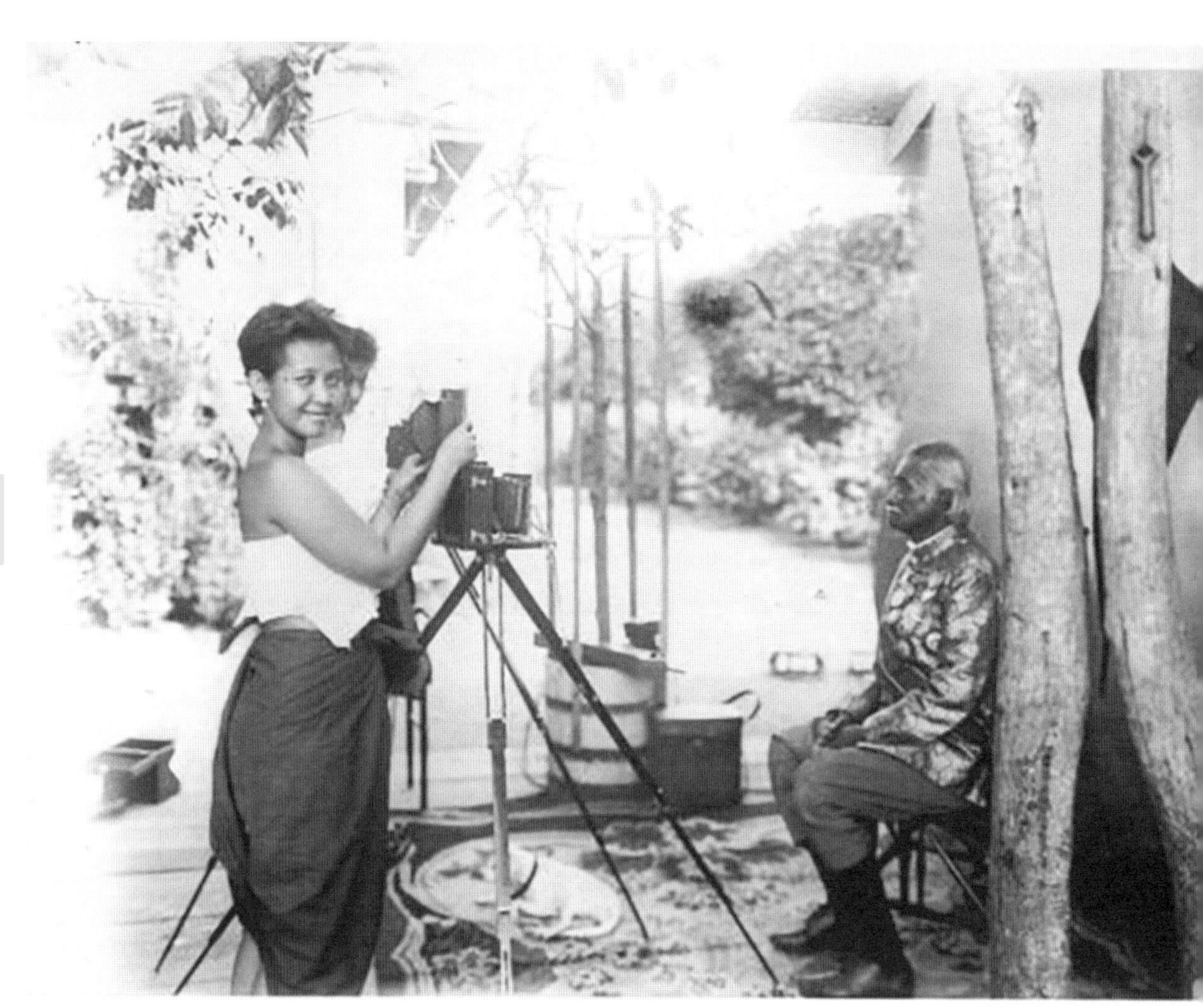

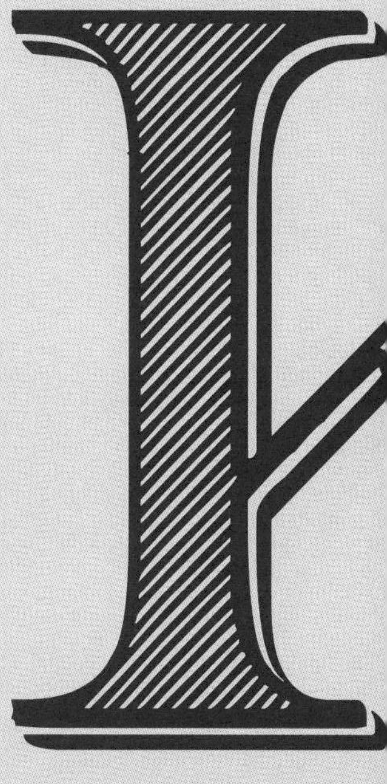

Erb Bunnag photographing her father, Tet Bunnag. Photographer unknown, c. 1906.

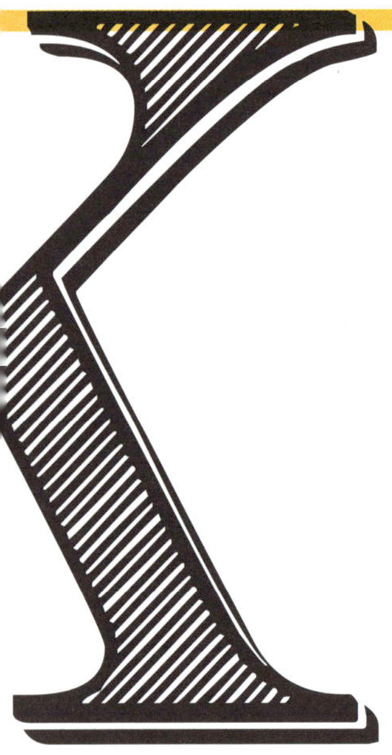

KINGS

What do princesses and queens, sultans and rajahs, princes and kings have to do with modern art in Southeast Asia? While the <u>modern</u> is often associated with the new, established seats of power have also played important roles in the emergence and development of modern art, just as royal courts had been the most significant sponsors for art and culture in premodern times.

One of the key ways in which monarchs contributed to the development of modern art was in the commissioning of art and architecture; some were even involved in creating these expressions themselves. Indeed, one of the most profound revolutions that <u>modernities</u> brought was an expansion of the roles available to women, which in turn made it possible for <u>women</u> to play new roles in the making of modern art. A potent example shows Thai royal consort Erb Bunnag, smiling and confident, as she photographs her father. Erb's newfound creative agency matched the privileged position that she and her sisters had won within the Bangkok palace. From the 1890s, royal women there had gained access to photographic technologies, according to art historian Leslie Woodhouse, often depicting each other engaged in <u>quotidian</u> activities. This made these women "newly accessible to eyes outside the palace," Woodhouse notes, reflecting broader social changes.

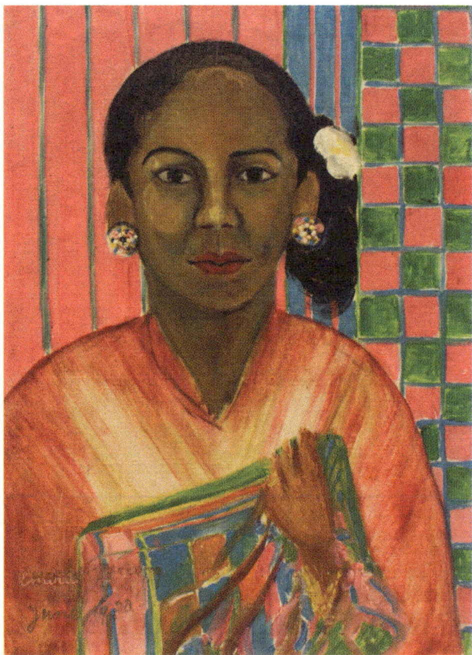

Emiria Sunassa. *Wanita Sulawesi* (Sulawesi Woman). 1958. Oil on canvas, 66 x 47 cm. Collection of Oei Hong Djien Museum, Magelang.

Emiria Sunassa, who claimed to be a princess from the sultanate of Tidore, also created art, and in so doing challenged previously expected roles for royal women. She made formally experimental paintings of armed Papuans and campaigned for Papuan independence. Details on Emiria's biography are uncertain, and art historians Heidi Arbuckle and Wulan Dirgantoro have argued that the artist deliberately constructed multiple subjectivities. This blurring of identity is mirrored in Emiria's painting, *Wanita Sulawesi* (Sulawesi Woman), in which the background pattern reappears on a cloth the subject is holding to her heart.

Emiria Sunassa
b. 1894, Indonesia; d. 1964, Indonesia

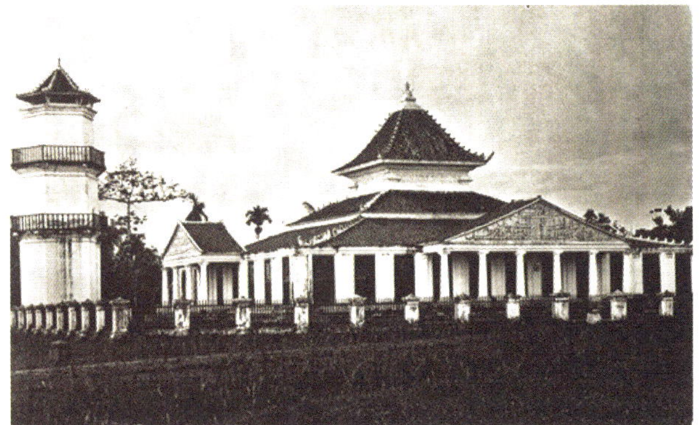

Palembang Great Mosque, or Masjig Agung, Sumatra, Indonesia. Constructed from 1738 to 1748, under patronage of Sultan Mahmud Badaruddin I (r. 1724–1758). Photographed c. 1857–1877. Collection of Tropenmuseum, Amsterdam.

Advances in architecture also came about under the direction of monarchs. Royal sultans throughout archipelagic Southeast Asia commissioned Grand Mosques, also known as Masjid Agung. As in art, such architecture reflects a tendency toward hybrid forms; combinations of new and old, foreign and local forms, they reflect connections made by diasporic populations of Malay, Javanese, Bugis and others. There "was a noticeable change in architectural culture in the eighteenth century," according to architectural historian Imran bin Tajudeen, "with a number of small mosques that are typologically Malayo-Javanese, but are strongly characterized by the contribution or intervention of Southern Chinese, Hadhrami (from Hadhramawt valley in southern Arabia, today's Yemen), and Tamil builders and patrons." Discussing the Grand Mosque in Palembang, Tajudeen argues that "Javanese techniques were thus used in Palembang to create a structural configuration that had no precedent in mosques found in Java," a "novel experimentation" he notes was commissioned by a political elite who had fled central Java to take up residence in the Sumatran city. That is, Javanese architectural methods were used in Palembang in entirely new ways that had never been used previously in Java. In other words, a diaspora population created a new style and technique through the transfer of different ideas from various places: a process echoed in the development of modern art in many parts of Southeast Asia.

Royal elites also introduced innovations and experimentation by inviting foreign artists to court, who thereby provided an <u>educational</u> model for local artists. This is captured in a 1906 photograph depicting Phra Soralaklikhit painting the Italian artist Cesare Ferro while Ferro, in turn, paints King Chulalongkorn.

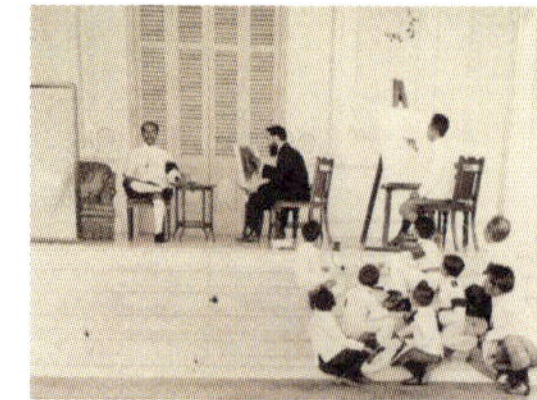

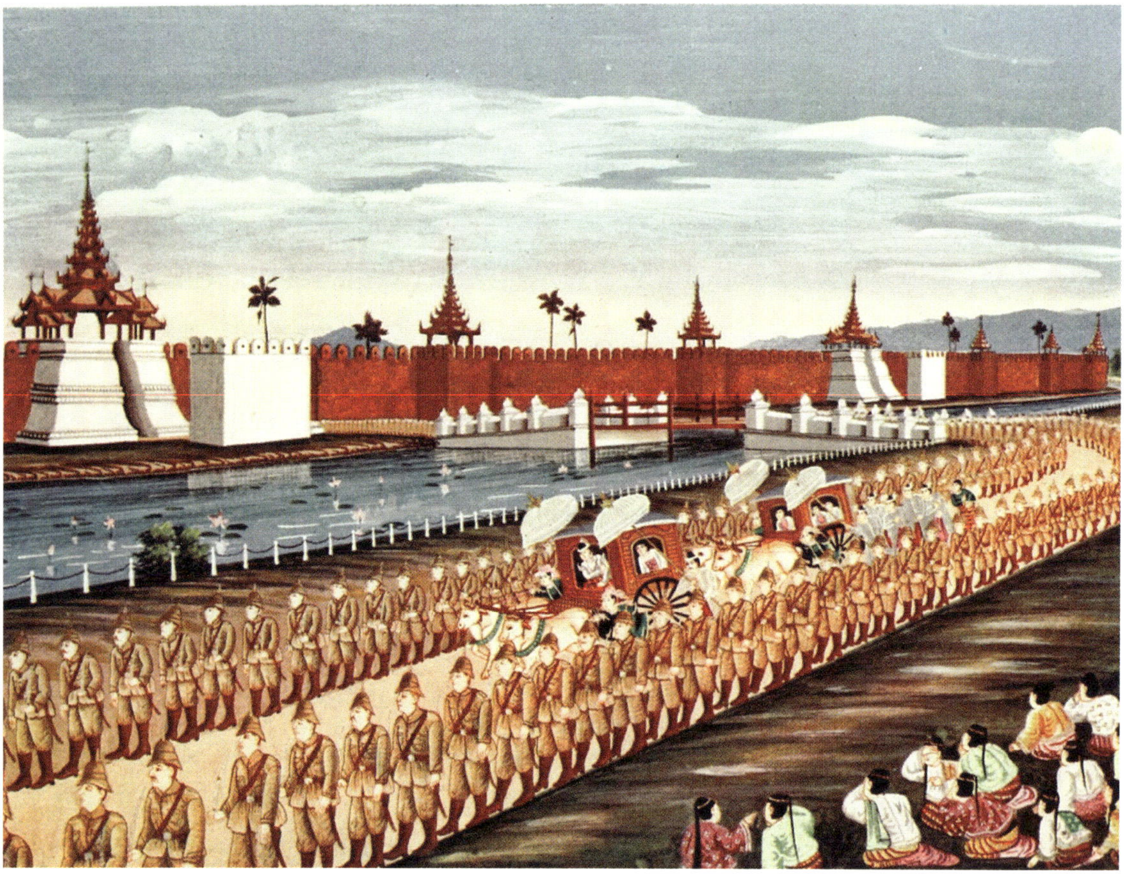

Phra Soralaklikhit depicting Cesare Ferro depicting King Chulalongkorn (King Rama V, r. 1868–1910). Photographer unknown, 1906.

Saya Chone. *King Thibaw and Queen Supayalat Leaving Mandalay For Ever.* c. 1900s. Opaque watercolour on paper, attached to cloth, 30 x 42 cm. Private collection.

U Ba Nyan
b. 1897, Myanmar; d. 1945, Myanmar

In Myanmar, Western-style <u>realism</u>, based in observation and verisimilitude, emerged outside of the court. Yet royalty continued to cast its shadow: U Ba Nyan, hailed as the first Myanmar artist sent abroad for schooling, also painted a formal <u>portrait</u> of Britain's King George V (although the painting's location is now unknown). Other artists, including Saya Chone, who had painted in the royal court in Mandalay

Saya Chone
b. 1866, Myanmar; d. 1917, Myanmar

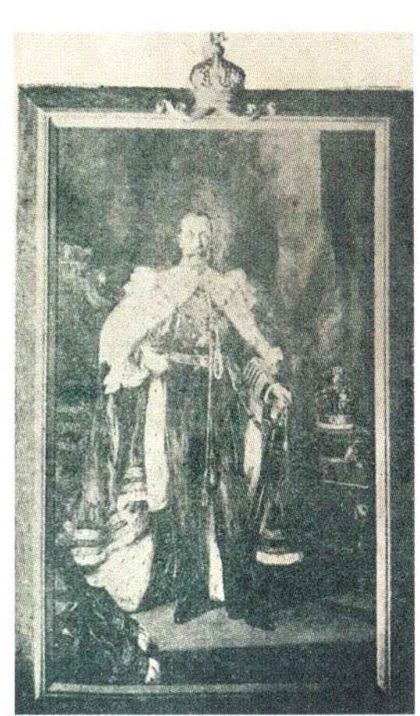

U Ba Nyan's portrait of King George V. Image published in *Dagon Magazine*, no. 132, August 1931.

prior to its defeat by invading British colonists in 1885, continued to paint in the court style, yet also incorporated modern elements, innovating within kingly tradition. For example, Chone's *King Thibaw Min Leaving Mandalay* combines the formality and repetition of traditional Burmese painting with modern compositional techniques like linear perspective. The depiction was made over a decade after the <u>historical</u> event it depicts: after being deposed in 1885, Thibaw was exiled in southwestern India.

Despite all of these and many other important modernisations led by royal figures, modern art has largely flourished due to a seismic shift *away* from courtly <u>patronage</u>, toward new networks for commissioning and disseminating art. Individuals as well as new kinds of institutions created through the emergence of modernities have become major sources of support for modern art, allowing new kinds of expression which might never have been permissible within royal or religious settings. In most parts of Southeast Asia, modern artists are also now less inclined than ever to make depictions of royalty.

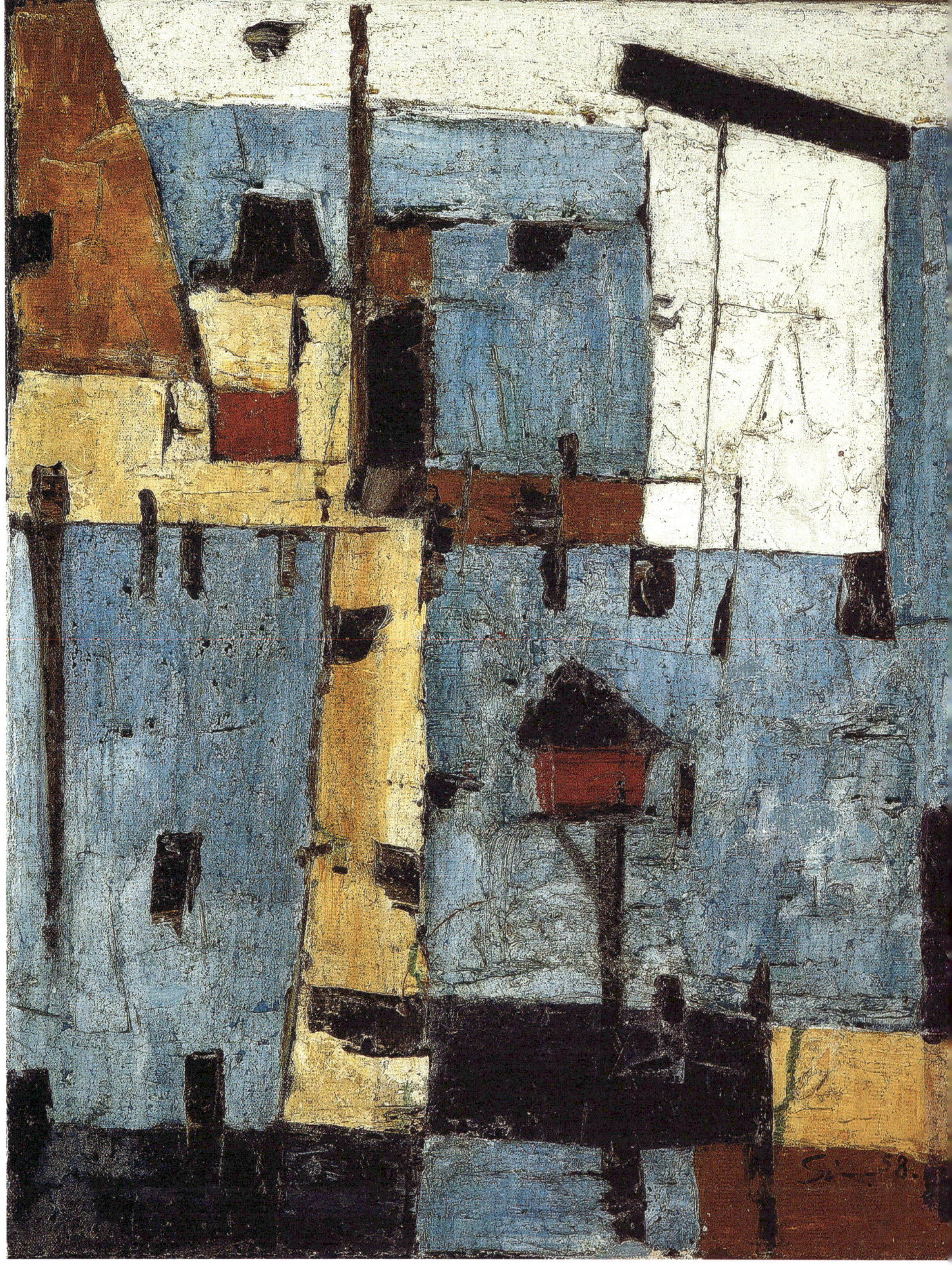

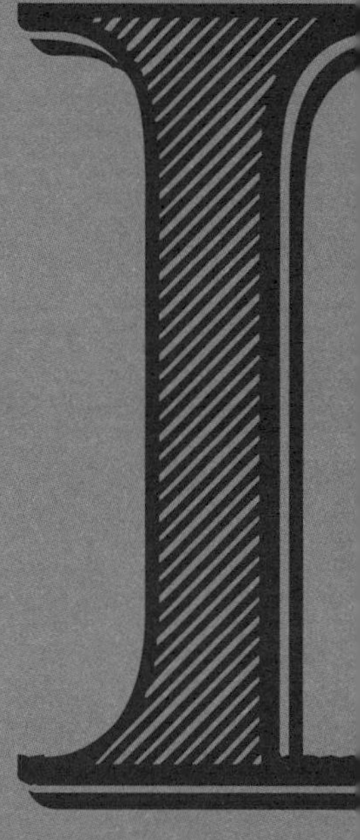

LANDSCAPE

At Borobudur, Angkor, and other premodern temples, bas-relief sculptures of deities and mortals often appear alongside depictions of trees, flowers, and animals, as well as <u>vernacular</u> housing. This suggests that people have long been drawn to the portrayal of nature and environments. Yet the landscape does not appear in such settings: the depiction of a large area of countryside is a distinctly modern phenomenon in art in Southeast Asia. In modern art, landscapes are often significant in a range of ways, including as ways for artists to imagine and visualise aspects of the <u>national</u> and the <u>spiritual</u>.

Early vistas of landscape by colonial artists often emphasised the encroachment of <u>urbanisation</u> into nature, and followed codified aesthetic conventions of the landscape genre as practised in Europe. The work of William Daniell, who worked in numerous British colonies during the 18th and 19th centuries, offers a typical example. Daniell first moved to India at the age of 16, and his first published artworks were made in collaboration with anonymous Indian artists, and his father. In almost all of Daniell's landscape paintings and prints, trees placed at the edge of the composition frame the scene. Moreover, human figures appear at small size; this is a device called "staffage," used to indicate the scale of the environment, and to make clear that the people are not the principal subject of the artwork. These compositional strategies are typical of European aesthetic conventions for depicting landscape in a genre known as "picturesque."

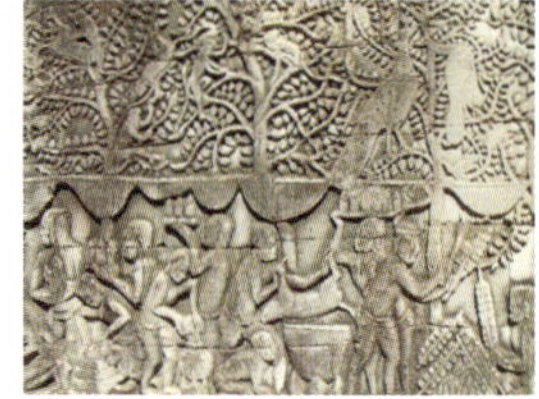

Vegetation, bas-relief, Bayon. 12–13th centuries CE, Siem Reap.

William Daniell
b. 1769, United Kingdom; d. 1837, United Kingdom

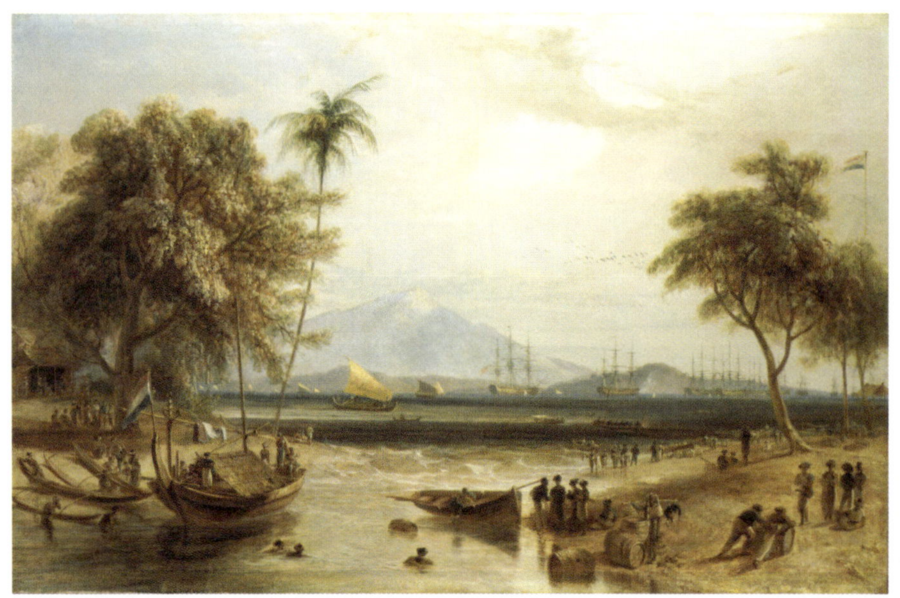

William Daniell. *The Watering Place at Anjer Point in the Island of Java.* 1794. Oil on canvas, 67 x 107 cm. Collection of Royal Museums Greenwich.

While staffage is rarely seen in 20th-century artworks, other elements of picturesque aesthetics remained popular after their transfer and use by Southeast Asian artists. As in Daniell's work, large trees painted at one side of many of Fernando Amorsolo's landscapes frame the scene, and convey a sense of its scale. Yet the figures in Amorsolo's landscapes—women and men engaged in the quotidian labour of farm work—are more realistic. Within his large oeuvre, Amorsolo often painted very similar scenes multiple times, repeatedly linking the landscape to agricultural labour. The abundance of the rice fields, and the productivity of the Philippine people, symbolise an idealised image of the nation in Amorsolo's work, as in paintings by his teacher Fabian de la Rosa and countless other artists.

As Amorsolo's paintings show, artworks featuring landscapes in Southeast Asia have often emphasised the fertility of the tropical terrain, and positioned the landscape as symbolising the nation. Depictions of landscapes dominated by rice cultivation, especially, abound in modern art from across Southeast Asia. Sometimes, as in the work of Nhek Dim, these images relate to political ideas specific to a single nation. Nhek Dim's paintings of rice farmers united in collective labour echo the policy of "Khmer Buddhist Socialism" propounded by the former king, Norodom Sihanouk. Elsewhere, as in some paintings by Basoeki Abdullah, as well as various early photographs, artists have used depictions of the landscape as a way to explore formal elements such as the flatness of rice paddies flooded with water.

Water is an omnipresent element in the Southeast Asian environment, and depictions of ports and the sea have been almost as common as images of rice fields. Some artists, like Kum Yuen Sim, have approached seaside landscapes through the lens of abstraction. Her flat, rectilinear blocks of colour evoke the atmosphere of a fishing village. Many other artists, including Eng Tow, Kim Lim, and Ithipol Thangchalok, have also conveyed the appearance and experience of landscape using abstract forms.

Some artists have been drawn to the interplay between natural environments and religious architecture, revealing the spiritual relationship many people have with the landscape. Examples include Latiff Mohidin, who explored the hybrid intersections of nature and culture in his artworks and poetry, and Chua Ek Kay. Although better known for his formally inventive work with Chinese ink in which topographical features are treated like abstract forms, Chua also

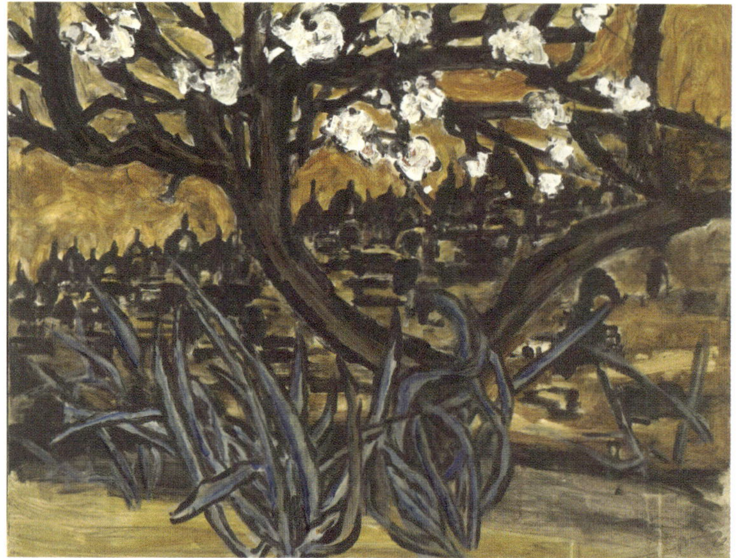

Chua Ek Kay. Untitled (*A Tree in Front of Borobudur*). Undated (c. 2006). Oil on canvas, 92 x 122 cm. Collection of Singapore Art Museum.

depicted in oil the harmonious integration of stupa structures into the landscape.

Just as the representation of landscape is a distinctly
modern type of art, so too has the land itself been transformed by <u>modernities</u>. Abdullah Ariff's watercolour paintings of tin mines adapt elements of pictorial aesthetics, yet
depict wholly unnatural environments. Tin mines desecrat-
ed the landscape, yet were crucial to the national economy
when Ariff was painting, and tin mining corporations were
important <u>patrons</u> of modern art in Malaysia.

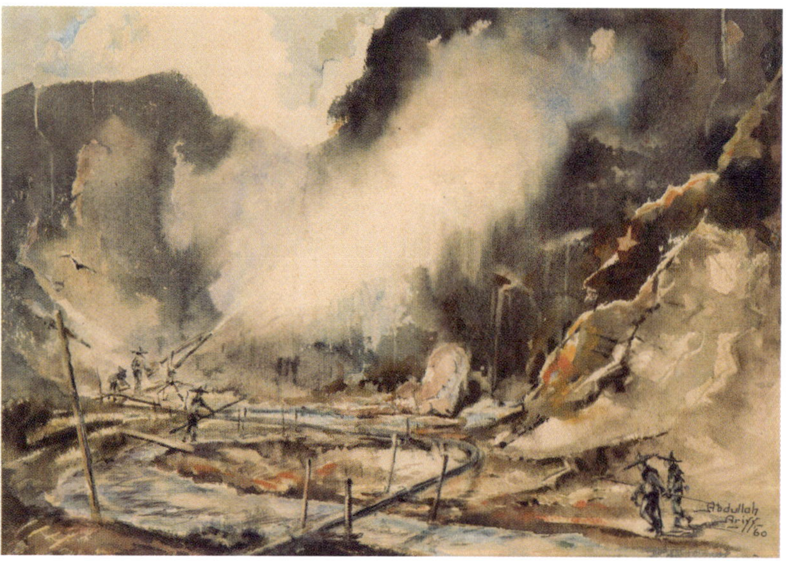

Abdullah Ariff. *Tin Mining*. 1960. Watercolour on paper, 37.7 x 55.1 cm. Collection of National Gallery Singapore.

Depictions of landscape are less common in <u>contemporary</u> art. Yet some contemporary artists, like Nge Lay, have ruminated on the landscape as a site of violence. This marks a significant shift away from the prevailing tendency to celebrate Southeast Asian landscapes as sources of beauty and life.

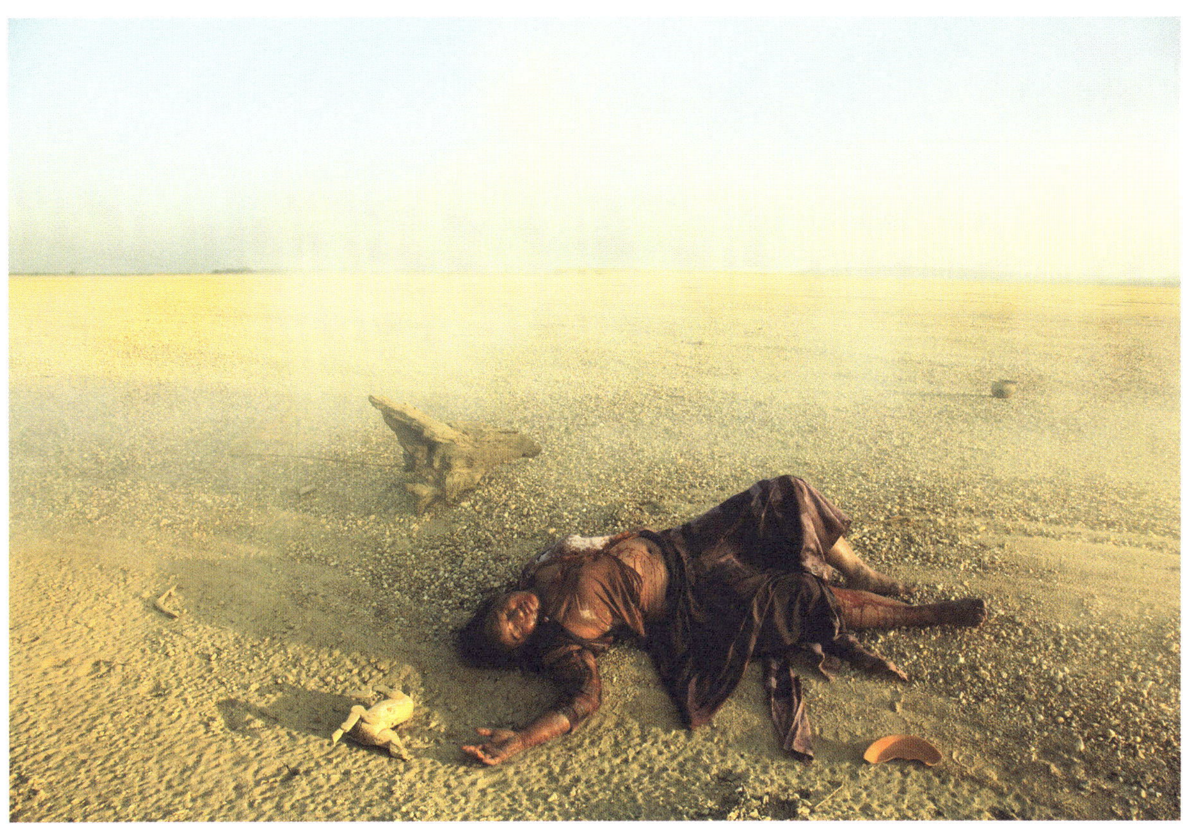

Nge Lay. *Observance of Self on Being Dead*. 2011. Archival print on rag, 116 x 160 cm. Collection of the artist.

It seems necessary from the outset to state that we are MODERN artists and as such, we are not involved with traditional Asian art forms. We are however borrowing from Asian philosophies in order to come up with an attitude which we hope will help enrich the international modern art movement which needs to be considered in global terms these days.

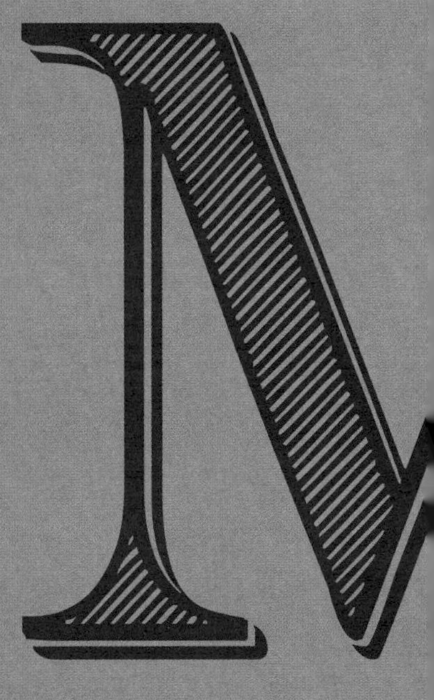

—Sulaiman Esa and Redza Piyadasa, 1974

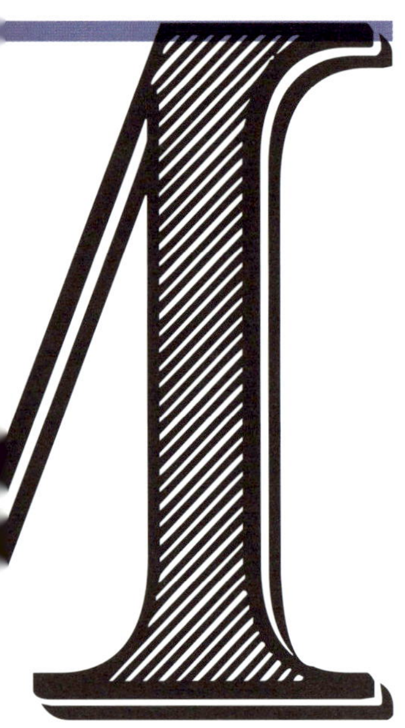

MANIFESTO

"That art is becoming a very dialetical and conceptual activity today is indicative of a new state of affairs which supposedly 'modern' Asian artists are yet to become aware of! Aesthetic and formalistic influences then become quite irrelevant and obsolete in the new scheme of things."

These confidently resounding words are typical of the strident and accusatory tone of many modern art manifestos, in Southeast Asia as elsewhere. They were written to accompany an exhibition—titled *Towards A Mystical Reality*—that was held in 1974 in Kuala Lumpur. The artists Sulaiman Esa and Redza Piyadasa caused quite a scandal for

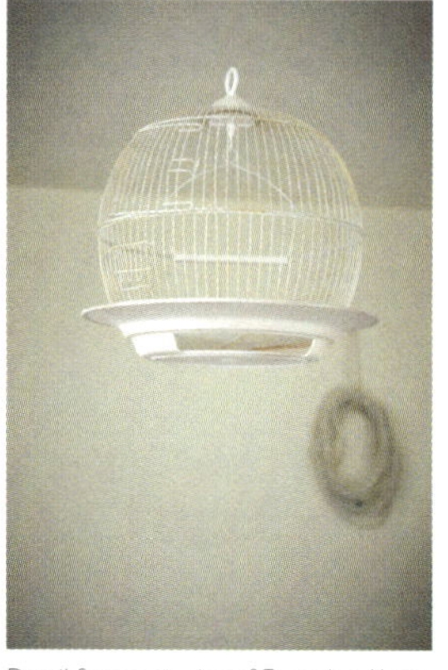

Detail from restaging of *Towards a Mystical Reality* 1974.

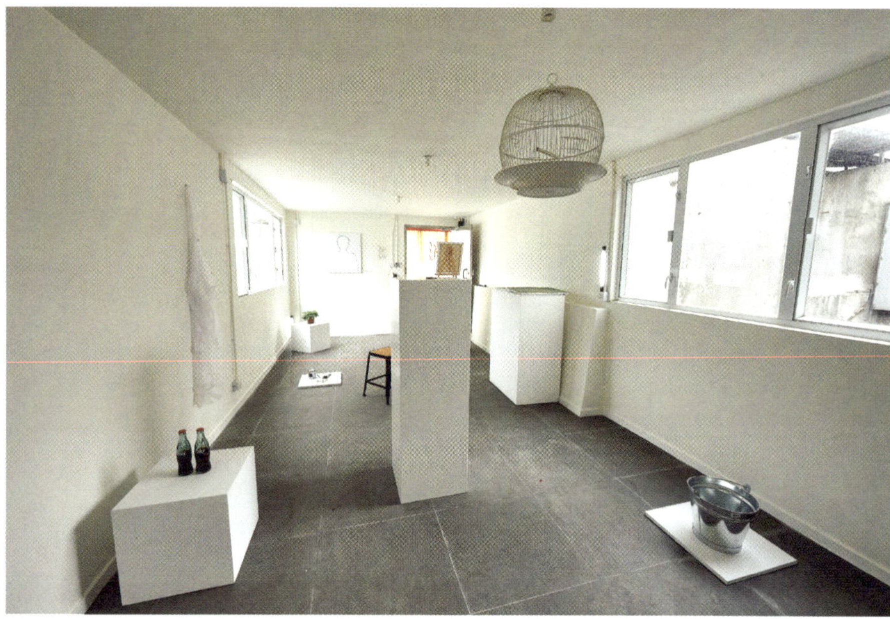

Simon Soon in collaboration with project managers from Para Site, Hong Kong. Restaging of *Towards a Mystical Reality* 1974. 2016. Mixed media, dimensions variable. Permission granted by the families of Redza Piyadasa and Sulaiman Esa.

exhibiting found objects, such as opened cola bottles and a store-bought birdcage, as conceptual artworks. But the impact of this exhibition, at the time and since, is equally due to the manifesto, which has also been used as a key tool for interpreting the exhibition and its artworks.

The word "manifesto" comes from the Italian *manifestare*, "to manifest." Its continuing use in art discourse is likely related to the prominence of an early European manifesto; written by Italian artist and poet Filippo Tommaso Marinetti and published on the front page of a Parisian newspaper in 1909, it marked the launch of a modern art movement called Futurism.

In Southeast Asia, the authors of many manifestos were not likely to have known much about Italian Futurist artists.

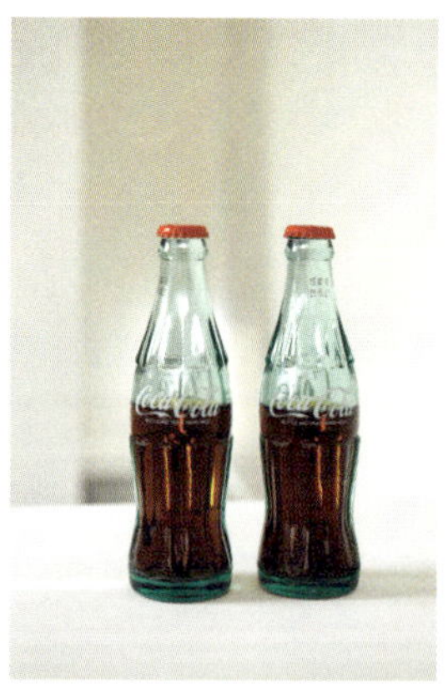

Detail from restaging of *Towards a Mystical Reality* 1974.

They made statements that were often, instead, interventions in <u>debates</u> and contexts quite specifically rooted in the local, <u>national</u>, and regional. These texts were also self-consciously declarative, intended as bombastic statements of an artistic mission, and usually had an impact as such among audiences at the time.

The 1970s saw a burgeoning of art manifestos in Southeast Asia. Many of these sought to articulate a turning point in modern art — often, as in the case of the excerpt quoted above, away from aesthetic and formalistic concerns, and instead toward a more conceptual, transmedia, and/or political approach. Other widely cited examples from this period include the Gerakan Seni Rupa Baru, launched in 1975 in Indonesia. Also producing exhibitions as well as a manifesto, this group of artists protested a "vision of 'art'… that is limited to only painting, sculpture, and drawing (prints)." Their manifesto called for various forms of art to engage with society and culture, arguing that "actual social problems are more important than private sentiments." Even more stridently political than this, the communist United Artists' Front of Thailand also issued a manifesto in 1975, taking a broad view of art's responsibility as including opposition to "all the misleading structures of the government," and announcing their "mission… to conserve, innovate, and develop Thai culture art and make it serve all Thai people."

Gerakan Seni Rupa Baru
(GSRB, Indonesian New Arts Movement)
Formed 1974, Indonesia;
disbanded after 1987

United Artists' Front of Thailand
Active 1974–1976; based Thailand

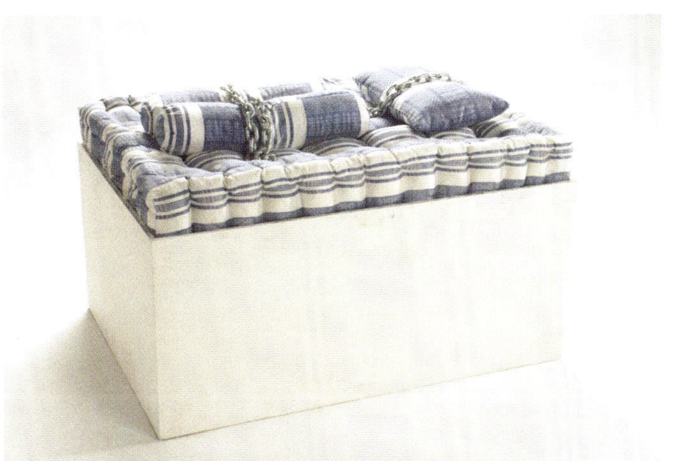

FX Harsono. *Rantai yang Santai* (The Relaxed Chain). 1975, remade in 2006. Steel chain and mattress, dimensions variable. Collection of National Gallery Singapore.

Of course, striking statements by and about Southeast Asian artists had been written and published before the 1970s. Best known is a 1939 diatribe against *Mooi Indie* ("Beautiful Indies") landscape paintings by S. Sudjojono, who saw these romanticised images of Indonesian <u>landscapes</u> as

Sindudarsono Sudjojono
b. 1917, Indonesia; d. 1986, Indonesia

pandering to European tastes. Sudjojono is <u>canonical</u> for his role in leading fellow Indonesian modern artists to reject the *Mooi Indie* genre, in favour of other kinds of realism and later abstraction. There are many other texts which have not yet been generally considered as manifestos. One example is Ho Chi Minh's 1951 letter addressed to an exhibition by painters, declaring "Culture and art is also a front. You are soldiers on that front."

Many other texts have been written by artists and collectives in the region, but only those issued as public declarations—made manifest—are generally considered manifestos. The use of equivalent terms in Southeast Asian <u>vernacular</u> languages—and the implications of these uses, in repositioning meanings and understandings of such writings—has yet to be fully researched.

MEDIUM

The general format of an artwork is referred to as its medium: for example, art may be in the medium of painting, sculpture, or printmaking, or other more recent forms like installation and performance, which are often called new media. The specific materials and techniques of an artwork can also be called its medium: for example, a painting may be further specified as being in the medium of oil on canvas, or acrylic on board. Any painting, sculpture or any other artwork made by combining several different materials can be described as mixed media.

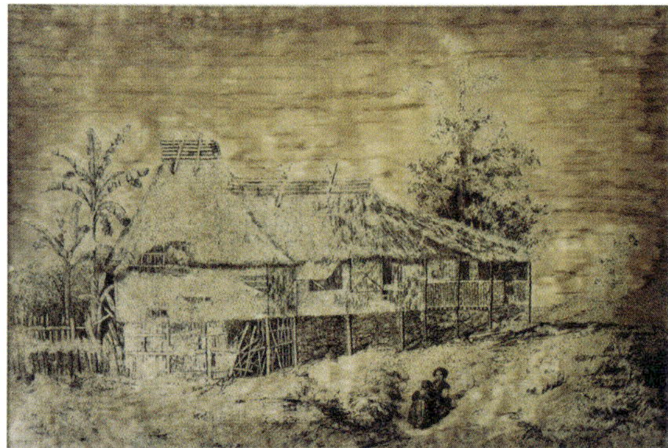

Adelaida Paterno. *Nipa House with Mother and Child.* c. 1880s. Human hair on Chinese silk, 28 x 43 cm. Collection of Bangko Sentral ng Pilipinas.

Describing the medium of an artwork is a way of categorising art. These categories are often perceived along an implicit hierarchy of <u>value</u>, in which some media—especially painting, sculpture, printmaking, and other visual arts—are regarded as superior to others, especially those associated

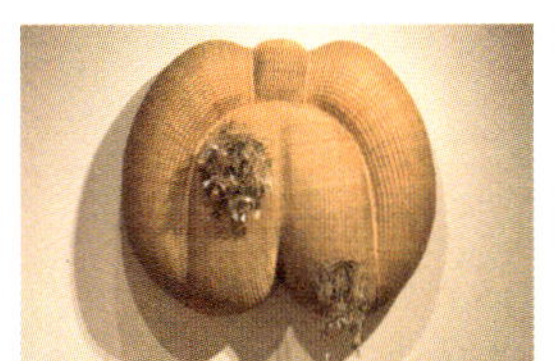

Nindityo Adipurnomo. *Hiding Rituals and the Mass Production II.* 1997–1998. Rattan, human hair, plastic bag, paper, string, 250 x 300 x 90 cm. Collection of Singapore Art Museum.

with <u>craft</u>. This ranking is a distinctly modern invention in Southeast Asia, which emerged alongside modern ideas of an <u>artist</u> as a creative individual. The hierarchy was structurally reinforced with the establishment of secular art <u>education</u>, which tended to prize painting and sculpture the most. The widespread (though certainly not universal) shift away from engaging with <u>spirituality</u> in modern art also helped to privilege artworks which were portable and often made for <u>exhibition</u> rather than to be displayed in a religious setting. The privileging of some media above others has also elevated men above <u>women</u>; this is because craft is typically seen as feminine, even though men may also engage in craft practices. Artists who worked in unconventional media—such as Adelaida Paterno, who made embroidery with human hair— often occupy secondary positions in the emerging <u>canon</u> of modern art. They may also be thought of as <u>naïve</u>.

Many <u>contemporary</u> artists have challenged the hierarchy that places some media ahead of others. This is one key reason for the increasing appearance of new media and mixed media in contemporary art, often including materials and techniques that are commonly understood to be specific to Southeast Asia. An example is Nindityo Adipurnomo, who often works with woven rattan among other media, and who is influential as co-founder of a prominent contemporary art space in Yogyakarta. Contemporary practices have emerged alongside and after <u>conceptual</u> artistic approaches, in which the idea behind an artwork is more important than its material or aesthetic form.

Intersections among different visual art media, and also between visual art and other cultural and artistic phenomena, have often been downplayed in discussions of modern art, including in Southeast Asia. Categorising art according to medium has also cleaved different artistic formats from one another. For instance, painting is often discussed (and, in books and especially in museums, often viewed) only or chiefly in relation to other painting, as well as other visual art forms. It is less common for painting and visual art to be seen or discussed in relation to music, dance, architecture, <u>fashion</u>, cuisine, ritual, <u>cinema</u>, or any of the myriad other cultural forms which can be discussed in aesthetic terms.

This separating of different media—which overlooks transmedia intersections within and between different art forms—misses out on the many rich examples of transmediality in modern art. In much of Southeast Asia, new forms of distinctly modern art emerged in a wide variety of media within just a few decades of each other, and there was a fertile exchange between these different media. In Cambodia, for example, the first modern Khmer novels appeared in 1938, painting and drawing from life (called "modern painting" in Khmer) were first taught at the national art school after 1945, the first formally trained Cambodian modern architects began practicing in the 1950s, and the first Cambodian film was produced around 1958. All these new forms flourished during the 1960s alongside other modern media, such as popular rock music. Painters like Nhek Dim painted record covers for musicians including Sinn Sisamouth, and

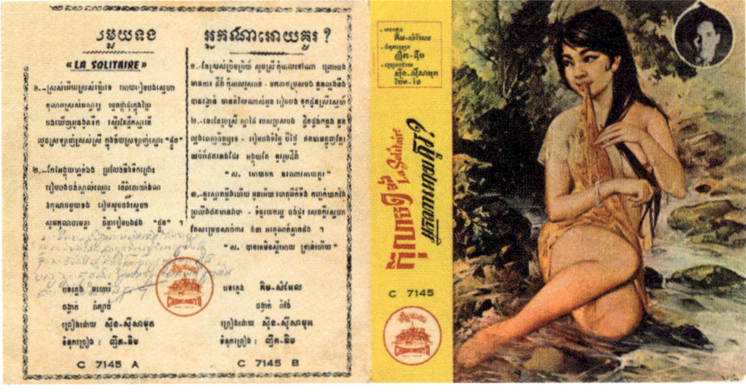

Album cover of *Kulab Muay Dang* (A Rose) and *Neak Na Oy Gur?* (Who Asked You to Paint?), sung by Sinn Sisamouth and released by Chanchhaya Records in 1974. The painting reproduced is Nhek Dim. *A Rose* (also known as *La Solitaire*). Early 1970s.

the two collaboratively wrote songs. Many art schools in Southeast Asia continue to teach modern arts in a wide variety of media, meaning that architects study alongside dancers, sculptors, and so on.

Focusing less on one specific medium, and instead examining transmedia exchanges, may reveal that meaning in art is produced through a complex and dynamic network of interaction. As the novelist Pramoedya Ananta Toer poetically suggests, "Painting is literature in colors. Literature is painting in language."

MODERN

"Modern" is a notoriously difficult term to define, and the concept means vastly different things to different people, its connotations changing in varying contexts and over time, altering between languages, and shifting in relation to art, culture, and other discourses.

Yet despite these challenges, it can be said that the modern is above all a kind of imagining. It is a conjuring into existence of something—an idea, an artwork, a way of thinking or doing or making—which did not exist before. That is, to be modern is to be new. Of course, to be modern can also mean many other things, but it is fundamentally to be concerned with newness and transformation as values in themselves.

The modern in art, in the context of Southeast Asia as elsewhere, refers to a critical reassessment of the art of the past. Modern art takes on countless different forms, yet in all of these, it is modern because it departs from the art of the past in some way. Modern art also engages with <u>modernities</u>, deeply and often inarticulably. That is, it emerges from the tumult of its times. Modern times seem to be more turbulent than ever before, and art reflects these unprecedented changes, while also sometimes anticipating the <u>zeitgeist</u> or spirit of the era. Some kinds of modern art are sometimes referred to as "modernism," usually referring to a self-consciously enthusiastic embrace of modernity, although the term "modernism" has not been as popular in this region as elsewhere, and its use can sometimes be confusing or imprecise. Generally speaking, the modern in art emerged in Southeast Asia during the 19th and 20th centuries, although in some places it may predate the 19th century, and ideas about the modern in art continue to emerge today, alongside the <u>contemporary</u>.

Many ideas about modern art are encompassed by *seik-ta-za-pangyi*, a Burmese term which refers to a painting or artwork deemed to be "psychotic" or "mad." First used to pejoratively describe illustrations published by Bagyi Aung Soe in 1953, the term became synonymous with that artist's works, and—according to art historian Yin Ker—subsequently with modern art in general, in the context of Myanmar.

There is no record of a similar term being used anywhere else in Southeast Asia, in any of the region's other vernacular languages, and yet despite this singularity, *seik-ta-za-pangyi*—"psychotic" or "mad" art—encapsulates many widely held attitudes to the modern in art. The use of the term conveys a sense of shock and incomprehension that many people have felt at the encounter with modern art. This may be driven by disdain or dislike, but it is also motivated by an irresistible fascination. Most importantly, the use of the neologistic term, *seik-ta-za-pangyi*, intimates that the art being described is not only crazy or deranged, but also emphatically new: so new that no existing vocabulary is sufficient to describe it.

In each of the major Southeast Asian <u>vernacular</u> languages, some of the many terms used for "modern" are predicated on a similar sense of newness and progress. A fundamental fascination with the new is reflected in many aspects of modern art, including its visualisation of <u>time</u> speeding up, its enmeshment with <u>globalisation</u>, and its ability to capture the zeitgeist. A commonly shared energetic embrace of novelty is evoked in the <u>poetry</u> of the Anak Alam <u>manifesto</u>, written in Malay in 1974. Its artist-writers affirm: "our generation is a vessel / of enthusiasm and readiness."

However, the modern is not solely or wholly new. Modern art, especially in Southeast Asia, has often redeployed pre-modern <u>traditions</u>, adapting old ways of doing things for new purposes. The old has existed alongside the new, together comprising the modern in this region. This may set Southeast Asian attitudes to being modern apart from those in the West. In his account of modernity in Western contexts, scholar Marshall Berman describes a commonly shared "drive that seems to be endemic to modernization: the drive to create a homogenous environment, a totally modernized space, in which the look and feel of the old world have disappeared without a trace." If this drive has been felt in Southeast Asia, it has certainly never held much sway. The "old world" remains ever-present alongside the modern in the art, culture, cities and landscapes of this region. For example, <u>urbanisation</u> has not eclipsed a love of the <u>landscape</u> as a symbol in art; <u>spirituality</u> has remained a persistent interest alongside the <u>quotidian</u>; and so on.

The modern is complex, contradictory, and ever-changing—because it is an idea that we make. Art makes that process of imagining visible and manifest.

MODERNITIES

Modernity refers to the state of being <u>modern</u>, and also refers to the historical period that has emerged gradually in Southeast Asia, mostly since the 19th century. While the meanings of the modern are vast and various, to be modern is fundamentally to be concerned with newness and transformation. There are many, varied ways of being modern: it can be seen in a rural outpost transforming into a city, or an attitude that rejects or departs from the past. The modern has taken on different characteristics in different locations, which have also changed with the times. Therefore, many scholars now speak of multiple *modernities*, rather than a singular modernity, in order to convey the plurality and diversity of ways to be modern, and to signal that ideas about the modern transform as they go through processes of <u>transfer</u> from one place to another.

In Southeast Asia as elsewhere, modernity is inseparable from coloniality. Its emergence and development has depended on colonialism, including colonial ways of thinking, seeing, and visualising in art. The expansion of European empires into this region, and the establishment of colonies here, enabled and fuelled modernisation in Southeast Asia, as well as in Europe and beyond. It is vital not to overlook the role of colonialism in the emergence of modernities in this region, yet it is also important not to over-simplify this dynamic, or to discount the agency and inventiveness of Southeast Asian people—including artists—within the colonial encounter.

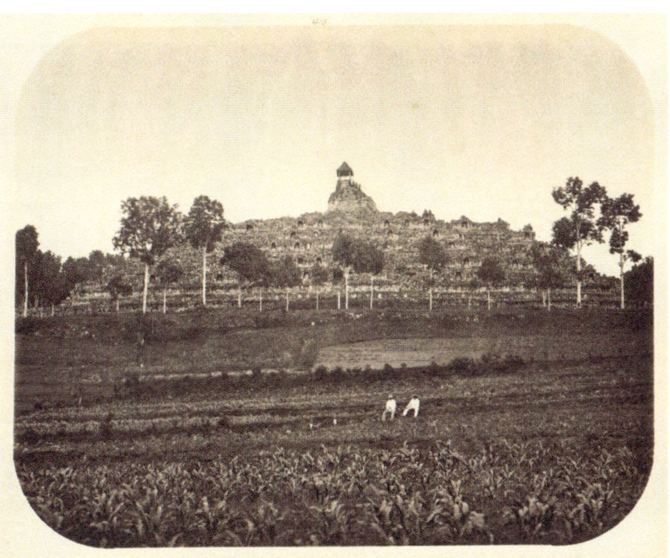

Woodbury & Page. *A View of the Borobudur Temple Complex.* Mid-to-late 19th century. Albumen print, 20 x 25 cm. Collection of National Museum of Singapore.

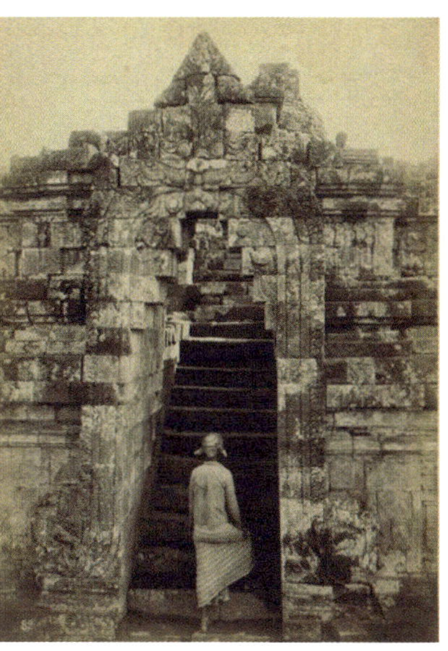

Kassian Cephas. *Javanese at the Foot of the Stairs in the Temple Complex of Borobudur near Magelang.* 1872. Albumen print, 25 x 19 cm. Collection of Museum Volkenkunde, Leiden.

For example, a photograph by Woodbury & Page showing formally posed European men in foreign <u>fashions</u> seated in front of Borobudur, as if it belongs to them, reminds us that new technologies for image-making emerged in tandem with the colonial project. Yet a contemporaneous photograph by Kassian Cephas showing a respectfully dressed Javanese man ascending the entrance to Borobudur complicates and adds nuance to this, by reminding us that Southeast Asians have always found ways to transcend colonial attitudes which regarded them as <u>exotic</u>, and instead to imagine new perspectives.

To be modern, after all, is to imagine that which has not existed before.

Some key common features of modernities include the emergence of <u>nations</u>, as well as processes of <u>urbanisation</u> and <u>globalisation</u>. Moreover, modernities have transformed social roles, especially for <u>women</u>, as well as creating a sense of <u>time</u> speeding up and secularising many aspects of life, including art <u>patronage</u> and <u>education</u>. These changes were

Woodbury and Page studios
Established by Walter Bentley Woodbury and James Page in 1857, Jakarta; active until 1908

Kassian Cephas
b. 1845, Indonesia; d. 1912, Indonesia

like revolutions, transforming society as a whole, and also the intimate experience of <u>quotidian</u> daily life. This is dramatised by a 1961 Cantonese film directed by Chiang Wai-Kwong, produced in Hong Kong but supported by Singapore-based <u>cinema</u> companies, in which the lingering novelty of household telephones is a small but telling sign of many of these thrilling upheavals that changed the way people lived and related to each other.

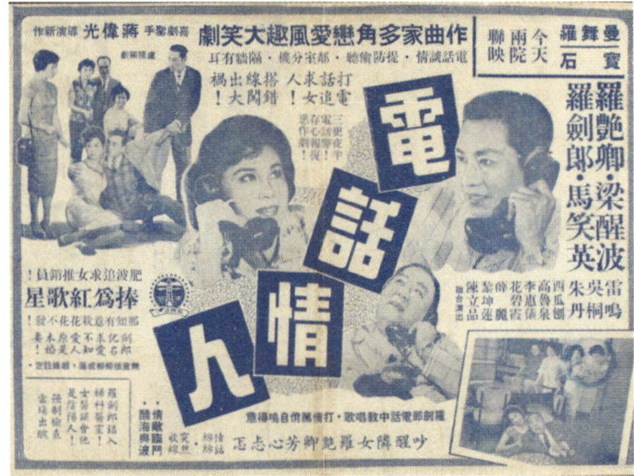

Handbill for *The Telephone Affair*, directed by Chiang Wai-Kwong, released 1961. Collection of National Museum of Singapore.

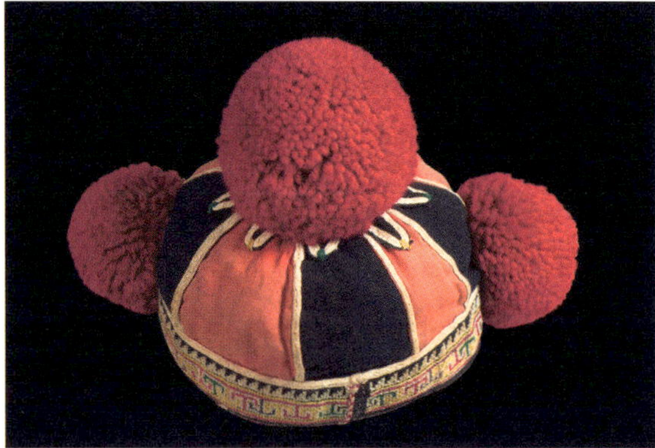

Maker unknown (Yao people, northern Thailand). Hat with pompoms and embroidery. c. 1960s. Indigo-dyed cotton, commercial fabric and threads, wool. Collection of the Asian Civilisations Museum, Singapore.

While these transformations are defining attributes of modernities, it is important to remember that older ways of living, thinking, and making art have continued alongside new, modern ideas. <u>Tradition</u> and <u>spirituality</u> retain a vital and dynamic energy in modern life and art. <u>Kings</u>, sultans and other royalty continue to play important roles alongside new forms of modern government, and new <u>patrons</u> for art. The photographs cited above are examples of the compelling allure of premodern objects as inspirations for modern art and culture. Decades later, repeated depictions in modern styles of premodern temples, by numerous artists including Chen Cheng Mei, Latiff Mohidin, Tran Binh Loc, and Chua Ek Kay, demonstrate the persistence of this fascination with the premodern among modern artists of Southeast Asia. Modernities transformed the world, but in the modern era, people continued to look to and learn from the premodern past.

Sometimes, the impact of modernity can be discerned in artworks and objects which at first may appear quite traditional. An example is a hat made in the Yao (or Mien) community, an ethnic group closely related to the Hmong, who live mostly in highland areas of northern Laos, Thailand, and Vietnam, as well as in southern China. The prominence and volume of the pompoms in the hat's design, and the vibrant colour of these pompoms, reflects the historically recent availability of commercially manufactured fibres even in remote, mountainous areas far from urban centres. In this way, the hat—which also features cotton dyed with indigo in the traditional manner—is clearly a product of modernity, by which commerce and new technologies spread into even the most distant and inhospitable terrains, transforming even the appearance of pompoms.

Pompoms might be uncontroversial, but many other aspects of modern life and modern art have prompted fierce <u>debates</u>. These debates have essentially been about what form modernity should take, and what the balance should be between the modern and the traditional.

One of the most important effects of debate within modern culture is that it facilitates an awareness of multiplicity—that is, of there being many versions of the modern, and many modernities rather than a single modernity. Disagreements at smaller scales, and even peaceful discussions between individuals and groups, have also had lasting and widespread effects, and made visible that modernity is plural and contested, and constituted from the ground up, not imported from on high, or from far away.

This has been further heightened in densely populated urban settings, where <u>connections</u> are formed between people who might never have met in a time before modernity. A sense of this is conveye d in a print by Josias Cornelis Rappard, a Dutch soldier and artist who spent time in Indonesia. He depicts an animated dialogue between men and women from diverse social classes and ethnic groups, taking place on board a sleek, modern tram. A more heated kind of exchange is evoked in *Riot*, by Lim Hak Tai, a <u>diasporic</u> artist with a crucial role in establishing art <u>education</u> in Singapore.

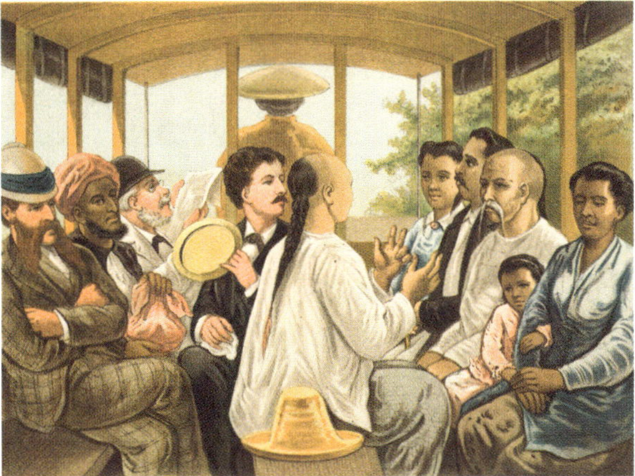

Josias Cornelis Rappard. *Interior View of a Tram Carriage.* c. 1881-1888. Chromolithograph, 17.2 x 23.3 cm. Collection of National Museum of Singapore.

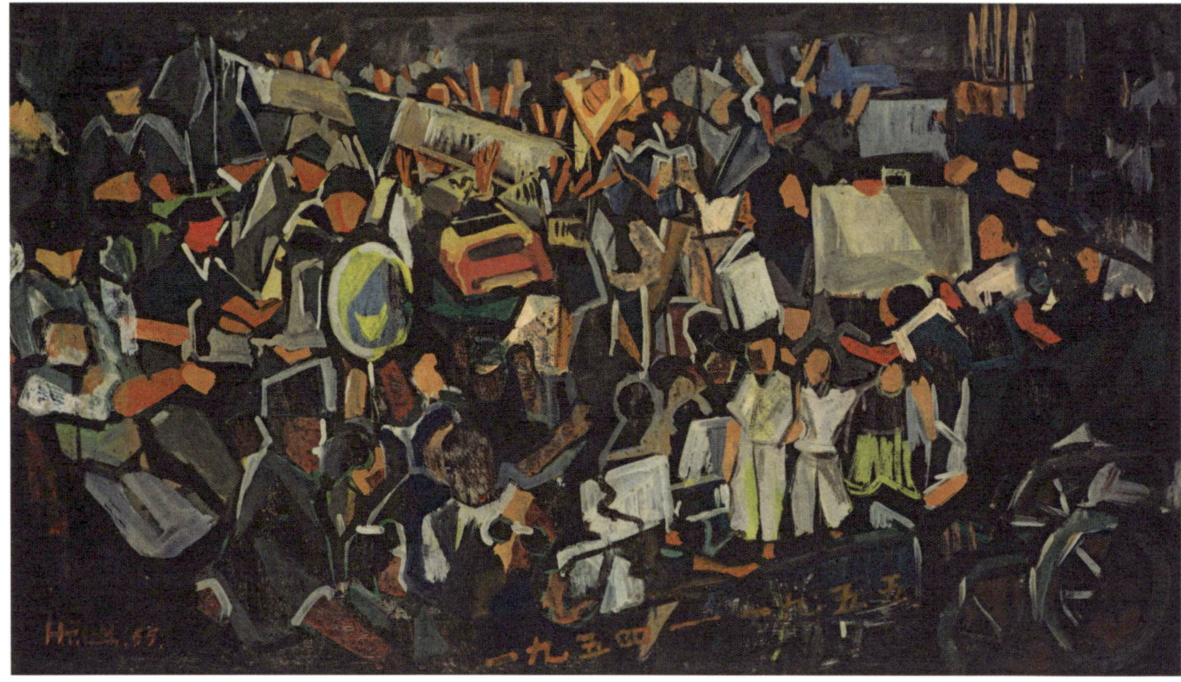

Lim Hak Tai. *Riot*. 1955. Oil on board, 49.5 x 89 cm. Collection of National Gallery Singapore.

These expressions of self-conscious diversity, difference and even disagreement within Southeast Asian modernities are important, in part, because they make clear that people have always been aware that there are multiple ways to be modern. By contrast, in scholarly theorising of art and culture, the concept of "multiple modernities" has emerged relatively recently, mostly discussed since the turn of the 21st century. This has led some commentators, like philosopher Peter Osborne, to argue that the idea of there having been many kinds of modernities has become legible only in hindsight, or only when viewed from the perspective of the contemporary.

This view does not hold for Southeast Asia; it overlooks the keenly felt and sharply articulated multiplicity that characterised the emergence and development of the modern here, in art as in other aspects of life. Modernities in Southeast Asia were always multiple and contested, and this is revealed vibrantly and poetically in modern art.

Despite this, theorising of modernities at the regional scale have thus far been limited in reach. In Southeast Asia, modernities emerged concurrently with, and inseparably from, an idea of the nation. It is therefore unsurprising that most discussions of modernity in relation to art have concentrated on single nations. As art historian T.K. Sabapathy observes, "there is a pronounced tendency for art writers/scholars in Southeast Asia to focus on the constituent parts of Southeast Asia rather than to develop a perception of the region as a whole and as a suitable object of study." The effects of this tendency are not only that most modern art has been discussed in relation to individual nations rather than the region of <u>Southeast Asia</u> as a whole, but also that most writing has been concerned with what Sabapathy terms "domestic turfs and micro concerns."

Have writers from, in or concerned with Southeast Asia written expansive texts philosophising on the meaning of the modern and modernities in this context? If they have, their writings are not widely known or easily accessible. As modernities continue to unfold in their many and varied forms, surely more will be said about the experience of the modern in Southeast Asia, and its manifestations in art.

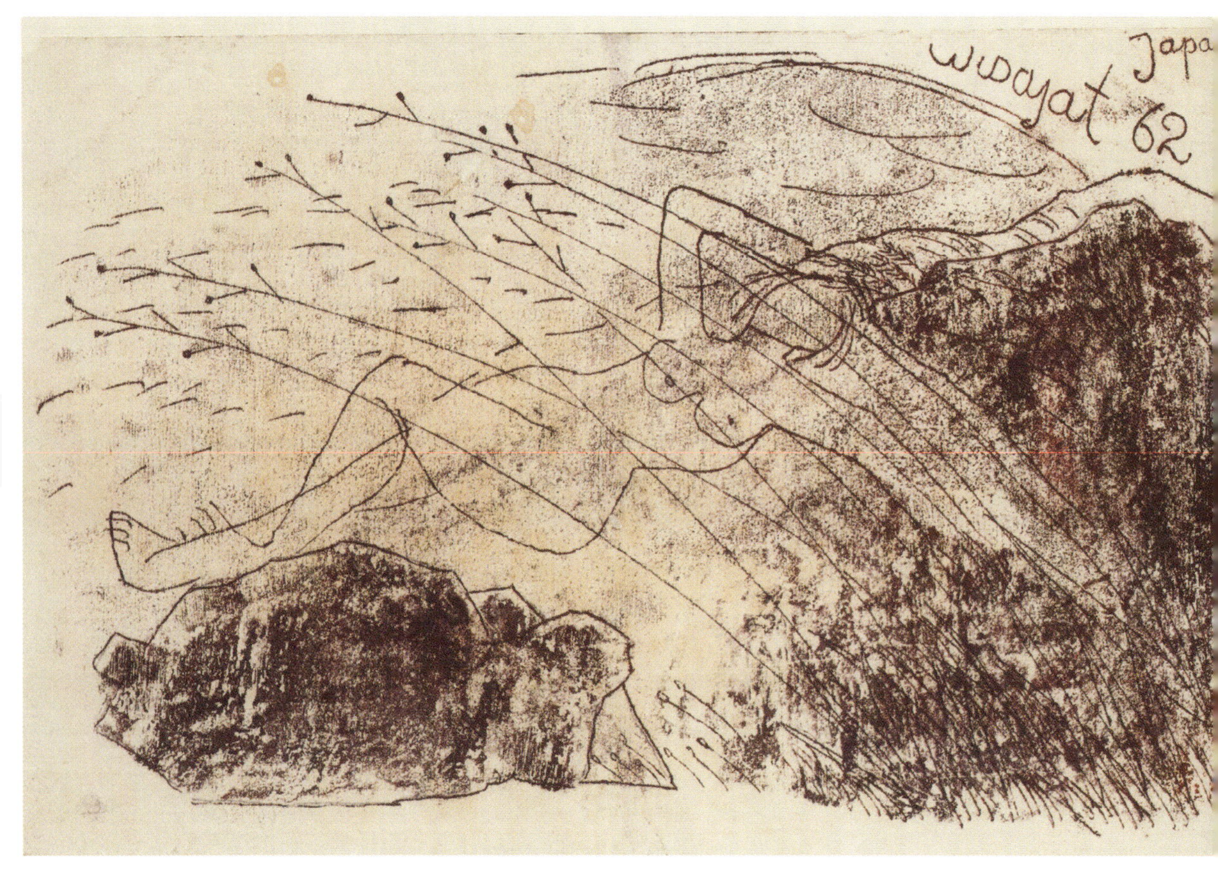
wioayat
Japa
62

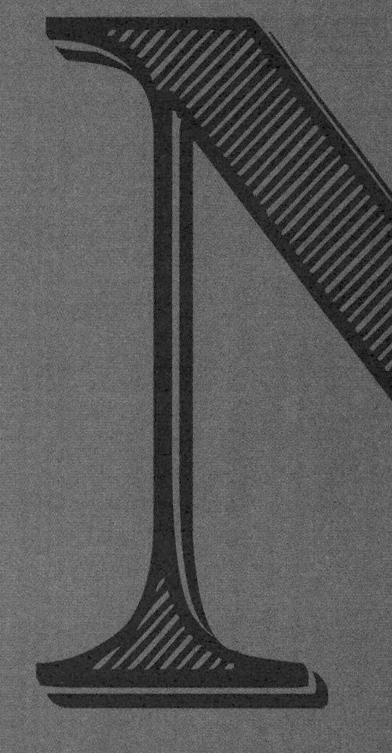

Widayat. *Nude (Wanita Telanjang)*. 1962. Etching on paper, 22 x 42 cm. Collection of National Gallery Singapore.

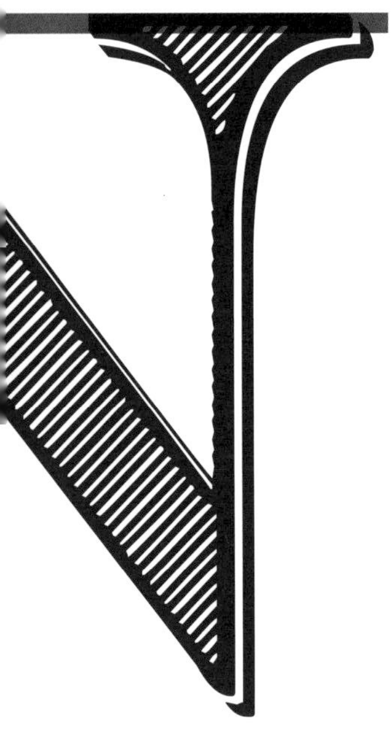

NAÏVE

Naïve art, sometimes also called outsider art, refers to work made by people without formal art training. Sometimes, the style or technique of artworks made by professionally educated artists can also be described as naïve. Nowadays, outsider art is widely celebrated, and naïve qualities in artworks are often admired. In the past, however, for an artist to be untrained or to be perceived as lacking in technical skill was generally looked down upon. This pejorative attitude to naïvety in art derived from both colonial misapprehensions of Southeast Asian <u>traditions</u> and practices, and from the emergence of the modern idea of an <u>artist</u> as an eccentric but nevertheless "professional," educated individual who possesses advanced technical skills in <u>realism</u> and other styles. This idea was embraced by both colonial authorities and Southeast Asian artists, shaped in part by the establishment of formal art <u>education</u>, in secular institutions across the region, during the 19th and early 20th centuries.

Naïve artists have, at times, missed out on a formal education not by choice but circumstance. <u>Women</u> were forbidden from enrolling in the earliest art schools, meaning that many 19th- and 20th-century artists who were women, like Misiem Yipintsoi, Paz Paterno and Adelaida Paterno, were self-taught. Perhaps as a result of this, some of them—most notably Adelaida Paterno—experimented with unusual <u>media</u>, a common feature in the practice of many naïve artists. As well as this, however, both Paz and Adelaida Paterno also mastered the conventions of academic realism that were fashionable at the time, completing both rural scenes and still life paintings that reflect their experience of <u>tropical</u> life.

Many women nowadays continue to practice art without formal training, as observed by Astri Wright, one of the few scholars to concentrate on self-taught artists in Southeast Asia. Writing of artists Kartika Affandi, Lucia Hartini and Murni, Wright declares that they "are all self-taught by circumstantial default rather than as a result of clear, conscious choices of their own," and furthermore, they "are self-taught in a society which increasingly seeks to reward artists with degrees from art academies." While this limits their access to some opportunities, Wright affirms that it also makes these artists' works arrestingly distinctive. "When I initially saw them, Kartika's, Lucia's and Murni's paintings reached out and grabbed me by the eyeballs," she enthuses. Similar celebrations of the idiosyncratic aesthetic of naïve art are found in the <u>reception</u> of self-taught artist Nim Kruasaeng. While Murni is acclaimed for her disregard of

<u>taboos</u>, Nim is championed for invoking, through her use of <u>abstraction,</u> a dream-like reverie, somewhere between meditation and mastery, or, a "dispersion of consciousness," in the words of curator Pier Luigi Tazzi.

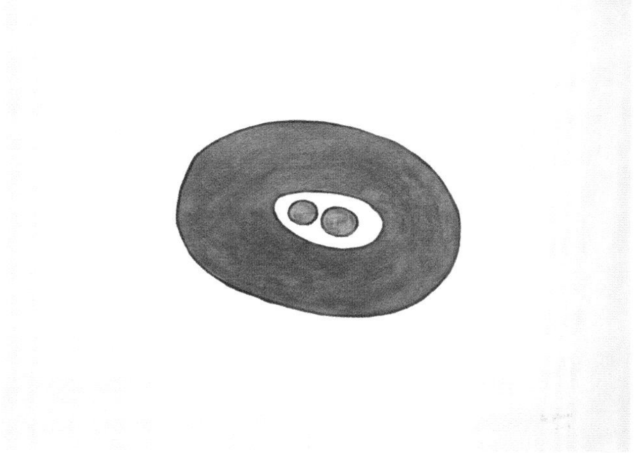

Nim Kruasaeng. *Untitled*. 2006. Acrylic on acid free paper, 56 x 76 cm. Collection of the artist.

Naïve art often does not adhere to the specialised techniques and conventions of realism, yet nevertheless often makes visible deeper truths which might otherwise go unseen. It is for this reason that many artists with extensive formal education, such as Widayat (who also taught art for over 30 years) and Nguyen Tu Nghiem (who was inspired by village <u>traditions</u>), have aspired to the immediacy and originality found in works by self-taught artists. Artworks by untrained people, including those disconnected from the norms of daily life, may often "reveal that which would otherwise remain hidden from view thanks to the special insight of their creators," according to art historian Colin Rhodes, a specialist on outsider art in the West.

This is seen in the paintings of Svay Ken, who began painting in his 60s, after a lifetime of working in menial jobs. When critics described his style as naïve, the artist's defenders retorted that the irregularities in scale in Svay Ken's paintings were not meaningless mistakes reflecting a lack of skill, but rather were deliberately used by the artist to communicate the relative importance of different figures in a composition. For example, the man on the stage in his *Monthly Mandatory Meeting* is the largest in the painting. This reflects his status as a Khmer Rouge military commander, whose authority was absolute during the period of <u>war</u> and <u>genocide</u> in Cambodia. The artist's decision to make this ominous figure the largest in the image disregards the conventional

Widayat
(also known as Haji Widayat)
b. 1919, Indonesia; d. 2002, Indonesia

Nguyen Tu Nghiem
b. 1918, Vietnam; d. 2016, Vietnam

Svay Ken
b. 1933, Cambodia; d. 2008, Cambodia

rules of perspective, by which the figure should be smaller, since he is positioned in the distance. A similar compositional strategy is seen in many of Svay Ken's works, depicting both <u>quotidian</u> subjects and momentously tragic episodes in <u>history</u>. The artist may have been self-taught, but his artworks are sophisticated and carefully considered, not naïve.

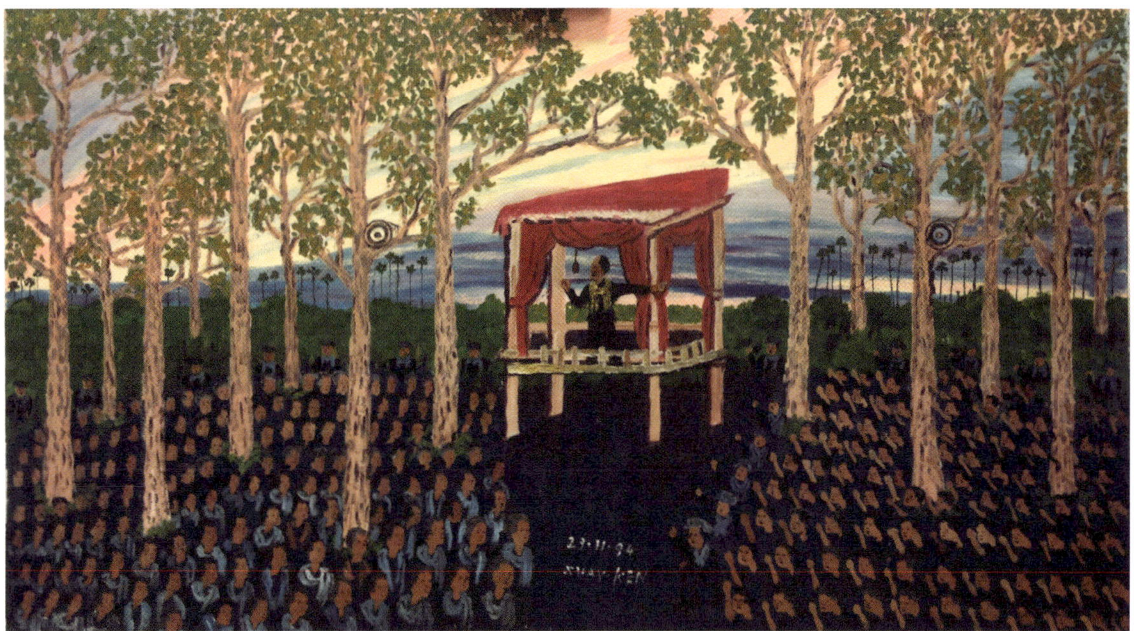

Svay Ken. *Monthly Mandatory Meeting*. 1994. Oil on canvas, 70 x 130 cm. Collection of National Gallery Singapore.

NATION

In 1983, the scholar Benedict Anderson put forth his now-famous definition of a nation as an "imagined community." The specialist on Southeast Asia explained: "[A nation] is imagined because the members of even the smallest nation will never know most of their fellow-members, meet them or even hear of them, yet in the minds of each lives the image of their communion." Although Anderson's ideas have been challenged, it is widely accepted that modern national identities are constructed, and culture plays a central part in this construction. This is seen especially vividly in much of the modern art of <u>Southeast Asia</u>, which has often been discussed in reference to national identities in the region.

In painting, <u>landscapes</u> are especially fecund symbols for nations, depicted as standing for a nation's fertility and abundance, and usually as feminine. Scholar Ashley Thompson traces the origins of this in premodern literary traditions of the region, describing "an old trope of power and sexual difference by which the king conquers and possesses the land as his wife." As this suggests, the earth is often characterised as feminine. This deeply held, often <u>spiritual</u> sentiment is evoked in Emiria Sunassa's *Sri, the Goddess of Rice*: the goddess rises from the earth, and is linked—through the colour of her skirt—to the heavenly skies which bring rain and fertility for the rice harvest. While popular media images may associate states with male politicians, <u>kings</u>, and other masculine figures, <u>women</u> have always been essential to the literal and symbolic construction of modern nations.

Another stylistically more typical example of landscape symbolising nation is seen in the work of Nhek Dim, who was the most popular artist in 1960s Cambodia, championed by the prince, politician and filmmaker, Norodom Sihanouk, and also supported by the United States as part of their Cold War-era cultural <u>propaganda</u> efforts. Nhek Dim's numerous paintings of rice farmers in idyllic countryside scenes allegorically position the rural landscape as a symbol for the postcolonial nation, filled with fertility and promise. He often depicted farmers wearing chequered scarves known as *krama*, which identify the figures as belonging to the Khmer majority, rather than Vietnamese or other minorities. Nhek Dim's *The Harvest*, shown in an <u>exhibition</u> organised by the US, was described in a 1962 review as "depict[ing] strikingly the sunburned face of the man of the soil, diligently doing the work that the nation depends on." This commentary makes explicit the powerful tie between depictions of landscape and the modern nation.

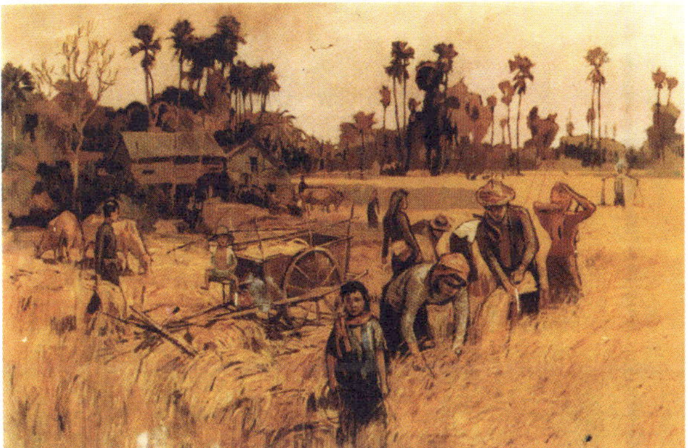

Nhek Dim. *The Harvest*. 1961. Oil on canvas, dimensions unknown.

<u>Portraits</u> have also been important for defining a country's image of itself. This has included not only depictions of recognisable political figures—especially those who contributed to struggles for <u>independence</u>—but also portrayals of ordinary people as national "types," making them iconic

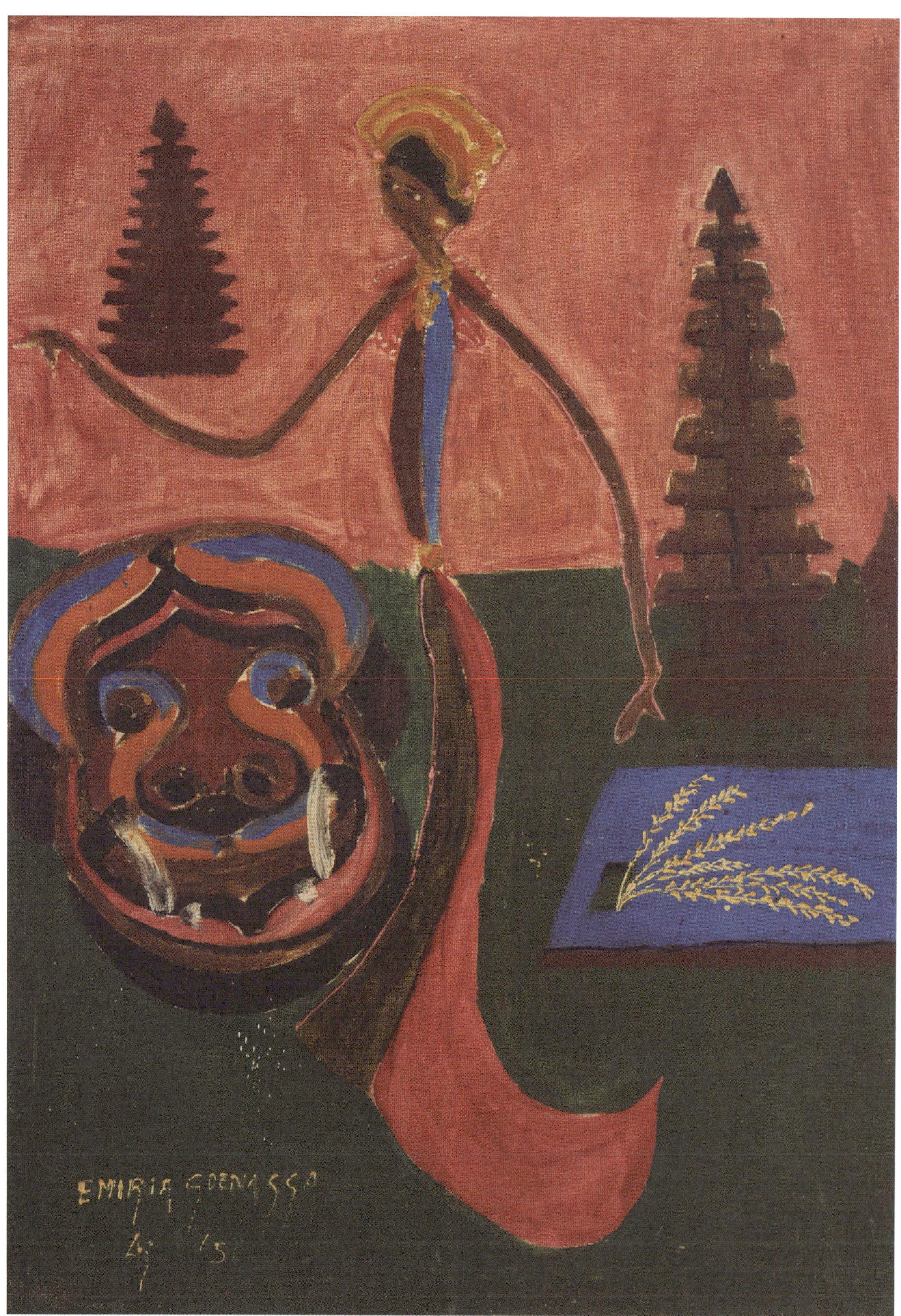

Emiria Sunassa. *Sri, the Goddess of Rice*. 1958. Oil on canvas, 65 x 46.8 cm. Collection of National Gallery Singapore.

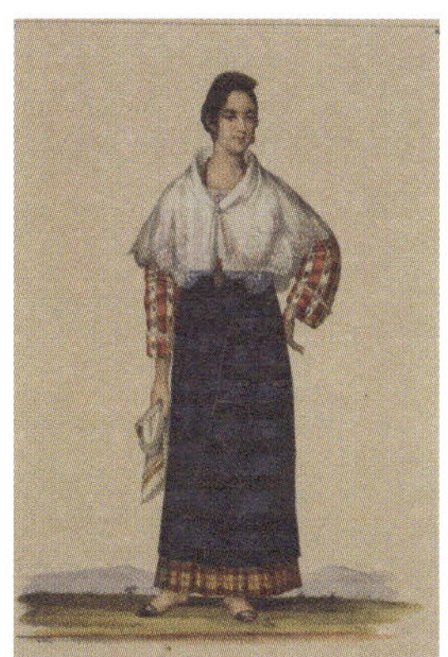

Justiniano Asuncion. *Una India de Manila*. Mid-19th century (after 1842). Lithograph with hand colouring on paper, 30 x 22 cm. Collection of National Gallery Singapore.

representatives of a country's diversity, and co-opting minority groups into the national majority in the process. Early examples of this are *tipos del pais* ("types of the country") by 19th-century artists in the Philippines, including Justiniano Asuncion, Damian Domingo, and Jose Honorato Lozano. Their portrayals of the different regional and social classes of the Philippines, each distinguished by detailed depictions of their <u>fashions</u>, were popular souvenirs. Similar depictions of "types" are found in many parts of Southeast Asia. In Myanmar, artists including M.T. Hla and Yatanabon Maung Su portrayed minorities who were seen as <u>exotic</u> by both British colonial authorities and the Burmese majority, also sometimes capturing their <u>hybrid</u> attire. These and other similar depictions of difference and diversity, even though often aimed at foreign markets, functioned to enfold minorities within nationalist narratives.

One approach taken to the diversity of several Southeast Asian nations was the introduction of "national languages" as a concerted attempt to unite linguistically, ethnically, culturally and spiritually disparate populations. The enthusiastic embrace of these language policies is captured in two works by Chua Mia Tee, a celebrated <u>social realist</u> artist at the time. He conveys the rapt attention of students and the evocative power of nationalist <u>poetry</u>. We might imagine students and others felt that by learning a national language, they were participating in the construction of the nation. Similar depictions appear elsewhere, as in Nguyen Khang's propaganda painting done in the craft material of lacquer, which depicts Ho Chi Minh with a group of students, one of whom holds a book, seemingly reflecting pride in the literacy campaign of the day.

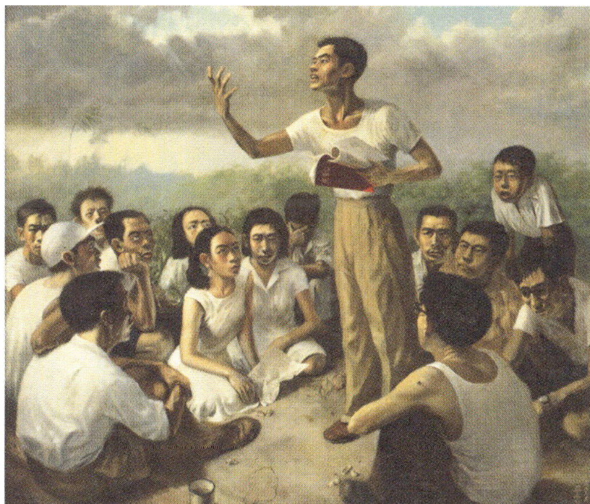

Chua Mia Tee. *Epic Poem of Malaya*. 1955. Oil on canvas, 112 x 153 cm. Collection of National Gallery Singapore.

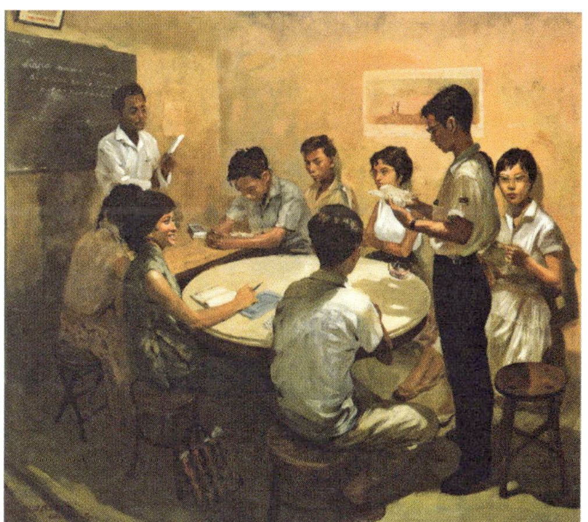

Chua Mia Tee. *National Language Class*. 1959. Oil on canvas, 112 x 153 cm. Collection of National Gallery Singapore.

Besides painting, there have been many other cultural expressions of the idea of the nation in Southeast Asia. These expressions were never linked to a single <u>medium</u>, but rather took place in all cultural forms, including literature, <u>cinema</u>, and performance, as well as in competitive sports and spectacles of various kinds. The emergence of national film industries, for example, was a source of national pride and a means for Southeast Asian stories and images to circulate internationally, forging new <u>connections</u> in the process. Indeed, manifestly modern—that is, historically new—media like cinema, novels, and perhaps especially easel paintings may have been especially suited to the imagining of Southeast Asia's modern—that is, new—nations, since Southeast Asian states are a distinctly modern and new phenomenon, even if they also draw on and repurpose older cultural tropes and traditions.

Just as movies, novels, and easel paintings were distinctly new media, so too was <u>realism</u> a recognisably new style. It allowed artists to literally depict the places and people that made up a nation. Many art historians and other scholars have suggested that realism is intimately linked with nationalism; this idea has been articulated in a Southeast Asian context by Patrick D. Flores, who describes the nation as a "cognate or *doppelgänger*" for realism. Flores argues that the nation is "construed as a narrative of representation and representative-ness." The diversity of "types" captured in modern portraits are, after all, united under the banner of the modern nation which purports to represent them. This is made literally apparent in a painting by Fernando Amorsolo which imagines the "first" Philippine flag being made by three <u>women</u>, who are understood as symbols of the three geographical regions within the archipelagic country.

Yet there are significant limits and exceptions to the dominant discourse of modern nations. One is the challenge posed by diversity to the idea of a nation as an imagined community. This is exemplified in Emiria Sunassa's many depictions of ethnic and cultural minorities in Indonesia, especially from the archipelago's eastern islands. These often-dreamlike scenes challenge the official narratives advanced by <u>kings</u> and other rulers, and suggest the contested nature of the <u>zeitgeist</u>, or spirit of the times. Emiria is celebrated by art historians including Heidi Arbuckle and Wulan Dirgantoro for her unusual choice of subject matter, including portrayals of armed Papuan people, whose fight for independence she politically supported. Perhaps unlike the "types" discussed above, this is a diversity which resists incorporation into a nationalist "image of their communion" (as Anderson describes it). Emiria depicts not genres of people but rather individuals whose difference seems to be irreducible, and cause for celebration rather than mere curiosity. Dirgantoro argues that Emiria's "paintings of tribes from Papua and Kalimantan do not merely represent the exotic other, they also problematize the idea of nation as an imagined community," referring to Anderson's famous phrase. Noting that Emiria often exhibited alongside leading modern artists of her generation, including S. Sudjojono, Dirgantoro emphasises "the contrast between her choice of subject matter and that of her contemporaries." Emiria's works may perhaps be seen as celebrations of the new Indonesian nation, but they are atypical ones: they present the nation as being joyfully jumbled and unruly in its diversity, and significantly, as populated and represented by women. Emiria's style may appear naïve, but her paintings are deceptively complex.

While it is still possible to tie artists like Emiria to nationalist narratives of modern art in Indonesia, this also challenges the coherence of that discourse. This exposes a fundamental contradiction in concepts of the nation in formerly colonised contexts. As noted by scholar Partha Chatterjee, who is one of Anderson's critics, "Nationalism denied the alleged inferiority of the colonized people; it also asserted that a backward nation could 'modernize' itself while retaining its cultural identity." Yet, as he observes, even as nationalism "challenged the colonial claim to political domination," by relying on a conception of the nation as a form of modern progress, the idea of nationalism "also accepted the very intellectual premises of 'modernity' on which colonial domination was based." Southeast Asian nations and modernities are inextricably entwined, as modern art reveals.

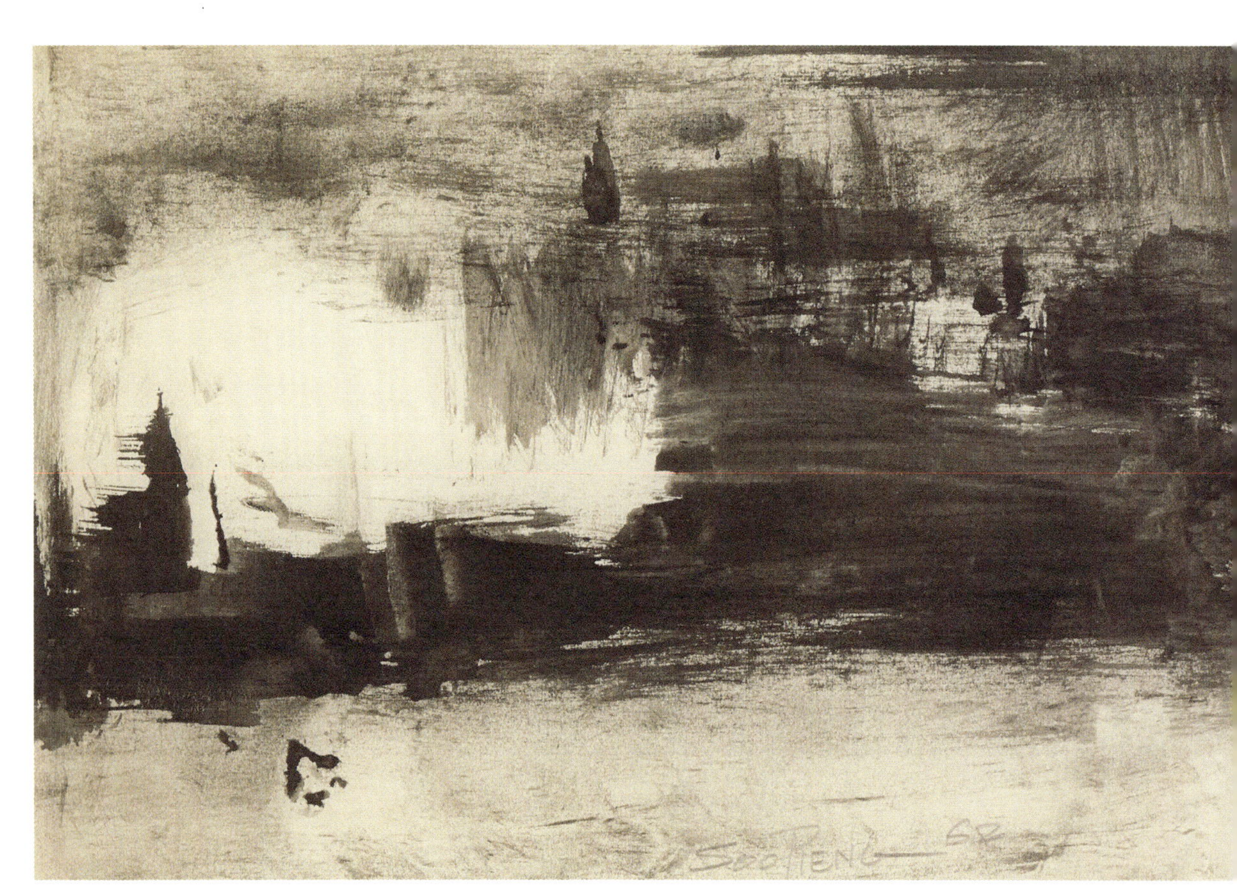

Cheong Soo Pieng, *Untitled (Abstract Landscape 7)*, 1962, Watercolour on paper, 15.6 x 23.3 cm. Collection of National Gallery Singapore.

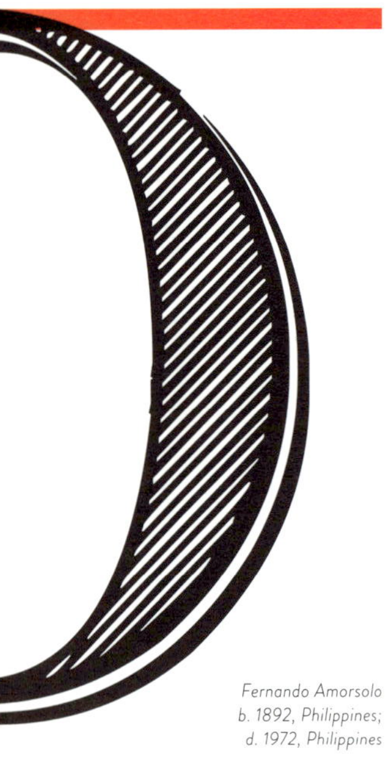

*Fernando Amorsolo
b. 1892, Philippines;
d. 1972, Philippines*

OEUVRE

An oeuvre usually refers to all the artworks that an artist has ever created. But what if only a few works by an artist are known to survive, or if an artist's oeuvre varies widely? How important is it to understand a modern artist's total oeuvre, particularly in Southeast Asia?

Elsewhere in the world, specialists will often create a *catalogue raisonne*: a comprehensive list of every work an artist has created. Yet very few *catalogues raisonnes* have been made for Southeast Asian artists, which might suggest that specialists on modern art of this region have had different interests and priorities, and might also reflect differences in available artworks, resources and archival materials. In this context, studying inconsistencies in an artist's oeuvre can be revealing.

Fernando Amorsolo was a highly prolific artist whose oeuvre varies widely in terms of style, subject matter, and perceived value. One of the Philippines' most celebrated modern painters, Amorsolo created many iconic images. His depiction of women sewing the Philippine flag epitomises a common way of imagining the birth of the nation, for instance, and his paintings of the 1940s Japanese occupation convey the tension and debate of war very effectively, highlighting the competing claims over the people, city, and nation set in motion by military occupation. His landscape paintings also typify several conventions of that genre.

Yet while these works embody key tropes found throughout the modern art and culture of Southeast Asia, they are not necessarily representative of Amorsolo's oeuvre. The artist reputedly made more than 10,000 paintings, many of which depict idealised and often scantily clad women in rural settings, and are commonly regarded as repetitive; some might even be considered kitschy souvenirs. It's been suggested that Amorsolo painted with American expatriate buyers in mind. While tastes vary, it could be argued that works like *Bather by a Stream* lack the originality of composition, clarity of conception, and subtlety of execution of Amorsolo's more celebrated works.

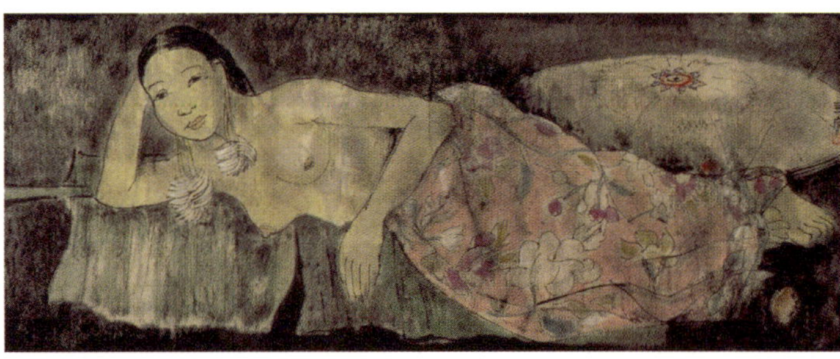

Cheong Soo Pieng. *Woman Lying Down.* 1949. Chinese ink and watercolour, 37.5 x 94.5 cm. Gift of the Loke Wan Tho Collection. Collection of National Gallery Singapore.

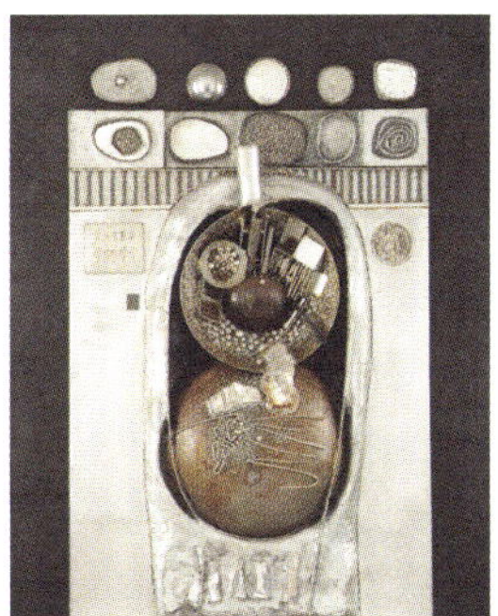

Cheong Soo Pieng. *Composition*. 1973. Metal relief, 119 x 89 cm. Collection of National Gallery Singapore.

Another example of an artist with a varied oeuvre is Cheong Soo Pieng, who is best known for his paintings of women whom he rendered as <u>exotic</u>, such as *Balinese Maidens*, which is very similar in composition to several of his other works. Cheong is also celebrated for depicting <u>quotidian</u> life in kampongs (villages). He painted in several quite varied styles, but repeatedly depicted this same subject matter from soon after his arrival in Singapore in 1946 until his death in 1983. Yet despite this consistent interest in village scenes and daily life, there are also striking deviations in Cheong's oeuvre, such as his experiments with <u>abstraction</u>. Some, like *Abstract Landscape 7*, closely resemble his village scenes, and reflect his interest in Chinese ink. But others, like *Composition*, appear strikingly different and deal with quite unrelated compositional concerns.

Is it necessary to explain such variations within an artist's oeuvre? Art historians continue to debate this. Attempts to locate a consistent narrative throughout may contribute to an idea of the <u>artist</u> as a genius figure with a singular vision. This may mean overlooking other possibilities for interpreting an oeuvre, including the impact of contextual factors like market <u>values</u>, demands of <u>exhibitions</u>, and changing interests and life experiences on an artist's work.

At the other end of the spectrum from the prolific Amorsolo and Cheong are artists whose oeuvres have been lost or destroyed. Very few artworks have survived the Cambodian <u>genocide</u> of the 1970s. Among them are a few hundred paintings by Nhek Dim that depict <u>landscapes</u>, <u>women</u>, and <u>urbanisation</u>; despite him being the best-known artist in Cambodia, the extent of his total oeuvre is unknown. Only a couple of dozen works by Nhek Dim's peer Sam Yoeun are known, most depicting rural life, including farmers embracing communist <u>fashions</u>.

The oeuvres of many <u>women</u> artists have also disappeared. An example is Mia Bustam, who is best known for being married to S. Sudjojono, whose work and approach to <u>realism</u> she chronicled in her <u>journals</u>. Mia was also an artist, working with embroidery and painting. Her self-<u>portrait</u> was exhibited with works by members of LEKRA, a communist-affiliated group prohibited after the genocide in Indonesia between 1965 and 1966. Very few of Bustam's works, however, have survived. This fact, in tandem with her gender and choice to work with <u>craft</u>, mean that she has never enjoyed the acclaim of her husband. <u>Canonical</u> artists like Sudjojono usually have a large and accessible oeuvre.

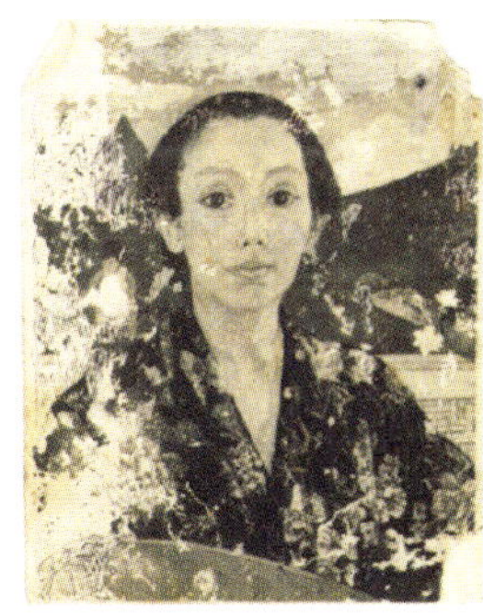

Mia Bustam. *Self Portrait*. 1960. Oil on canvas, dimensions unknown, location unknown (presumed lost).

Cheong Soo Pieng
b. 1917, China; d. 1983, Singapore

Nhek Dim
b. 1934, Cambodia; d. 1978, Cambodia

Sam Yoeun
b. 1933, Cambodia; d. circa 1970, Cambodia

Mia Bustam
b. 1920, Indonesia; d. 2011, Indonesia

Sindudarsono Sudjojono
b. 1913, Indonesia; d. 1986, Indonesia

LEKRA
Lembaga Kebudayaan Rakyat
(Institute for the People's Culture)
Active 1950–1965; based Indonesia

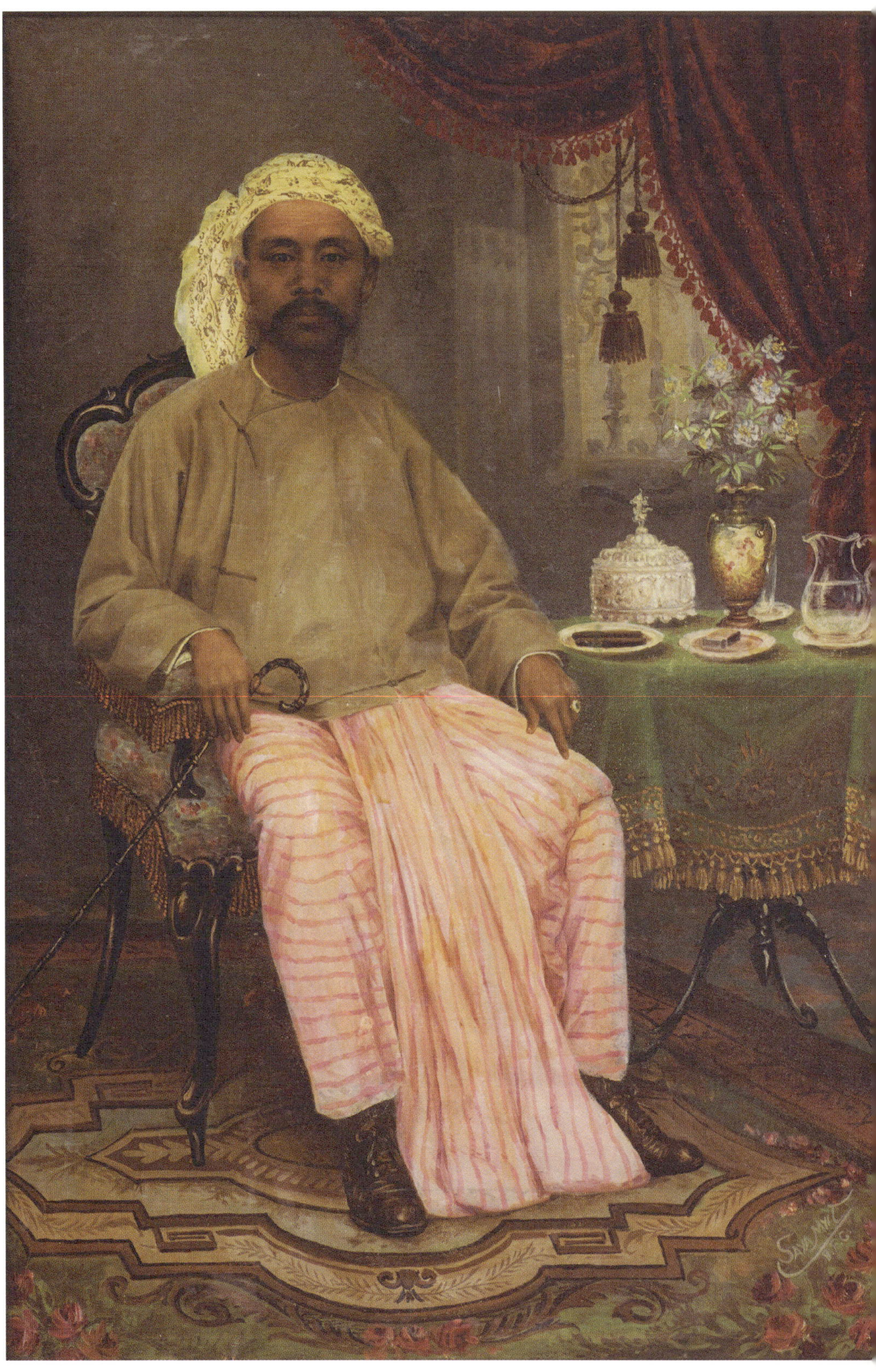

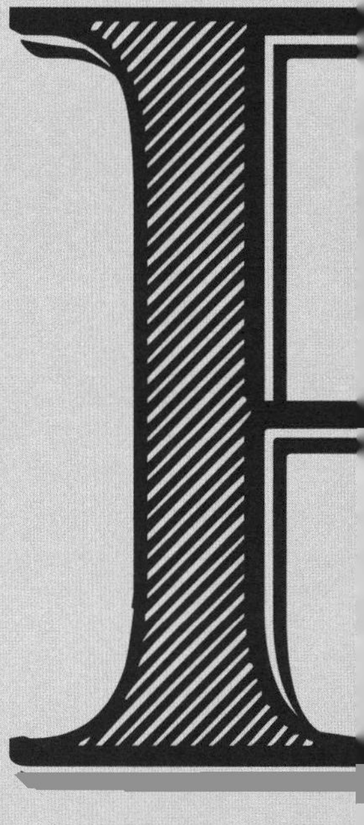

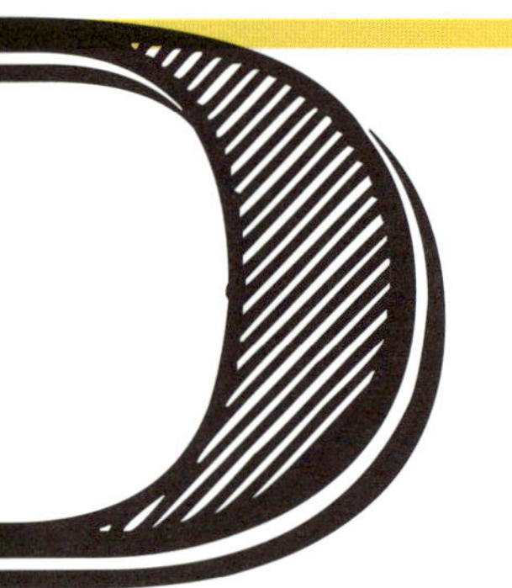

PATRONAGE

Patronage is, simply put, the support given to a person, organisation or cause. In premodern times, most paintings, sculptures, temples, textiles, and other objects which today we might call artworks were commissioned by royal courts, or else by religious institutions. By contrast, modern art enjoys patronage from a staggering variety of sources which had never been available before the emergence of <u>modernities</u>.

New kinds of patronage for modern art—comprising financial and other kinds of support—often comes from individuals who assemble collections of artworks, usually buying them from <u>exhibitions</u>, galleries, artists' <u>studios</u>, or other distinctly modern institutions. Support for modern art also comes from corporations, charities, museums, and other large public bodies. Governments and political organisations are also important patrons, including both those in charge of the <u>nation</u> where an artist is born or lives and works, as well as those in countries far away.

Alongside all of these and many other kinds of patrons, <u>kings</u>, sultans and other royalty continue to play a role in supporting modern art as well as architecture, and <u>spirituality</u> remains an important source of inspiration and support.

Shifts in patronage not only reflect the emergence of modern art, they have also shaped its development in many key ways, allowing for the proliferation of fresh ideas, novel techniques, and new styles. After all, the <u>modern</u> is largely characterised by an enthusiastic embrace of all things new.

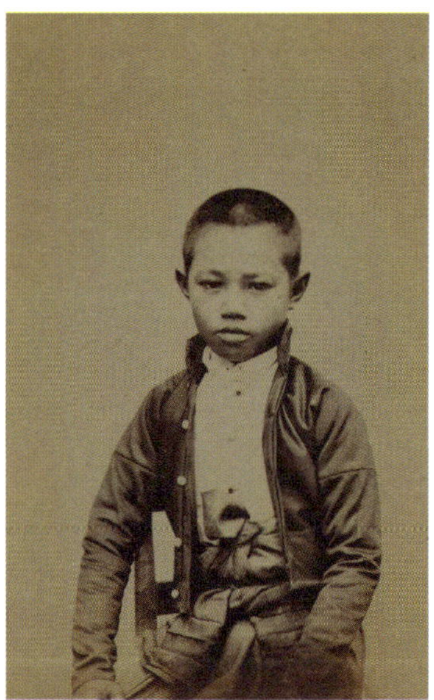

Francis Chit. *Portrait of Siamese Boy (Carte de visite).* c. 1866. Albumen print, 8.9 x 5.6 cm. Collection of National Gallery Singapore.

From the 19th century onwards, following the <u>transfer</u> of new art styles and techniques to Southeast Asia, many artists made <u>portraits</u> of local elites, as well as souvenirs for tourists and travellers. Photographs, such as visiting cards made by Francis Chit, were popular souvenirs. Painted portraits, generally in a <u>realist</u> style, often not only depicted the commissioning patron's appearance, but also conveyed their social status. Saya Myit's *Sitting Man with Mustache* is an example. The sitter's wealth is revealed in the artist's depiction of his fine Western crystalware and elaborate tasselled curtains, while his <u>hybrid</u> combination of Burmese and European <u>fashions</u> further underscores his cosmopolitan sophistication.

By the mid-20th century, large multinational corporations had become important patrons. For example, in 1963, Shell commissioned a major body of paintings by Hoessein Enas, a celebrated portraitist, for a book titled *Malaysians*. At the same time, Shell was desecrating the country's <u>landscape</u> through tin mining. Companies like Shell not only commissioned, but also collected. Major works by Lai Foong Moi and other artists were acquired by Singapore Airlines and other corporate collections.

Around this time, patrons commissioning art as <u>propaganda</u> also began to play an important role in shaping modern art, in the context of the Cold War. Many <u>socialist realist</u> artworks, including posters, were made at the direction of national governments and political parties. In an effort to counterbalance this, the American state sponsored many Southeast Asian artists to pursue an education in the United States, or simply to visit the country to see its museums. This forged unexpected <u>connections</u> among artists from across the region, and beyond. Many artists subsequently navigated a path between <u>abstraction</u>—which was heavily favoured in the United States at the time—and realism.

Many patrons, like Loke Wan Tho, were amateur artists themselves, or formed close personal relationships with the artists they supported. Loke invested in <u>cinema</u>, practised photography, and collected paintings and sculptures. His collection ultimately formed the basis for Singapore's national collection of modern art, and included works by many celebrated artists based in Singapore and Malaysia, including Cheong Soo Pieng, Tchang Ju Chi (who died during World War II), as well as Mohammed Abdul Kadir (co-founder of the Angkatan Pelukis Aneka Daya, a group championing Malay artists), and many others. One of Loke's many photographs of Cambodian antiquities depicts a sculpture in the

Bayon style, widely regarded as a portrayal of King Jaya-varman VII, who was also a celebrated premodern patron.

With the gradual transition to <u>contemporary</u> art, sources of patronage have continued to shift and expand. <u>Biennials</u> have become important sources of financial and other forms of support, such as by providing funding and space for the creation and display of newly commissioned works. Cura-tors—both those working independently and those affiliated with museums or other institutions—have also emerged as mediators between artists, patrons and publics.

Paying attention to patronage helps make visible the complex network of multi-directional exchanges which have made modern art possible. Artists, of course, are undeniably important. But they do not work in isolation.

POETRY

Are they windows, doorways, or perhaps city towers? The three vertical rectangles structuring *Black and White Series (3 Panels)* by artist and poet Arthur Yap are ambiguous and suggestive. So too are the curved shapes and lines which appear in the square frames within these rectangles. Their organic forms resemble elements of topography—perhaps serpentine rivers, as glimpsed from afar or seen from above. Yet the repetition of these bulbous shapes compounds their mystery and appeal, mitigating the possibility of reading them as representing real <u>landscapes</u>. They appear, instead, almost anthropomorphic. Eluding mimesis, Yap's repeated forms point us in imaginative directions, perhaps toward what another artist and poet, Latiff Mohidin, calls a "mindscape."

Rather than depicting a place, the <u>abstract</u> features in Yap's monochromatic painting might be considered a kind of rhyme within the picture. There is an experiential pleasure in allowing our eyes to move across these lyrical lines and shapes, as if we are reading a poem. We may find rhythms in the repetition and variation of the forms, and perhaps a mood or cadence in the grain of the shading as white paint dissolves through grey toward black. The experience of viewing any artwork involving repeated visual motifs—for example, sculptures by Kim Lim or drawings by Bagyi Aung Soe—may also invoke this association with rhythm and rhyme, melody and metre. Lim spoke of "being aware of the pulses and rhythms in nature," while Aung Soe wrote that he "had to read millions of poems" in order to illustrate poetry.

Arthur Yap was a celebrated poet as well as a painter; his artworks appeared on the cover of some of his publications. Yap's verse—which rarely rhymes—is known for its evocations

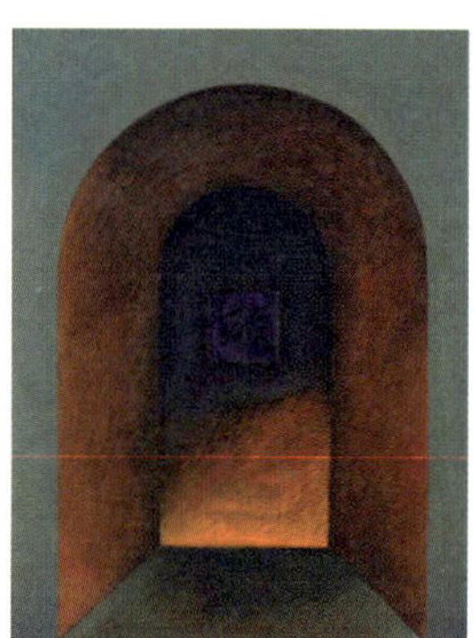

Latiff Mohidin. *Mindscape 17.* 1983. Oil on canvas, 82 x 64 cm. Gift of Bin-jaiTree in memory of Chia Yew Kay and Tan Kim Siew. Collection of National Gallery Singapore.

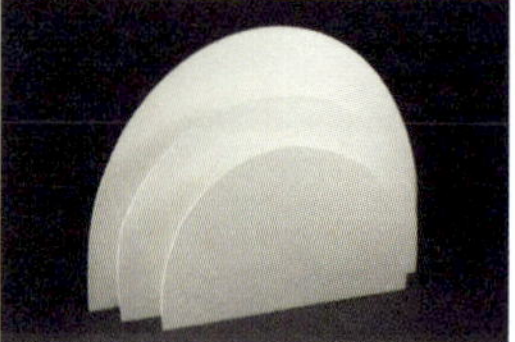

Kim Lim. *Steps.* 1967. Stainless steel, enamel paint, zinc coating, 92 x 129 x 24 cm. Gift of William Turnbull. Collection of National Gallery Singapore.

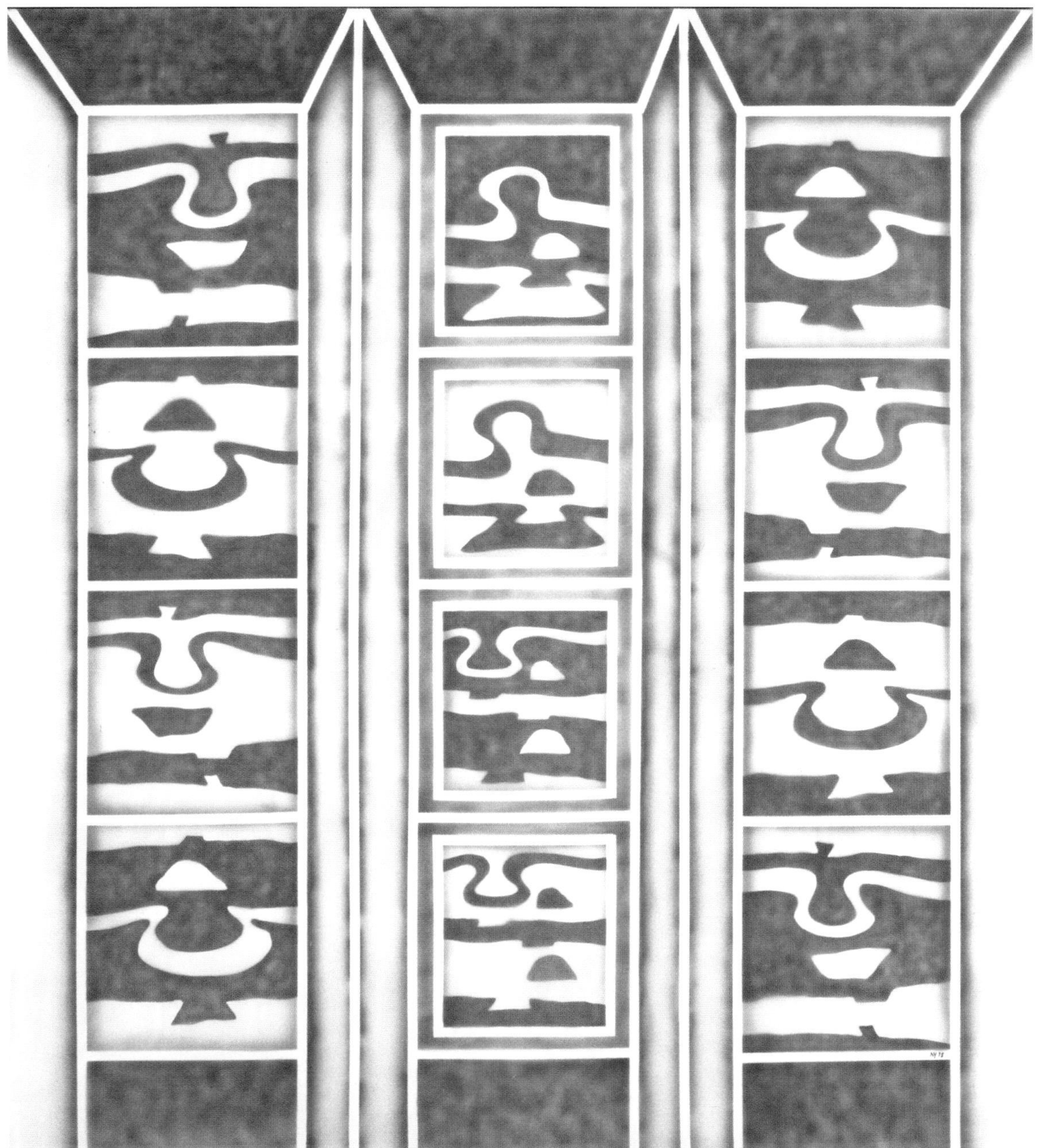

Arthur Yap. *Black and White Series (3 Panels)*. 1975. Acrylic on canvas, 136.5 x 126.5 cm. Gift of Fanny, Jenny and Alice Yap. Collection of National Gallery Singapore.

of <u>urban</u> environments and forms of sociality, especially in Singapore, and its fond appropriation of the grammar and vocabulary of Singapore English. While Yap's paintings are abstract, his poems usually feature people who seem quite real, often occupying recognisable places, and speaking in familiar ways. Thus, in *2 mothers in a h d b playground* (1980), he writes: "ah pah wants to take you chya-hong in new motor-car."

The colloquial mixing of Chinese dialects with English is common in Singapore, where most people live in a kind of social housing referred to as "HDB." Yap distils the essence of <u>quotidian</u> informality, and casual, neighbourly <u>connections</u>.

There are many other modern artists who are also poets. Some, like Latiff Mohidin, use poetry to issue declarations, as in his *Generation Anak Alam* ("Children of Nature") manifesto (1974). It asserts: "all around us are miscarriages of words about / 'art' / and / speeches on art from people who know not / let alone appreciate art." Many artists who worked in the idiom of Chinese ink painting, like Fan Chang Tien, integrated calligraphic poetry and image; Fan often rhymed vertical lines of text with depictions of stems of bamboo and other plants.

Artists' poems and artworks may be mutually illuminating—but not always, and not directly. Latiff, for example, rejects the idea that his poetry and painting are connected. The relationship between different media like art and poetry can be richer than simply registering a <u>biographical</u> fact about an artist and employing it to aid interpretation.

Poetry—with its attention to form, as inseparable from content—may also help us to think and write about art, especially about the experience of apprehending art. A description of facts, no matter how skillful, inevitably falls short of being able to capture the feelings we have upon encountering an artwork—when we see the depiction of light in a photograph, for example, or the way that light falls on a sculpture, animating it, even many years after it was made.

Writing, speaking, and thinking about art in ways that honour these embodied, affective responses needn't involve the use of floral, fancy, or specialist language. When <u>contemporary</u> artist Araya Rasdjarmrearnsook films Thai villagers discussing canonical European artworks, their fresh and unexpected interpretations offer startling insights, making us see familiar old paintings in novel ways. This, too, may be a kind of poetry.

PORTRAIT

Ranging from official depictions of authority figures to informal records of private moments, portraits have taken many forms in Southeast Asian modern art, and serve a wide variety of purposes. Whether they embody authority and status or express an individual's private inner state, portraits are undoubtedly powerful, and can evince strong emotions, and sometimes even sub-rational responses. They also offer an entry point to many broader art historical issues.

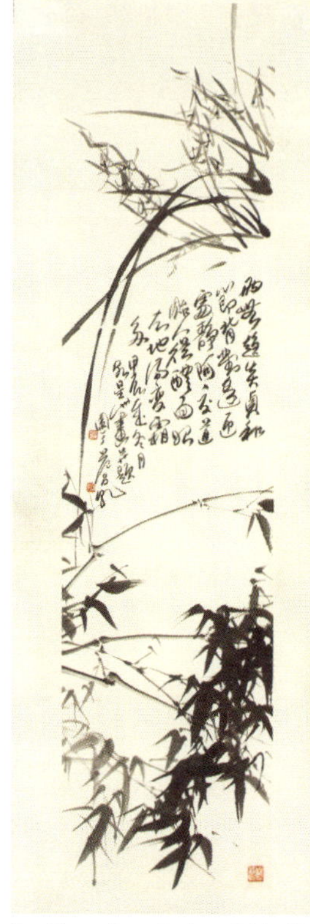

Fan Chang Tien. *Bamboo*. 1964. Chinese ink on paper, 145 x 35 cm. Gift of Heng Siew Leng. Collection of National Gallery Singapore.

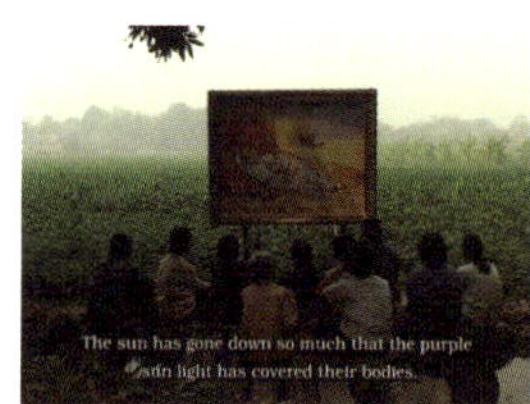

Araya Rasdjarmrearnsook. Still from *Two Planets: Van Gogh's The Midday Sleep and the Thai Villagers*. 2008. Video, single channel, colour, sound, 18 min 18 sec.

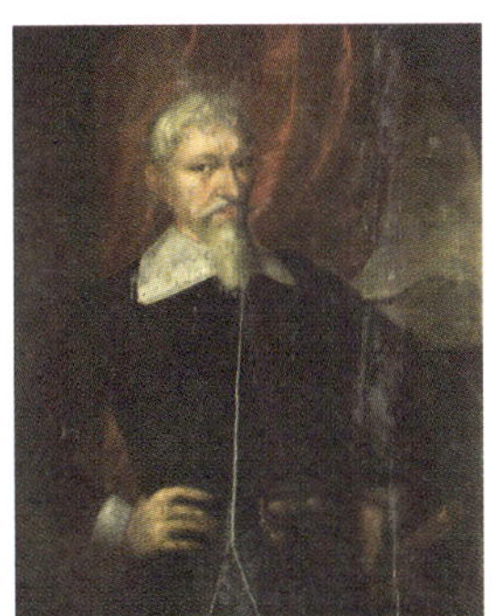

Anonymous. *Portrait of Hendrik Brouwer, Governor-General of the Dutch East Indies.* c. 1632–1675. Oil on panel, 98 x 79 cm. Collection of Rijksmuseum.

Portraits have often been used to denote power and prestige. Official portraits of elites are found throughout Southeast Asia: the genre first gained appeal in this region as a means to communicate the authority of both colonial and local rulers. Early examples date to the 17th century, when portraiture was the most celebrated genre of Dutch painting. However, at that time only less-skilled Dutch artists travelled to the islands now called Indonesia. As art historian David van Duuren remarks, these Dutch artists were "usually well-routined at putting together a likeness, [yet] entirely lacked the vision, expressive force and presence of their greater colleagues." A Dutch portrait of a 17th-century Governor-General, for example, conveys little of his personality or political stature.

In Thailand, depictions of royalty—originally forbidden—were allowed from the mid to late 19th century onwards. The resulting portraits, like Phra Soralaklihkit's portrait of King Nangklao, emphasise royal supremacy: the king's pose is rigid and formal, and his costume and jewels further underscore his wealth and might. The fact that it is illegal, in Thailand, to deface royal portraits further demonstrates the power of portraits to convey an aura of power equivalent to the persons they depict.

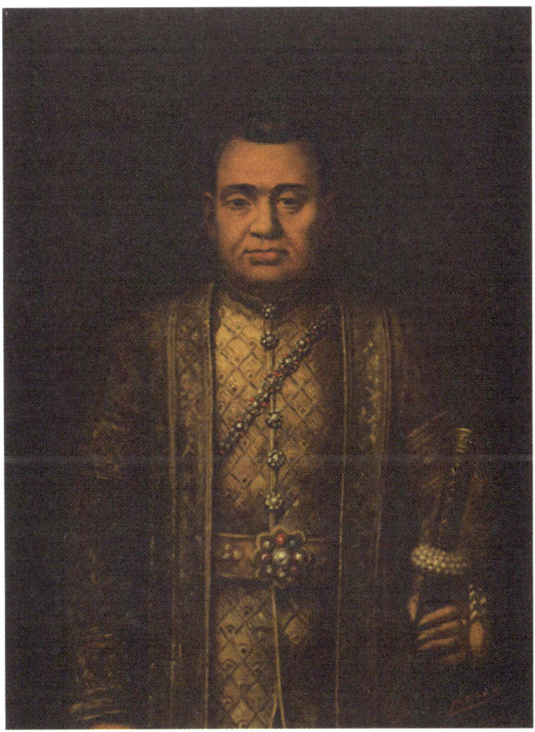

Phra Soralaklikhit. *Portrait of King Nangklao.* 1916. Oil on canvas, 42 x 32 cm. Collection of National Gallery Singapore.

The law about royal portraits in Thailand also indicates that portraiture has often been an especially charged site for transformations brought about by the emergence and development of the <u>modern</u> in art. Depictions of <u>kings</u> and other royalty sometimes require context to be intelligible as modern. In Soralaklikhit's portrait of King Nangklao, we may also discern a radically modern artistic reappraisal of past <u>traditions</u>. During Nangklao's reign, it had been forbidden to make depictions of royalty. After his successor, King Mongkut overturned this rule, embracing photography, painting, and sculpture as <u>media</u> for portraits, artists began to make images of kings who had never been allowed to be portrayed during their own lifetimes. Soralaklikhit's painting was made in 1916, over half a century after the death of Nangklao, and it demonstrates the total turnaround in attitudes to likenesses of kings, as well as a realist style of painting completely new in the Thai context, transformed during processes of transfer from the West. The painter's signature, prominently painted in red, indicates his intention to be identifiable, in keeping with the modern idea that an <u>artist</u> should be a recognisable individual.

Individuality is often important in modern portraiture: not only the artist but also the sitter must usually be readily identifiable. In the 19th century, Indonesian artists mastered European-style portraiture, and began serving a diverse range of wealthy and powerful <u>patrons</u>, not only colonial masters. An 1879 portrait of a local ruler by Raden Kusumadibrata, who is thought to have studied under Raden Saleh, is described by art historian John Clark as especially able to "bewitch," as its "commanding" subject "appears to be there in reality, looking at us as we dare to observe him." This is an evocative description of the power of <u>realism</u>.

Official portraits take many forms, sometimes emphasising private moments more than public prowess. In Burma during the late 19th century, family portraits of royalty and wealthy elites emerged as a popular genre, following the innovations of Saya Chone. His *Family Portrait* revels in sumptuous details of fabric and architecture, depicting aristocrats at one with their elegant and luxurious surroundings, although it's unclear if this is a depiction of specific or identifiable individuals. Saya Chone usually painted in a <u>hybrid</u> style, while other artists followed conventions of realism more closely. A sub-genre of Burmese portraits from this period is dubbed "candid" by art historian Andrew Ranard, and features "attempts by the artists to capture subjects in authentic settings, with the focus on an incident or event."

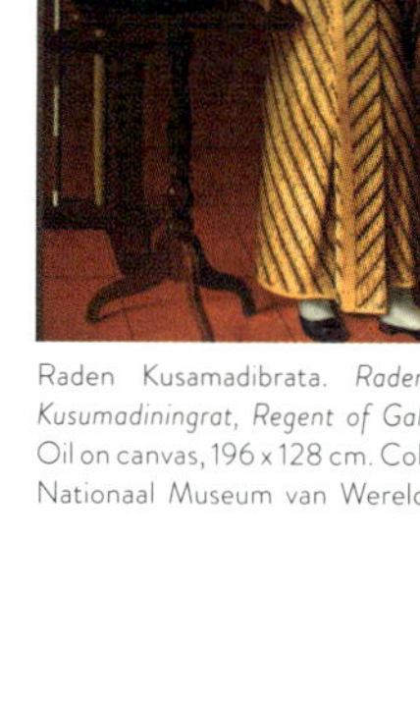

Raden Kusamadibrata. *Raden Adipati Kusumadiningrat, Regent of Galuh.* 1879. Oil on canvas, 196 x 128 cm. Collection of Nationaal Museum van Wereldculturen.

Saya Saw and Saya Maung Tin Maung were proponents of this sub-genre. At first glance, their work may appear similar to Chone's, but the posture of the figures and the action taking place sets their compositions apart. The candid nature of such works is more closely aligned with realism, and less with the traditional courtly style as followed by Chone.

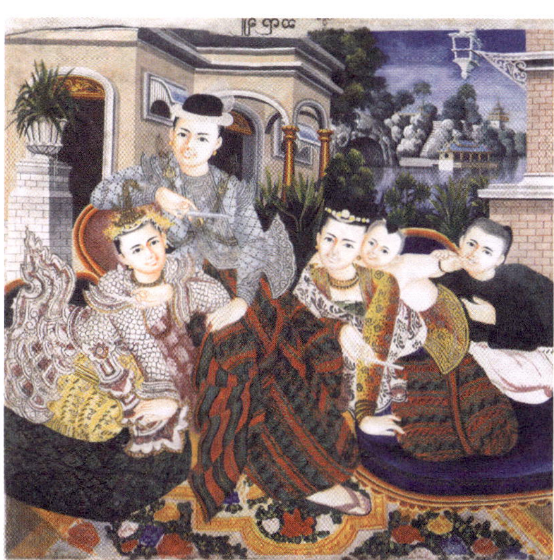

Saya Chone. *Family Portrait*. c. late 19th to early 20th century. Gouache on cloth, 67 x 67 cm. Collection of Fukuoka Asian Art Museum.

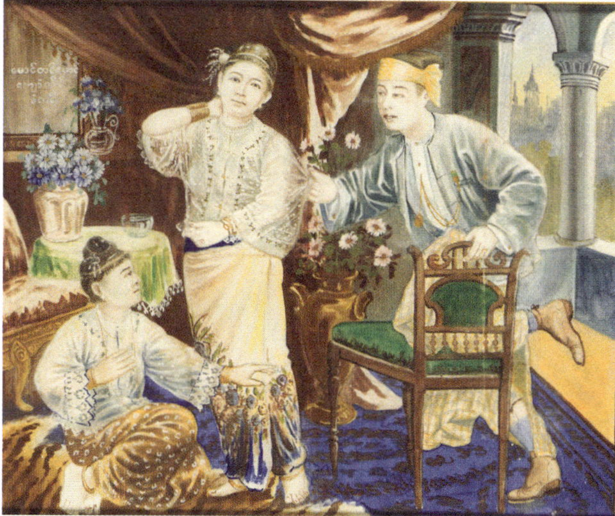

Saya Maung Tin Maung. *Startled Chaperone*. c. 1920s–1930s. Opaque watercolour on cloth, 51.5 x 64 cm. Collection of National Gallery Singapore.

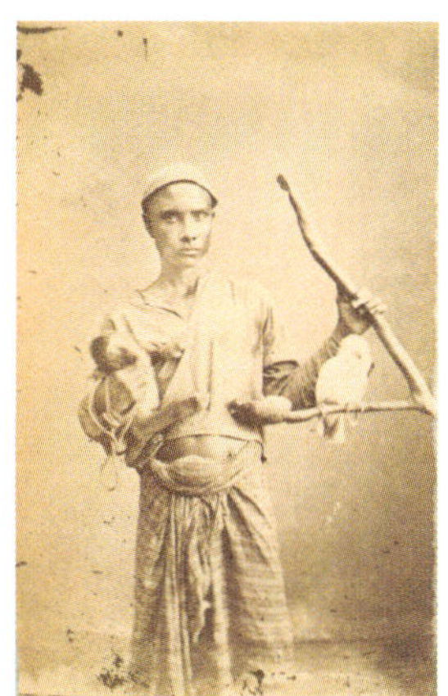

John Thomson. *Malay Man with Bird*. 1862. Albumen print, 10.9 x 6.8 cm. Collection of National Museum of Singapore.

While portraits can stand for unrivalled power and authority, they can also provide a window into the disenfranchised in society, or into moments of uncertainty and ambivalence. An example is a photographic portrait of an anonymous "Malay man" depicted by John Thomson. Looking uncertainly at the camera, appearing frightened and impoverished, the man cuts a stark contrast to the assertive confidence seen in portraits of rulers and elites. He is a haunting symbol of the subjugation and objectification of Southeast Asians under the colonial gaze, which was often made manifest in portraiture. Thomson was one of the earliest travelling photographers to practice in Southeast Asia, operating a studio in Singapore from 1862, and then in Bangkok from 1865, where he took some of the first portraits of King Mongkut.

A more recent example is Aye Aye Mar's 1980 portrait of five women, which is one of many in the artist's oeuvre now lost. Titled *The Flames of Artery*, the painting features five women in a state of deep, desperate distress, as spelt out by their gaunt faces and haunting expressions. The women are grouped closely together—thereby creating a claustrophobic sense of tense constraint—and their tautly

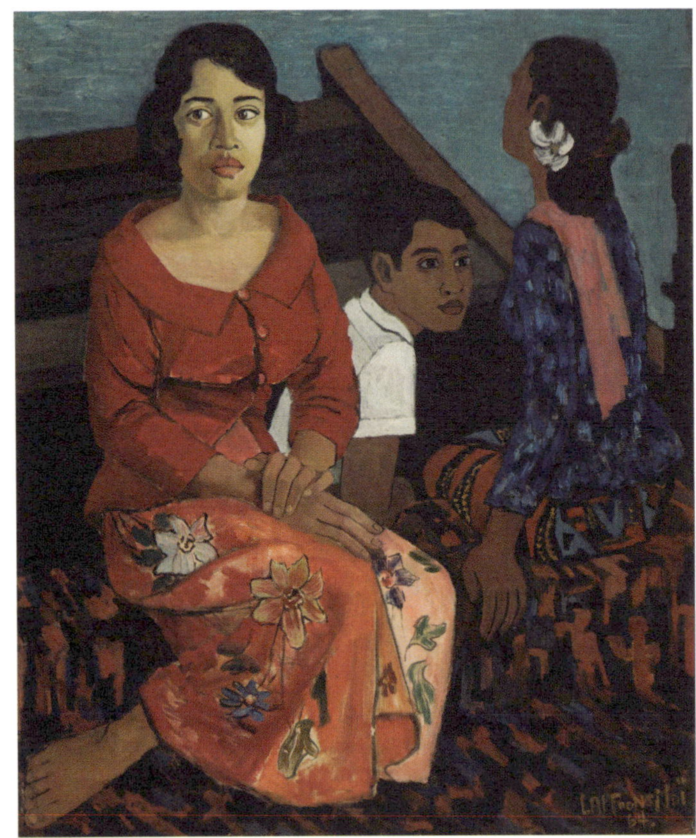

Lai Foong Moi. *Home Coming*. 1964. Oil on canvas, 77 x 65 cm. Collection of Singapore Airlines Limited.

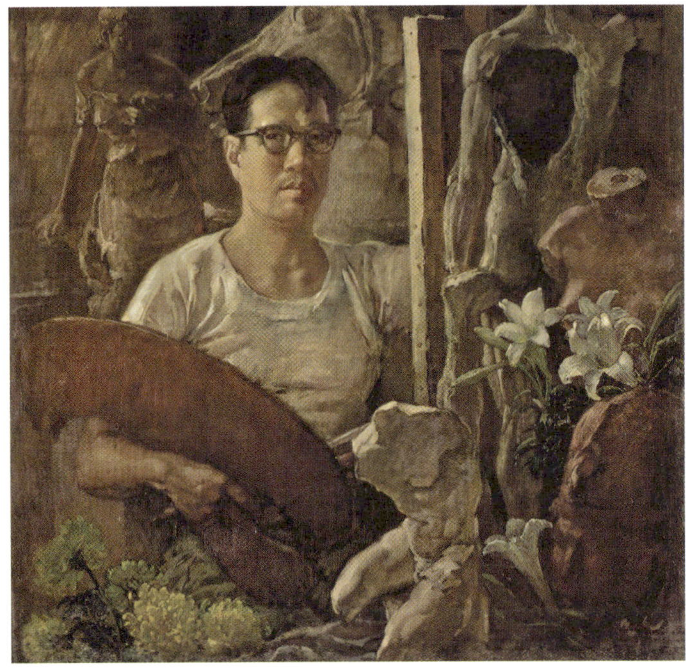

Lee Man Fong. *Self Portrait*. 1958. Oil on canvas, 99 x 102 cm. Gift of Mr and Mrs Putra Masagung. Collection of National Gallery Singapore.

drawn faces are rendered as exaggerated angular planes. This portrait was censored in a violent act of literal defacement: Burmese government censors "stamped 'no permission' all over the women's faces," the artist later recalled, in an interview with researcher Melissa Carlson. Paintings by many other artists suffered a similar fate.

Candid portraits that appear to freeze a moment in <u>time</u> became popular in many places during the 20th century. An example is Lai Foong Moi's *Home Coming*. Lai was one of few women associated with <u>social realism</u>; she also often depicted <u>vernacular</u> architecture she encountered during her inspirational travels in Southeast Asia. Celebrated as the first Malaysian artist to receive an <u>education</u> in Paris, Lai perhaps felt an affinity with the experience of <u>diasporic</u> people and travellers, as depicted in *Home Coming*. The people pictured in the work appear uncertain but hopeful; there is a rare and enchanting air of mystery in the painting.

Self-portraits made throughout the 19th and 20th centuries helped to articulate a modern conception of the figure of the <u>artist</u>: artists were depicting themselves as individuals with their own identity and creative agency. Many artists, like Lee Man Fong, choose to depict themselves in their <u>studio</u>, with details that reveal more about their self-image. In Lee's self-portrait, for instance, the artist depicts himself wearing light and informal clothing, which makes it apparent that he is working in a <u>tropical</u> environment. Lee lived most of his adult life in Singapore and Indonesia, where he enjoyed the special <u>patronage</u> of President Sukarno. Yet here he depicts himself as surrounded by Western-style sculptures, perhaps reminders of his six years spent living in Europe immediately after World War II. Lee was essentially self-educated, yet his work avoids a <u>naïve</u> appearance, often featuring dense and complex compositions.

Portraits come in a range of forms and styles, and artists also explore the distinction between portraiture—depictions of specific individuals—and the representation of human figures more generally. An example in sculptural form is But Mochtar's strikingly elongated, semi-<u>abstract</u> rendering of a woman embarked on a <u>spiritual</u> journey. Artists have also painted portraits and rendered human faces and figures in semi-abstract styles. Ta Ty, for instance, rejected the <u>socialist realist</u> style of North Vietnam, moving from Hanoi to the South in order to pursue his interest in abstraction. He was later punished for this, and fled to live in a <u>diaspora</u>. Another example of a semi-abstract depiction of a person is Fua Haribhitak's *Face*, made while the artist was living in Italy. It is unclear whether the work portrays a specific individual or not. Fua had been in the first generation of students to study modern art under Silpa Bhirasri, and his experiments with abstraction inspired by cubism, like this work, had a great impact on his peers and subsequent generation. While he worked in a diverse range of styles, Fua consistently returned to portraiture, using the human form as a starting point for abstractions in various styles—a testament, perhaps, to the seemingly limitless possibilities of portraits.

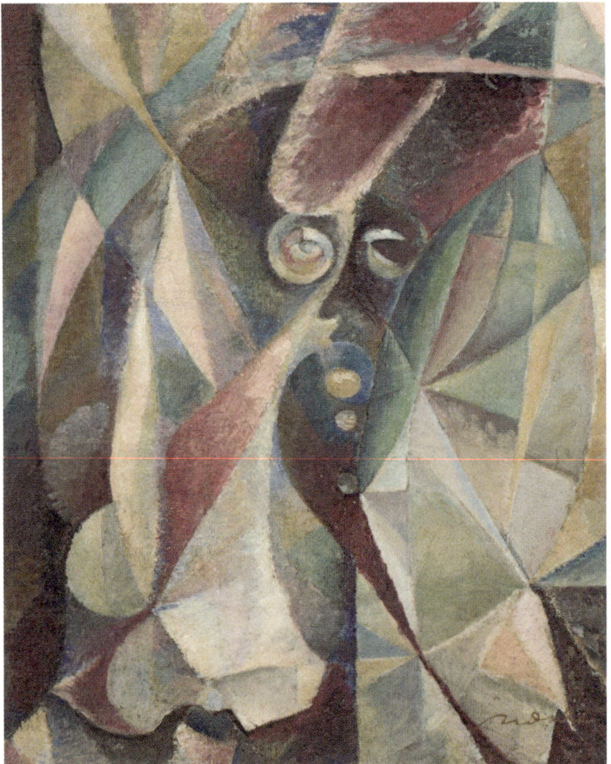

Fua Haribhitak. *Face*. c. 1956. Oil on canvas, 65 x 55 cm. Collection of National Gallery Singapore.

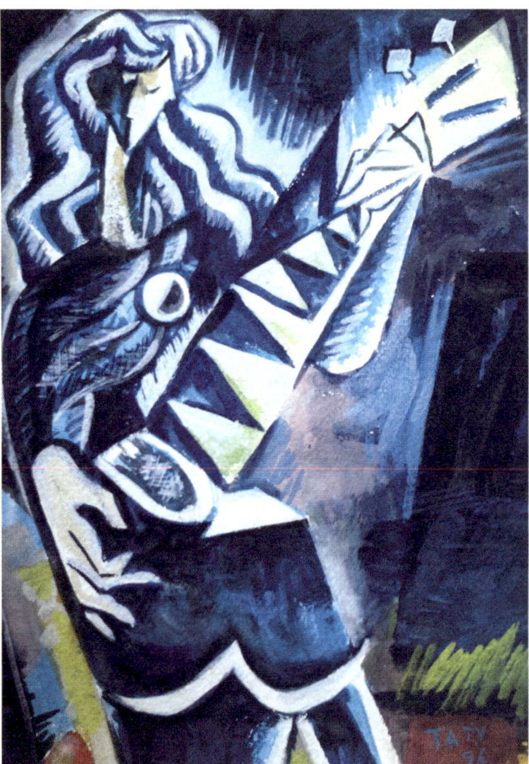

Ta Ty. *Untitled (Abstract)*. 1956. Gouache on paper, 52 x 37 cm. Albert I. Goodman Collection.

PROPAGANDA

Any biased communication promoting a particular opinion, especially a political position, can be called propaganda. How does propaganda relate to art? There is a prevailing view, developed during the 20th century and chiefly in Western discourse, that propaganda is of lesser value and should not be viewed as art. In this view, with propaganda it is the message that matters, instead of the form or appearance it takes. This notion, however, is too simplistic.

In Southeast Asia, the difference between art and propaganda is not so clear-cut. Modern art has often been used to communicate political messages. In Laos, Vietnam, and

164

to a lesser extent Cambodia, artists have been obliged to work in a <u>socialist realist</u> style due to official directives from communist parties and/or governments, within the context of <u>war</u> and its aftermath. Many were engaged to make posters which advanced a certain ideology. One example, by Pech Song, depicts <u>artists</u> alongside revolutionary workers, peasants and soldiers, positioning them as being equally central to the revolutionary struggle in Cambodia. In Laos, Anoulom Souvandouane, who was employed by the state to design banknotes, ministry logos and the national emblem, also designed posters and greetings cards. While such works can thus be considered propagandistic, they are also of significant aesthetic interest. Song and Anoulom both also continued to make paintings alongside these other activities.

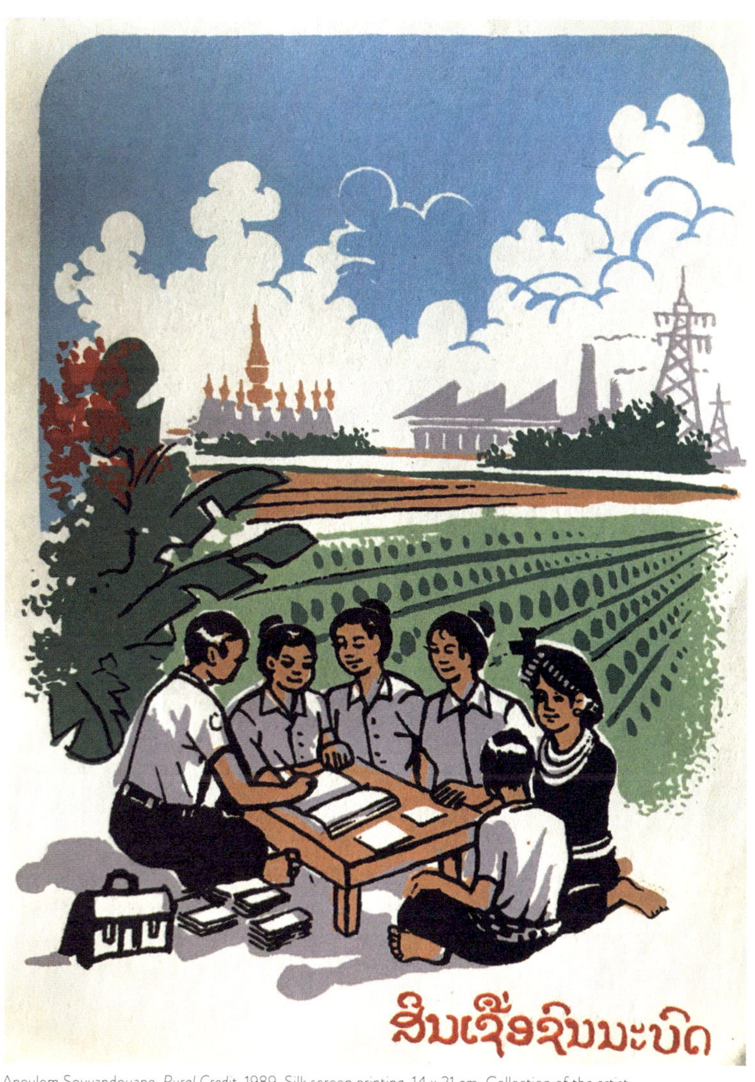

Anoulom Souvandouane. *Rural Credit*. 1989. Silk screen printing, 14 x 21 cm. Collection of the artist.

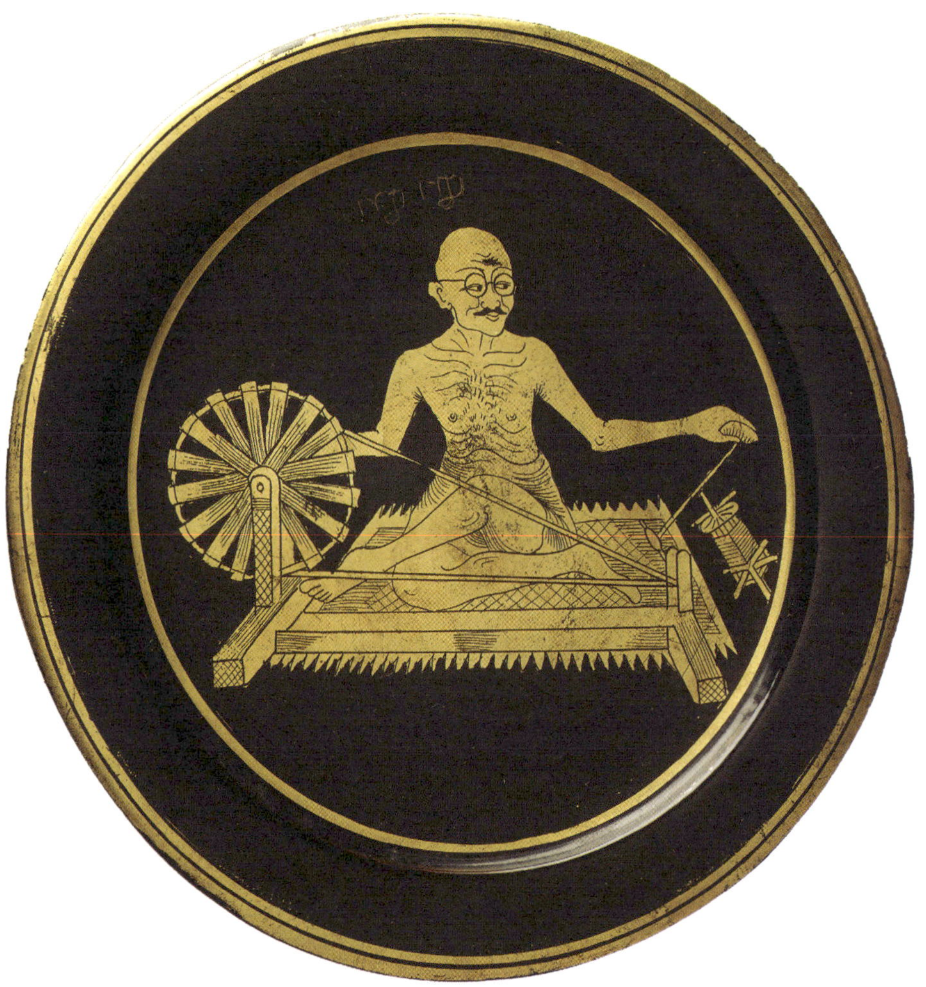

Maker unknown. Plate with depiction of Mahatma Gandhi. 1930s. Made in Myanmar, possibly Pagan. Lacquer, gold leaf and bamboo, 15.2 x 15.2 x 1.5 cm. Collection of British Museum.

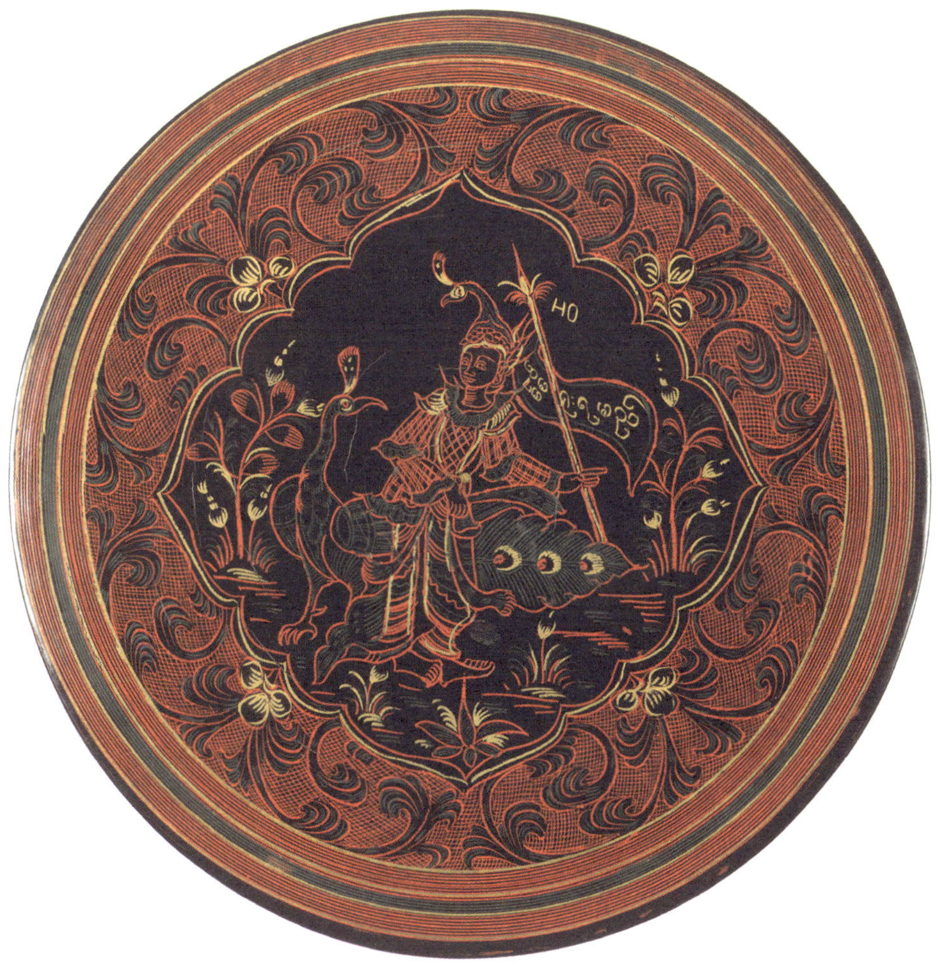

Maker unknown. Betel box with depiction of banner which reads "We shall get home rule." Early 20th century, possibly 1924. Made in Tangyi, Myanmar. Lacquer and bamboo, 21 x 21 x 20 cm. Collection of British Museum.

The terminology of propaganda in many Southeast Asian <u>vernacular</u> languages also suggests a different understanding of the category. In Khmer, Lao, and Thai, for instance, the term used for propaganda is *khosana*, derived from Pali. Writing of the Lao case, historian Simon Creak argues that "the term 'rhetoric' better encapsulates the complexities of state production of language [than the term] 'propaganda.'" Creak notes that *khosana* has a meaning which is "very broad, referring in different contexts to 'information,' 'promotion,' and 'advertising,'" and that "in Laos there is no clear distinction between the medium and the content; *khosana* can refer to both."

More research is needed on Southeast Asian articulations of propaganda, yet this example suggests that the form (including aesthetic appearance, which Creak refers to as "medium") and message (which Creak calls "content") may be closely linked, or even indivisible, in vernacular understandings of propaganda, as in art.

It is not only under communist regimes that art and propaganda align, and not only in the style of socialist realism. Sometimes, even <u>craft</u> techniques have been used to convey a political agenda. Lacquerware made in Myanmar during the campaign against British colonial rule offers some striking examples, including a 1930s plate decorated with the *shwe-zawa* method of gold-leaf lacquer, popular in Pagan, which displays the image of anti-colonial figure Mahatma Gandhi, and a betel box decorated with the *yun* method of incisions, on which a banner proclaims, "We shall get home rule," a common anti-colonial slogan at the time. These are quirky illustrations of how decorative <u>traditions</u> can be adapted and extended for modern purposes, including in the struggle for <u>independence</u>.

Besides artworks, <u>exhibitions</u>, institutions, and performances can also be deployed as a form of propagandistic cultural diplomacy, where soft power is used to advance an ideology or political stance. For instance, when Agus and Otto Djaya lived in the Netherlands from 1947 to 1950, they mounted three exhibitions in Amsterdam, and showed their works in four other European cities. Recent research has revealed that these activities were part of a covert mission using cultural diplomacy to promote support for the Indonesian National Revolution, which led to independence from Dutch rule in 1948. With this in mind, the artworks the brothers made during their European sojourn—many of which depict scenes of conflict from mythological stories popular in Java—may be interpreted as anti-colonial propaganda. Nonetheless, they are also undoubtably works of art.

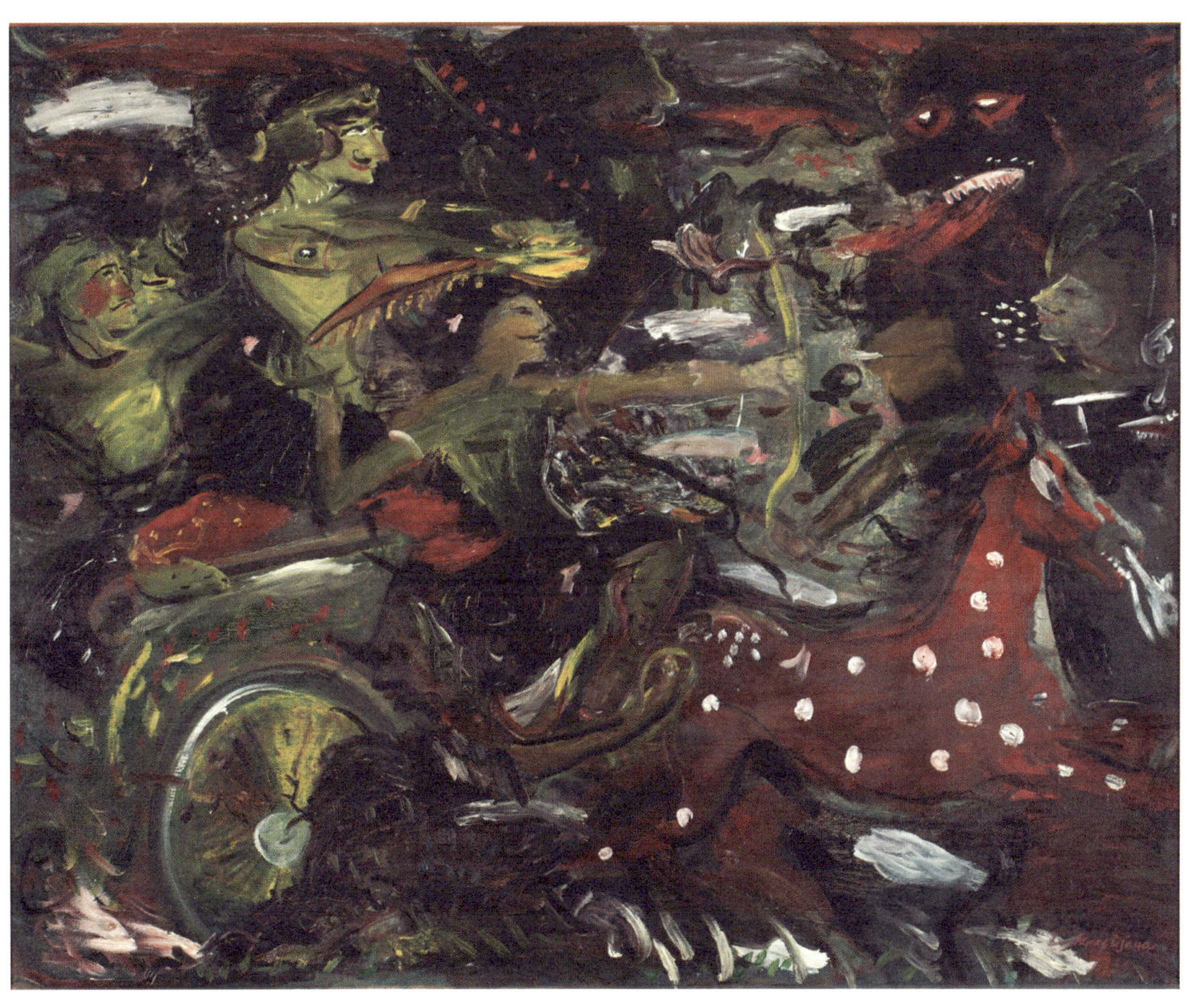

Agus Djaya. *Fight*. 1944. Oil on plywood, 120 x 150 cm. Collection of Stedelijk Museum Amsterdam.

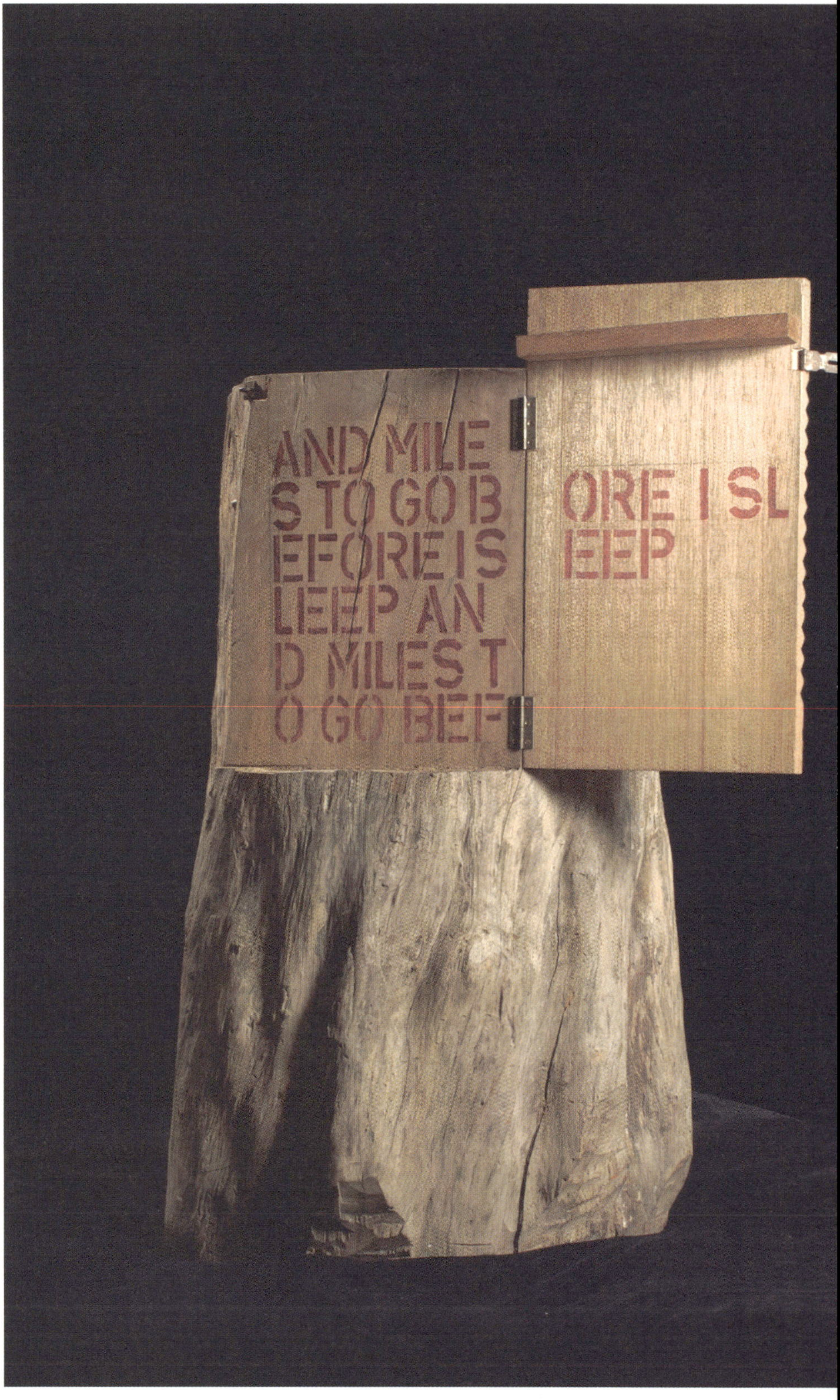

AND MILE
S TO GO B
EFORE I S
LEEP AN
D MILES T
O GO BEF
ORE I SL
EEP

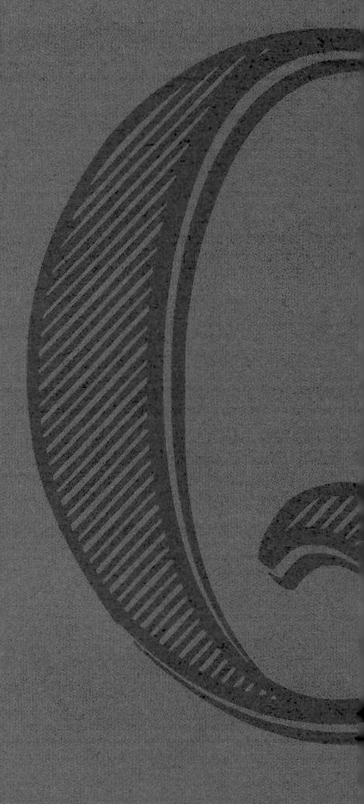

Cheo Chai-Hiang. *And Miles to Go Before I Sleep*. 1975. Wood, metal and ink, 90 × 54 × 40 cm. Gift of the artist. Collection of National Gallery Singapore.

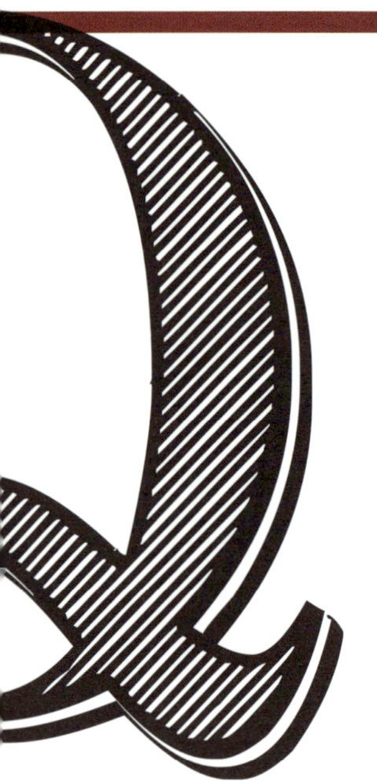

QUOTATION

"Art is inevitably engaged with what came before it, and that engagement is an active reworking," says art historian Mieke Bal about the concept of quotation. Artists quote in different ways—sometimes referring to the written word, a visual <u>trope</u> or even a specific artwork—and for varied purposes. In the process, they propose new understandings of whatever they quote.

And Miles to Go Before I Sleep by Cheo Chai-Hiang is titled after a line from the <u>poem</u> *Stopping by Woods on a Snowy Evening* by American poet Robert Frost. In using this quotation, Cheo invites viewers of his work to also think of the complex concepts in Frost's poem.

The line "And miles to go before I sleep" appears twice in Frost's poem. This repetition shifts our understanding of the poem, from one of straightforward description to allegory. We imagine that the "miles to go" may refer to the distance the narrator has left to travel before he reaches home, as well as the life that he still has left to live, with all its obligations. We also imagine that "sleep" may refer to actual slumber the narrator looks forward to, or death. Cheo's sculpture, which also quotes the line twice, reproduces these allegorical allusions: the wooden washboard brings to mind the mundane obligations of <u>quotidian</u> life, such as laundry, while the tree stump hints at the inevitability of death. This foregrounding of ideas, as well as Cheo's use of found objects, are strategies commonly used by many <u>conceptual</u> and <u>contemporary</u> artists.

Some artworks quote not only from written texts, but also from other artists. For example, Basoeki Abdullah's *Djataju Fights Ravana for Princess Sita* depicts a character from the Ramayana. The composition echoes Dutch artist Rembrandt's *The Abduction of Ganymede* and is thus a kind of visual quotation, as suggested by art historian John Clark. By quoting from European depictions of mythology, Basoeki aligns his depiction of Ramayana characters with Western classical traditions.

Other artists use visual quotations as a form of ironic commentary. Semsar Siahaan's *Olympia, Identity with Mother and Child* is a painting of a naked, blonde woman reclining on a bed. This principal element in the composition is a reference to *Olympia*, a well-known painting by French artist Edouard Manet. Yet whereas Manet's was a portrait of a female Parisian sex worker, Semsar's painting depicts different social groups in contemporary Indonesian society, each identified largely by their <u>fashions</u>.

Clearly, while Semsar is quoting Manet's painting, he is radically changing its meaning, as well as obviously deviating

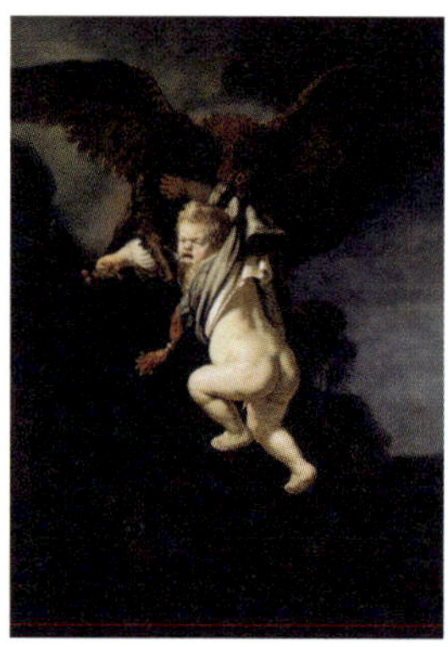

Rembrandt. *The Abduction of Ganymede.* 1635. Oil on canvas, 177 x 129 cm. Collection of the Gemaldegalerie Alte Meister.

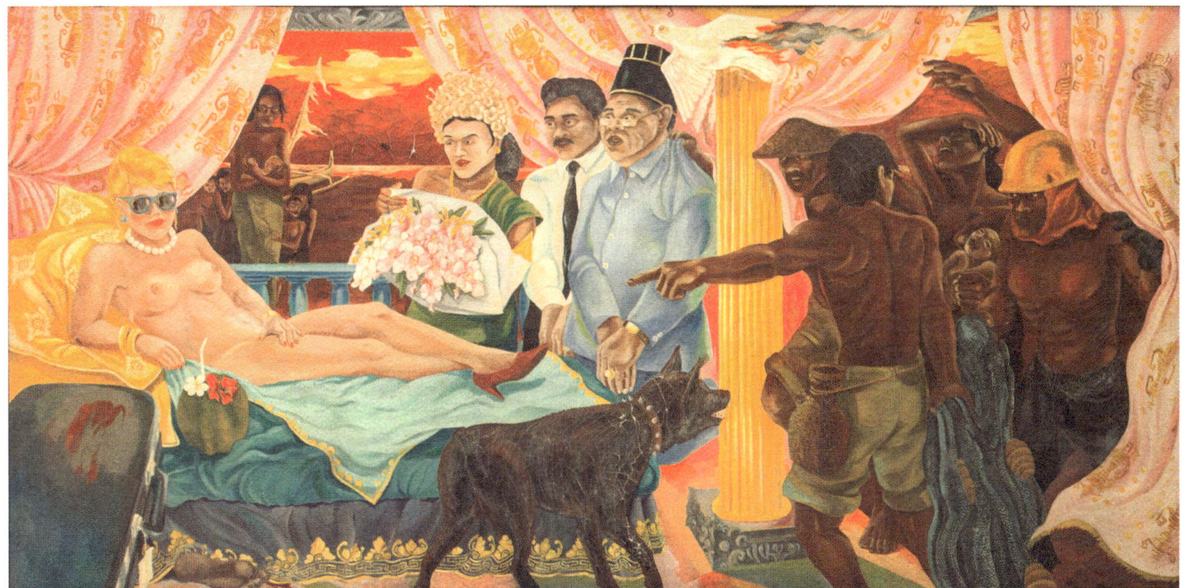

Semsar Siahaan. *Olympia, Identitas Ibu dan Anak (Olympia, Identity with Mother and Child)*. 1987. Oil on canvas, 140.5 x 290 cm. Collection of National Gallery Singapore.

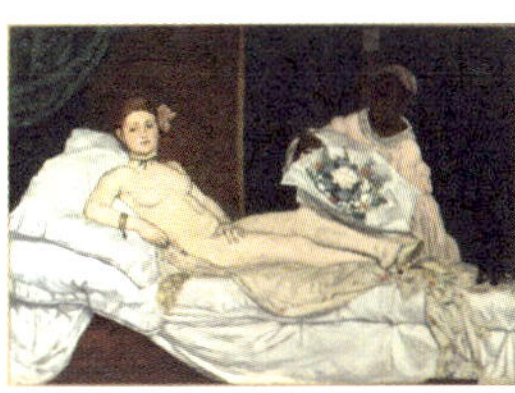

Edouard Manet. *Olympia*. 1863. Oil on canvas, 130 x 190 cm. Collection of Musee d'Orsay, Paris.

from its appearance. In one way, this continues in Manet's footsteps, since Manet's *Olympia* was also composed with reference to similar paintings by Titian, Ingres, and several other European artists. Yet Semsar is also distancing himself from Manet in important ways. This painting has been described by art historian Aminudin T.H. Siregar as "represent[ing] actual social, political and economic conditions of the time in Indonesia." Semsar was unafraid of criticism, having caused a stir in 1981 for burning a sculpture by his professor, which he deemed exploitative of the arts of Indonesia's ethnic minorities.

Art historian T.K. Sabapathy proposes that Semsar's appropriation of Manet "distinguish[es] his practice of painting from an acknowledge[d] watershed moment in Western painting's history without being captive to it and on his [own] terms." This kind of ironic visual quotation thus functions to signal Semsar's mastery over Manet and the Western canon. In other works, he refers to paintings by several other Western modern artists, including Pablo Picasso.

These and other instances of quotation of words, images, and ideas demonstrates that the modern art of Southeast Asia, as elsewhere, has developed through manifold dialogues between artists and others, some of which take place within the space of artworks themselves.

Titian
b. circa 1488–1490, Italy; d. 1576, Italy

Jean Auguste Dominique Ingres
b. 1780, France; d. 1867, France

Pablo Picasso
b. 1881, Spain; d. 1973, France

QUOTIDIAN

The ordinary and everyday—also called the quotidian—has been a preoccupation of modern artists in Southeast Asia, as elsewhere. Although quotidian scenes appear in some pre-modern images, modern artists embraced the unexceptional with unprecedented fervour. This happened as art shifted away from being made primarily for religious purposes, or for patrons.

The everyday, as a subject, has been explored in various ways. In the mid-20th century, photography was one important means of doing so. *The Memorial Bridge* by 'Rong Wong-Savun is typical of the genre referred to as street photography. The images in the series are carefully composed—'Rong is celebrated for using idiosyncratic camera angles—but they are not posed. Rather, these are snapshots, depicting ordinary people going about their daily lives in central Bangkok.

Photographs of quotidian moments and scenes, such as 'Rong's, can be understood as attempts to expand the aesthetic possibilities of photography and its subject matter. Earlier photographs were usually carefully composed, from <u>studio</u> <u>portraits</u> to formal depictions of scenes that were deemed more significant than the mundane everyday.

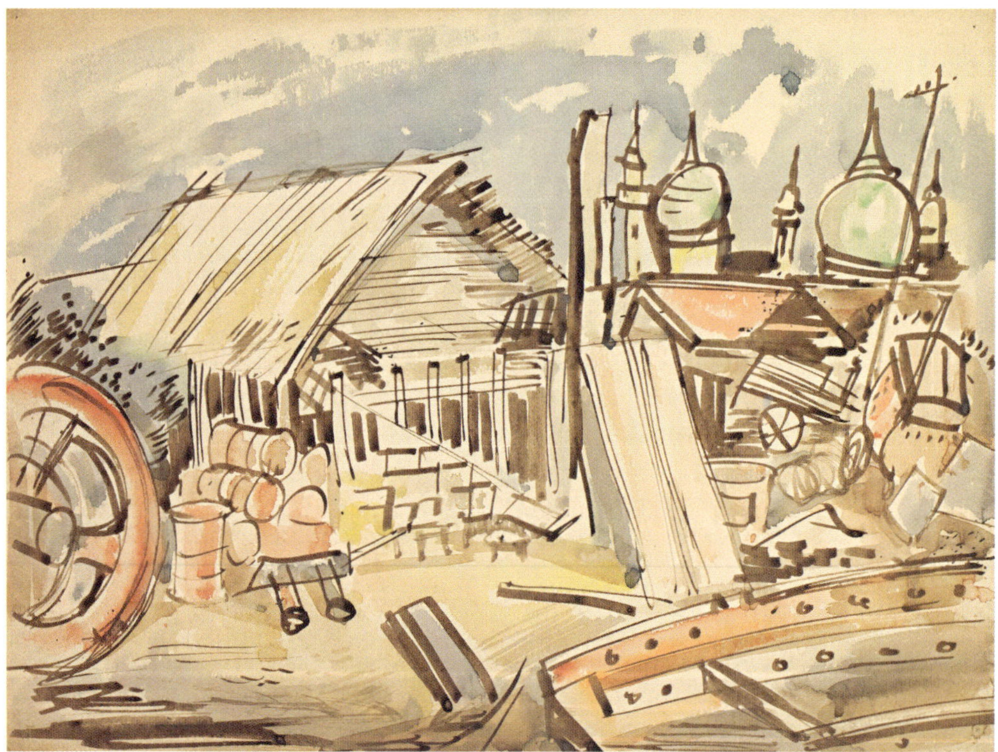

Cheong Soo Pieng. Untitled (*A Rubbish Dump*). c. 1950s. Watercolour on paper, 27.4 x 37.5 cm. Collection of National Gallery Singapore.

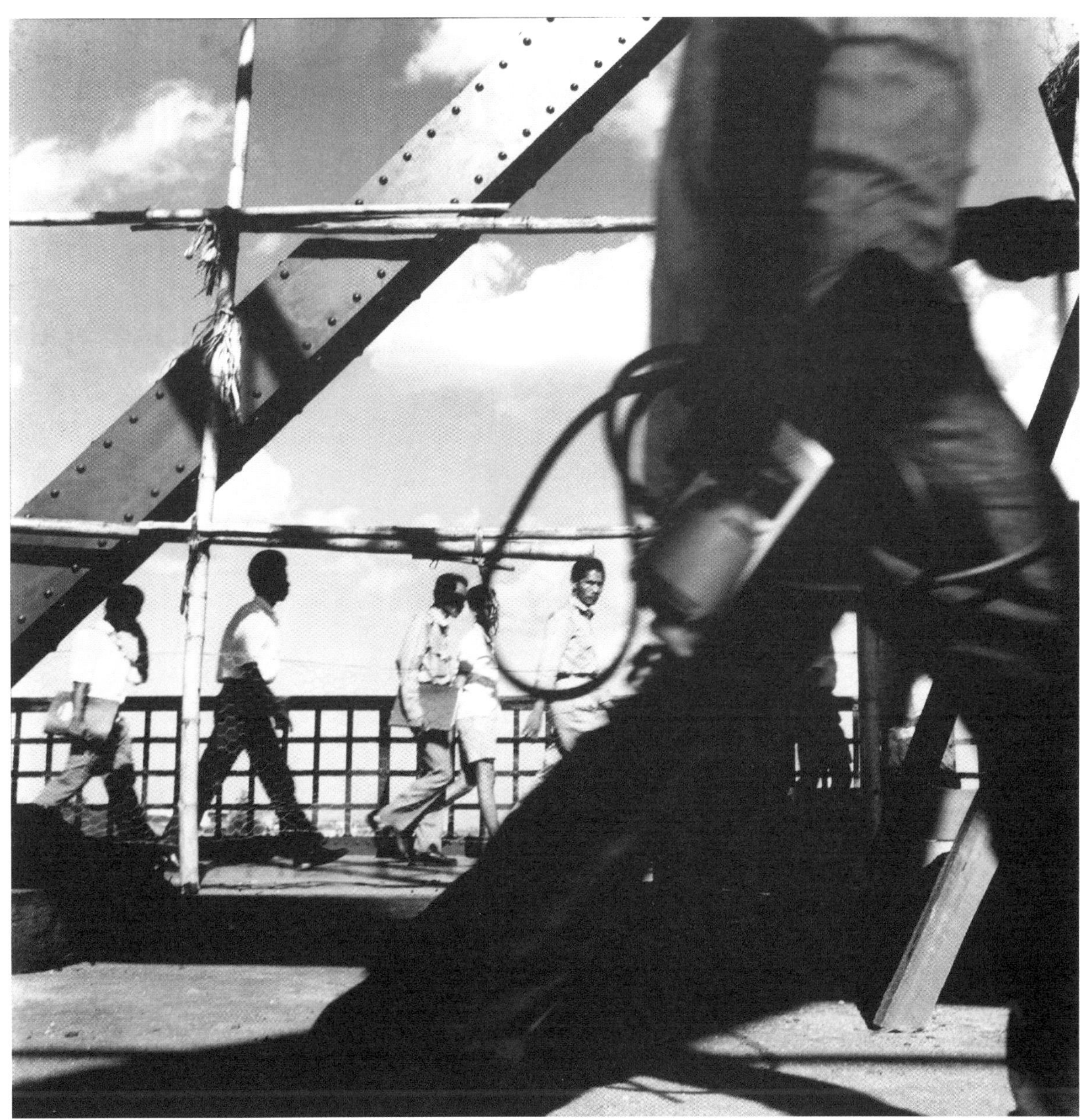

'Rong Wong-Savun. *Rama I Bridge*. c. 1958, printed 2017. Silver gelatin print, 25.5 x 25.5 cm. Collection of National Gallery Singapore.

Around the same time, painters like Cheong Soo Pieng were also depicting everyday life in stylised compositions that combined elements of several aesthetic traditions, including Chinese ink painting. Like many other Chinese emigre artists who settled in Singapore during the 1950s, Cheong often painted scenes of Malay villages, or kampong. This approach, known generally as the Nanyang style, usually involved affected and exoticising representations, but nevertheless usually focused on depicting the anonymous and everyday, rather than the exceptional. Cheong also took an interest in corners of village and urban life which are often overlooked or forgotten, as in his painting of a rubbish dump.

These modern artists embraced depictions of the quotidian to expand art's aesthetic and conceptual parameters. However, long before them, the everyday had already made some striking appearances. The bas reliefs at Cambodia's Bayon temple (12th century CE) are famed for including depictions of everyday places and activities, from markets to farming and cooking.

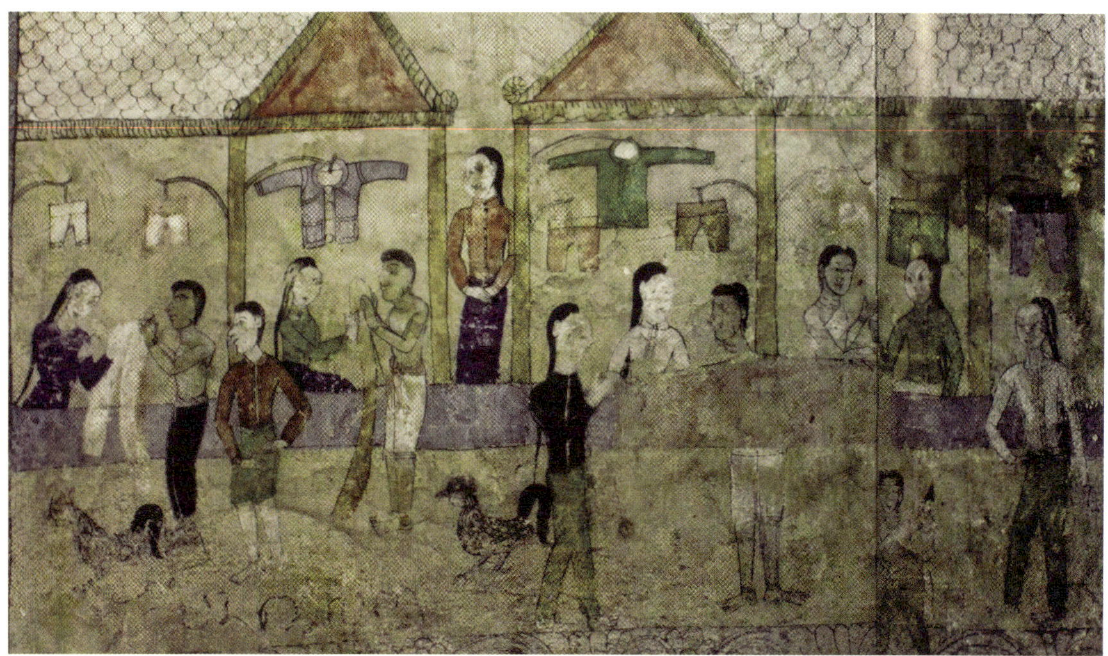

Artist unknown. Detail of Chinese merchants depicted in mural painting at Wat Photharam, Maha Sarakham, Thailand. c. early 20th century.

More recent Buddhist temple paintings also include images of the everyday alongside religious tales. Anonymously authored temple murals in the Lao-speaking region of Northeast Thailand include images of Chinese garment merchants and their customers, portrayed in a more naturalistic style than is used for depicting religious activities

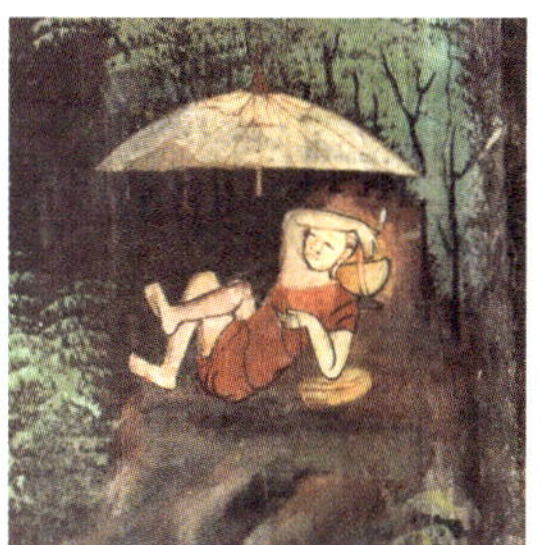

Attributed to Khrua In Khong. c. 1850s. Detail of sleeping monk in mural painting at Wat Bowonniwet, Bangkok.

and figures. In several celebrated temple murals in Bangkok, Khrua In Khong painted monks going about their daily activities, such as collecting alms and even napping, alongside canonical Buddhist scenes. This interest in the quotidian, along with his adoption of elements of European perspective and other novel compositional techniques, marks Khrua In Khong as an early example of the modern in Southeast Asian art.

Southeast Asian artists who travelled far from home during the late 19th and early 20th centuries were also drawn to depicting the quotidian, possibly inspired in part by trends among European artists at the time. <u>Realism</u> had signified an interest in showing everyday life as it was—unidealised and unspectacular—that was further extended in Impressionism, which bathed casually composed scenes of the everyday in impressions of natural light. This spirit is captured in *Rome* by U Ba Nyan, who was <u>educated</u> both in Burma and at London's Royal College of the Arts. This watercolour depicts the lively disarray of Italian street activity. Like the artist's studio portrait paintings, it denotes a fascination with the effects of natural light, ranging from subtle tonal shifts to sharp contrasts between light and dark.

From the late 20th century onward, contemporary artists in Southeast Asia have often referred to the quotidian not through depicting scenes of daily life, but instead through their use of everyday materials in sculptures, installations, and performances.

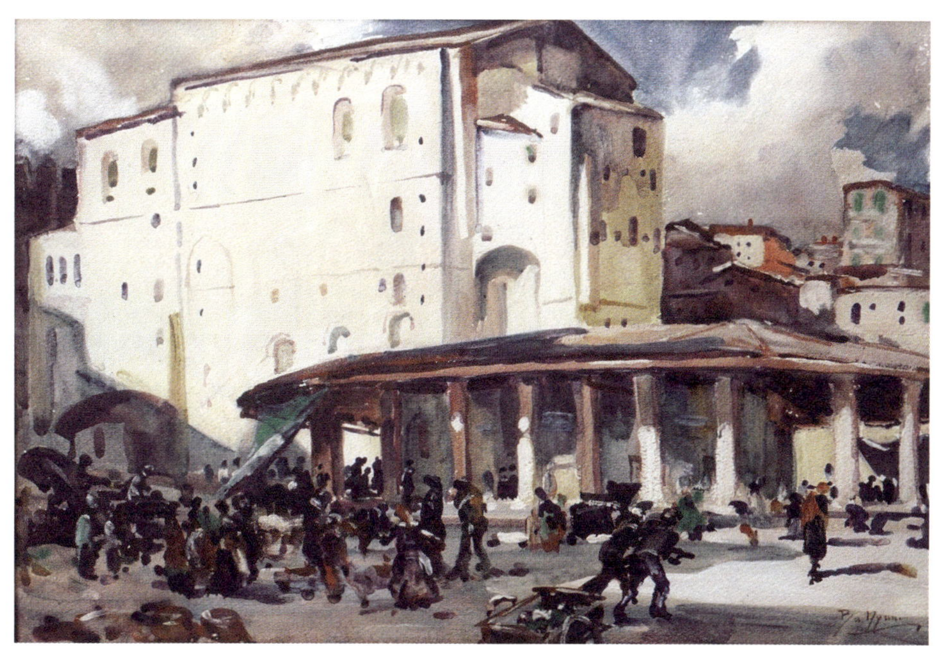

U Ba Nyan. *Rome*. c. 1927. Watercolour on paper, 33 x 49 cm. Private collection.

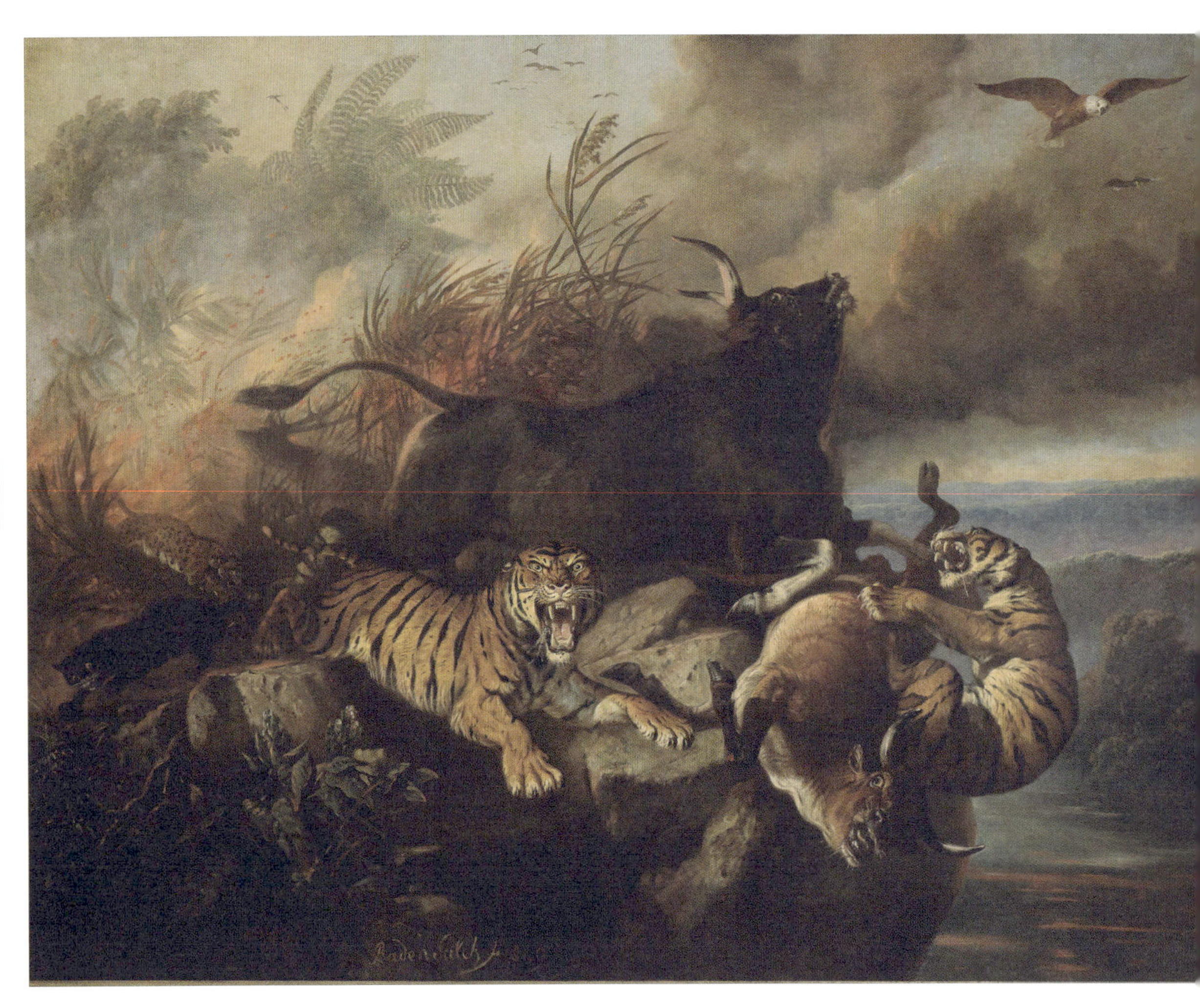

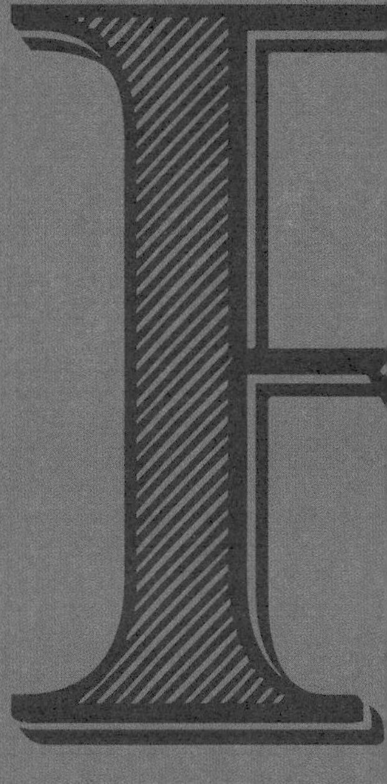

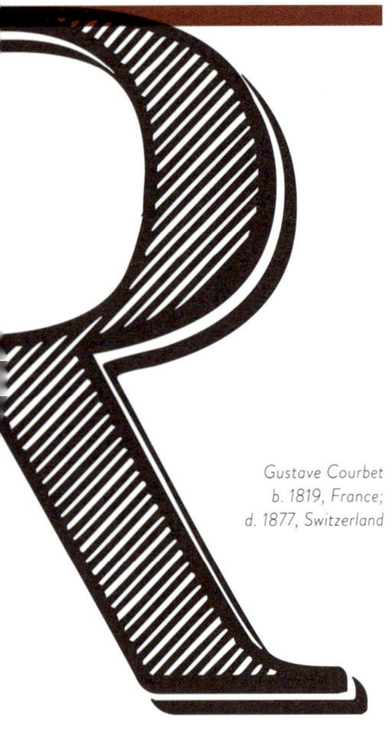

REALISM

In discussions of the modern art of Southeast Asia (as of many other parts of Asia), realism is a term with an extraordinarily broad range of meanings. It is usually understood to refer to any kind of representation in art in which a person, place or object is depicted in a way that is true to life. There have been many different approaches to realism, and it has taken on a variety of distinct and often opposing political connotations as well.

Realism also refers to a specific artistic movement in France during the mid-19th century, in which artists like Gustave Courbet depicted quotidian (rather than historical) scenes, in naturalistic styles that departed from the stiff formality of posed portraits, rejecting the exaggerated manner of preceding artists.

The broader range of meanings attached to realism in relation to Southeast Asia may reflect the region's great internal diversity. The development of modern art in the region during the 19th century was closely linked to various kinds of realism. Through the transfer of European techniques of drawing and painting from life, especially (although not only) in the medium of oil on canvas, artists produced convincing representations of people, places and things. They did so by using illusionistic depth of space, achieved by using linear perspective in compositions, as well as precise brushstrokes, in which shapes, colours and volume are conveyed through gradual shading from light to dark, as if the depicted scene is illuminated by a single light source. The technical term for this kind of shading is chiaroscuro.

Yet it is important to note that even though this kind of painting is called realism, it is not a literal or direct representation of reality. The scenes depicted in Raden Saleh's paintings of tigers are not believable, and the episodes depicted in history paintings by Felix Hidalgo or Juan Luna are not actual events. No family would really gather in the configuration seen in Simon Flores' portraits of wealthy Philippine families. Flores was one of the most celebrated realist painters of his period who received his education in the Philippines, and his clearly posed compositions follow the conventions of the genre of realist portraiture, allowing the artist to show off his skills in rendering fine details of fashions and architectural space, while also conveying the social class of the depicted family.

These examples show just how expansive the term "realism" is, perhaps especially in Southeast Asia—realist artists may not represent anything that might actually happen in

Gustave Courbet
b. 1819, France;
d. 1877, Switzerland

Raden Saleh
b. circa 1811, Indonesia; d. 1880, Indonesia

Felix Hidalgo
b. 1855, Philippines; d. 1913, Spain

Juan Luna
b. 1857, Philippines; d. 1899, Hong Kong

Simon Flores
(also known as Simon Flores y de la Rosa)
b. 1839, Philippines; d. 1904, Philippines

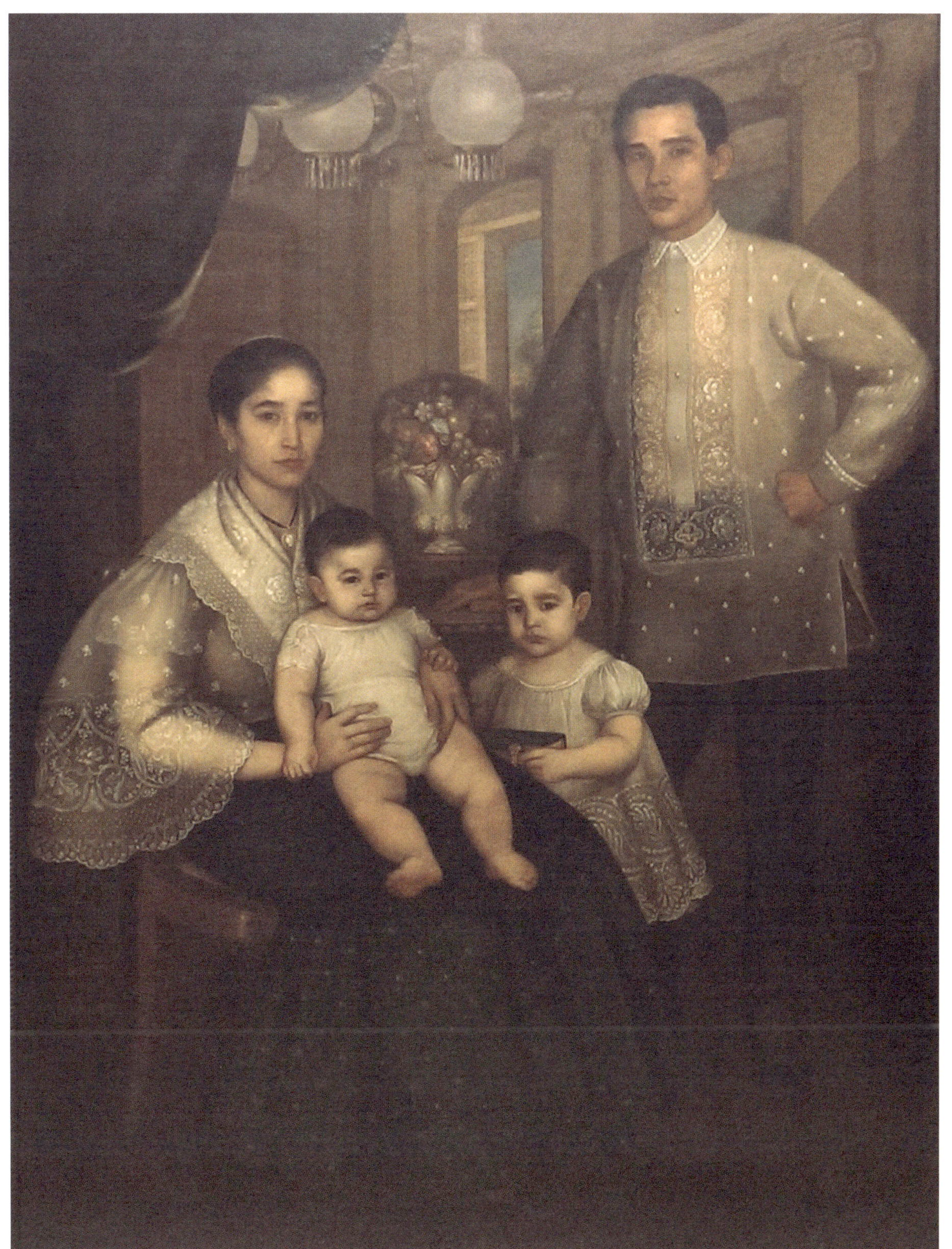

Simon Flores. *Portrait of Cirilo and Severina Quiason and Their Two Children.* c. 1880. Oil on canvas, 140 x 107 cm. Collection of Bangko Sentral ng Pilipinas.

real life, although the people, places and things they depict may be rendered in a convincing manner.

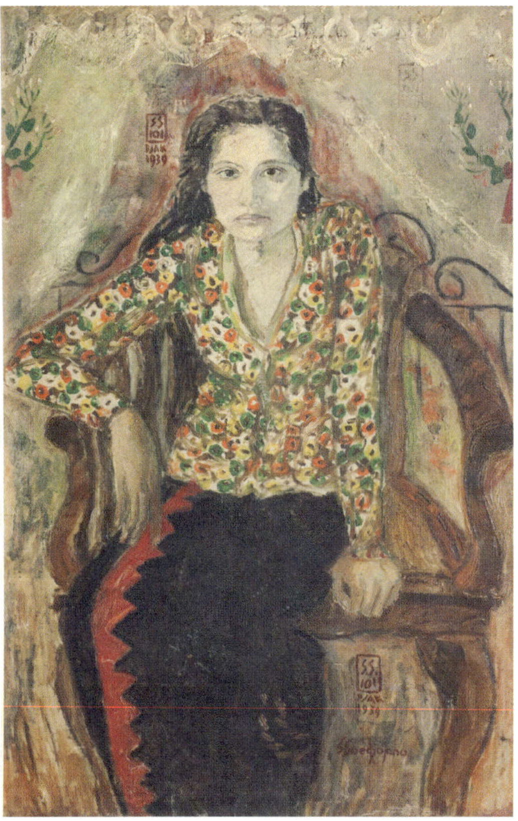

S. Sudjojono. *Di Depan Kelambu Terbuka* (Before the Open Mosquito Net). 1939. Oil on canvas, 89 x 66 cm. Koleksi Istana Presiden.

On the other hand, there are also artists who have deliberately set about painting scenes that they feel cohere more to lived reality. Realism has been championed by artists who railed against what they saw as overly embellished depictions of <u>landscapes</u>. S. Sudjojono, for example, famously wrote a <u>manifesto</u> rejecting paintings which, he charged, were overly exotic evocations of the *Mooi Indie* or "Beautiful Indies," by artists including Wakidi. Sudjojono's hyperbolic vision for realism called for "visible soul." His paintings often include unnatural compositions, semi-<u>abstract</u> brushstrokes and other marks, and other deviations from realistic representation. Yet they evoke a sense of emotional complexity which he felt was not found in the work of his predecessors.

There are other understandings of realism which depart even further from naturalistic representations. For instance, according to historian Adrian Vickers, in Bali "artists and texts talk about 'giving life' in the artistic process." Vickers explains that "'Giving life' refers in part to accuracy of representation, a Balinese sense of realism very different from that found in the West." The shading in Ida Bagus Ketut Siring's work, for example, is clearly not a naturalistic chiaroscuro. But might it constitute another kind of realism, representing not just physical forms but also <u>spiritual</u> energies?

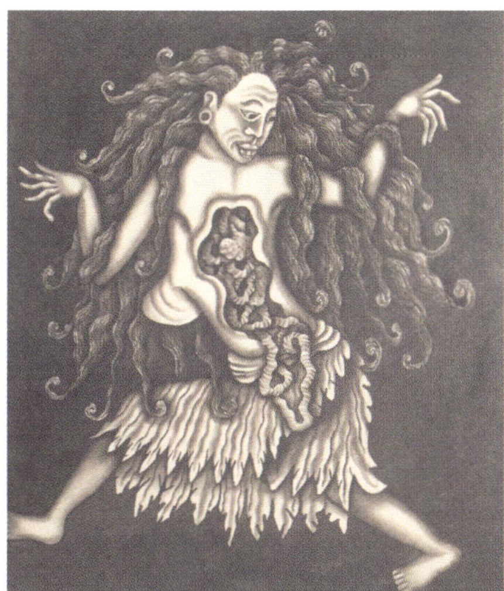

Ida Bagus Ketut Siring. *Striding Female Spirit with Entrails Exposed.* 1937. Ink on paper, 22 x 25 cm. Collection of the American Museum of Natural History.

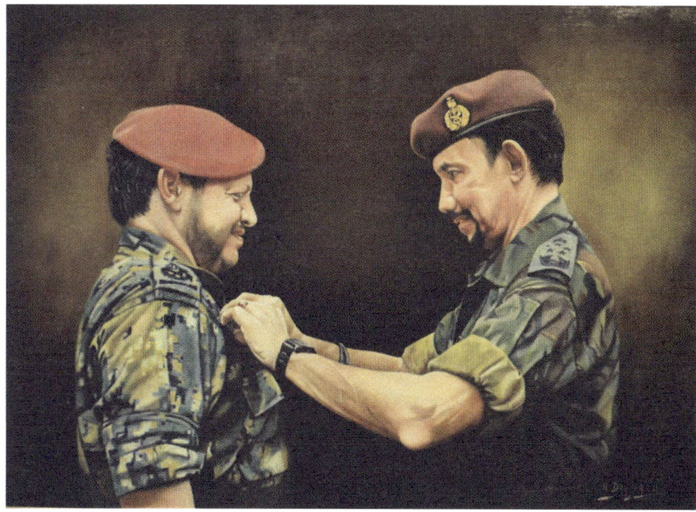

Haji Dayang Haji Mutalip. *His Majesty the Sultan and the King of Jordan.* 2013. Oil on canvas, 91 x 152 cm. Collection of His Majesty Sultan of Brunei.

In the 20th century, two of the best-known kinds of realism in Southeast Asia have been <u>social realism</u>, which refers to sympathetic depictions of hardships among working people done by left-leaning artists of various persuasions, and <u>socialist realism</u>, a more stylised kind of art, usually closely affiliated with explicitly socialist states or organisations.

Realism is less common in <u>contemporary</u> art, yet remains the preferred style for much <u>propaganda</u> and state communication, having often been closely associated with the imagining of <u>nations</u>. An award-winning portrait of the Bruneian sultan by Haji Dayang Haji Mutalip is an example of this using photo-realism, a sub-genre which reveals the links between different media.

Realism is not just seen in painting. Small bronze sculptures made in Bago (formerly Pegu), Myanmar are an example of realism appearing in objects made primarily for trade. Many of these bronze sculptures feature poses and subjects from paintings and photographs, replicated in sculptural form. This trans-medium phenomenon demonstrates realism's expansive nature and broad appeal, and also reinforces that realism is not an objective depiction of reality, but rather an artistic style and convention.

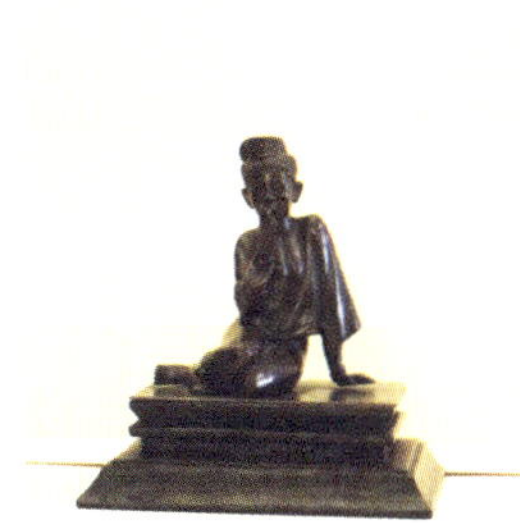

Mg Ban Wa. *Not Titled* (Sitting Lady with Cheroot). c. 1900s. Approximately 15 x 15cm. Collection de Flogny.

Raden Saleh
b. circa 1811, Indonesia; d. 1880, Indonesia

RECEPTION

When trying to understand modern art and its histories, we often focus on how artists make artworks, or perhaps on how patrons and exhibitions help facilitate that production. Yet considering how artworks are received by various publics is also fascinating and revealing.

Three important ways of studying reception can be seen through examples from the oeuvre of Raden Saleh, one of the first Southeast Asian artists regarded as modern.

Perhaps the most intimate and difficult to articulate way of studying reception considers the encounter between viewer and artwork. A viewer's gaze at and bodily relationship with an artwork helps to animate and complicate it. Raden Saleh's *Forest Fire*, his largest painting, dwarfs its viewers: it is three metres tall and almost four metres wide. Moreover, the scene it depicts—tigers and other wild animals being driven from a cliff face by a raging inferno—is exceedingly remote from the lived experience of almost all its viewers. Yet despite these distancing devices, the artist also brings the viewer into a disarmingly close encounter with the

image. The largest tiger, also the one depicted closest to us, confronts us with a direct look, and compellingly draws our gaze. Its carefully painted eyes are placed below the mid-point of the canvas, perhaps intended to be at the eye level of most viewers. These and other compositional strategies allow us to appreciate the painting not only from afar, as a grand object signifying the skill of its maker and the prestige of its possessor, but also at close range. When near to the image, we might be frightened by its details at the same time as we are drawn into its spatial field. This phenomenological or embodied perceptual experience creates the possibility for the viewer to feel empathy with the tigers fleeing the fire.

A second way of studying reception, which is grounded in historical rather than perceptual or phenomenological research, investigates how understandings of artworks have varied, often quite dramatically, according to differing social, political and cultural contexts and interpretations. An example is the debate over Raden Saleh's *The Arrest of Prince Diponegoro*, which depicts the 1830 capture of a symbolically important Javanese prince by a Dutch general, an event that heralded the end of the anti-Dutch Java War. Some art historians, notably Werner Kraus, have acclaimed the painting an anticolonial statement that depicts an historical event from the perspective of the colonised. Yet other analyses have emphasised Raden Saleh's closeness to Dutch authorities, and suggested the painting might even have been commissioned by them. (Raden Saleh had been presented with a royal award by Dutch King Willem II in 1844, among several other elite honours, and was named King's Painter by Willem III in 1851. In total, he spent more than two decades in Europe.) S. Sudjojono—an artist widely seen as foundational to new kinds of modern art in Indonesia, including <u>realism</u>— sharply criticised Raden Saleh's conciliatory relationship with the colonisers. Yet Sudjojono also celebrated Raden Saleh's important influence on Indonesian modern artists.

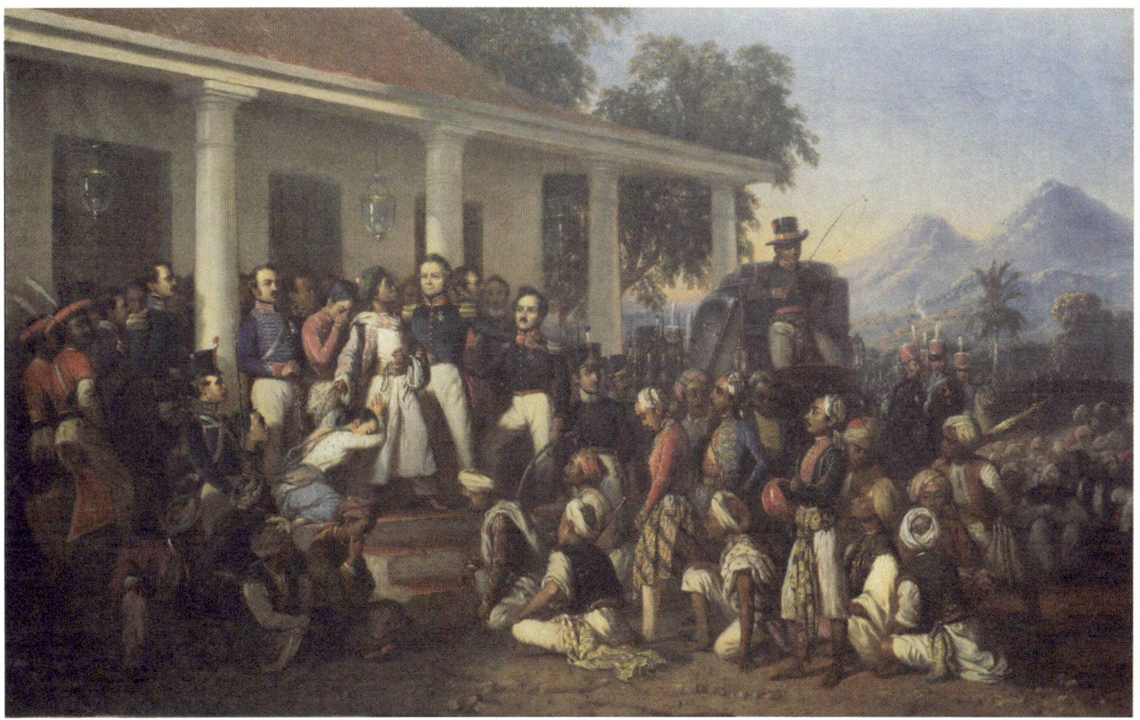

Raden Saleh. *Penangkapan Pangeran Diponegoro* (The Arrest of Prince Diponegoro). 1857. Oil on canvas, 112 x 179 cm. Koleksi Istana Presiden.

A third approach to reception focuses on how artworks have been mediated, and how this might shape people's understandings. Raden Saleh has been hailed as the "father" of Indonesian art since at least the 1940s, when Sudjojono praised him lavishly. Thus, many will see his work with that preconception already in mind, and might be less inclined to form their own critical assessments of its <u>value</u>. Also, many people will only see Raden Saleh's works through reproductions in books (and now online), at small scale and sometimes in poor quality or without colour. One consequence of studying artworks through reproductions can be to focus on composition and iconography, rather than on elements of scale, colour, or brushwork which can only be seen in person.

RETROSPECTIVE

Some terms have taken on specific meanings in specialised art discourse, while also being commonly used in general discussion. In everyday usage, "retrospective" is an adjective meaning to look back on the past. Yet in art contexts, a "retrospective" is an <u>exhibition</u> surveying an <u>artist's</u> <u>oeuvre</u>, usually from its early beginnings, and typically demonstrating its development over time.

Retrospectives tend to secure an artist's reputation and position in the <u>canon</u>. This kind of exhibition has emerged relatively recently in Southeast Asia. For example, the <u>reception</u> of Raden Saleh as "father" of Indonesian modern art has been prominent since at least the 1940s, but the first retrospective of Raden Saleh's work was not held until 2012.

A retrospective necessarily involves some degree of looking back in time, but many retrospective exhibitions of Southeast Asian modern artists have been held while the artist is still alive, and still making artwork. This limits the possibility for critical assessments based on hindsight and introduces other complicating factors, such as desires for financial or other forms of profit and <u>value</u>. Some large-scale retrospective exhibitions organised by museums and other non-profit institutions have been accompanied by smaller coinciding exhibitions, organised by commercial galleries, showing works that are comparable or contemporaneous to those displayed in the retrospective exhibition, yet are available for purchase. Increasingly common internationally, this practice may be especially prevalent in some parts of Southeast Asia.

Two of the earliest book-length studies to deal with modern art in Southeast Asia—Marco Hsu's *A Brief History of Malayan Art* (1963, in Chinese) and Claire Holt's *Art in Indonesia: Continuities and Change* (1967, in English)—both also discussed artists who were still living and working at the time of writing. This has since become standard, with many texts on Southeast Asia's modern art history including consideration of recent works by artists who were the authors' peers, alongside discussion about artworks from earlier periods, made by artists no longer living. As a result, retrospective art history—writing which looks back on the past—has been consistently intermixed with more speculative accounts of present-day developments.

This enfolding of the retrospective with the recent in many historical and exhibitionary accounts of Southeast Asian modern art has been accepted as the norm in this region, but has previously been considered unusual or even inadvisable in other parts of the world. In the 1960s, American art historian Rosalind E. Krauss elected to write her doctoral dissertation on the work of David Smith, an American sculptor. This would have been the first doctoral study of a living artist completed in any American university, had the artist not died just before Krauss began work. As art historian Richard Meyer later quipped, "Smith's art could at last be scrutinized, interpreted… but only, and almost literally, over his dead body." This anecdote suggests that the approach of Hsu, Holt, and other early historians of Southeast Asian modern art were quite at odds with their counterparts elsewhere.

Much has changed in recent decades. According to art historian Terry Smith, most applicants to graduate schools in some parts of the world now intend to specialise in contemporary art, usually by living artists. Smith notes that many scholars are still grappling with questions about how to approach contemporary art historically, and what might become of notions like critical distance and scholarly objectivity, given the collapsing of the temporal distance between the making of an artwork and its appearance in an art historical account.

The prevalence in Southeast Asia of retrospective exhibitions of work by living artists, and of historical accounts of modern art which combine hindsight with recent observations, may be linked to a sense that modernity in this region is not only located in a <u>time</u> past, but also continues to unfold.

RUINS

A ruin is a relic from a past which is no more. Ruins—and artistic depictions of them—therefore often evince intense emotional responses, from melancholy to awe.

Ruins have taken on a range of symbolic meanings in Southeast Asian modern art. Many colonial artists during the 19th and early 20th centuries saw the region's ancient temples as ruins, and thus as indexes of the passage of <u>time</u>. They wrongly perceived the decline and decay of Southeast Asian civilisations. By contrast, many artists dealing with the effects of <u>war</u> during the mid and late 20th century depicted ruined buildings and cities as symbols of the enemy's brutality, the violence and wasteful destruction of battle, and the rapid transformation of <u>urban</u> and rural <u>landscapes</u> by modern, technologically enhanced warfare.

A drawing by Dutch draughtsperson H.C. Cornelius epitomises colonial attitudes to ruins. The drawing depicts the 1807 survey of Candi Sewu temple (8th century CE), near Prambanan, central Java. Europeans formally dressed in <u>fashions</u> of their day—conveying their assumed authority—

direct Javanese workers who conduct menial labours, indicating that Europeans believed that only they could properly survey the temple, and that the role of the Javanese was to serve them. The temple appears overgrown with vegetation, its overall shape rhyming with the volcanic mountain behind it, which the artist has carefully included in the composition, emphasising the temple's age and dilapidation.

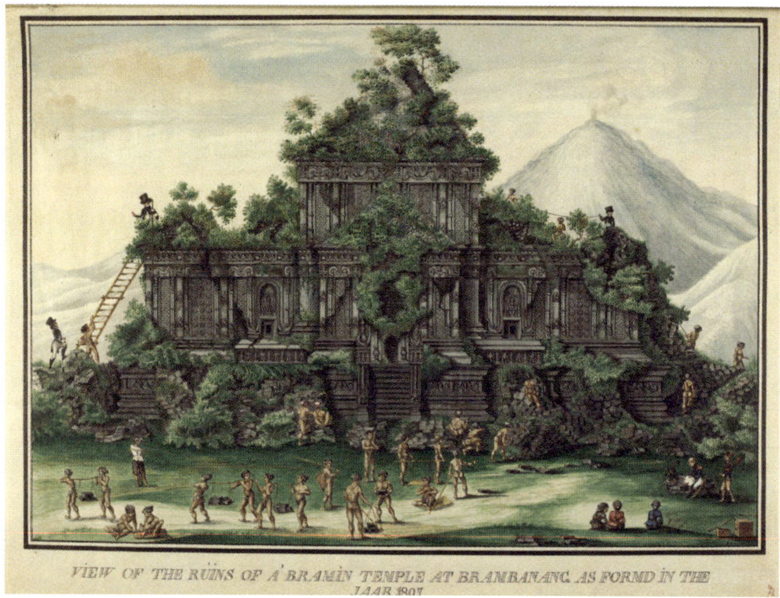

H.C. Cornelius. *The Cleaning of Candi Sewu, Prambanan, Central Java.* 1807. Watercolour, pencil, pen and ink on paper, 35 x 47 cm. Collection of British Library.

At the time that Cornelius and his peers travelled to Java, many European scholars believed that "artistic endeavour might effectively function as a barometer of civilisation, shedding light on the broader socio-political condition of a people rather than merely providing an indication of their aesthetic tastes," according to art historian Sarah Tiffin, who also discusses Cornelius' drawing. Therefore, Europeans were impressed by the ancient people who had built the temples, but many had little respect for the modern-day Southeast Asians who they thought had allowed these temples to fall into disrepair. George Groslier, an artist and writer who helped to establish formal art education in Cambodia, believed Khmer dancers to be "the sole, fragile vestige of [the] country's glorious past" along with "the immense ruins whence she came." Groslier regarded other art forms as in "turmoil" and "decline," requiring "rescue" through formalisation of schooling, and establishment of a museum in Phnom Penh.

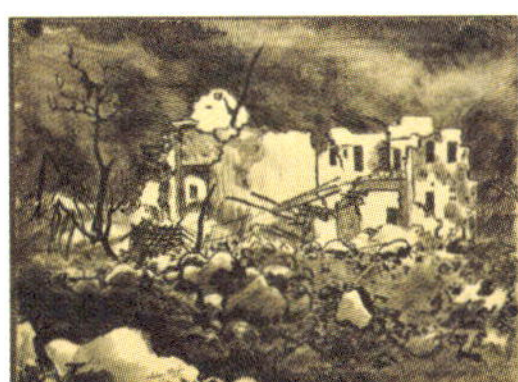

Phan Ke An. *Kham Tien Street, Hanoi— The Cruelty of the American Invaders, Night of 26.12.72 (Christmas Bombings)*. 1972. Black ink on paper mounted on the back of front hard cover of artist's sketch book, 29.5 x 40 cm. Collection of Ambassador Dato' N. Parameswaran.

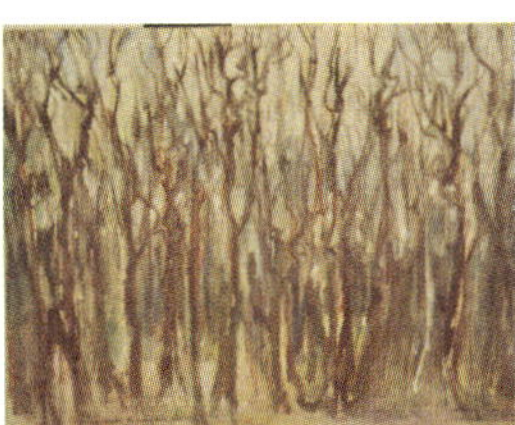

Huynh Phuong Dong. *The Forest Was Damaged by the Chemicals of Americans, Tiem Quong, 15/7/64*. 1964. Mixed media on paper, 18.8 x 24 cm. Collection of Ambassador Dato' N. Parameswaran.

Southeast Asian artists later turned the trope of ruins back on their colonial oppressors. War artists in Vietnam including Phan Ke An lamented the devastation of Vietnamese cities by American bombing, while Huynh Phuong Dong captured the ruination of forests by American chemical warfare. In Indonesia, the optimism of the revolutionary movement for independence was tempered by mass violence between 1965 and 1966, which has been described as <u>genocide</u>. With this in mind, S. Sudjojono's *Seko, Prambanan* (The Guard, Prambanan) seems a bittersweet image of lament.

In English, "ruin" can refer to any kind of complete destruction, including financial loss or reputational dishonour. The etymological root of the English term, however, is in literal collapse or falling down. This helps to explain the pregnant symbolic potential of apparently "ruined" structures to ignite the imagination.

More research needs to be done, however, on the conceptualisation of ruins in Southeast Asia's <u>vernacular</u> languages, many of which have no equivalent term. We know that Cambodians and Javanese did not perceive the temples of Angkor or Borobudur as ruins, like many 19th- and early 20th-century Europeans did, because they saw that these temples had remained in use as sites of <u>spiritual</u> pilgrimage and worship: they had not been neglected, as the Europeans wrongly believed. But how did the concept of ruins shift as it was translated into Southeast Asian languages, and how has this linguistic shift affected understandings of the concept among artists of this region? Given the wealth of artworks depicting ruins in Southeast Asian modern art, this would be a rich area for further study.

Phan Ke An
b. 1923, Vietnam; d. 2018, Vietnam

Huynh Phuong Dong
b. 1925, Vietnam; d. 2015, Vietnam

Sindudarsono Sudjojono
b. 1913, Indonesia; d. 1986, Indonesia

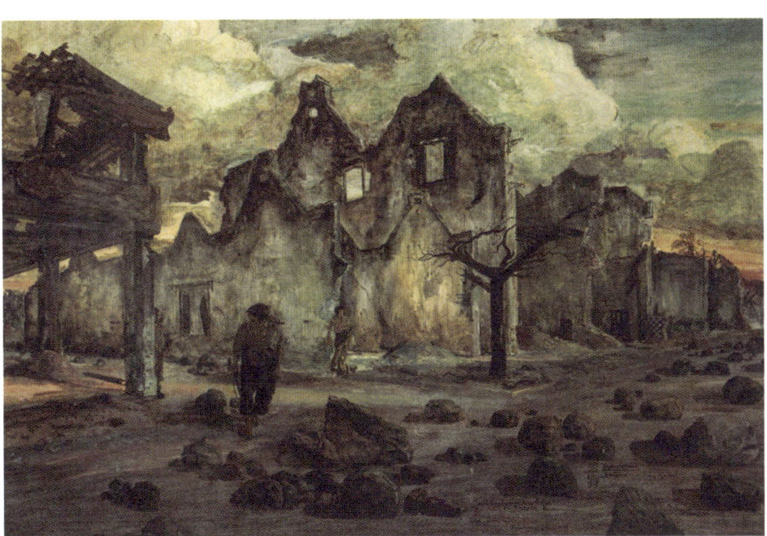

S. Sudjojono. *Seko, Prambanan* (The Guard, Prambanan). 1968. Oil on canvas, 201 x 298 cm. Collection of Museum of Fine Arts and Ceramics, Jakarta.

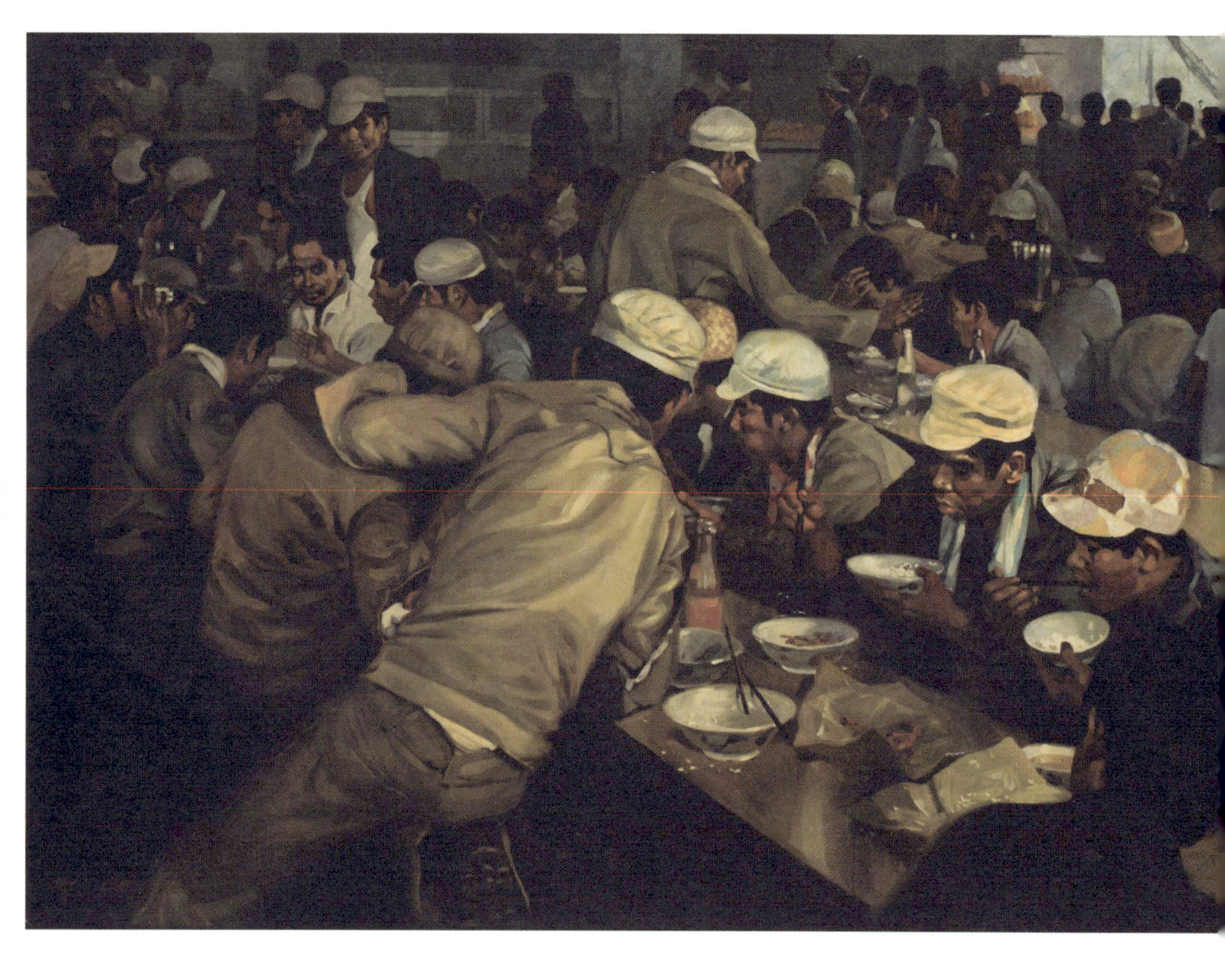

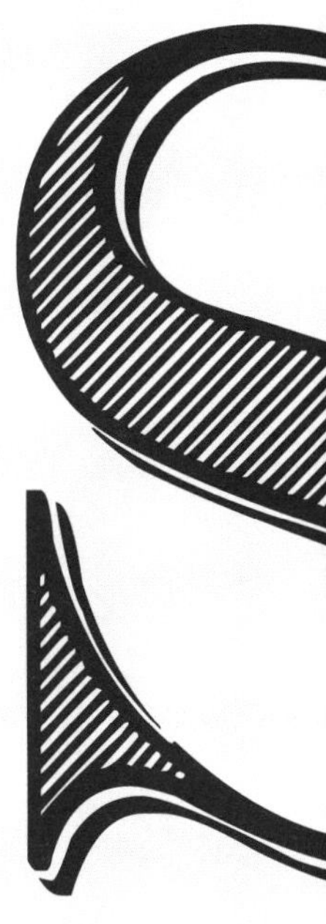

Chua Mia Tee. *Workers in a Canteen*. 1974. Oil on canvas, 92 x 120 cm. Gift of the artist. Collection of National Gallery Singapore.

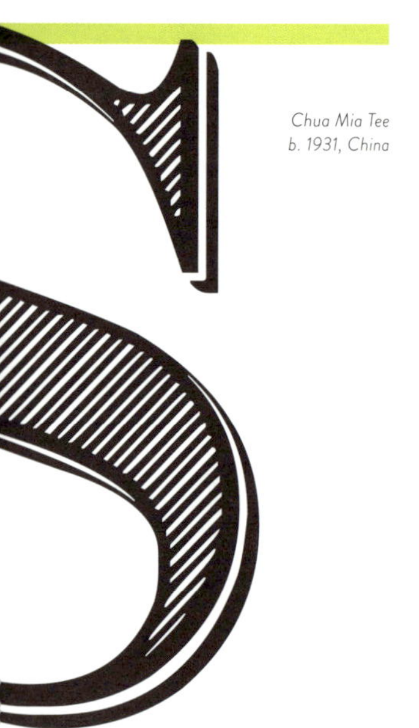

SOCIAL REALISM

"I was moved by the workers' life and plight," recalled Chua Mia Tee of his visit to a shipyard in Jurong, Singapore, where he made sketches and photographs in preparation for his painting, *Workers in a Canteen*. While optimistically championing the promise of his new <u>nation</u>, Chua also observed the desolate life of Singapore's less fortunate, engaging with social issues and underprivileged classes. He felt that "being an artist was a meaningful vocation," he later said, as "I was not merely painting sceneries."

These words, and Chua's *Workers in a Canteen*, are typical of social realism. While the style takes quite diverse forms, social realism is characterised by a desire to depict the often harsh realities of <u>quotidian</u> life for working people, especially those engaged in <u>urban</u> manual labour, like the shipyard workers in Chua's painting. His composition evokes the din of activity in the dimly lit canteen and the rough-and-ready attire and behaviour of the workers, exemplifying the gritty naturalism of Singapore social realism. Mealtimes were a popular subject matter for social realist artworks, with artists like Lai Foong Moi—one of few <u>women</u> associated with the style—often picturing the weariness of workers during brief moments of rest. An earlier painting by Lee Boon Wang—Chua's former classmate and a fellow member of the Equator Art Society, a prominent group of social realist artists—also emphasises a worker's worn and discoloured apparel, in a radical departure from the fine <u>fashions</u> often seen in formal <u>portraits</u>.

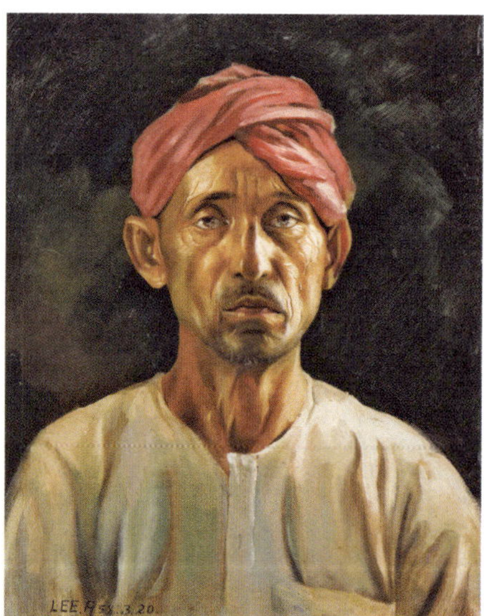

Lee Boon Wang. *Potong Pasir Dairy Farmer*. 1958. Oil on canvas, 53.3 x 43 cm. Collection of National Gallery Singapore.

Social realism differs from <u>socialist realism</u>, which also portrays working people, because socialist realist artists are usually affiliated with an explicitly socialist state or political party, and make more stylised depictions, which are often used as <u>propaganda</u>. By contrast, social realist artists occupy various broadly left-leaning political tendencies. The style was practised by artists in locations across much of Southeast Asia, especially during the years leading to and following <u>independence</u>. Social realism was especially popular in Singapore, among artists like Chua who were associated with the Equator Art Society, and slightly later in the Philippines, where artists in the Kaisahan (Solidarity) collective and other groups advocated a version of social realism which was more stylistically eclectic.

As mentioned, social realist works have manifested in different styles and forms. For example, many Equator Art Society artists—like their peers in LEKRA and elsewhere across the region—enthusiastically embraced woodcuts, inspired by the popularity of the medium among communists in China, and its easy reproducibility. *Illegal Hawking* by Koeh Sia Yong is an example of the dramatic use of contrast to evoke itinerant hawkers' struggles with economic precarity, legal crackdowns, and the <u>tropical</u> climate.

Kaisahan
Active since 1976; based Philippines

LEKRA
Lembaga Kebudayaan Rakyat
(Institute for the People's Culture)
Active 1950–1965; based Indonesia

Koeh Sia Yong
b. 1938, Singapore

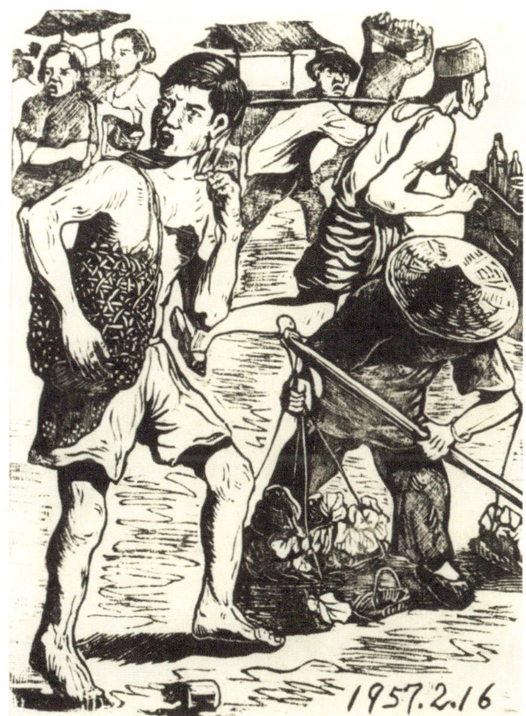

Koeh Sia Yong. *Illegal Hawking*. 1957. Woodblock print on paper, 21 x 15 cm. Collection of National Museum of Singapore.

Pablo Baen Santos
b. 1943, Philippines

Social realists in the Philippines often made greater use of symbolism in their artworks, as observed by art historians Alice Guillermo and Patrick D. Flores. *New Christ* by Pablo Baen Santos, a founding member of Kaisahan, typifies this deployment of social realist allegory. Like Chua, Lee, and other artists in Singapore, Santos renders in emphatically sympathetic detail the torn and dishevelled clothing worn by the labourer, who is the principal subject of his painting. The man's slumped posture communicates his physical exhaustion, and the generally downtrodden atmosphere of struggle is reinforced by the crowd gathered in the background. Yet Santos, like other Philippine social realists such as Antipas Delovato, not only depicts poverty and hardship, but also polemically charges that American imperialism—graphically symbolised here by the United States flag—is to blame for the woes of the Philippine working class.

Antipas Delovato
b. 1954, Philippines

Santos, like many of his peers, strove to reach audiences outside of galleries and <u>exhibitions</u>, often through publishing cartoons or painting public murals. Such actions can be said to further exemplify the belief of social realist artists, in the words of Alice Guillermo, "that art has a vital role to play in society and that it can be a catalyst for social change."

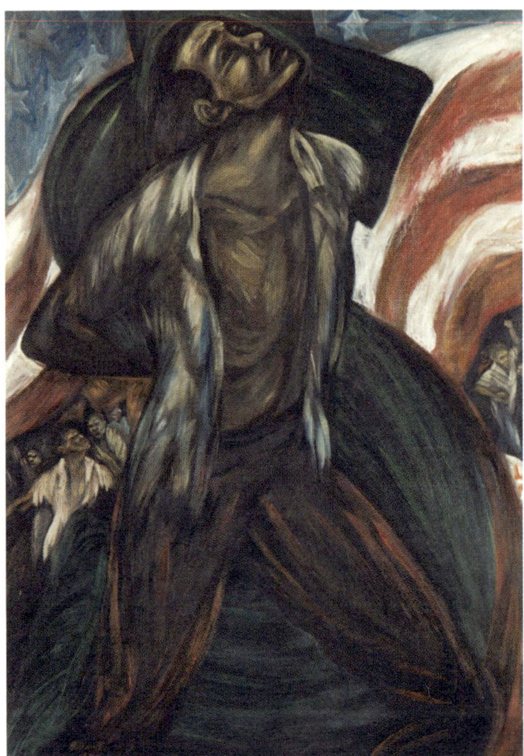

Pablo Baen Santos. *Bagong Kristo* (New Christ). 1980. Oil on canvas, 122.4 x 86.6 cm. Collection of National Gallery Singapore.

SOCIALIST REALISM

"I'm using my time to study and learn about the problems of the poor, who are so much poorer than we, who don't eat three meals a day, and who have to do heavy work as manual laborers, hiring themselves out for low wages. When they demand fair pay, and appeal for help, how could you have me standing idly by, Mother?" This impassioned plea for social action expresses the spirit of socialist realism. It is from a short story written in Thai in 1975 by Wat (Wirawat) Wanlanyangkun.

Socialist realist artworks are those that represent the conditions of the working class and peasantry, with a view to changing them, as well as soldiers and revolutionaries, to celebrate and heroise their efforts. Socialist realist artworks feature stylised and exaggerated depictions of human figures and simplified environments; these works are often reproduced as posters.

Socialist realism has the distinction of being the only style of modern art that has been officially insisted on by several states in Southeast Asia; typically socialist realist artists are members of socialist organisations or work for socialist governments, and must adhere to a range of rules about their professional activities.

Not to be confused with social realism—which encompasses a broad range of approaches to depicting social problems—socialist realism refers to a quite specific aesthetic and ideological attitude. It is explicitly political. Whereas social realist artists may have a broad range of left-leaning political inclinations, most socialist realist artists follow "party-line" socialist ideology: that is, the official and usually strictly enforced policy of a communist party, often one which was in charge of a state. Socialist realist art not only depicts social realities, but also advocates for and celebrates concrete, left-wing change. In this regard, it is a form of propaganda. In the excerpt from Wat's short story, quoted above, socialist realist qualities include direct references not only to poverty, but also to political demands and appeals. The story also deals directly with real-life topical events, thus intervening in actual political debates of its day.

Contemporaneous with Wat's story, a manifesto by the United Artists' Front of Thailand was also published in 1975, championing "art for life, art for people." They organised outdoor exhibitions along a busy and symbolically significant Bangkok avenue, displaying billboard-sized paintings. These paintings featured stylised depictions of people engaged in armed political conflict, bright colours painted in flat blocks (rather than the tonal gradations of naturalistic realism), and

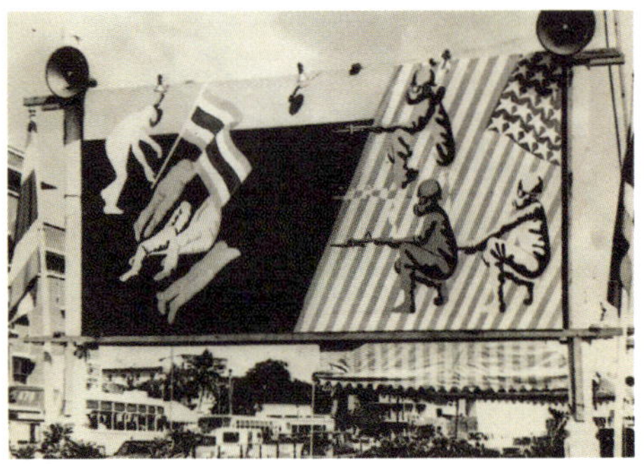

A view of the United Artists' Front of Thailand's exhibition along Rajadamnern Avenue, Bangkok, in 1973.

simplified, poster-like compositions: all hallmarks of socialist realist style.

Whereas the United Artists' Front of Thailand adopted socialist realism as a subversive strategy during a period of political upheaval, socialist realism was the official state style in North Vietnam after the revolution of 1948, and in Cambodia, Laos, and unified Vietnam after the revolutions of 1975. It had also been the official communist party style for some time before this; artists in these countries were required to adhere to its principles. Vietnamese propaganda posters are the best-known examples of this state- and party-mandated socialist realism. Some of these posters were aimed at international audiences, demonstrating <u>connections</u> within the communist bloc. Most, however, were aimed at domestic publics, demonstrating the efficacy of art as a tool for communicating ideology. Their affiliation with socialist realism is seen not only in their employment of simplified, stylised compositions, and flatly painted, bright colours, but also in their subject matter. Nguyen Tien Canh's depiction of workers against a background of industrial mechanised transport is one such example.

In Cambodia, few examples of socialist realism from during the Khmer Rouge period (1975 to 1979) survive. However, posters from the 1980s demonstrate the role of <u>artists</u> within the new socialist regime. The enforcement of socialist realism as the official state style during the 1980s was uneven, as the emphasis was on rebuilding <u>education-al</u> and other institutions, and returning to <u>traditional</u> arts, chiefly performance, after the devastation of <u>genocide</u>.

In Laos, like in Vietnam, many socialist realist artists were employed by the state. Anoulom Souvandouane de-signed banknotes, ministry logos, and the national emblem for the post-1975 socialist state, while also making neo-tra-ditional paintings which demonstrate the incorporation of Buddhism and other <u>spiritual</u> beliefs into the Laotian state's socialist ideology.

Nguyen Tien Canh
b. 1937, Vietnam

Anoulom Souvandouane
b. 1948, Laos

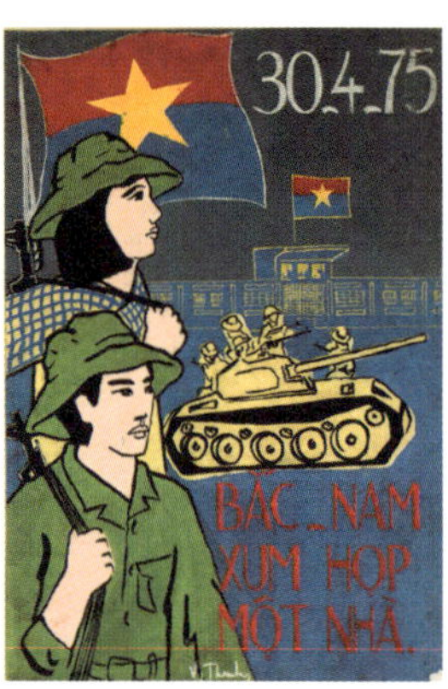

Artist unknown. *Ban Nam xum hop mot nha* (North South united as one home). c. 1975. Gouache on paper, 55 x 78.5 cm. The Dogma Collection.

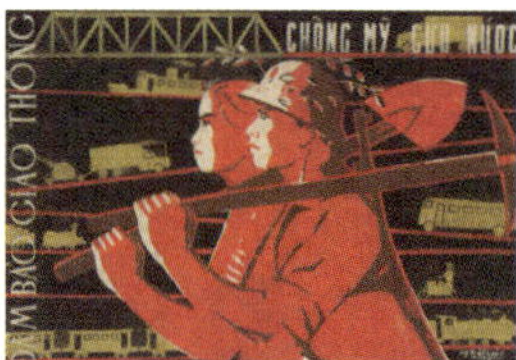

Nguyen Tien Canh. *Ensure Good Traffic to Fight Against America and Save Our Country.* 1968. Gouache on paper, 48.5 x 71.9 cm. Collection of National Gallery Singapore.

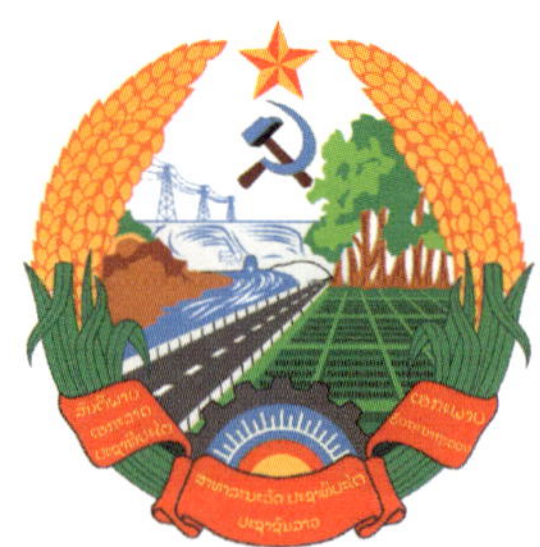

Anoulom Souvandouane. National emblem of Laos from 1975 to 1991. Designed 1975.

Nowadays, in discussions of art as in other contexts, Southeast Asia is usually understood to refer to ten countries: Brunei, Cambodia, Indonesia, Laos, Malaysia, Myanmar, Singapore, the Philippines, Thailand, and Vietnam. Yet this understanding of the region that lies south of China, east of India, and north of Australia emerged and cohered only recently. Southeast Asia as a category for thinking and analysis is not fixed or stable, but rather has shifted significantly over time. It draws in part on older names used to describe parts of the region, such as Nusantara and Suvarnabhumi, Nanyang and Nampo. These older toponyms are Javanese/Malay, Indic, Sinitic, and Japanese, respectively. While Southeast Asia is increasingly taken up as a frame for discussing art, a sense of the region as a distinct and unified whole rarely appears within artworks themselves.

The name "Southeast Asia" was first popularised during World War II, when it was adopted by Western military strategists. In the wake of that war, the region (together with its new name) received increasing outside attention, because it was a key node within the global Cold War between capitalist countries and the communist bloc. The geopolitical importance of Southeast Asia in the Cold War related chiefly to two events: the escalation of the two Indochina Wars in Vietnam, Laos and Cambodia, which raged from 1946 until 1975, and the hosting of the first mass meeting of Asian and African states in Bandung in 1955. Many of the participants in the Bandung conference were "non-aligned," meaning that they refused to take a side in the Cold War ideological divide between capitalism and communism.

These two events captured the attention of the world, including masses of people in both former colonial powers and newly independent, formerly colonised countries. Yet despite this worldwide interest in newly named Southeast Asia, inside the region most countries were preoccupied with the struggles of decolonisation and the building of new national identities. Southeast Asian modern artworks from the decades following World War II continued the pre-existing trend of articulating a vision of the nation (and implicitly, its distinctness from other countries), rarely taking up the task of picturing the region as a whole. Yet despite this, many features shared across Southeast Asia are made manifest in art. Examples include the remarkably similar depictions of landscape and tropical fruits in far-flung locations by artists without any apparent connections—an example of art reflecting the zeitgeist or spirit of the times—as well as the use

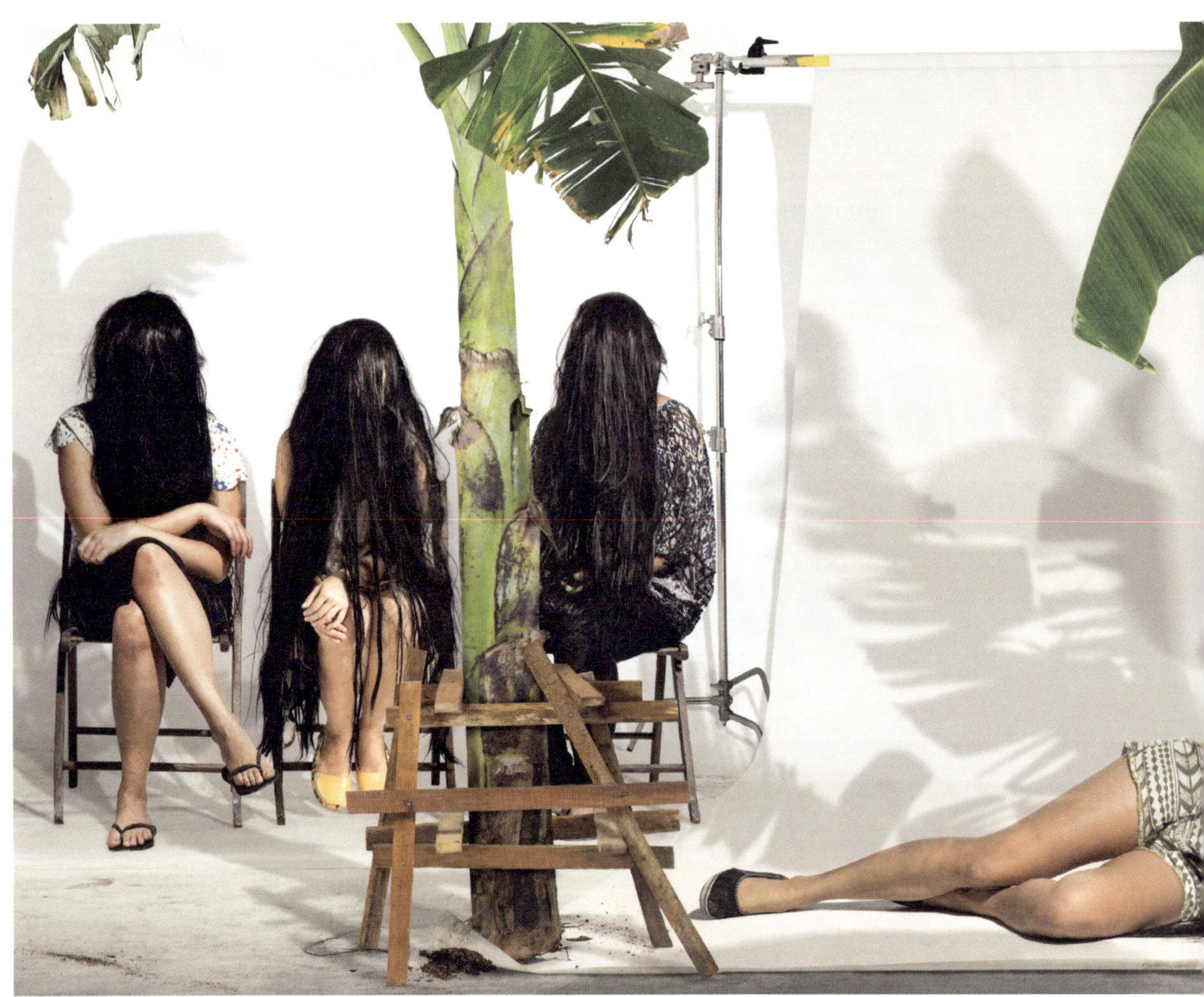

Yee I-Lann. *Like the Banana Tree at the Gate: A Leaf in the Storm*. 2016. Giclee print on Hahnemühle PhotoRag© paper, 61 x 160 cm. Collection of the artist.

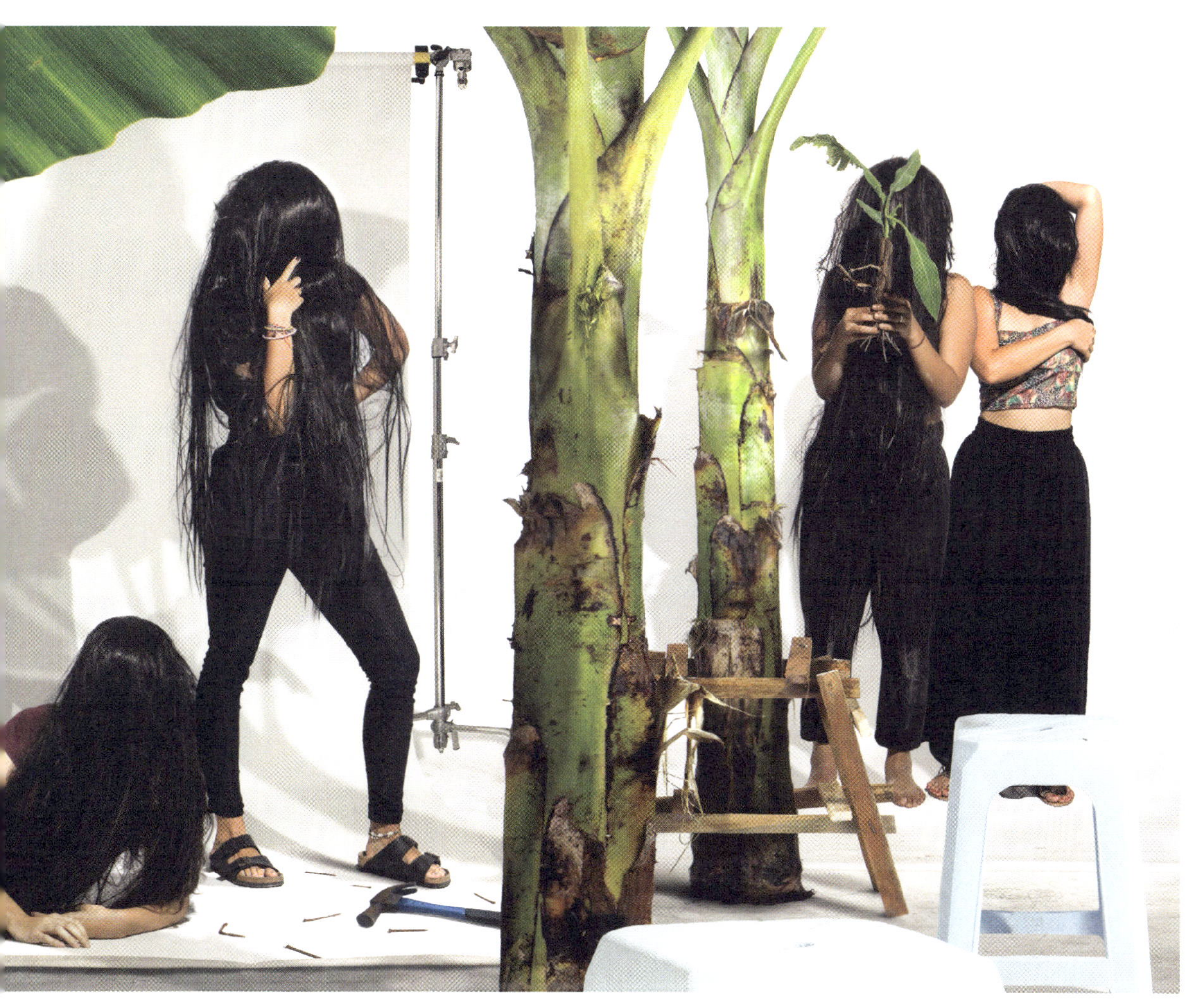

of batik and other <u>craft</u> techniques across wide terrains, and the <u>poetic</u> explorations of recurring visual forms by artists like Latiff Mohidin.

The territory encompassed by Southeast Asia has been contested, too, with some <u>exhibitions</u> and accounts including Hong Kong, Sri Lanka, and Taiwan within the region at various times. Its present borders have been defined chiefly by the Association of Southeast Asian Nations (ASEAN), an intergovernmental organisation established in 1967 with five constituent countries, gradually expanding between 1984 and 1999 to encompass its present ten member-states.

In recent years, many <u>contemporary</u> artists have been drawn to ideas, images and tropes that transcend national borders, and convey a sense of Southeast Asia as sharing elements of a common <u>history</u> and identity. An example is Yee I-Lann, whose work has explored the *pontianak*, a long-haired, vampiric ghost-<u>woman</u> believed to exist in places across Southeast Asia (Yee cites examples from <u>cinema</u>, including films made in Cambodia, Indonesia, Malaysia and Singapore). The artist also explores banana trees as symbols for the region. For Yee, the banana tree relates specifically to an episode from the history of Borneo, where she was born. According to historian Michael Dove, in the 17th century a sultan suggested that Borneans should avoid planting banana trees near their gates. Banana trees, the sultan believed, revealed the abundance of the island and its soil. Avoiding planting them in prominent positions was therefore a strategy to conceal from potential colonial invaders the great wealth of the fertile <u>tropical</u> land. Thus the banana tree, in Yee's work, represents many features shared across national borders in Southeast Asia, including <u>spiritual</u> beliefs, nature and <u>landscape</u>, encounters with colonialism, and climate.

Interestingly, both the *pontianak* and the banana tree transcend not only national borders, but also the territories encompassed by older regional terms: they can be found both in Nusantara (a term, associated with Malay cultures, that refers to the archipelagic parts of Southeast Asia) and Suvarnabhumi (an Indic term which in premodern literature referred to vast stretches of mainland or peninsular Southeast Asia).

While Southeast Asia as it is understood today is a recent invention, and one closely linked to geopolitical events, perhaps artists might begin to reimagine the region as one that belongs to its residents, and can be defined (or not) by them, rather than by their rulers, or external forces.

SPIRITUALITY

In 1994, the artist Arahmaiani, then based in Indonesia, created an artwork that caused her to receive death threats, and to flee her country in fear for her life. Titled *Etalase*, this work presented a Qu'ran and statue of the Buddha—sacred objects and symbols of spiritual devotion—in a vitrine alongside profane items including a packet of condoms, a box of soil, and a bottle of Coca-Cola. The artwork was one of several made by the artist questioning the relationship between religion and commercialism, as well as between Islam and other religions, including Buddhism, Hinduism, and Javanese animist beliefs. Arahmaiani has said that she is critical of "religious conservatives and fundamentalists [who] don't want to lose the legitimacy of their power."

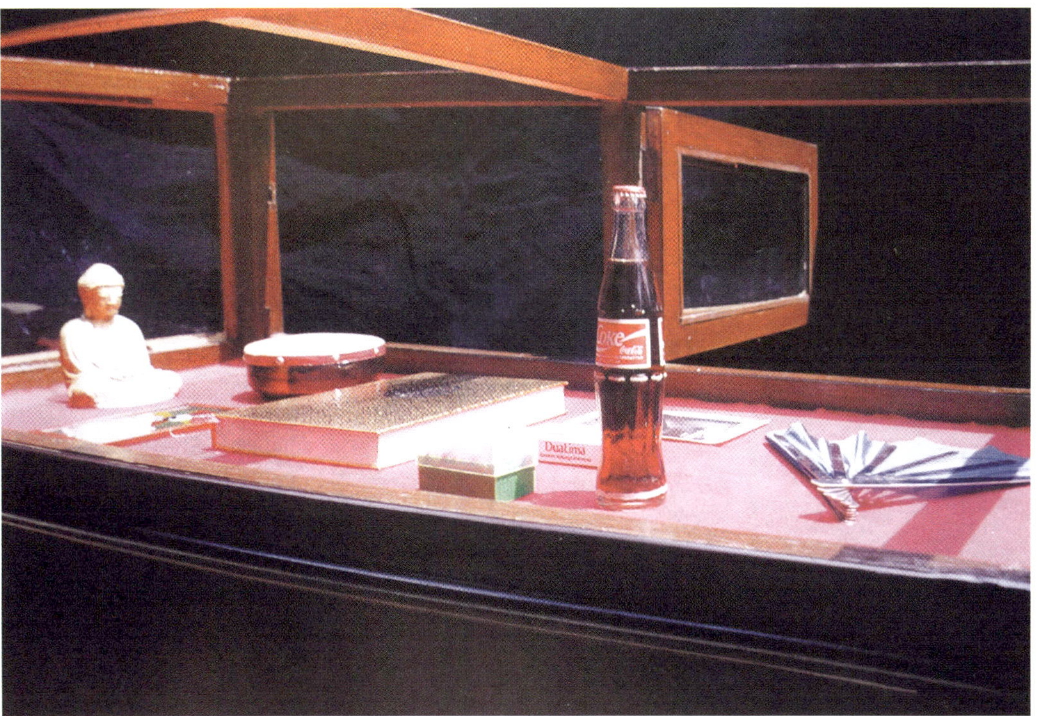

Arahmaiani. *Etalase*. 1993. Installation with found objects, 95 x 147 x 66 cm. Collection of the artist.

The violent response to Arahmaiani's work demonstrates the deep passion that spiritual beliefs can inspire. Religion and spirituality are profoundly important to many Southeast Asian people, and have played significant roles in shaping the cultures of the region. Spirituality has also been a great source of inspiration for modern art here, including to provide a purpose for art, and to locate sources for art that relate to longstanding and continuing traditions in the region.

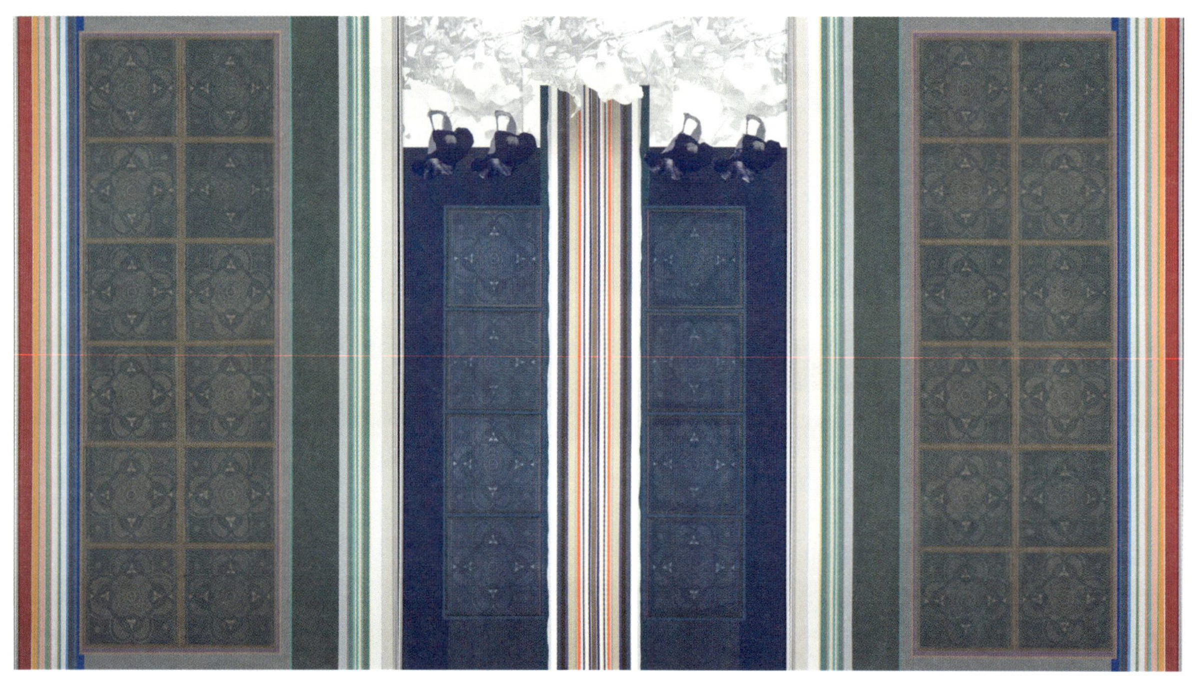

Ismail Zain. *From There to Now*. 1986. Print, collage and acrylic on canvas, 151.5 x 90.5 cm. Collection of National Gallery Singapore.

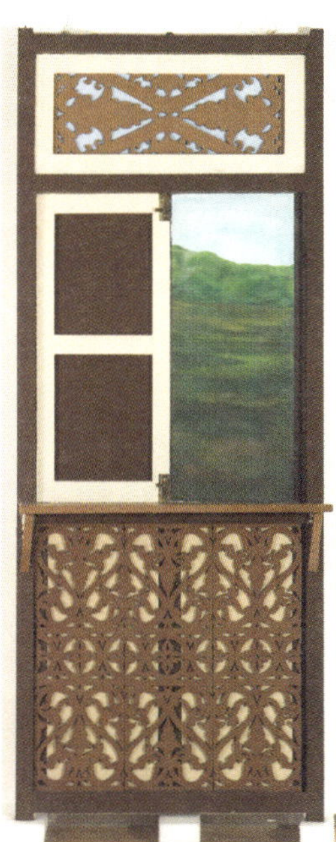

Ruzaika Omar Basaree. *Dungun Siri II.* 1978. Wood and emulsion paint, 73 x 92 cm. Collection of Muzium and Galeri Tuanku Fauziah, Universiti Sains Malaysia.

An example of spirituality providing inspiration for art can be seen in the various ways that artists respond to Islamic ornamentation and calligraphy, and the convention of avoiding representational depictions in some kinds of Islamic art. For example, Ismail Zain's seemingly decorative <u>abstract</u> artworks are deceptively complex compositions, in which repeated shapes and images taken from <u>quotidian</u> life are juxtaposed to "create a relationship in pattern and surfaces," as the artist explains. Ruzaika Omar Basaree also plays with the tension between abstraction and representation, transposing elements of traditional Malay architecture and Islamic patterning into mixed-<u>medium</u> paintings which suggest an open-ended, <u>poetic</u> sensibility. And A.D. Pirous' heavily textured paintings mimic the appearance of Arabic or Jawi script, but the cursive lines protruding from their surfaces are in fact unintelligible inventions, and thereby perhaps communicate a sense of spirituality in a more universal "language." Pirous began making works like *Epitaph IV* after visiting the United States; his combination of <u>abstraction</u> (which was promoted by American cultural <u>propaganda</u>) with Islamic spirituality demonstrates the artist's ability to create a <u>hybrid</u> synthesis of these two aesthetic modes.

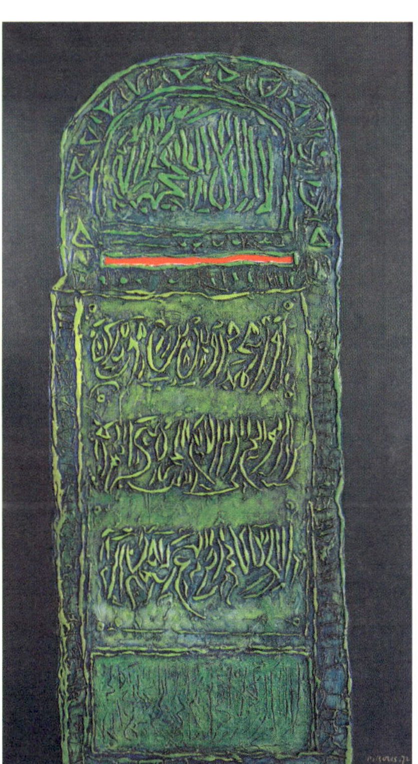

A.D. Pirous. *Epitaph IV.* 1972. Oil on canvas, 165 x 115 cm. Collection of National Gallery Singapore.

Other artists have conjured feelings of universal spiritual connection, evading association with any single religion. For example, the hyper-elongated forms of But Mochtar's *Statue of a Woman Carrying Offerings on Her Head* evoke the tribulations of existence, and the widespread use of devotional practices to ameliorate suffering. Other artists have used abstraction to explore spiritual ideas which are not easily communicated in words or representational images.

Some of the earliest Southeast Asian examples of what we may now describe as modern art are religious in nature. If part of what makes an image or object <u>modern</u> is a reappraisal of past traditions, then both the *Black Nazarene* (a sculpture made by a Mexican artist and brought to the Philippines in 1606) and the *Santo Nino de Cebu* (a sculpture made by a Flemish artist and brought to the Philippines in 1521) may perhaps qualify as modern, since despite functioning as revered objects in the usual manner, they do not follow the predominant established Western conventions for the depiction of Jesus. In these and other early Philippine religious icons, the image of Jesus is instead widely considered to resemble Filipino people, who Spanish colonial missionaries sought to convert to Catholicism. The need for artists to produce religious artworks was one key factor leading to the early <u>transfer</u> of techniques of <u>realism</u>, and the early establishment of art <u>education</u> in the Philippines.

Later, artists who rejected the predominance of Western painting styles in the Philippines used new, more local aesthetics to articulate syncretic understandings of Christianity. *Mother Nature's Bounty Harvest*, by Victorio Edades, Galo Ocampo, and Carlos "Botong" Francisco, reimagines the tree of life, which is mentioned in the Bible, as a <u>tropical</u> papaya tree, and suggests an integration of Catholic and <u>vernacular</u> beliefs. These artists, who also painted a famous mural in a <u>cinema</u> and sparked heated <u>debates</u> about modern art in the Philippines, nevertheless saw spirituality as integral to their culture and identity.

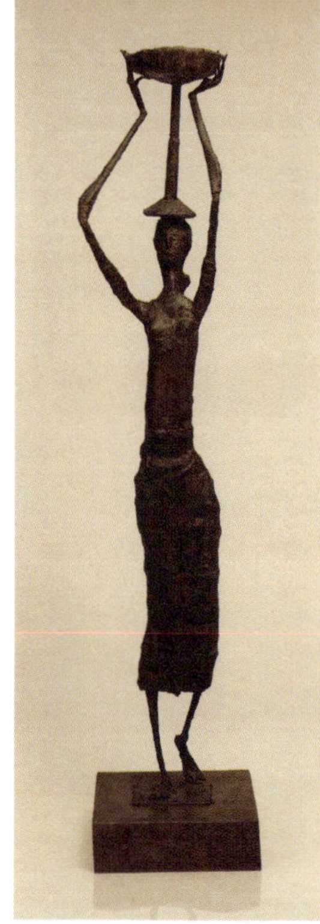

But Mochtar. *Statue of a Woman Carrying Offerings on Her Head*. 1963. Bronzed copper, zinc, tungsten, iron, 124 x 26 x 26 cm. Collection of National Gallery Singapore.

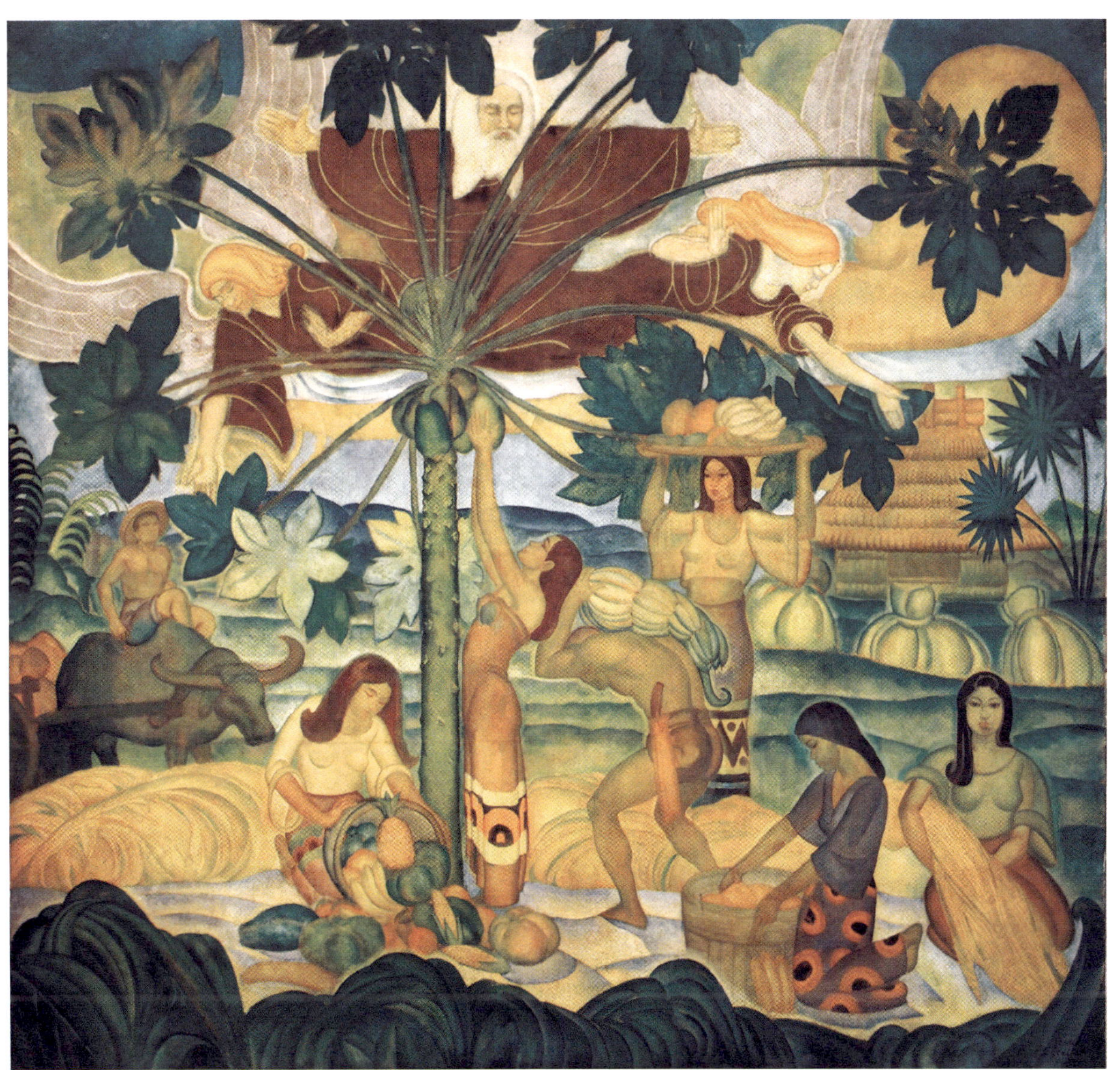

Victorio Edades, Galo Ocampo and Carlos "Botong" Francisco. *Mother Nature's Bounty Harvest*. 1935. Oil on canvas, 258 x 273 cm. Private collection.

The studio—the artist's place for contemplation and creation—has often been considered essential to being a modern <u>artist</u>. The rise of artists' studios in the 19th and especially 20th centuries was important to the emergence of the modern in Southeast Asian art, because previously, most paintings and sculptures were made in religious or royal settings. The use of studios signalled a broader shift toward secular themes and <u>patrons</u> for art.

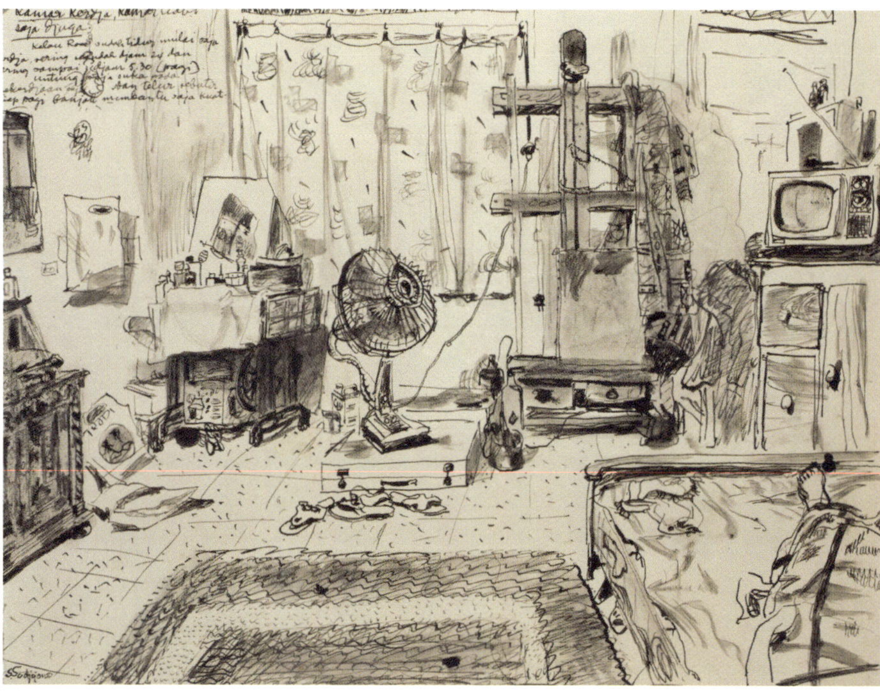

S. Sudjojono. *My Work Room Is My Bedroom Too*. 1969. Gift of Cynthia and John Koh. Collection of National Gallery Singapore.

Sometimes, the studio is a predominantly private place, one which is not only used for contemplation and creation but that also sometimes doubles as a living space. This is seen in *My Work Room Is My Bedroom Too*, from a sketchbook by S. Sudjojono. At the centre of this ink sketch is an electric fan, placed on top of a paint box. Next to it sits an easel on which an unfinished canvas rests, and some clothes are hung. A working desk faces a television. These various details emphasise the entwining of domestic and artistic functions in Sudjojono's studio. To further underscore the intimate nature of the room, a pair of shoes have been kicked off, and a bare foot is visible at the right edge of the image, resting on the bed.

In several other images from the same sketchbook, Sudjojono depicts singer Rose Pandanwangi, his second wife.

Sindudarsono Sudjojono
b. 1913, Indonesia; d. 1986, Indonesia

Rose Pandanwangi
b. 1929, Indonesia

While she is not visible in this drawing of the artist's studio, her presence there may be presumed, as the handwritten inscription notes that "when Rose goes to bed, I start working, often after midnight." This suggests also the invisible domestic and spousal labour of <u>women</u> that sustains and facilitates the work of male artists.

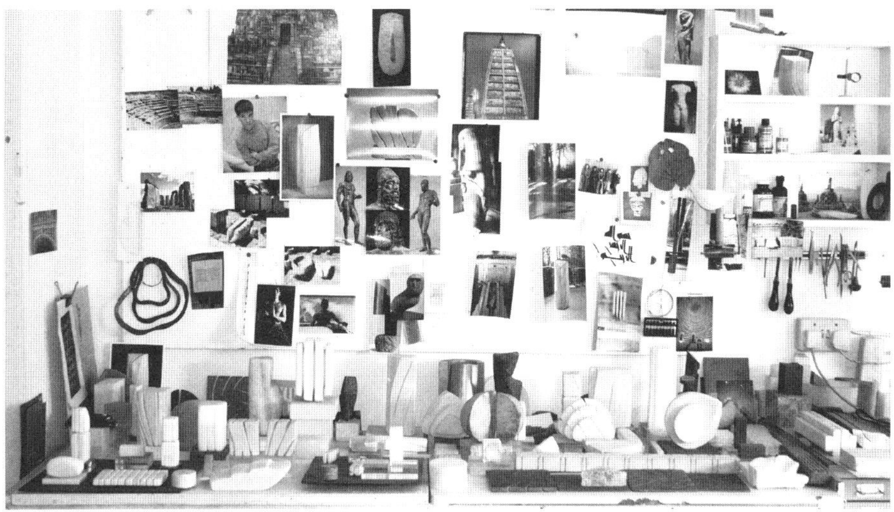

Kim Lim's studio in London, c. 1995.

While studios can be enclosed and domestic, like the one Sudjojono depicts, they are also almost always social spaces where art is made not only in isolation, but through dialogue. Many artists, like Kim Lim, display other artists' works in their studios, creating another kind of dialogue, through images and inspirations.

Some studios are more overtly social in nature, and are sites where people meet and, sometimes, collaborate. Images of Juan Luna in his Paris studio reveal it to be opulently decorated, and thus seemingly intended for the reception and entertainment of visitors. In one photograph from around 1885 to 1890, the artist poses in a <u>fashionable</u> starched collar and overcoat. Such images are quite common. A 1943 photograph shows Le Van De in his Hanoi studio, dressed in a formal suit and surrounded by several paintings, which all share the same composition. Another image from Juan Luna's Paris studio shows the artist's friend, Philippine nationalist hero and writer Jose Rizal, posed amusingly in a headdress and lying on a bed. The costume and pose is similar to that in Luna's *Cleopatra*.

From the 19th century onward, studios became popular not only for practitioners of so-called "fine arts" like painting, but also for the more popular medium of photography.

Kim Lim
b. 1936, Singapore; d. 1997, United Kingdom

Juan Luna
b. 1857, Philippines; d. 1899, Hong Kong

Le Van De
b. 1906, Vietnam; d. 1966, Vietnam

Jose Rizal
b. 1861, Philippines; d. 1896, Philippines

In photography studios, customers—who were often like <u>patron</u> and model combined—would pose against specially decorated curtains and screens which were used as the backgrounds for <u>portraits</u>. Photography studios often changed owners but continued under the same name, suggesting that their reputation derived not only from individual photographers, but from a wider constellation of factors, including their position in society.

Whether private or social in nature, an artist's studio is usually thought of as an individual space. Yet some modern artists also advocated for collective forms of studios. From the 1940s onwards, Sudjojono was an early and important proponent for the idea of communal places for groups to study and make art. Called *sanggar* in Indonesian, perhaps these were one precursor to "post-studio" artistic practices today. Many <u>contemporary</u> artists do not need a dedicated workplace, instead working with performance, video, or socially engaged practices that are more sited in various contexts.

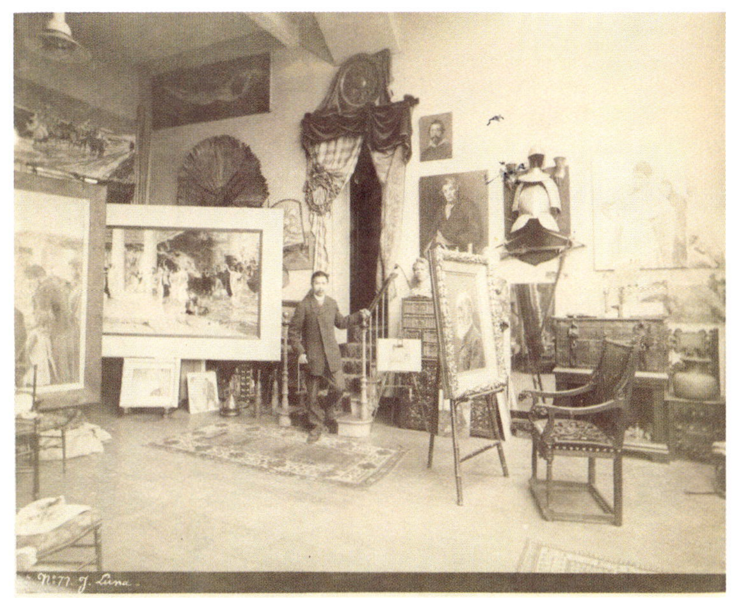

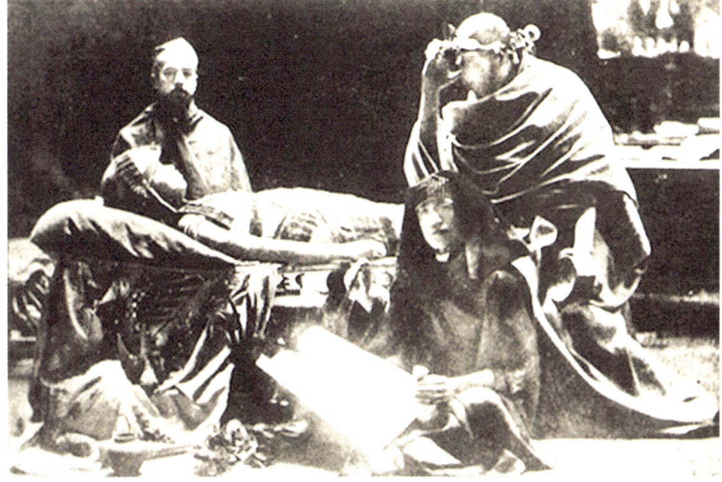

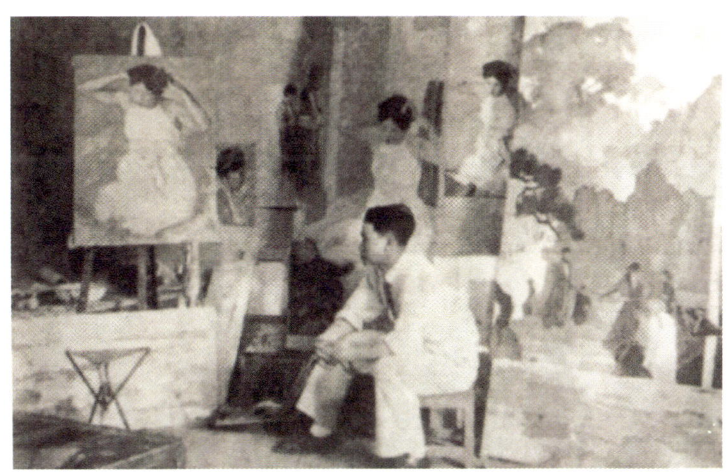

(top to bottom)

Juan Luna in his Paris studio, c. 1890.

Juan Luna recreates a tableau from *Cleopatra* in his studio with Jose Rizal and the Pardo de Tavera brothers, Paris, c. 1889.

Le Van De in his Hanoi studio, 1943.

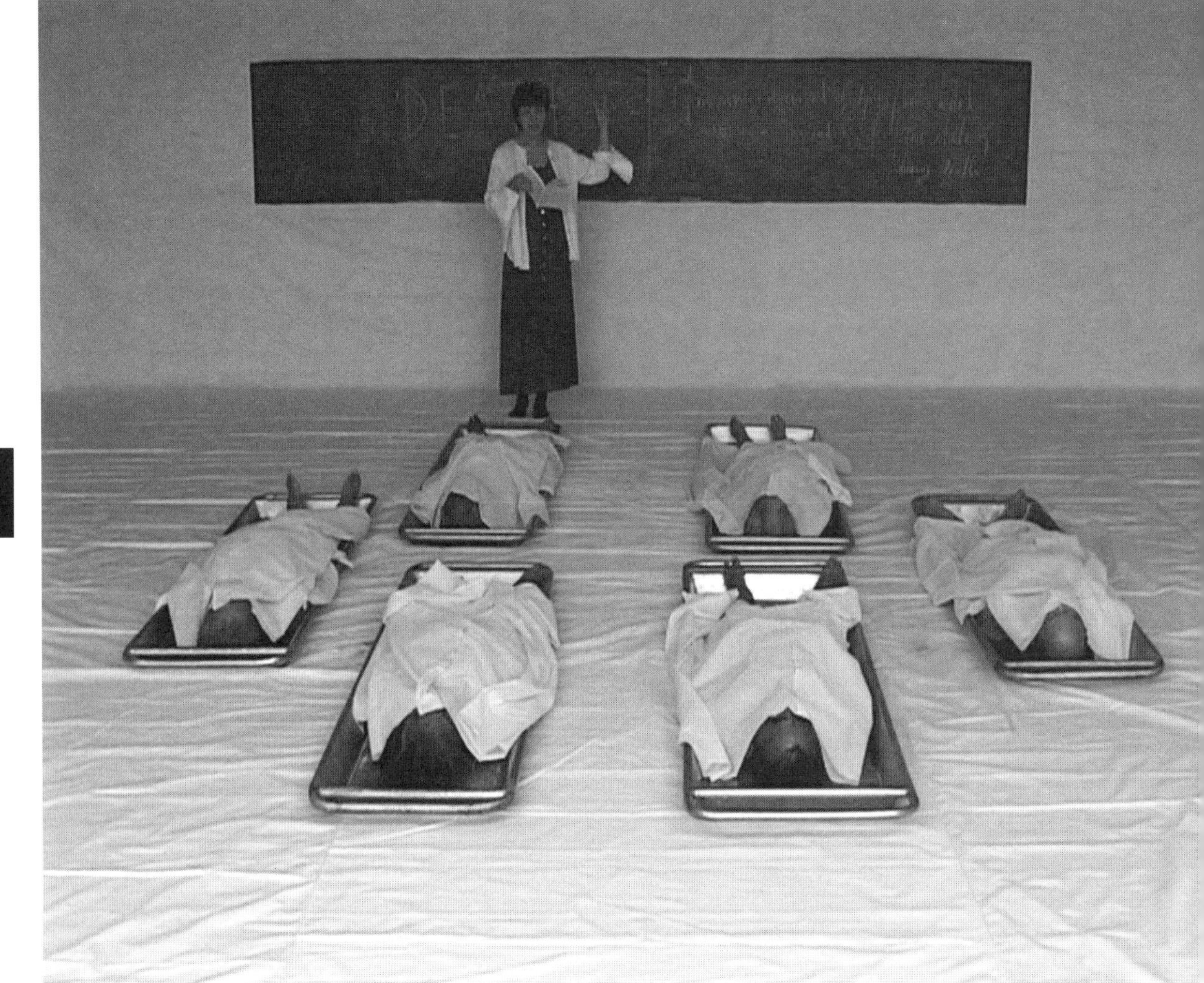

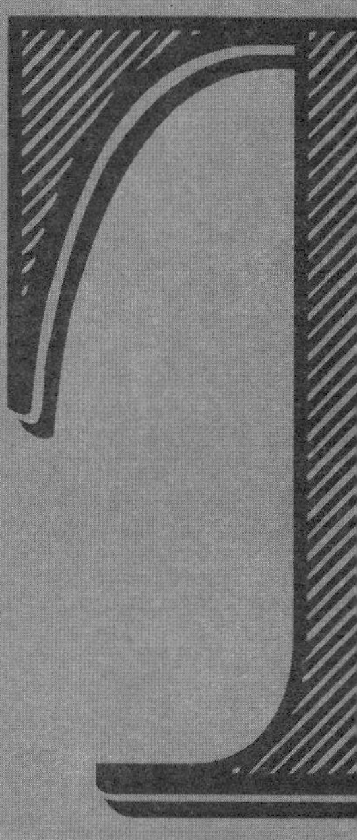

Araya Rasdjarmrearnsook. Still from *The Class*. 2005. Video, colour, sound, 16 min 30 sec.

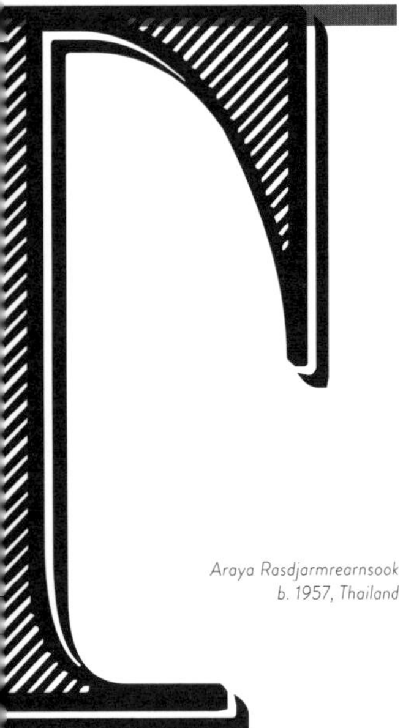

TABOO

What is taboo, or even obscene? Does reading to dead bodies or drinking one's urine count? Taboos are a fertile source of inspiration for modern art in Southeast Asia. Artists have often pushed boundaries, exploring attitudes and cultural norms about what is considered acceptable in society. Our ideas and definitions of taboos and obscenity, however, are shifting and subjective; these are not fixed or objective categories.

Taboos often centre on the human body. In most cultures and at most times, to be in the presence of dead bodies is considered taboo, except in special circumstances of grief and bereavement. Corpses are seen as unclean, and as confronting reminders of mortality. Yet there are artists who address this subject head-on. An example is Araya Rasdjarmrearnsook, whose artworks—which are <u>contemporary</u> and trans-<u>medium</u>, encompassing performance, installation, video, and text—involve her reading to or "teaching" dead bodies.

Araya plays with seemingly universal attitudes to death, while also pointing to cultural and linguistic specificities in Thailand. In her work, it is not death that is obscene, but rather aspects of how we live. "In Thailand we compare a dead person that looks poor and lonely to 'dying like a dog at the side of the road,'" Araya says, in a veiled critique of materialistic prejudices. With biting humour, she also observes, "Ghost movies have become exceedingly popular in Thailand… What I cannot understand is that at the same time that ghost movies became so popular, a very spicy kind of instant noodles became equally popular." Later, she pretends to hear a response from one of the corpses. "Ah, you say that know why it is that ghost movies and instant noodles are similarly popular where I come from? You guess that life there might be very boring. Thank you." The complaint is heightened by Araya's playfully pointed pivot from the taboo and seemingly nonsensical act of speaking to corpses, to the denigration of indecently "boring" aspects of daily life.

Nudity is another taboo that artists often deal with in their works. Early depictions of nakedness, such as U Ba Nyan's *Before*, considered the first nude in Myanmar, and Patrick Ng's *Youth Embarbed*, a rare example of a male nude, may have excited controversy when they first appeared. Records of the early <u>reception</u> of these works are scant, yet the rarity of nudes in Myanmar, and the scarcity of male nudes throughout Southeast Asia, may suggest that they were understood as at best daring, and at worst perhaps obscene. Records do show that Vincent Leow caused outrage when, in 1992, he drank his own urine in a performance, and soon afterwards, offered bottles of urine for sale as artworks. Headlines from Singapore newspapers at the time reveal the scale of the scandal: for example, "Drink Urine? Urgh! But…" and "But Is This Really Art?" Decades later in 2018, a drawing by Vincent Leow was removed from public exhibition in Singapore when it was deemed offensive.

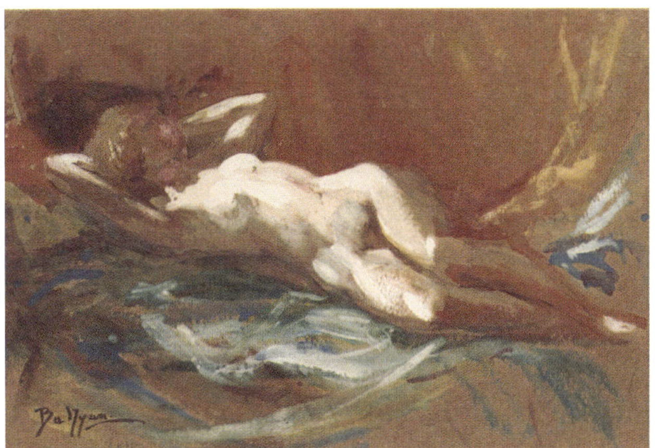

U Ba Nyan. *Before.* c. 1925–1930s. Gouache on paper, 18 x 26 cm. Collection of National Gallery Singapore.

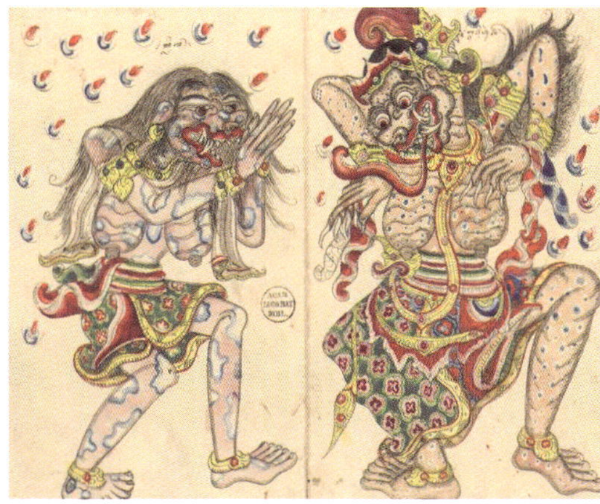

I Ketut Gede. *Klika honours Durga with a sembah.* Before 1890. Paint and ink on Dutch paper, 34 x 42 cm. Collection of Leiden University Library.

The depiction and exposure of human bodies is not the only way in which modern art can challenge taboos. I Ketut Gede's 19th-century Balinese drawings may appear to viewers today to be grotesque because of their exposed breasts, protruding tongues, and menacing poses. Yet according to historian Adrian Vickers, for viewers familiar with the Balinese *Calon Arang* story, the drawings would originally have appeared transgressive for quite another reason. According to belief, artists "who depict the power of witchcraft" take significant risks. Performers who dare to tell this story in shadow puppet theatre are believed to endanger their health and even life by challenging the "power or *sakati* of witches and warlocks in the community."

Thus, these drawings may be considered taboo to different audiences and for different reasons—viewers today may be concerned with their depiction of bodily immodesty, while their original viewers would have seen in them a dangerous provocation of <u>spiritual</u> forces. As this example demonstrates, taboos are shifting and subjective; regardless, they are a fertile source of inspiration for modern art in Southeast Asia.

I Ketut Gede
Active 19th century,
Singaraja, Bali, Indonesia

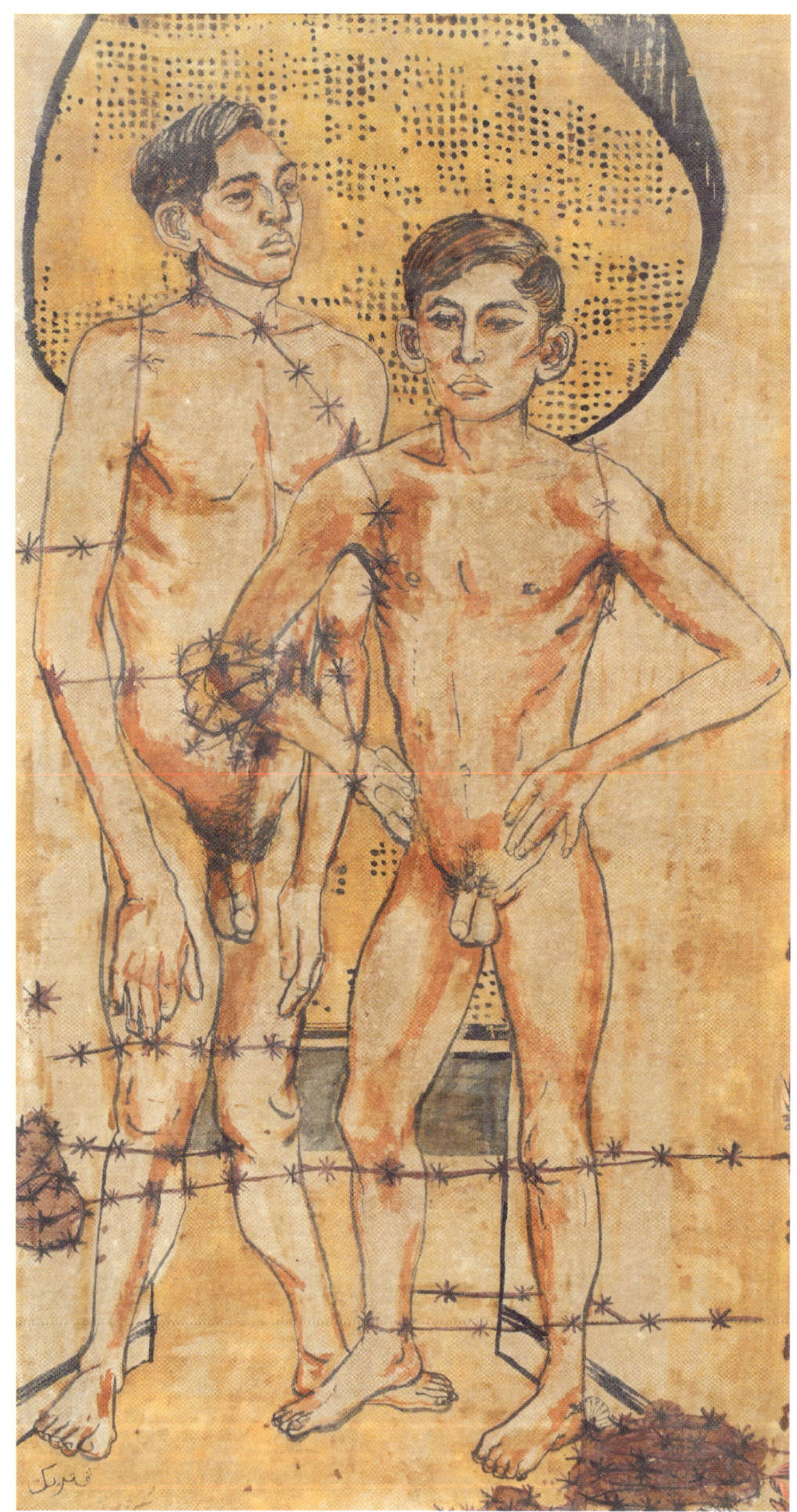

Patrick Ng. *Youth Embarbed*. 1962. Batik, 86 x 40 cm. Tuanku Fauziah Museum and Gallery, Universiti Sains Malaysia, Penang.

TIME

With today's digital technologies, we often feel that life moves faster than ever before. But this experience of time speeding up has roots in the 19th and 20th centuries, when modernities transformed people's relationships to time.

Over a century ago, art historian Ananda Coomaraswamy also sensed the world's acceleration. In 1916, he described "a world of rapid communications," in terms remarkably similar to those used today. Shortening the time for communicating or travelling between far-flung places seemed to collapse the distance between them, and <u>globalisation</u> revolutionised our temporal sensibilities, making time seem to go faster than ever before.

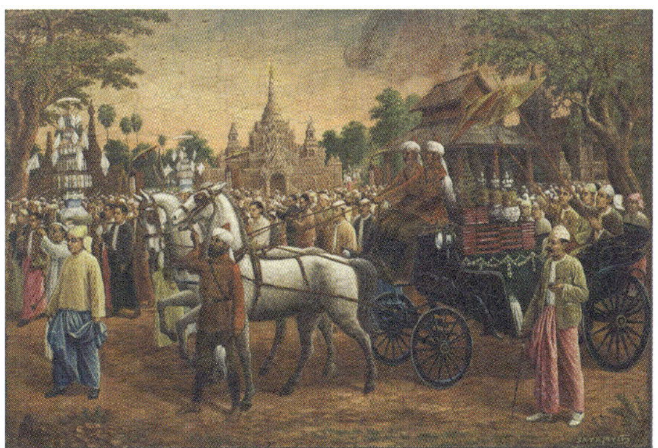

Saya Myit. *Carriage Procession (An Auspicious Charity)*. c. early 1930s. Oil on canvas attached to board, 51 x 77 cm. Collection of National Gallery Singapore.

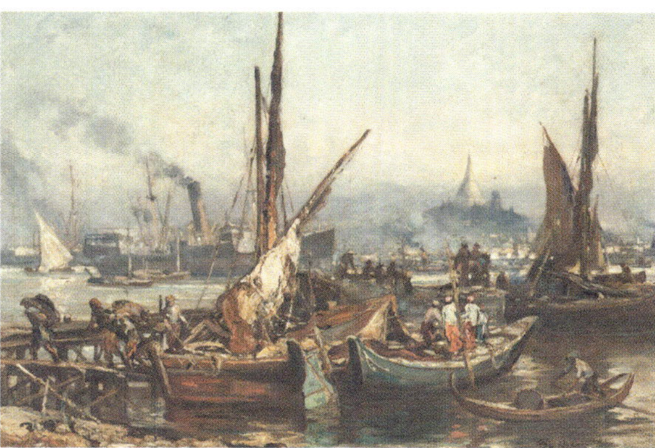

U Ba Nyan. *Rangoon Harbor*. c. 1930s. Oil on canvas, 46 x 76 cm. Collection of Mary Ann and Jimmy Chua.

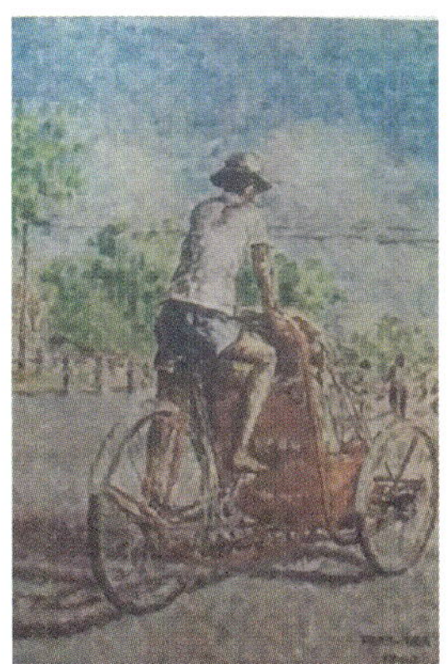

Pann Tra. *Cyclo*. 1960. Medium unknown, dimensions unknown. Location unknown, presumed lost.

Vehicles were often symbols of this process, which was further intensified by <u>urbanisation</u>. Historically new modes of transport were represented like ambassadors of the modern. This is apparent in depictions of a gleaming pedalled rickshaw in *Cyclo* by Pann Tra and a modern steamship in *Rangoon Harbor* by U Ba Nyan, its streamlined form contrasting with ramshackle old sailboats. Saya Myit made a series of paintings depicting vehicles of different kinds in procession through rapt crowds. One portrays an elegant horse-drawn carriage, while another shows a shiny new motor car.

Increases in the volume and speed of trade, travel and communication were factors that shifted experiences of time. Alongside these, modernities also heralded new ways of working and studying, and new architectures to house these activities. Two photographs by Emile Gsell, taken one year apart in Hanoi, reveal an interaction between French and Tonkinese that reflected new, distinctly modern attitudes to time.

Pann Tra
b. 1931, Cambodia; d. 2009, Cambodia

U Ba Nyan
b. 1897, Myanmar; d. 1945, Myanmar

Saya Myit
b. 1888, Myanmar; d. 1966, Myanmar

Emile Gsell
b. 1838, France; d. 1879, Vietnam

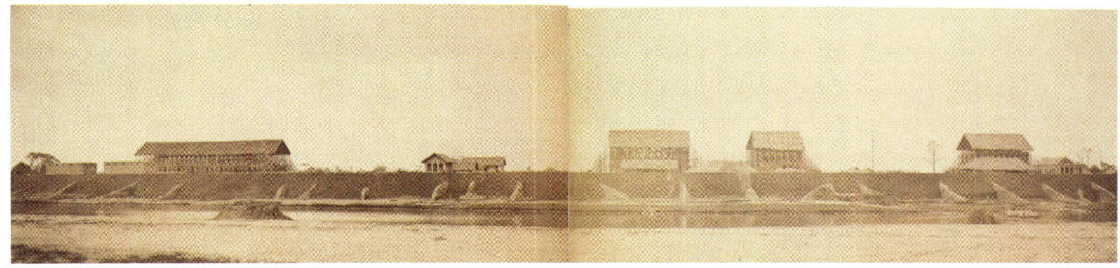

Emile Gsell, *Construction de la concession francaise en bordure du fleuve Rouge a Ha Noi* (Construction of the French Concession Along the Red River in Hanoi). late 1875. Collection Musee national des Arts asiatiques-Guimet [AP9383].

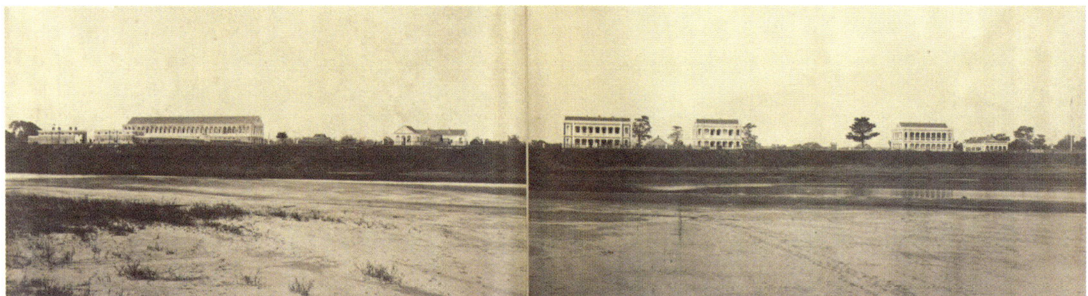

Emile Gsell. *Hanoi—Vue de la concession francaise au Tongking* (The French Concession Along the Red River in Hanoi). Late 1876. Universite Cote d'Azur. BU Lettres Arts Sciences Humaines. Fonds ASEMI. PH03-2-5. (CC-BY)

One photograph, taken in 1875, shows a group of buildings being constructed, including large colonial offices which regularised working hours. The architecture appears recognisably European, yet the building techniques are Southeast Asian, as seen in the use of thatched palm roofing and bamboo scaffolding. These construction methods were "old," yet the designs were "new": these were the first European-style stone buildings erected in Tonkin.

A year later, another photograph taken from precisely the same vantage shows the same scene completely finished. We see <u>hybrid</u> combinations of European and Southeast Asian architecture, such as deep eaves, high ceilings, and ventilation for the tropical climate. Yet most striking is simply that construction has been completed so rapidly. The riverbanks have also been expanded by extensive back-filling. The <u>landscape</u> has been wholly transformed, in the space of just one year. Such efficiency and speed was necessary to the colony, and integral to modernity.

Photography is often used to visualise time's passing. Gsell was among the first to photograph ancient temples in Cambodia, Thailand, and Vietnam, and his compositions contributed to European misconceptions of these sites as <u>ruins</u>. Later, photo-portraits commissioned annually over an entire lifetime by senior Lao Buddhist monks such as Pha Khamchan Virachitta Maha Thela explore Buddhist con-

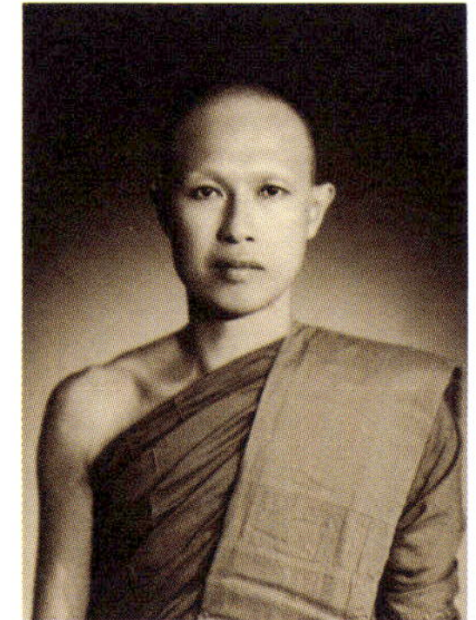

Pha Khamchan Virachitta Maha Thela
b. 1920, Laos; d. 2007, Laos

Photographer unknown. Studio portrait of the late Most Venerable Pha Khamchan Virachitta Maha Thela (1920–2007), taken at Fashion Studio, Bangkok, 1960. The text on the photograph says "Bangkok, 19.5.60, at the age of 40." Silver gelatin DOP print, 8.8 x 13.7 cm. Collection of Vat Saen Sukharam/ Buddhist Archive Photography.

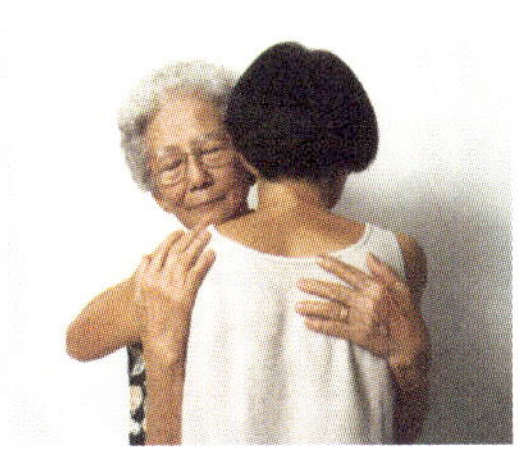

Amanda Heng. *Another Woman.* 1996–1997. C-print, 75.4 x 100.9 cm. Collection of Singapore Art Museum.

cepts of impermanence. The duration of these series emphasise processes of aging.

Aging and impermanence are also manifested in Amanda Heng's self-portraits with her elderly mother, which she has revisited over the course of two decades, as the two women grow older. Like many feminist artists, Heng often uses time-based media, including performance; such artworks take time to experience, foregrounding their relationship to a specific historical moment.

Whereas many modern artists like Saya Myit, U Ba Nyan, Pann Tra and Emile Gsell were entranced by visualisations of speed, Heng and many other contemporary artists explore possibilities for reclaiming and exalting slowness.

All artworks exist in plural conceptions of time which overlap and intersect. These include the moment in which an artwork is made, the instant in which we encounter it, and the time that has passed in between. Many artworks also depict complex comminglings of old and new, which together comprise modern experiences of time.

TRADITION

A tradition is typically understood as an idea or activity passed on from generation to generation. Yet scholars have observed that new customs or beliefs can very quickly come to be considered traditions, and that something is only legible as traditional when contrasted with the new and modern.

Modern art, by definition, critically reassesses and in some way departs from the art of the past, and reflects the changing times in which it is made. Yet modern art also frequently celebrates traditions. Many modern artists depict traditions as subject matter in their artworks, or else adapt traditional techniques or styles, using old forms in new ways.

Lim Mu Hue's paintings and woodblock prints depicting quotidian village scenes, as well as puppet theatres and other forms of charmingly old-fashioned yet still dynamic entertainment, are examples of modern art taking traditions as its subject matter. Lim's artworks were often social realist in nature; he generally focused on capturing the daily labour of ordinary people, including those working in diasporic Chinese performance troupes. In these works, Lim emphasises the liveliness of these activities and traditions which enjoyed continuing popularity in modern times. Chen Cheng Mei, who like Lim studied at Singapore's Nanyang Academy of Fine Arts, also emphasises the colour and vibrancy of Sinitic traditions in her depiction of a fortune teller in Chinatown. Chen's and Lim's depictions of traditions are typical of their generation of diasporic painters in Singapore and Malaysia, often referred to as Nanyang artists; the term derives from both the Chinese term used to refer to <u>Southeast Asia</u>, and the name of the art school in Singapore. Yet Chen travelled very widely, forging <u>connections</u> across the world, and she often depicted <u>exotic</u> people, places, and activities wherever

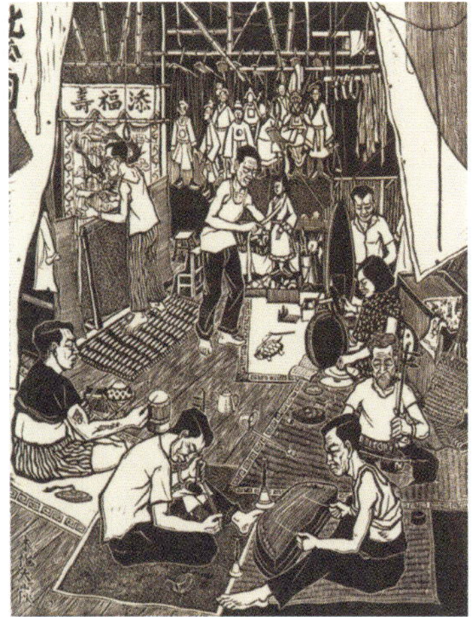

Lim Mu Hue. *Chinese Puppet Theatre*. 1966. Woodblock print on paper, 41 x 33 cm. Collection of National Gallery Singapore.

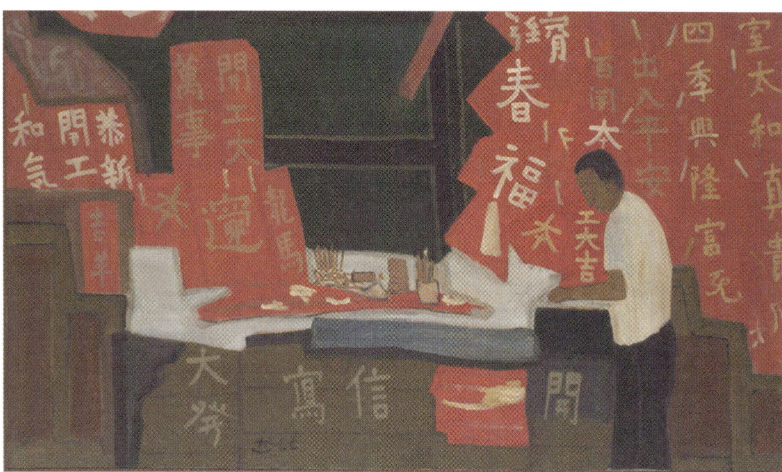

Chen Cheng Mei. *Fortune Teller (Chinatown)*. 1977. Oil on canvas, 61 x 106.7 cm. Gift of anonymous donor. Collection of National Gallery Singapore.

she went. Her eclectic subject matter and global travels transcend the Nanyang artists' focus on traditions found specifically in Southeast Asia, instead positioning longstanding customs and forms as a seemingly universal source of influence.

For many other artists, though, traditions have frequently been approached through the lens of the <u>national</u>. Nguyen Tu Nghiem, for example, celebrated traditions in an attempt to revitalise modern art and to imbue it with a distinctly Vietnamese sensibility. His paintings and lacquer works typically feature semi-abstract geometric forms, and often depict village scenes, <u>vernacular</u> architecture and culture, or <u>spiritual</u> practices. Nghiem won a National Exhibition Prize in 1957; yet three years later, the artist resigned from the Communist Party, and worked mostly in isolation for the following two decades. In his work during that period, he did not adhere to the <u>socialist realist</u> style mandated in North Vietnam at the time. Instead Nghiem's style combines the <u>naïvety</u> of children's art with the sophistication of an artist seeking to articulate a vision of his nation that did not adhere strictly to <u>propaganda</u>.

Nghiem was taught by To Ngoc Van. While the former artist often painted with lacquer, Van often painted on silk: both techniques functioned to ensure their works were recognisably Vietnamese. Van's silk painting, *A Girl Gazing at a Painting Representing a Belle*, captures the deeply contingent nature of traditions, which shift with the <u>times</u>. The work shows a woman wearing an *ao dai* dress which was then distinctly modern, having only recently been invented; this modern woman, in her modern <u>fashion</u>, gazes at a painting of a woman in strikingly different attire—perhaps one we might call traditional. Both the painting and the style of dress in this painting can best be understood in the context of <u>debates</u> about the role of <u>women</u> in 1930s Vietnam; it makes manifest the radical transformations in modern culture. It is also worth noting that today, the *ao dai* is widely considered a traditional form of dress; this demonstrates how quickly traditions can be formed.

Artist Ismail Zain wrote in 1989 about "tradition and past values," asking "how these might sustain their legitimacy and their 'communicability' within environments that have undergone considerable changes." This has been a persistent anxiety for artists in Southeast Asia. Yet tradition demonstrates a clear ability to rapidly adapt to modern demands. This is seen in the example of a top hat from 19th-century Philippines. When this hat was made, it represented a traditional take on something of the moment: traditional basketry was used to create a top hat, a fashionable and modern accessory at the time. This usage of local weaving techniques suggests perhaps the desire of its creator to appropriate this originally European fashion. Yet the <u>xenophilia</u> of this desire is tempered by the hat's transformation. The traditional and the novel are literally woven together in this object, just as they are fused in many examples of modern art.

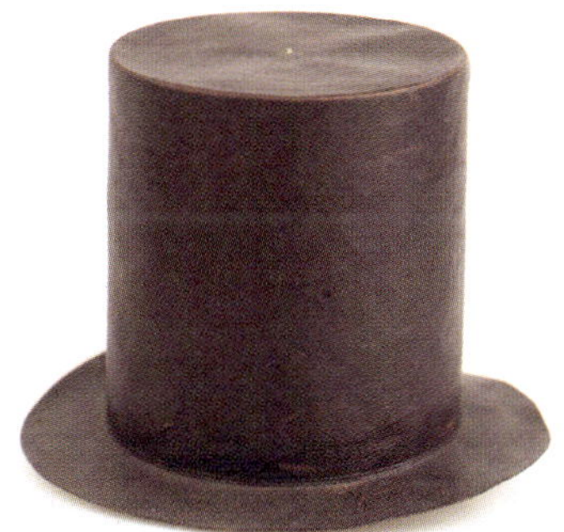

Hat, 19th century. Maker unknown, the Philippines. Basketry, pigment, 19 x 26 cm. Collection Nationaal Museum van Wereldculturen. Coll. no. RV-566-1.

TRANSFER

Many ideas, techniques, and styles in modern art have developed through contact between one place and another. These <u>connections</u> have often been a result of colonialism and <u>globalisation</u>. In Southeast Asia, art first began to become modern during early exchanges with Europe and North America. Indeed, art historian John Clark claims that "modernity in all Asian art cultures has developed out of contact with that of Euramerica."

Following Clark, we may ask: how can we think about this as a process of transfer, rather than imitation? Specifically, how can we conceptualise the transfer of art ideas to emphasise the ways in which they were selectively adapted and transformed by the "receiving" culture, in Southeast Asia, instead of privileging the perceived "origin" or "source" of those ideas, usually in the West?

Jose Honorato Lozano offers a helpful example. His *Maria Santiago* is titled after its commissioning <u>patron</u>, whose name comprises its principal image and who is depicted in the letter "M." The letters are formed from painted figures of all walks of life who are differentiated by the outfits and <u>fashions</u> they wear. Such works are known as *letras y figuras* ("letters and figures"), and they form a genre which is likely to have been originated by Lozano.

Compositions like *Maria Santiago* recall Christian illuminated manuscripts. According to researcher Jose Carino, the origin of Lozano's *letras y figuras* "can be traced to Europe in the Middle Ages, when calligraphers embellished the first letter of each chapter of the Bible or psalm of the prayer book, with artworks." Examples of illuminated Christian texts were found in the Philippines from as early as 1650, meaning Lozano would probably have seen these.

Yet Lozano did not simply imitate the European genre. Rather, he adapted and transformed it in several key ways. As Carino observes, Lozano illuminated not just the first letter, but the whole word. Furthermore, his *letras y figuras* do not depict biblical stories but secular scenes, spelling out the patron's name as well as presenting his observations of the <u>landscape</u> and inhabitants of rapidly <u>urbanising</u> Manila. (Curiously, *Maria Santiago* features fewer identifiable Manila landmarks than many of Lozano's other works, which Carino speculates may be because its commissioning patron was "not a visitor… and thus had no need to bring mementos of these places with her back home," since she was, rather, among "the earliest locals who commissioned a *letras y figuras*.")

Jose Honorato Lozano
b. circa 1821, Philippines; d. 1885, Philippines

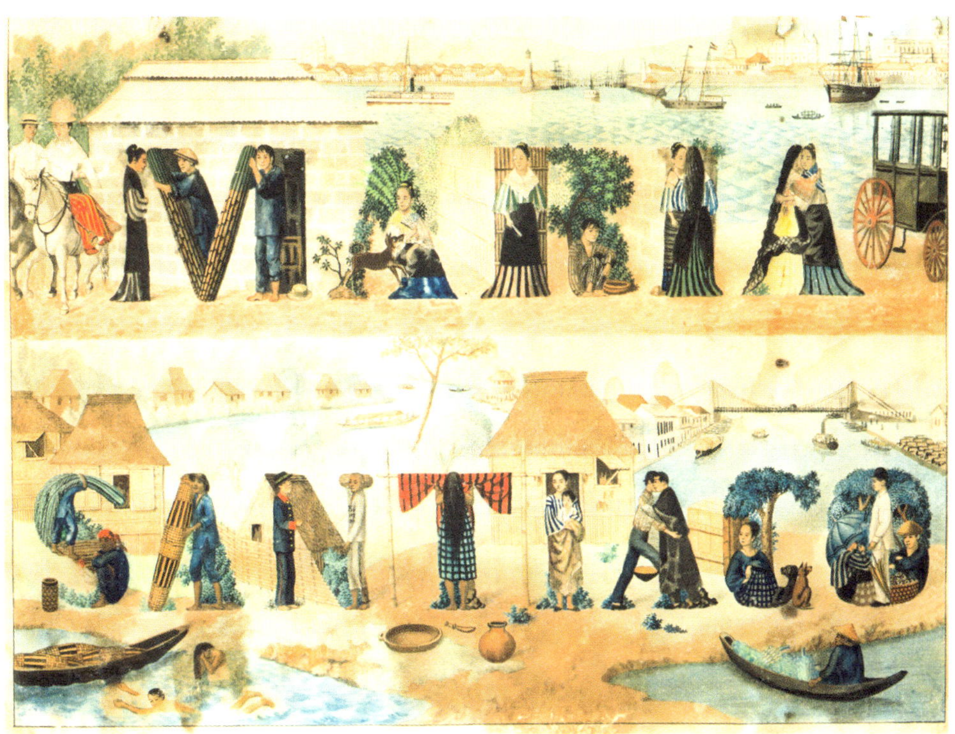

Jose Honorato Lozano. *Maria Santiago*. c. 1865. Watercolour on paper, 40 x 55 cm. Collection of Jaime C. Laya.

Moreover, the artist's style is <u>hybrid</u>, displaying an awareness of Chinese as well as European painting techniques. The use of perspective to represent spatial depth is distinctively European, whereas the light handling of paint and stylised depiction of shadow recalls Sinitic painting styles. This suggests Lozano was familiar with the work of Chinese artists who produced depictions of fashions for export, as were other Filipino artists, such as Damian Domingo, a pioneer of art <u>education</u> in the Philippines. Art historian Florina Capistrano-Baker argues that links between Philippine and Chinese export paintings include not only the use of similar techniques and materials, but also the collocation of some Philippine and Chinese drawings within a single album. Even in his use of Chinese painting techniques, Lozano adapts and transforms this <u>tradition</u>. As Carino observes, "Lozano's albums covered the gamut of Philippine flora, fauna, architecture, music, native practices and local traditions, while the Chinese devoted each album to a single subject or theme."

As this quote affirms, Lozano's *letras y figuras* were created not in imitation of a European genre, but through the transfer of styles. This process of artists actively transforming ideas and aesthetics received from elsewhere has been theorised by John Clark. He proposes that "The art culture

Damian Domingo
b. 1796, Philippines; d. 1834, Philippines

that receives does a great deal more than simply accept," because this process "is above all governed by the receiving art culture's demand for the transfer of a specific art style at a given epoch." In Clark's conception, the transfer of an art style from Europe to Southeast Asia is primarily shaped by artists and "art culture" in Southeast Asia, not by Europe.

TROPICALITY

Not withstanding the great diversity of <u>Southeast Asia</u>, a tropical climate is shared across the region, resulting from its location between the Tropic of Capricorn and the Tropic of Cancer, near to the Earth's equator. The typically warm and humid conditions in this area, as well as the plentiful rainfall, affect the region's vegetation, and shape aspects of culture and daily life. These conditions have also given rise to powerful metaphors, including of abundance and otherness. Indeed, the tropicality of Southeast Asia may be considered a key trope—a significant and persistent theme or motif—in the region's modern art.

In the tropics, the sky's appearance changes more swiftly, and storms occur more commonly, forcefully, and suddenly, than in temperate climates. Early depictions of the <u>landscape</u> in Southeast Asia by both European and local artists reveal a fascination with the possibilities of capturing this climatic phenomenon, and deploying it as a metaphor.

In works by Belgian artist Antoine Payen, who lived in Java from 1817 until 1829, the tumultuous skies and seas seem to symbolise emotional turmoil, as well as the danger and allure of exotic environments far from home. Payen's use of sharp contrasts in his compositions is also seen, in

different forms, in several works by Raden Saleh, who was Payen's student in Java before travelling to Europe for further <u>education</u>.

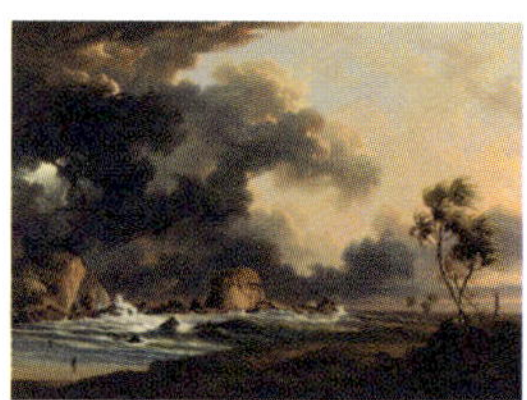

Antoine Payen. *Rising Thunder on the South Coast of West Java, Near Gajah Karang (the Elephant Rocks) in the Cidamar District.* 1844. Oil on canvas, 80 x 110 cm. Collection Nationaal Museum van Wereldculturen. Coll.no. RV-200-2.

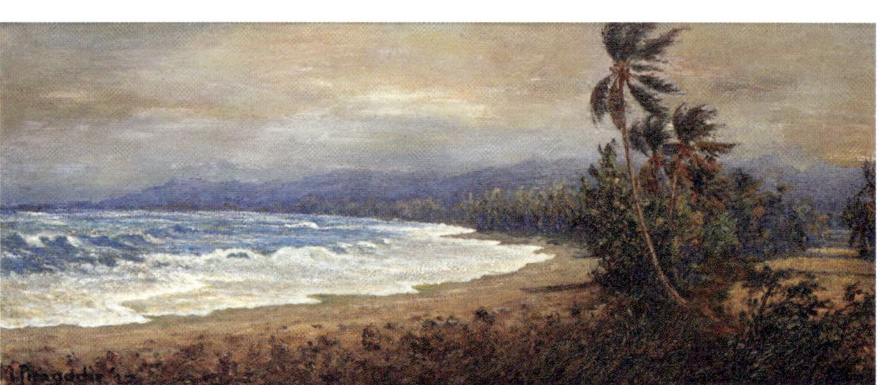

Mas Pirngadie. *Pantai Pelabuhan Ratu.* 1927. Oil on canvas, 30 x 75cm.

Later, the Javanese artist Mas Pirngadie also painted landscapes with dramatic, tropical skies. His depiction of the southern coast of western Java bears a striking compositional resemblance to Payen's earlier painting of the same area. But whereas the Belgian artist's scene is imbued with foreboding and danger, in Pirngadie's painting the colours, while vivid, are harmoniously balanced, conveying a sense of being at ease with the turbulent environment.

The vibrancy in Pirngadie's depictions of Java's tropical climate was seen by the artist's peers to symbolise a mood of nationalist possibility amid growing discontent at Dutch colonial rule. Writer Sutan Takdir Alisjahbana announced, in a 1934 profile of Pirngadie, that "now is not the time to feel sad over livelihood; for the young Indonesians, the time to fight has come. We will leave this darkness behind, advancing towards a glorious new dawn." According to art historian Simon Soon, "Sutan Takdir saw in Mas Pirngadie's landscape painting an agency that was able to shift one's perception from the question of inheritance towards a strategy of appropriation," and the artist represented for the writer "the ideal modern national subject." The similarity of Pirngadie's composition to Payen's can thus be understood not as unthinking mimicry, but rather as deliberate <u>transfer</u>. The previously colonial trope of depicting the tropical climate and landscape as exotic and threatening was redeployed by Southeast Asian artists, with new intentions and effects.

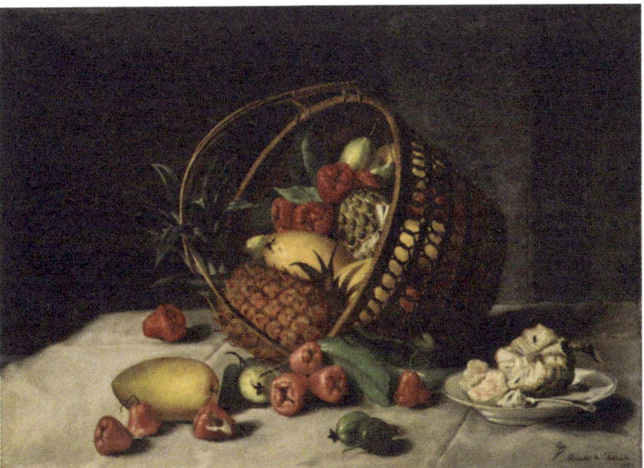

Paz Paterno. *Still Life with Atis, Macopa (Still Life with Sugar Apple, Rose Apple)*. 1884. Oil on canvas, 58 x 80 cm. Collection of Bangko Sentral ng Pilipinas.

Tropical fruits are another recurring motif in modern art of this region, also rich with metaphorical possibility. A painting by Paz Paterno which features ripe and colourful mangoes, custard apples, a pineapple, and other fruits endemic to this region, is typical of early depictions of tropical bounty. The artist—who had no formal <u>education</u>, as the Philippine art school was not yet open to <u>women</u> then—displays an awareness of the still life genre. Yet whereas European still life paintings are often allegories for the passage of <u>time</u> and human mortality, Paterno's painting instead conveys a feeling of lively vitality. This <u>naïve</u> yet sophisticated painting is one of the earliest known surviving artworks made by a Southeast Asian woman. Later artists like Georgette Chen also emphasised the fertile and vibrant appearance of tropical fruits.

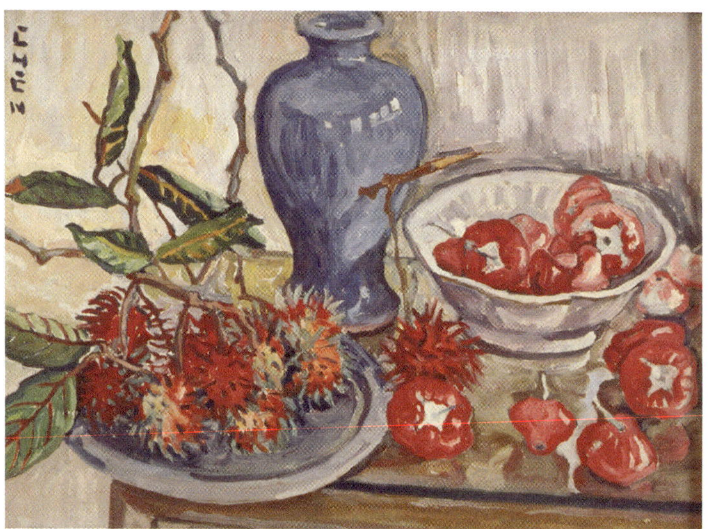

Georgette Chen. *Still Life with Blue Vase*. 1960. Oil on canvas, 34 x 47 cm. Gift of the artist's estate. Collection of National Gallery Singapore.

Southeast Asia's tropical climate has produced unique <u>vernacular</u> architectural forms, which many artists have responded to in their work, as well as many <u>fashions</u> which shield wearers from sun and rain, as depicted in 19th-century *tipos del pais* drawings made in the Philippines, for example.

Sometimes, though, tropical downpours catch us unaware. The experience is evocatively captured in paintings by Hendra Gunawan and Svay Ken, which show people sheltering from rain under large palm leaves. Both artists often depicted aspects of <u>vernacular</u> life which were fleeting, or transforming as a result of <u>urbanisation</u>, <u>globalisation</u>, and other changes. Their paintings of monsoonal rains are imbued with freshness and life, further extending the evocative potential of the trope of the tropical.

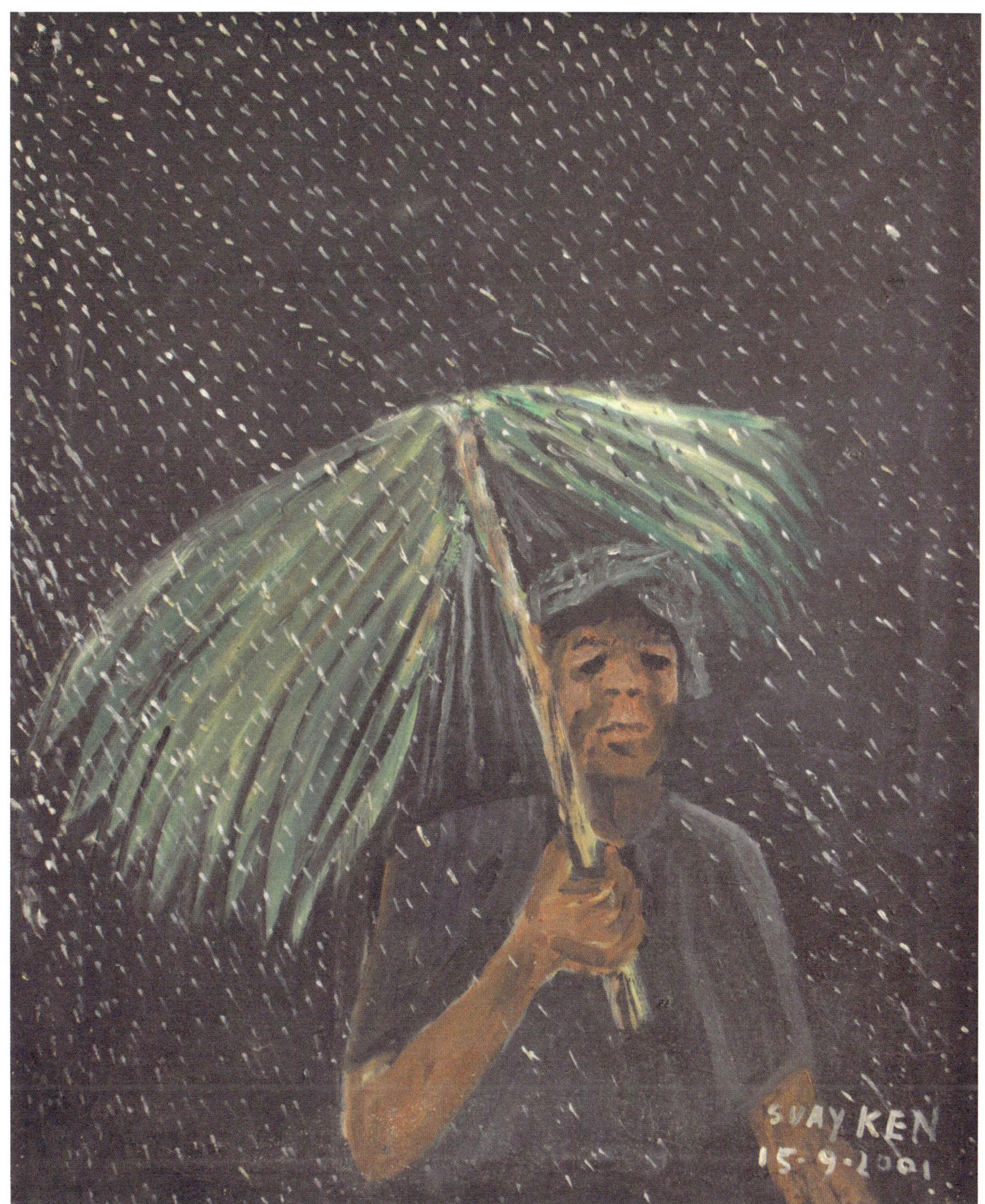

Svay Ken. Untitled. 2001. Oil on canvas, 60 x 49.5 cm. Collection of René Anant Feddersen.

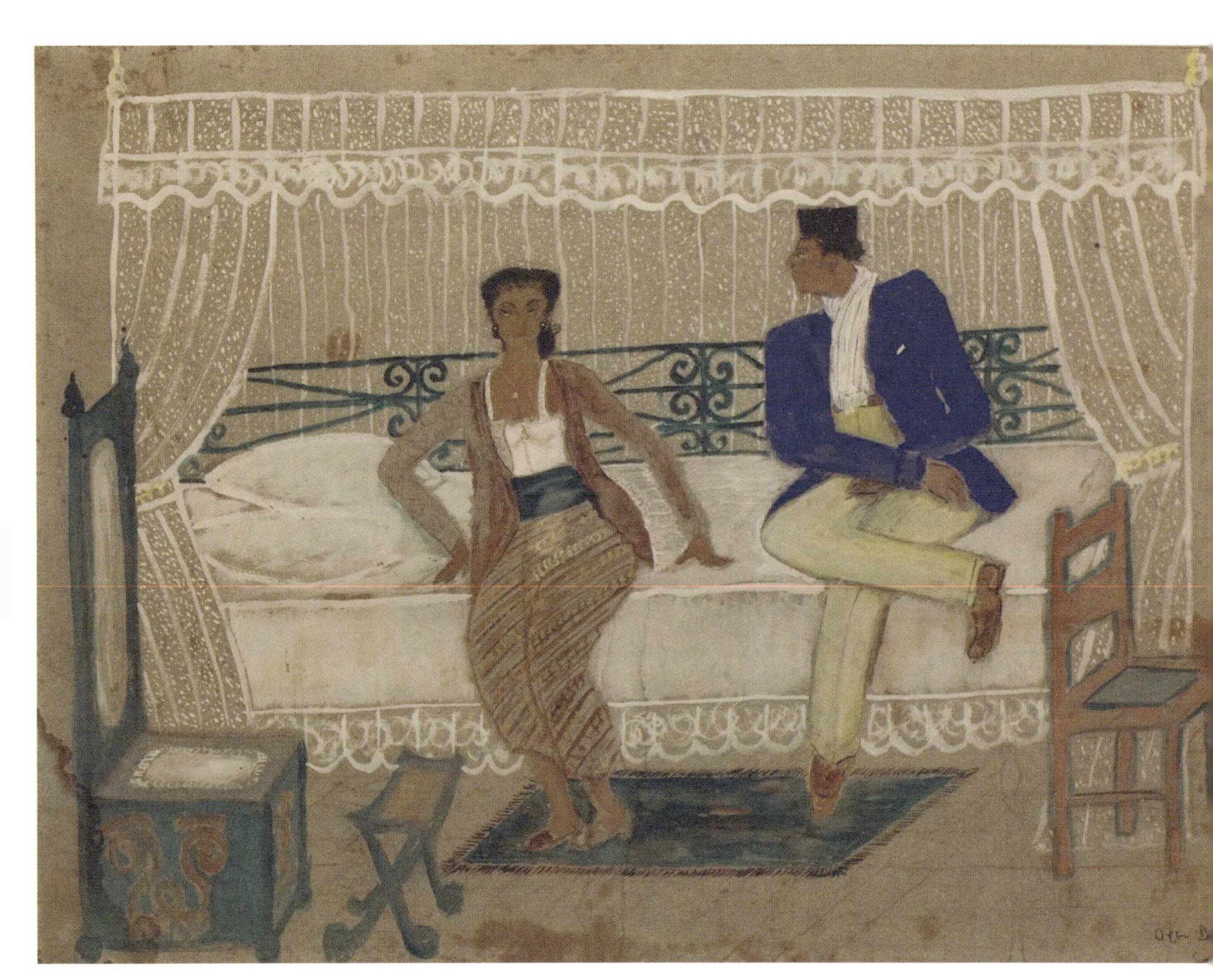

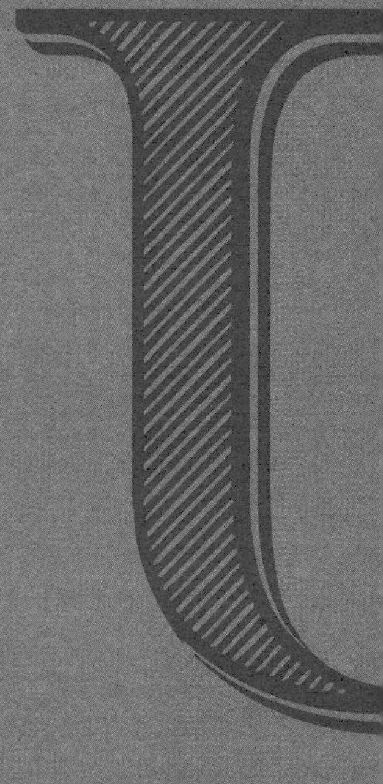

Otto Djaya. *Pertemuan* (Rendezvous). 1947. Watercolour on paper, 88 x 65 cm. Collection of Galeri Nasional Indonesia.

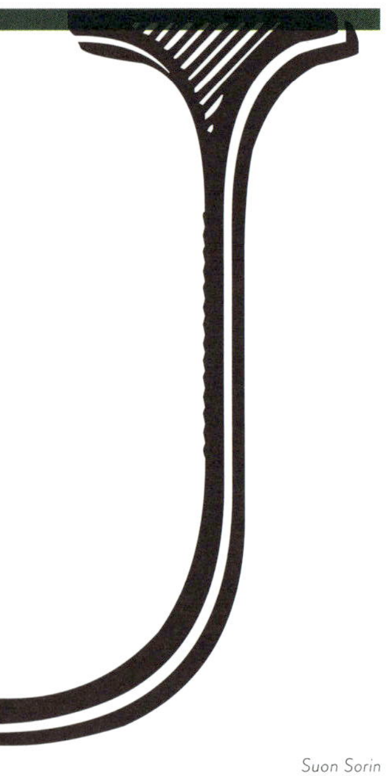

URBANISATION

"Within just two minutes of setting foot in Phnom Penh, Sam could see that the capital was much more crowded and busy than it had been seven or eight years earlier... The traffic was never-ending, but the city was also very neat, orderly and well-organized."

This passage is excerpted from an award-winning 1961 novel by Suon Sorin, written in Khmer. In it, he praises the new buildings and monuments in the Cambodian city, and the sudden proliferation of roads, running water, and electricity.

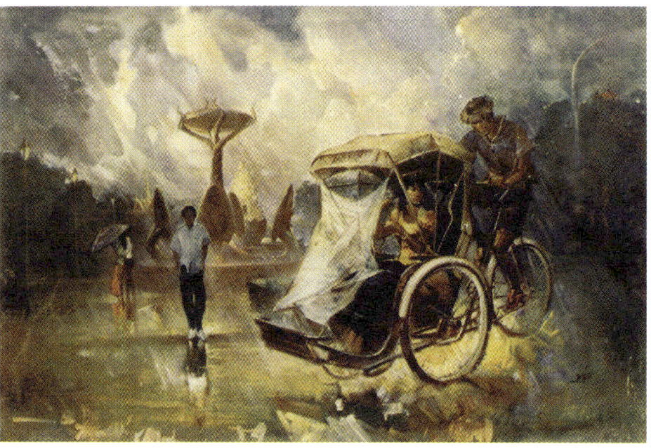

Nhek Dim. Title unknown. c. 1960s. Medium unknown, dimensions unknown. Location unknown.

Urbanisation—the transformation not just of the built environment but the way people live and work—was a development that excited many in Southeast Asia, including modern artists. Sorin's passage is one of many expressions of this optimism and zeal. Records show, for instance, that many Cambodian artists in Sorin's day painted scenes of Phnom Penh, especially the Independence Monument that was built to commemorate freedom from colonial rule, and designed by architect Vann Molyvann. Very few of these paintings survive, but one by Nhek Dim encapsulates the exhilaration that the city inspired. Like Sorin, Nhek Dim also carefully depicted electrical lights, including old-style lampposts on the left of the image, and a modern-looking curved one on the right. These details, while small, are telling about the impact of electricity on the experience of modern Phnom Penh.

Urbanisation was a sign of modernisation in the region, and stood for progress and growth in a postcolonial era. Expanding and improving urban environments was crucial to nation-building in Southeast Asia in both a literal and symbolic way: as Sorin described, the sights of the modern city were "like the face of the nation." Many <u>abstract</u> artworks from this period evoke the appearance and atmosphere of modern cities.

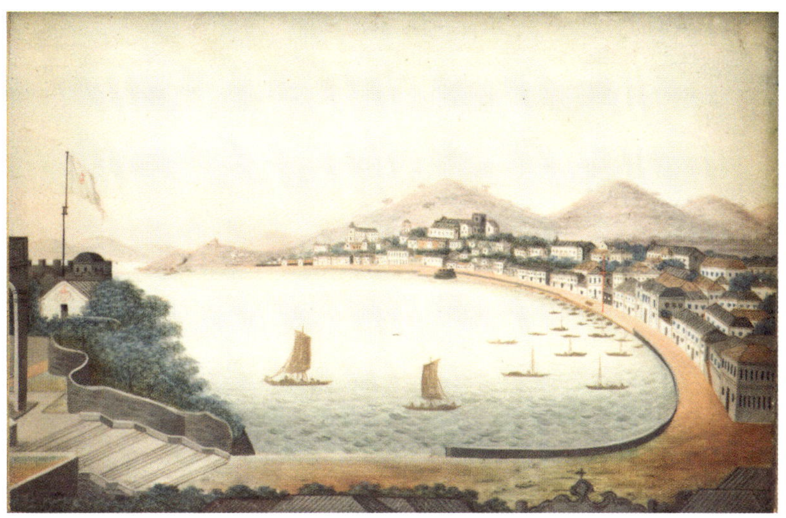

Unknown Chinese artist. *The Praya Grande, Macau.* c. 1820s. Oil on ivory, 8.5 x 13.5 cm. Collection of National Gallery Singapore.

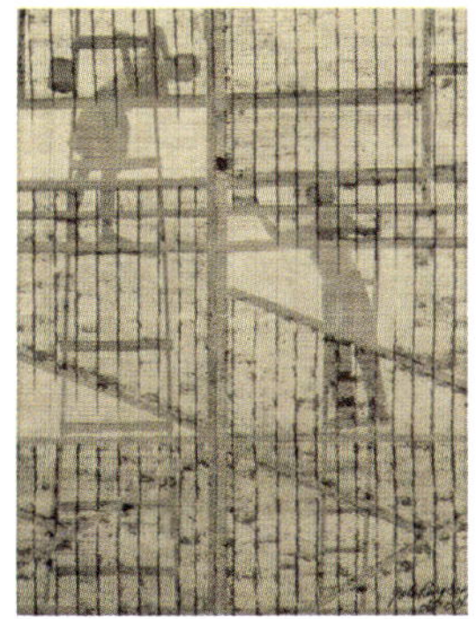

Wu Peng Seng. *Painters.* 1958. Gelatin silver print, 46.5 x 35.5 cm. Gift of Wu Peng Seng and family. Collection of National Gallery Singapore.

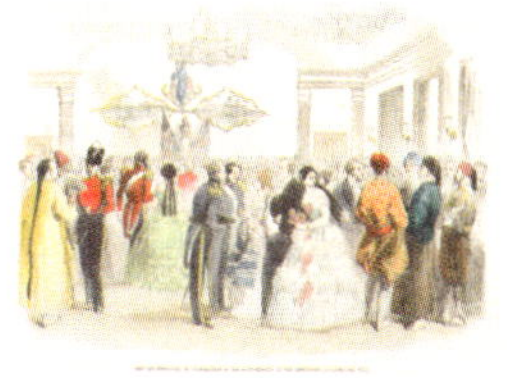

Artist unknown. *Ball at Singapore, in Celebration of the Anniversary of the Settlements.* 1854. Wood engraving on paper, 17 x 23 cm. Collection of National Museum of Singapore.

Representing urbanisation was also a key reflection of modernisation since colonial times. In as early as the 18th century, maps of Manila emphasised its orderly gridded streets. Early 19th-century images of other port cities, such as *The Praya Grande, Macau* by an unknown Chinese artist, also carefully depict neat rows of buildings, with consistent designs, in dense formation. Colonial artists often painted panoramas of cities, many of which were reproduced as prints in European periodicals, and which functioned as advertisements for commercial opportunities offered by a rapidly urbanising Southeast Asia. Some of the earliest photographs of the region, such as a daguerreotype view of Singapore taken in 1844—just five years after the introduction of the technology in Europe, and one year after the opening of the first photography studio on the island—are composed to emphasise the tidy shapes of city buildings. These examples demonstrate the importance of representing urbanisation in early depictions of modern Southeast Asia, alongside <u>landscapes</u> and images of <u>exotic</u> nature.

Urbanisation not only transforms the built environment, but also affects its human inhabitants, bringing people of different nationalities, cultures and religions together. Wu Peng Seng's photographs, such as *Painters*, convey the enmeshing of workers and the city. Colonial images of fashionable balls, such as an 1854 engraving published in the *Illustrated London News*, depict British society men and women engaging with Chinese, Indian, Malay, and other people.

<u>Women</u> have always been active in urban society, playing a wide variety of roles. For example, Southern Chinese migrants, known as Samsui women, were prominent at

Wu Peng Seng
b. 1915, China; d. 2006, Singapore

many construction sites in Singapore from the 1930s until the 1980s. Identifiable by their bright headdresses, these women appear in artworks from the period, by artists such as Lai Foong Moi and Liu Kang. Girls enjoying city life also appear in postcards produced by the Ahuja studios in early 20th-century Yangon.

Such opportunities notwithstanding, urbanisation also often intensifies and makes visible the subjugation of some groups, especially women. The exhausting labour that Filipina domestic workers perform, as well as the bond they often form as a diasporic community, is captured by Brenda V. Fajardo, in a work from her *Tarot Card Series: Pilipina*. In another example of an occupation often associated with city life, the complex subjectivity of female sex workers is evoked in Otto Djaya's painting of a couple seated on a bed, pictured in what historians claim is a brothel in a Javanese city. Djaya exhibited in Amsterdam's Stedelijk Museum, and like many Southeast Asian artists, seems to have also been interested in evocations of city life that he encountered on his travels.

Many contemporary artists, like Anida Yoeu Ali, continue to explore the effects of urbanisation in the 21st century, often through performances at significant urban locations in the region and beyond. Ali's photographs taken in Phnom Penh suggest a fascination with the city and its bright lights, recalling Suon Sorin's impressions of the Cambodian capital over half a century earlier.

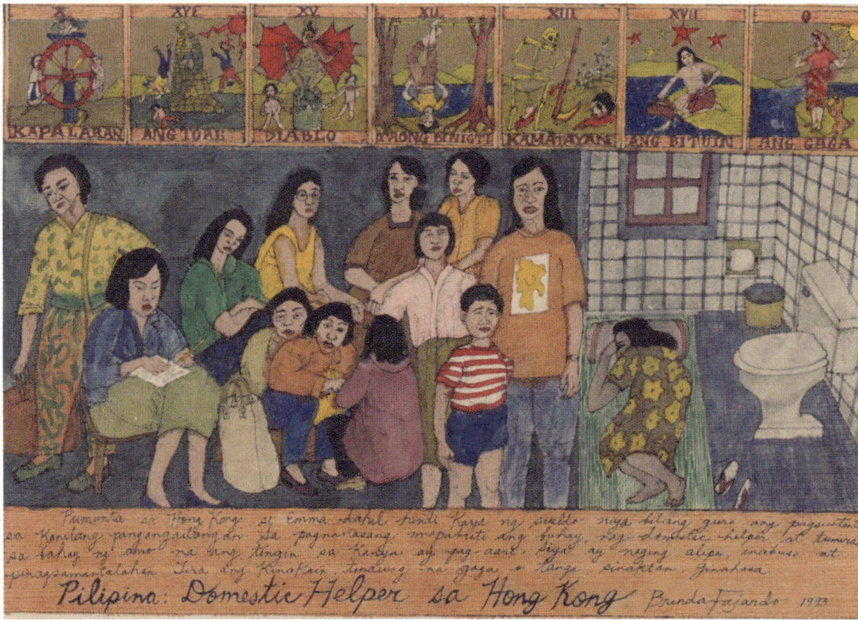

Brenda V. Fajardo. *Domestic Helper in Hong Kong*, from *Tarot Card Series: Pilipina*. 1993. Pen, ink, tempera on cogon grass paper, 63 x 78 cm. Museum of Contemporary Art Tokyo.

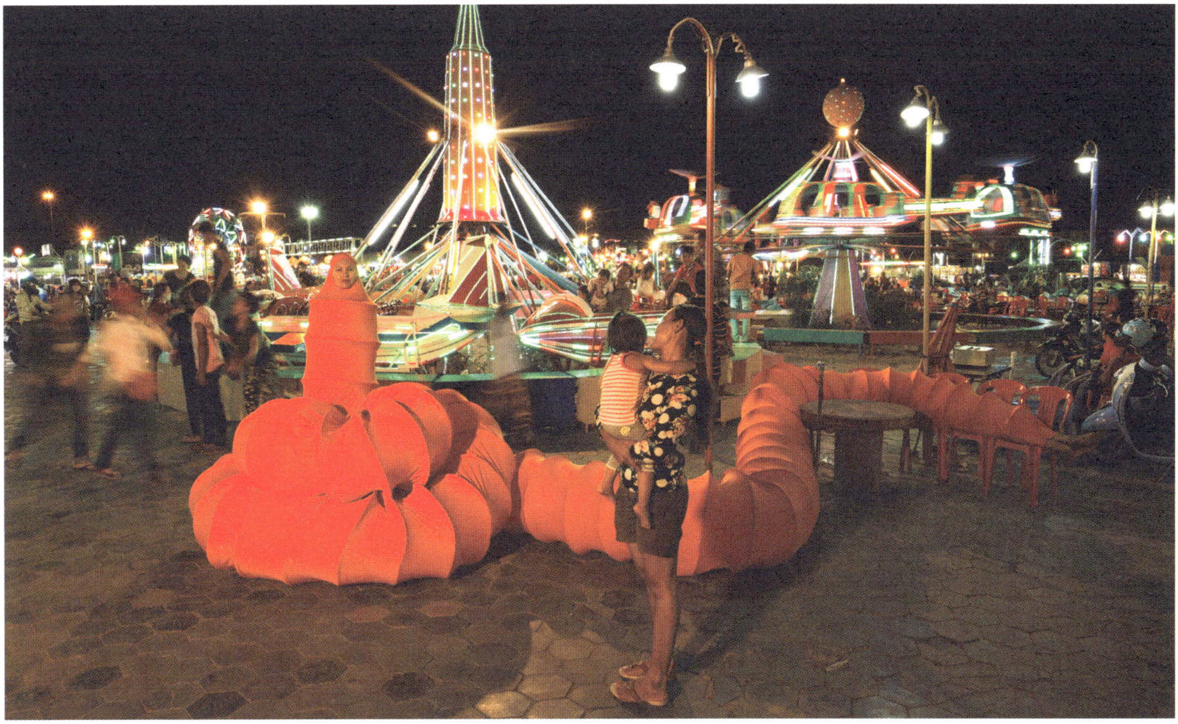

Anida Yoeu Ali. Still from *The Buddhist Bug, Into the Night*. 2015. Two-channel HD video projection, colour, sound, 7 min. A project of Studio Revolt.

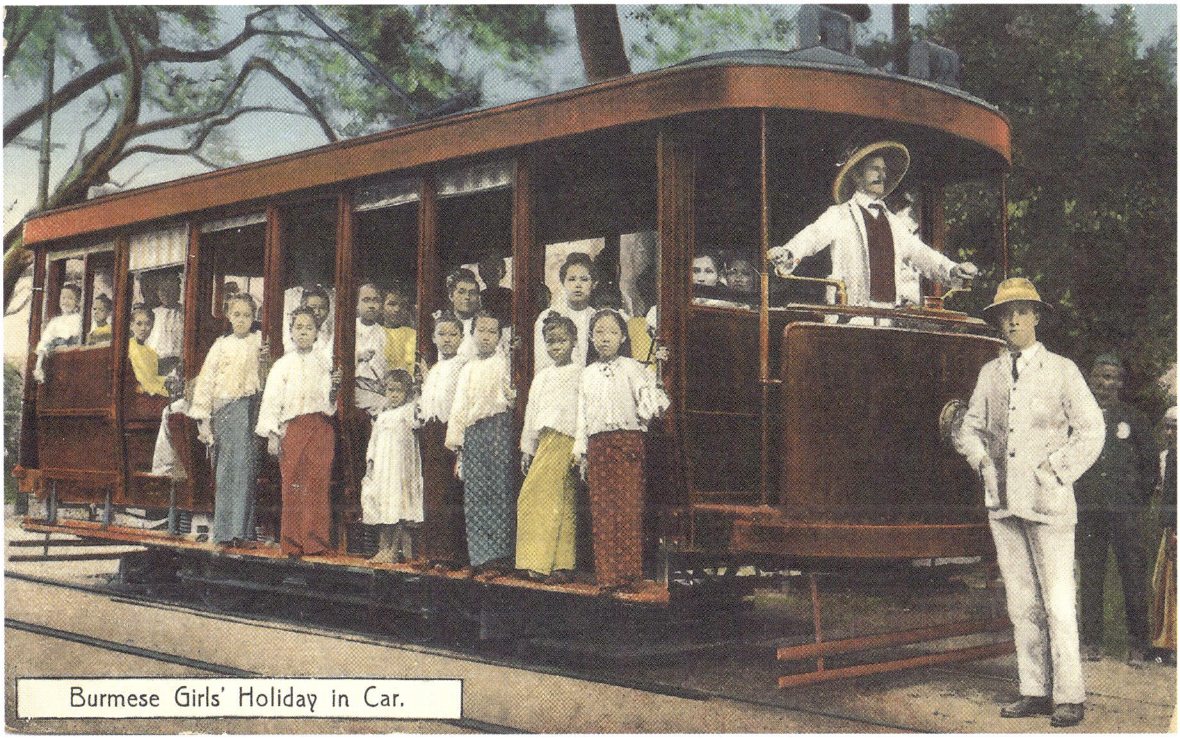

Burmese Girls' Holiday in Car.

D.A. Ahuja studio. *Burmese Girls' Holiday in Car*. Postcard. c. 1907–1909. The Sharman Minus collection of early postcards of Burma.

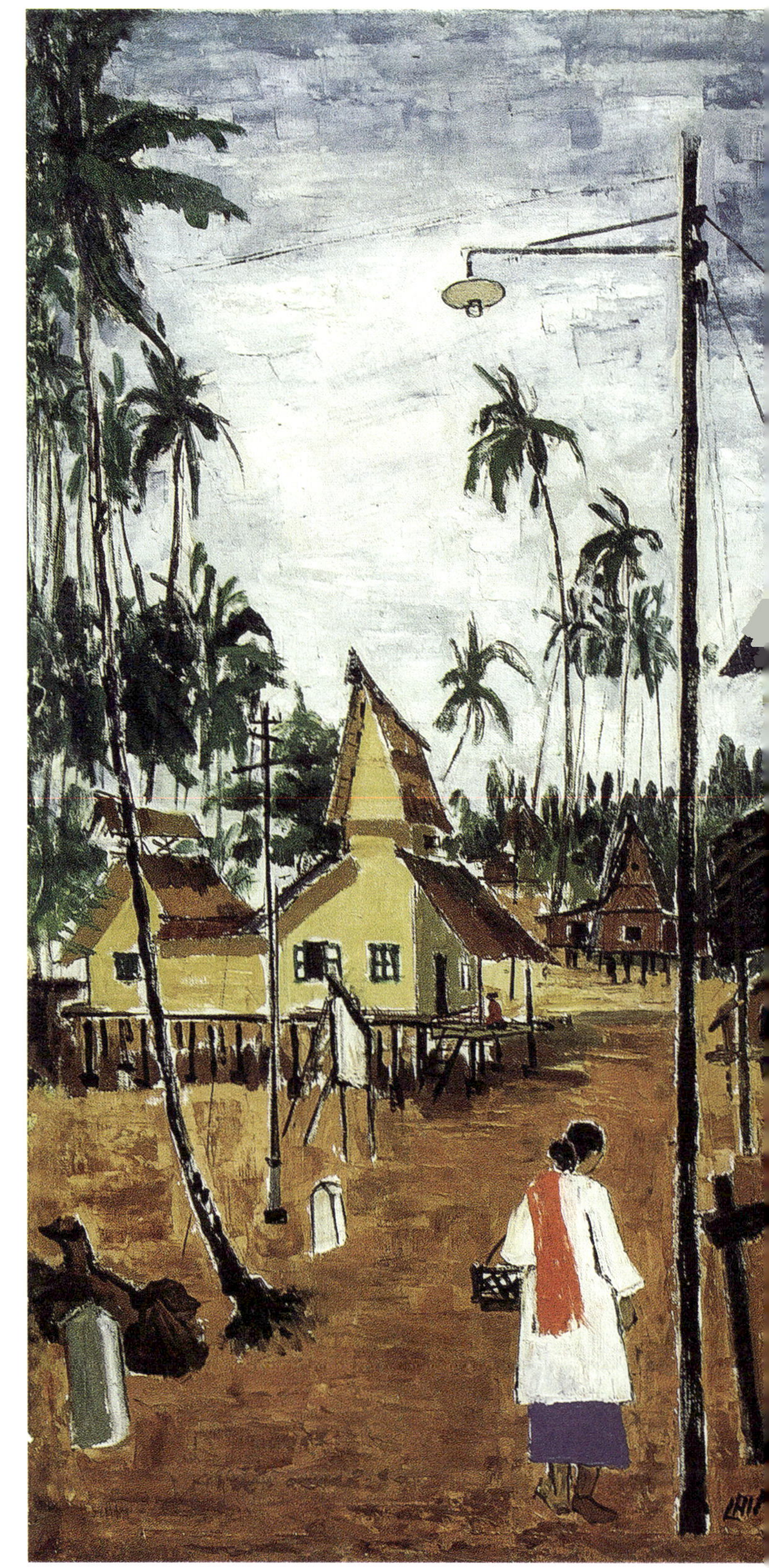

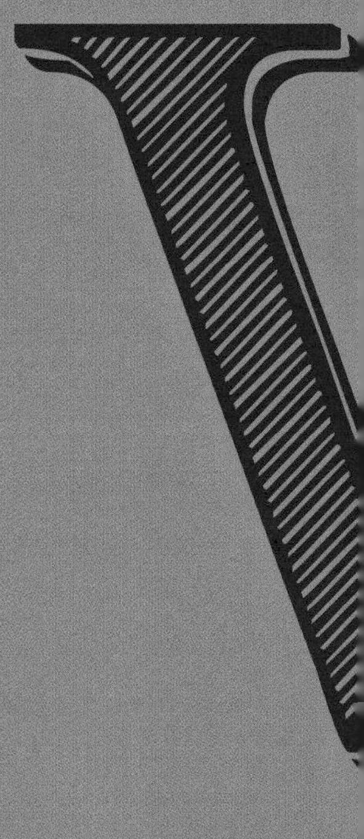

Lai Foong Moi. *Pagi Hari di Kampung* (Morning in the Kampung). 1959. Oil on canvas, 24 x 76 cm. Collection of Malaysia's National Visual Arts Development Board.

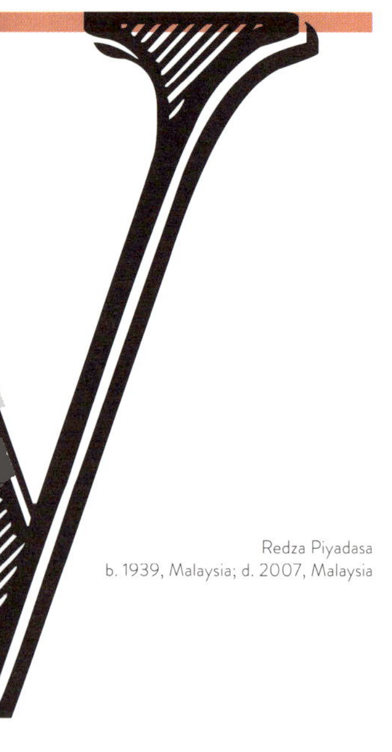

Redza Piyadasa
b. 1939, Malaysia; d. 2007, Malaysia

Anuar Rashid
b. 1958, Malaysia

VALUE

When we write about, exhibit, or even speak about a work of art, we are often making an implicit claim for its value. This perceived value may be aesthetic in nature, and thus highly subjective. Or claims may be made for an artwork's historical value, because of its connection to people or events of broader significance, sometimes beyond the realm of art. Artworks also have a financial value, which—like their aesthetic and historical worth—may fluctuate, and alters with the passage of time.

All judgements of value are contested and arbitrary: the value of an artwork is not an unchangeable and inherent fact, but something that is contingent on many factors, some external to the work. Redza Piyadasa's work, *Art Proposition*, is an illustrative case study. In this work, Piyadasa highlights issues of financial value in the text he has stencilled over the image. "After buying this 'oil painting' by Annuar [sic] Rashid for 130 Malaysian Dollars, I decided to black out most of it," the text declares. As an implied consequence of this action, the text continues, "This Piyadasa 'Art Proposition' is now offered for sale at 500 Malaysian Dollars." The asking price of the object, according to this statement, had increased more than threefold—effectively instantaneously—as a direct result of Piyadasa's technically simple intervention. Encountering the work at a later date, viewers may also be aware that its market value has likely increased further since then.

The work makes explicit that an artwork's financial value is arbitrary and mutable, and is often dictated largely by the name and reputation of its maker. Simply put, Piyadasa enjoyed greater fame and acclaim than Anuar Rashid, who had been one of his students, and thus could demand a much higher price than Anuar could.

The explicit claim for financial worth in *Art Proposition* is linked to an implicit claim for the work's aesthetic and <u>conceptual</u> value. The work employs various aesthetic devices to convey the identity of its author, distinguishing Piyadasa in ways consistent with the modern concept of an <u>artist</u> as a singular individual. *Art Proposition* is one of a series of works with the same title, and its use of stencilled lettering, in a recognisable font, is featured in many other works by Piyadasa. Moreover, the piece is adorned with a signature which is both legible and visually distinctive. As a result, this is immediately identifiable as the work of Piyadasa, suggesting that the aesthetic consistency within the artist's <u>oeuvre</u> contributes to its monetary value. Despite the fact that Piyadasa is often hailed as a pioneer of conceptual approaches in the

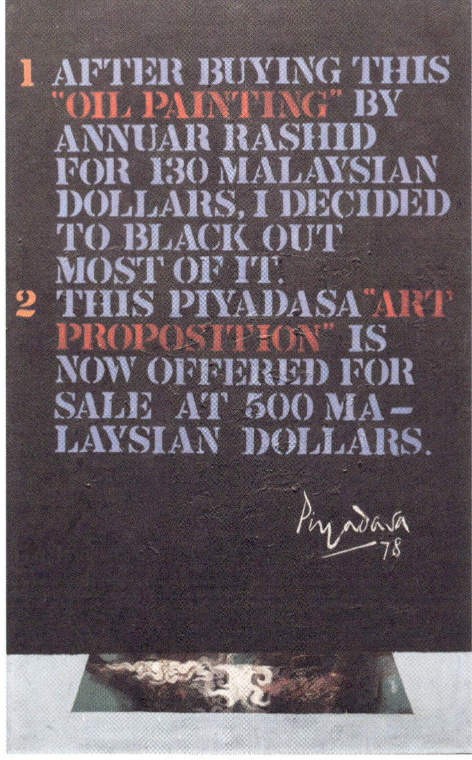

Redza Piyadasa. *Art Proposition*. 1978. Oil on canvas, 112 x 71.4 cm. Collection of Dato' Baharuddin Zainal.

region—a kind of practice sometimes thought to displace aesthetic aspects of art in favour of ideas—he clearly also took care with the appearance of his works.

That *Art Proposition* is often discussed without substantial reference to Anuar Rashid demonstrates that, as well as commanding a higher price for his works, Piyadasa also enjoys a position of greater significance within the emerging <u>canon</u> of Southeast Asian modern and contemporary art history.

Inclusion in the canon is inevitably linked to financial, aesthetic and historical value. The more highly priced an artist's works, the more demand there is for research about and <u>exhibitions</u> of that artist, thereby positioning him as part of the canon; by the same token, once art historians have written about an artist, or when museums or prominent curators have exhibited an artist's work, that artist's work will usually enjoy increased prices. The same principle can be seen in artworks made by <u>women</u>. They tend to be priced lower, and also to be written about and exhibited less often, included in fewer museum collections, and ascribed a lower value in other ways, both quantifiable and abstract. Exclusions from the canon thus affect not just financial value, but also aesthetic and historical value.

VERNACULAR

The word "vernacular" suggests a sense of domesticity, because it refers, in a very broad sense, to the architecture and
language that one is likely to encounter in daily life.

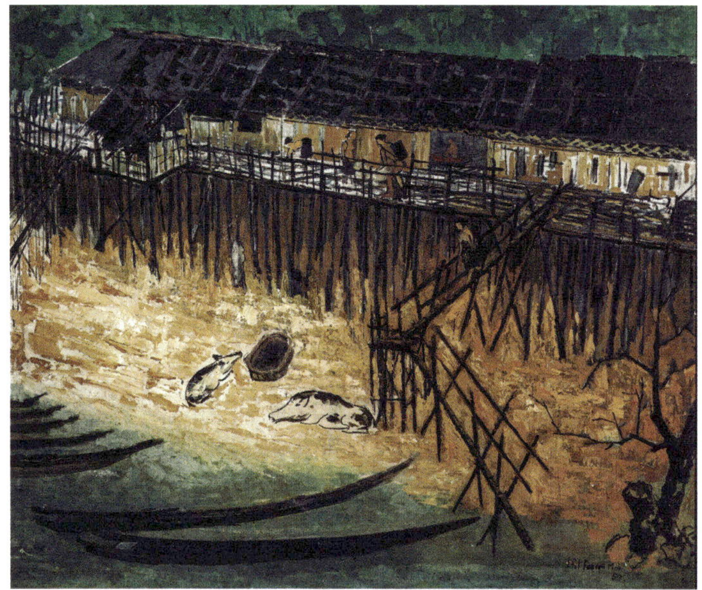

Lai Foong Moi. *Rumah Panjang Dayak* (Dayak Longhouse). 1959. Oil on canvas, 71 x 84 cm. Collection of Malaysia's National Visual Arts Development Board.

Lai Foong Moi
b. 1931, Malaysia; d. 1994, Singapore

Consider *Rumah Panjang Dayak* (Dayak Longhouse), a painting by Lai Foong Moi. The longhouse—the typical do-mestic accommodation of the Dayak peoples of Borneo—dominates the composition in this work, occupying the entire width of the canvas. A longhouse is an example of vernacu-lar architecture: a building that is domestic and functional, in contrast to monuments and structures made for official, public use (such as the museum in which Lai's painting now hangs). Languages commonly used for everyday speech in a specific locale are also called vernacular, in contrast to lan-guages—often cosmopolitan in nature, or of foreign origin—used for more formal communications. The various Dayak languages are vernacular, for example, whereas Malay, Indo-nesian and English are not, even though they are now widely spoken in the regions where longhouses are found.

Another painting by Lai, *Pagi Hari di Kampung* (Morning in the Kampung), also demonstrates the artist's interest in vernacular architecture. Here, Lai depicts village houses with distinctively shaped roofs. Rising to a high peak, the roof de-signs rhyme with the narrow, vertical orientation of the canvas.

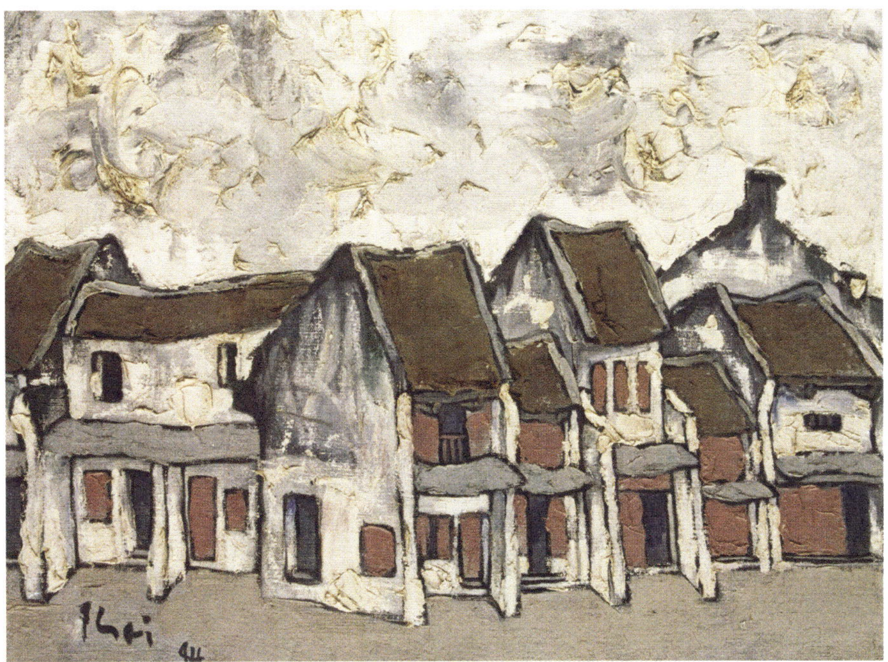

Bui Xuan Phai. *Pho Hang Mam* (Hang Mam Street). 1984. Oil on canvas. Collection of Vietnam Museum of Fine Arts.

Art historian T.K. Sabapathy describes *Morning in the Kampung* as a "fusion of elements selected from Chinese painting traditions and those from the School of Paris... an instance in which devices from the hanging scroll format have been grafted onto the technical requirements of easel painting." This is an example of <u>transfer</u>, whereby styles and formats which might be foreign to the artist are synthesised with other types of composition which might be more familiar. Lai was the first Malaysian woman to study art in Paris, and like many of her peers referred to as Nanyang artists, she often painted scenes of <u>quotidian</u>, village life, especially among ethnic groups that were <u>exotic</u> to her. This interest in domestic environments and vernacular architecture was not uncommon among the Nanyang artists, including the Ten Men Group that Lai joined. The group frequently travelled across Southeast Asia, seeking inspiration. Other members of the group, such as Shui Tit Sing and the group's de facto leader Yeh Chi Wei, also depicted longhouses and other domestic environments that they encountered on their travels. This approach is shared by many artists elsewhere, such as Bui Xuan Phai, who obsessively painted his hometown of Hanoi, focusing on its many shophouses and other anonymous domestic buildings.

Perhaps the oldest known image of Southeast Asian vernacular architecture appears in a bas relief at the 9th-century temple of Borobudur, in central Java. The sculpted friezes there mostly depict tales from Buddhist scriptures, but also some scenes of Javanese society, such as stilted houses. Yet ancient temples, like Borobudur, are also important sites for the early appearance of vernacular languages, in stone inscriptions. In many cases, early inscriptions feature both a vernacular language and Sanskrit. For example, the Karangtengah inscription (824 CE), thought to refer to Borobudur, is written in Old Javanese and Sanskrit, and the famed Sdok Kok Thom inscription (1053 CE), originating in present-day eastern Thailand, is written in Old Khmer and Sanskrit.

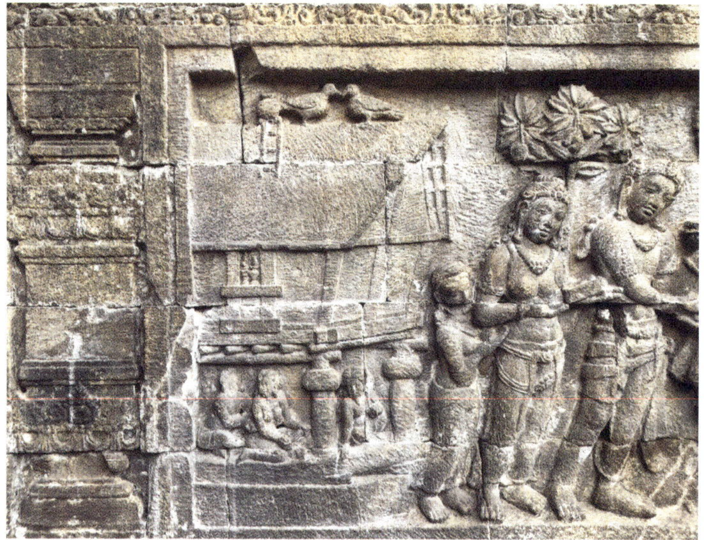

Vernacular housing, bas-relief, Borobudur. 9th century CE, central Java.

Some texts on modern Southeast Asian art have been written in the region's many vernacular languages, although their relationship to Anglophone discourse remains uncertain. Certainly, a large number of critical writings have appeared in some languages, such as Indonesian, Malay, and to a lesser degree Thai. Yet many of the significant texts about modern art elsewhere in the region seem to have been written in English, or else in the former colonial languages of Spanish, French, and Japanese, and also in Chinese. More research is needed on vernacular writings about modern Southeast Asian art—and some major projects on this topic, including translations, are currently underway.

It is known that terms for "modern" and "art" appear in all of Southeast Asia's most widely spoken vernacular languages. These terms emerged at varying times during the 19th and 20th centuries, and have taken on sometimes quite distinct meanings and connotations.

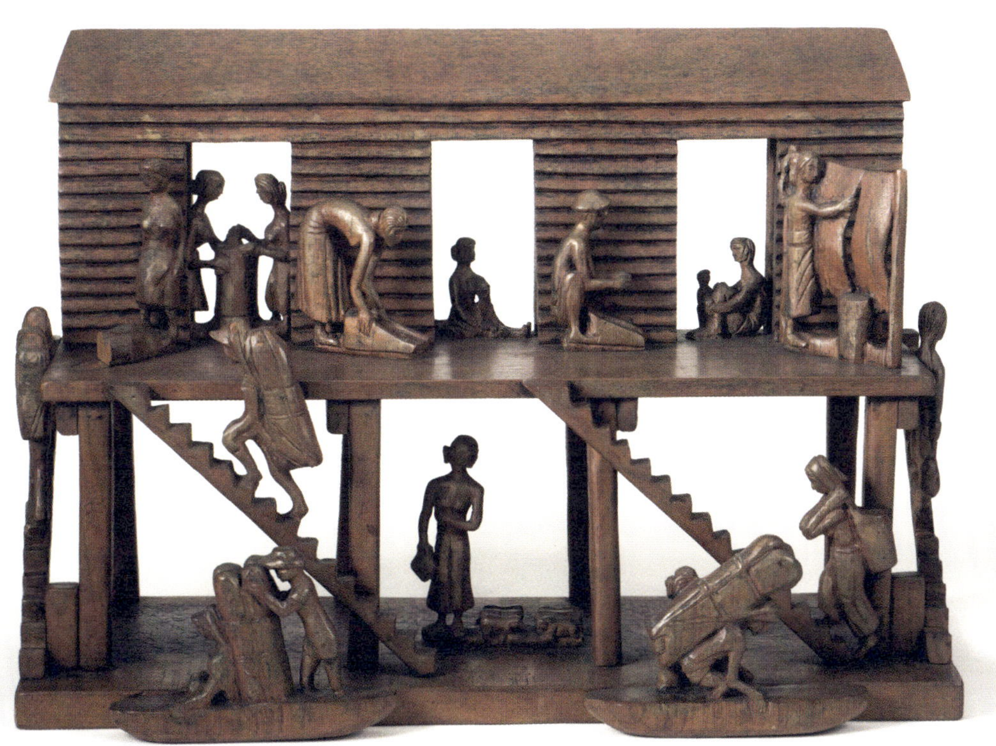

Shui Tit Sing. *Longhouse*. 1980. Teakwood, 47 x 69 x 29 cm. Collection of National Gallery Singapore.

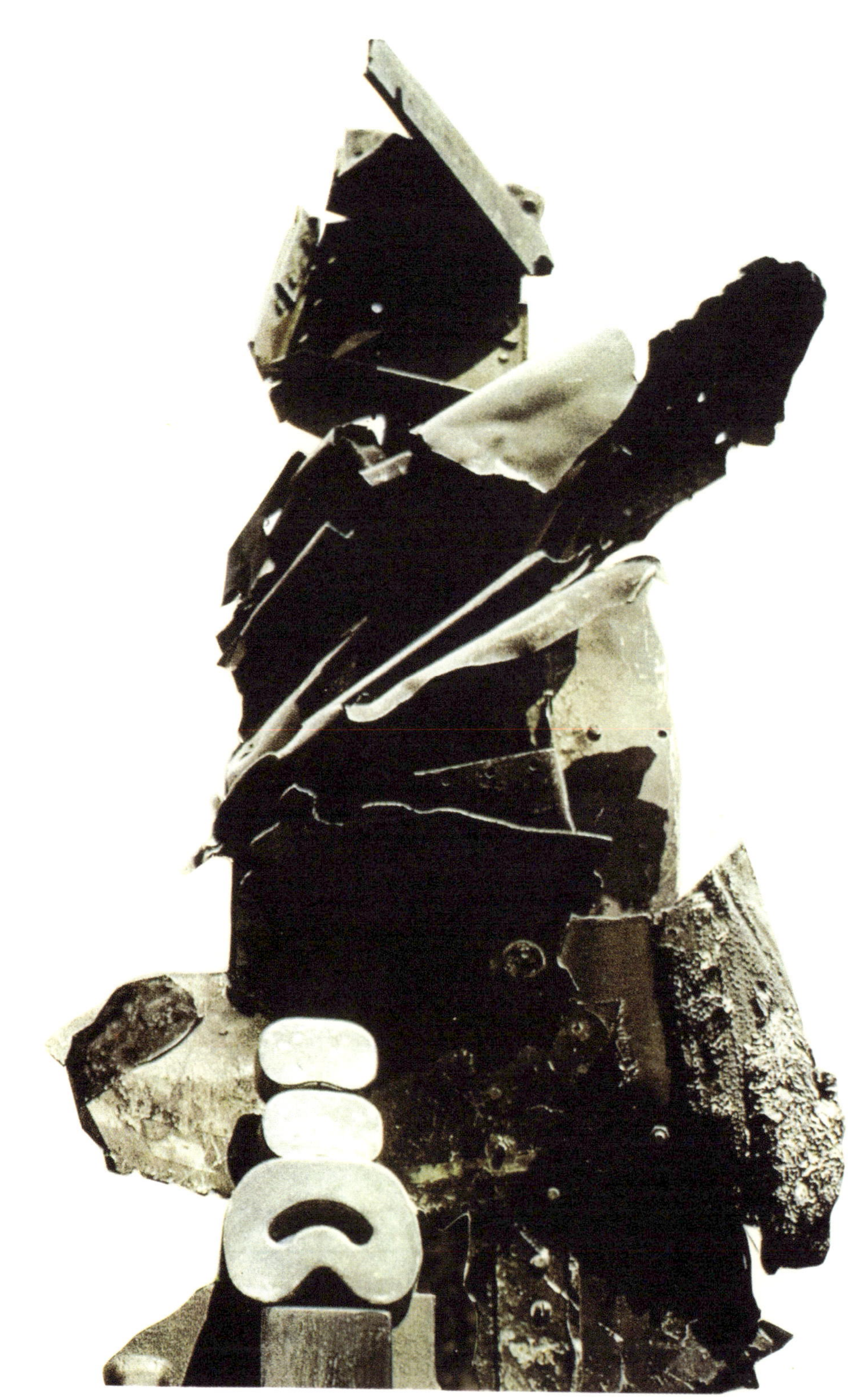

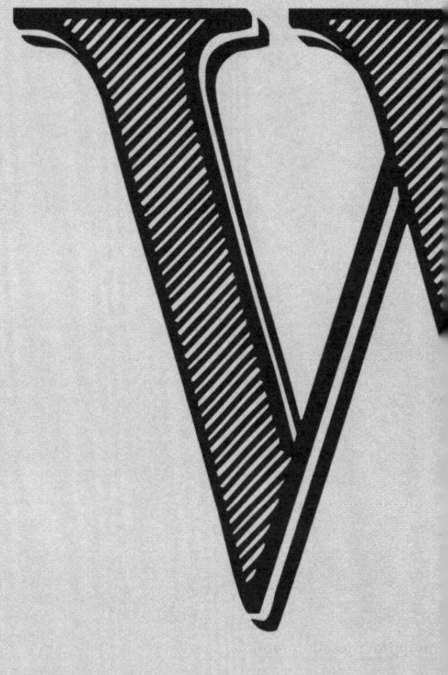

Diem Phung Thi. *The Soldier of Liberation*. 1973. Assemblage with scraps of B52 bomber, 120 cm (height). Location unknown.

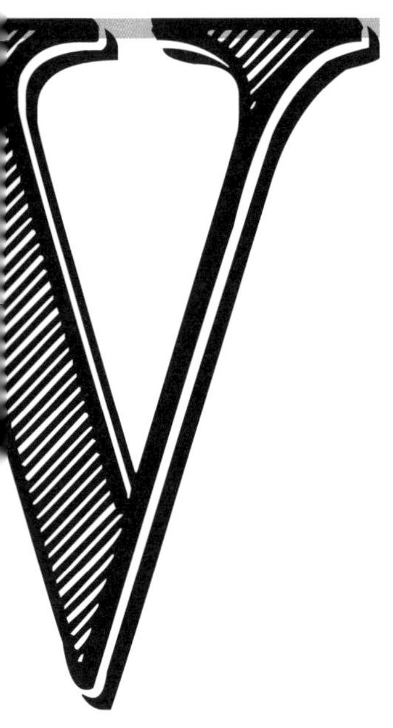

War is, above all, a terrible force of suffering and destruction. Like <u>genocide</u>, war perverts the course of art history through the death and mass migration of artists (as well as collectors, <u>patrons</u>, and other key figures), the loss and dispersal of artworks and archives, and the trauma many experience in the aftermath of violent conflict. Yet war has also been an undeniable source of inspiration for many artists. Moreover, war has caused societal transformations—especially for the roles of <u>women</u>—which have often had positive effects, despite the devastation.

"The depiction of the events and experiences of war has been an intrinsic part of representing the national in most Asian states," according to art historian John Clark. Many parts of Southeast Asia experienced war with colonial powers during the 19th and 20th centuries, and Vietnam, Cambodia and Laos further endured war with the United States, as part of the global Cold War. Every Southeast Asian state was occupied by Japanese forces during World War II, and the impact of this experience on the development of modern art was compounded by its coinciding with <u>debates</u> on transformations that were already underway, including the growing influence of forms of <u>realism</u>, and changes in art <u>education</u>. The Japanese interregnum was also part of the process of ending colonial rule, in most states.

The Soldier of Liberation by Diem Phung Thi is emblematic of many of the complexities of war as it has figured in Southeast Asian modern art. "The period during which Vietnam was submerged in bombs and shells with the threat of 'bombing to the Stone Age' was also the very time for nurturing, maturity fulfillment, and emergence of many talents," wrote art historian Nguyen Ngoc Tran about Thi, who had had been trained as a dental surgeon, but began practising as an artist, specialised in sculpture, after her relocation to France while the Second Indochina War raged in Vietnam. Tran suggested that the art of Thi and other Vietnamese "settling overseas" might be understood as "their affirmation that bombs had not brought Vietnamese people to submission and that Vietnamese culture would live forever."

Thi's *The Soldier of Liberation* is made from scraps of B52 bombs, and explicitly addresses Vietnam's survival through decades of war. Yet this artwork is not reducible to national or militaristic narratives. The rounded, organic forms at its base are clearly identifiable as elements from an idiosyncratic selection of sculptural modules Thi devised, which recur throughout her <u>oeuvre</u>, and which are often described as a

Diem Phung Thi
b. 1920, Vietnam; d. 2002, France

kind of alphabet. The presence of these <u>abstract</u> forms thus marks this sculpture as personal and individual: it is the artist's own vision of wartime, not the Vietnamese nation's. The sculpture implies an affiliation with the soon-to-be-victorious communist ideology of North Vietnam in its valorisation of the figure of the soldier, its use of remnants from American bombs, and its titular reference to the "liberation" of Vietnam by the communist forces. Yet it does not appear to function as <u>propaganda</u>, and is not in the <u>socialist realist</u> style that was mandated by that regime.

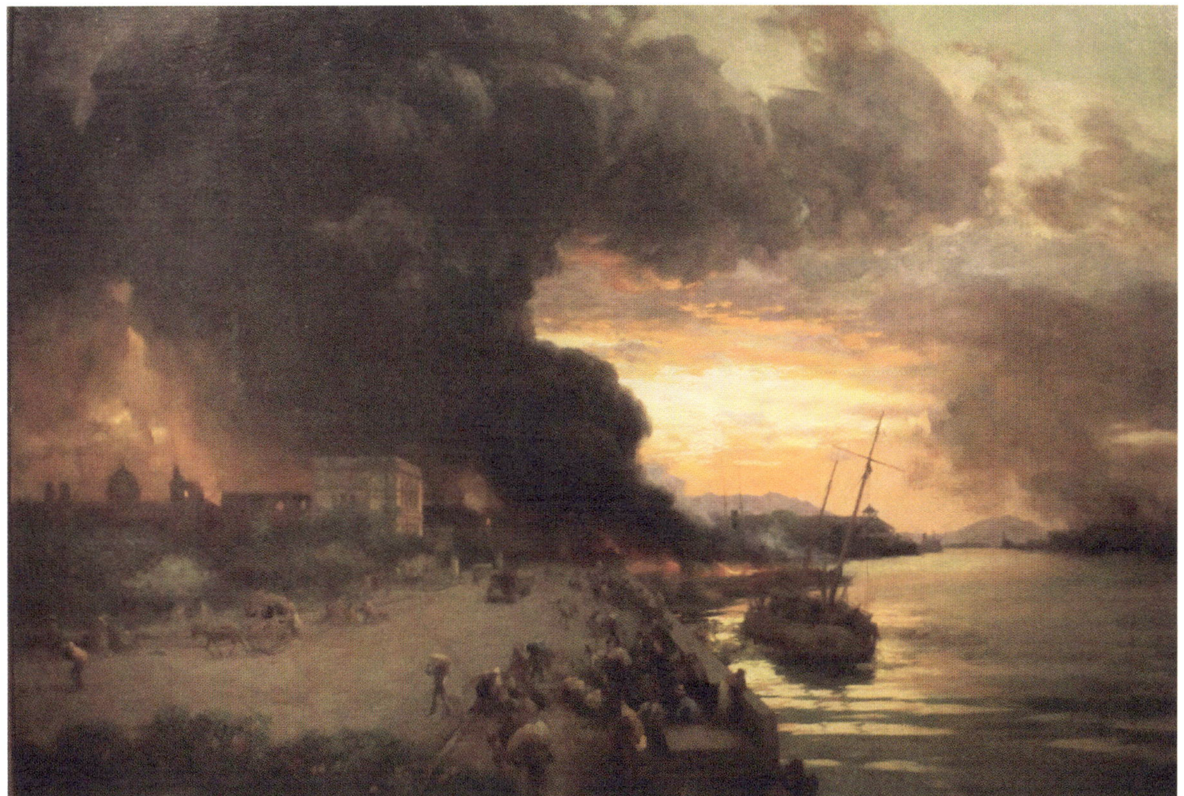

Fernando Amorsolo. *The Burning of Manila*. 1942. Collection of National Museum of Fine Arts, Manila.

Sometimes, depictions of war can be both beautiful and hideous, and in this fine balance, capture the <u>zeitgeist</u>, or spirit of the times. Diem Phung Thi's sculpture combines sharp edges that evoke violence with soft, invitingly lifelike forms. In another example, Fernando Amorsolo's paintings depicting the devastation of Manila during World War II are among the most effective and moving works in his large and varied <u>oeuvre</u>. These images of <u>ruins</u> capture war's brutality, but also its ability to inspire a kind of awe, akin to the experience of the sublime.

Fernando Amorsolo
b. 1892, Philippines; d. 1972, Philippines

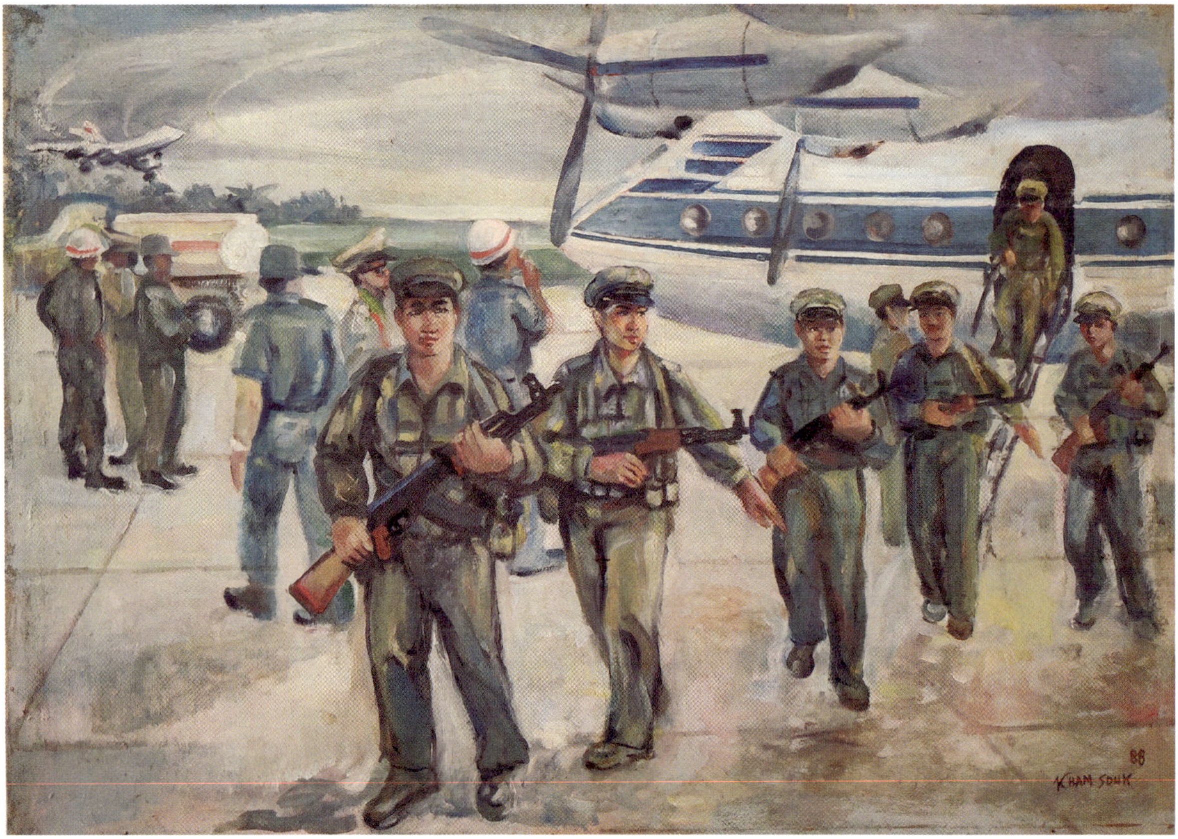

Khamsouk Keomingmuang. *Untitled.* 1988. Oil on canvas, 70 x 100 cm. Collection of MAIIAM Contemporary Art Museum.

The effects of war linger long after battle ends. For example, Laos has officially been at peace since 1975, yet since then, works by Khamsouk Keomingmuang, a National Artist, and Bounpaul Phothyzan, a contemporary artist, have continued to illuminate the looming shadow of wartime.

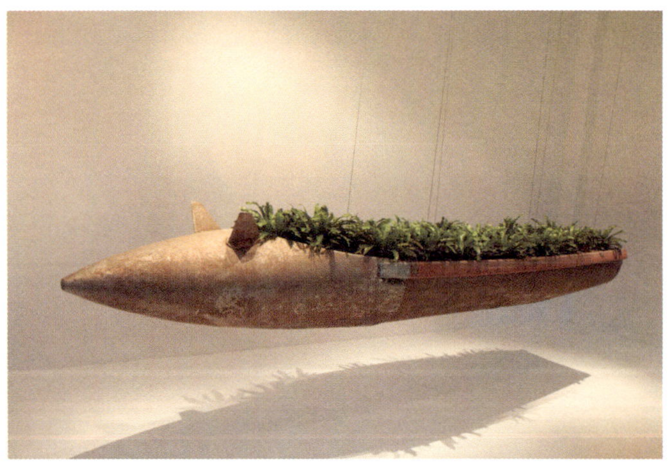

Bounpaul Phothyzan. *Lie of the Land.* 2017. Aluminium, wood, soil, seeds. Two parts, each 80 x 400 x 80cm. Collection of the artist.

WOMEN

Women are essential to the story of modern art, in Southeast Asia as elsewhere, and to processes of <u>modernities</u> more generally. The modern could not have emerged, in art or in life, were it not for women. Yet women are often absent or marginalised in historical accounts. Most exhibitions and museum collections and books—including this one—feature many more male than female artists. And while a great deal of attention has been paid to how modern art articulates national or regional identities and reflects political ideas, much less scholarly regard has been given to how modern art articulates the complex, shifting and often contradictory position of women in modern Southeast Asia.

For a glimpse of some issues at stake, consider the following depictions of women in modern art.

One of the earliest known surviving modern artworks made by a woman in Southeast Asia portrays a female figure sitting on a cart filled with stalks of rice, being driven back from the fields. This woman, who is nursing an infant, is simultaneously conducting maternal and agricultural labour, as observed by art historian Eloisa Hernandez. She is depicted in an embroidery made with human hair, instead of the more usual silk or cotton thread, demonstrating artist Adelaida Paterno's inventive adaptation of a conventionally feminine <u>craft</u>.

Adelaida Paterno
b. 1880, Philippines; d. 1962, Philippines

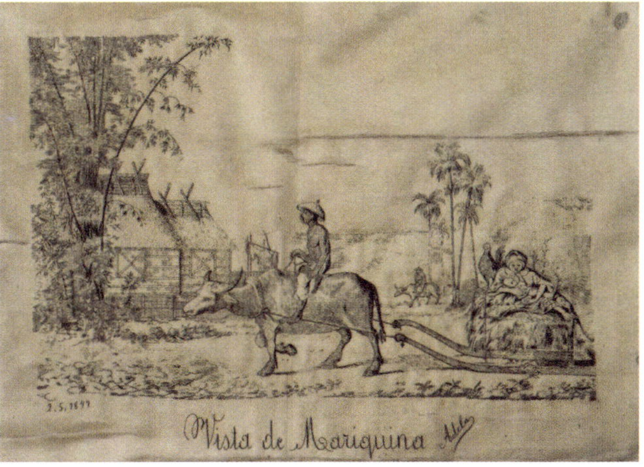

Adelaida Paterno. *Vista de Mariquina*. 1897. Human hair on Chinese silk, 34 x 46 cm. Collection of Bangko Sentral ng Pilipinas.

Many other artworks relate to motherhood, and frequently depict it as a complex, or even uneasy experience. An example is Kartika Affandi's painting *My Daughter Cilla & Lulu*. Lively and expressive swirls of paint express the boundless energy of youth: in some areas, the artist has pressed the

Kartika Affandi
b. 1934, Indonesia

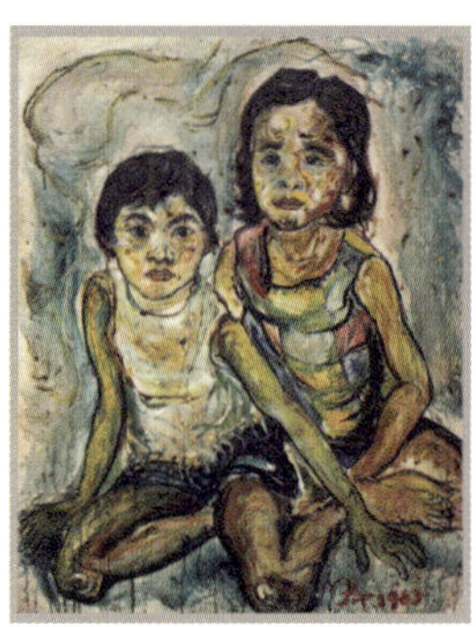

Kartika Affandi. *My Daughter Cilla & Lulu.* 1963. Oil on canvas, 84 x 64 cm. Collection of the artist.

pigment into the canvas, and in other parts the paint stands out in a thick impasto. Yet the rendering of the children's faces suggests an emotional range stretching far beyond childish vigour. The heavy expressions on these open yet seemingly tense faces reflect, perhaps, the mixed feelings of a mother as much as they do the earnest sensibility of a child. As art historian Astri Wright observes, "Many of [Kartika's] portraits achieve a psychological depth rarely seen." The artist is inescapably framed by her <u>biography</u>, being the child of Affandi, a paradigmatically masculine and individualistic <u>artist</u> who encouraged Kartika to paint from an early age. According to Wright, Affandi "wanted to experiment with [Kartika] to see if it was possible to bypass the stage of realistic studies and still produce a good artist. Clearly, this made it all the more difficult later for Kartika to liberate herself from her father's strong influence."

Affandi
b. 1907, Indonesia; d. 1990, Indonesia

As Kartika captures the fatigue of motherhood, Julie Lluch conveys the exhausting nature of women's domestic labour in *Cutting Onions Always Makes Me Cry*. The woman Lluch caricatures has a lifeless-looking face, and the foods she is preparing appear grotesquely unappetising. These features "suggest or intimate interiority," in the words of art historian Alice Guillermo, and prompt us to ask, "are the onion tears not also a subterfuge for the real tears that she weeps from her conventional role of woman for kitchen and bedroom?" Lluch's use of ceramics, usually associated with craft, challenges the valuing of some <u>media</u> over others, a process which parallels the privileging of men over women.

Julie Lluch
b. 1946, Philippines

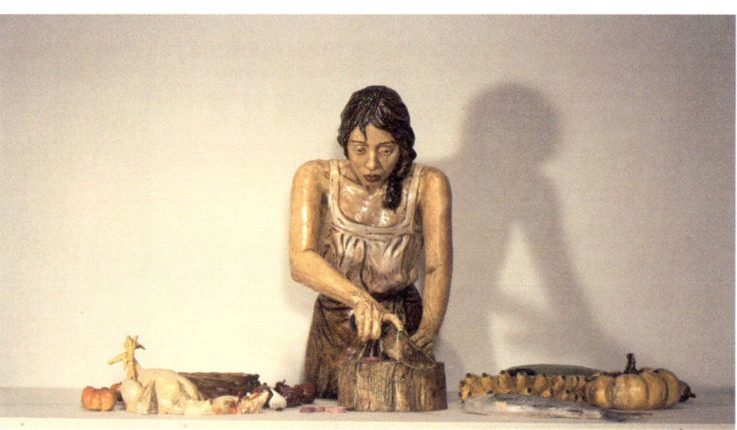

Julie Lluch. *Cutting Onions Always Makes Me Cry.* 1988. Acrylic on ceramics, 72.8 x 140 x 83.5 cm. Collection of Fukuoka Asian Art Museum.

Tith Kanitha
b. 1987, Cambodia

While Lluch laments the sorrows of housework, Tith Kanitha rejects it entirely. "I don't like the idea that women can't move away from the kitchen," Kanitha declares. For

Women Can Move Away from the Stove, she assembled in a shopping mall several clay stoves, of a kind commonly used for cooking in Cambodia, then publicly destroyed them with a hammer. The violence of this action contravenes usual expectations of women's behaviour, yet according to Kanitha, it also elicited curious and engaged responses from passers-by, which was her aim. Many artists have used performance to challenge usual perceptions of women's role in society.

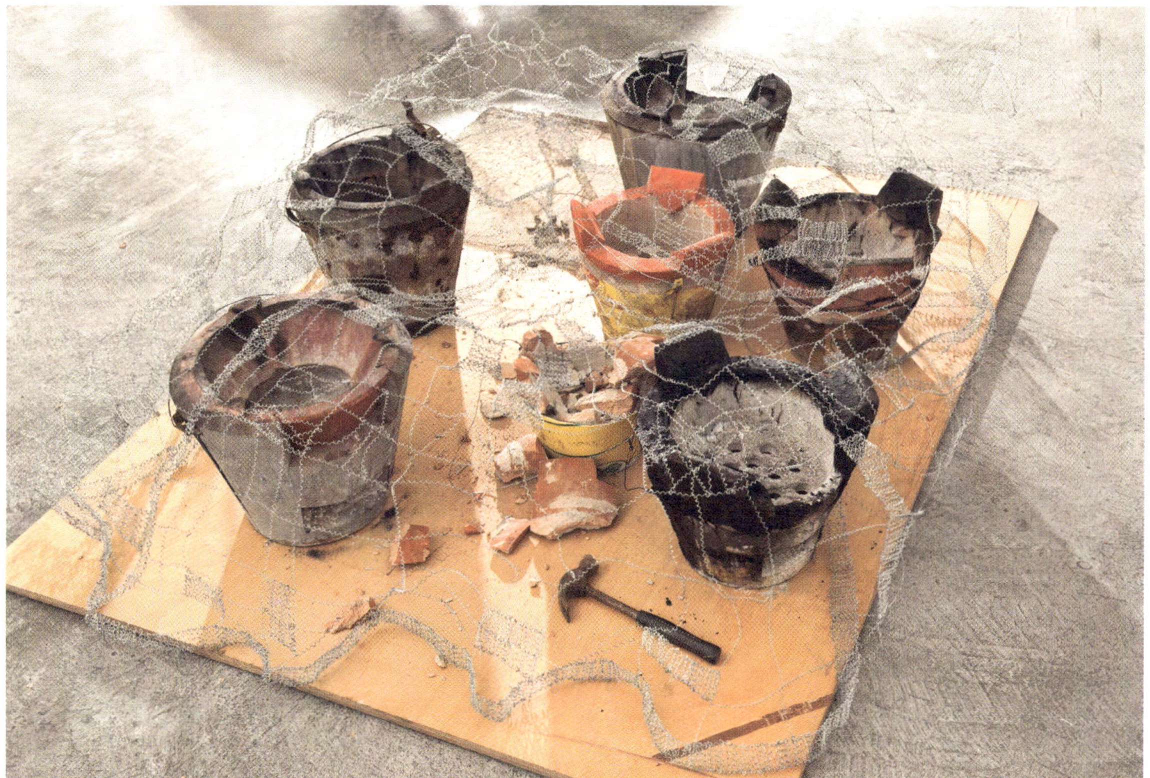

Tith Kanitha. *Women Can Move Away from the Stove*. 2010. Performance and installation with plywood, used clay stoves, hammer, woven wire, dimensions variable.

These depictions of women in modern art add nuance to and challenge familiar stereotypes which cast women as passive and placid. They reveal that modern women have been called on by modern life and ideology to play very active roles.

One such role relates to the concept of <u>nation</u>. The pervasive association of women with the <u>landscape</u>, seen in countless paintings by artists including Fernando Amorsolo and Nhek Dim, make women seem peaceful and calm, but also show women participating in vigorous agricultural labour. In this way, women also function to symbolise the nation, since farming is essential to national economies and imaginaries. Amorsolo takes this further, in a painting which imagines the first Philippine national flag being sewn by

Fernando Amorsolo
b. 1892, Philippines; d. 1972, Philippines

Nhek Dim
b. 1934, Cambodia; d. 1978, Cambodia

three women, representing three Philippine regions—again, associating the female body with land. Juan Luna also uses figures of women to allegorise the relationship between the Philippines and colonial Spain.

Modern art has also highlighted women's crucial role in armed conflict. During the Second Indochina War, for example, women in North Vietnam took up arms and joined communist militias. Many <u>socialist realist</u> artworks, by Nguyen Thu and Ton Duc Luong among others, show women proud of their physical strength and confidence with artillery. This contrasts sharply with earlier armed groups, such as an all-male, all-white "citizens militia" established in Jakarta in 1622, depicted in a 19th-century photograph made by Woodbury and Page.

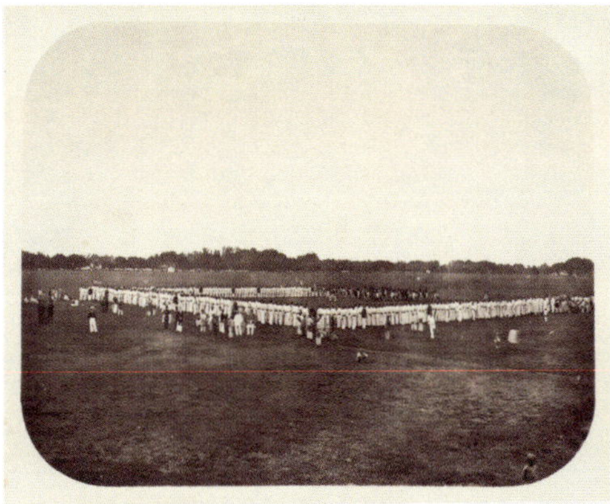

Woodbury and Page studio. *A View of the Citizens' Militia of Batavia on a Field.* Mid-late 19th century. Albumen print, 20 x 25 cm. Collection of National Museum of Singapore.

As in the example of this photograph, we can learn about gender relations in society not only through depictions of women, but also by studying their absences.

The scarcity of artists who are women in many accounts of modern art in Southeast Asia can be explained in part by their exclusion from formal institutions. Women were excluded from early art schools; Hernandez has argued that in the Philippines, this meant that many early artists (like Adelaida Paterno and her sister Paz Paterno) were self-taught. The first woman to be admitted to Manila's School of Drawing and Painting (Escuela de Dibujo y Pintura) was Pelagia Mendoza, who commenced study in 1889. Several of her artworks, and those of Carmen Zaragoza, were reproduced in prominent periodicals at the time, and both artists won prizes in 1892. However, both stopped making art after they married—a familiar and recurring scenario—and their artworks have been lost or destroyed. Elsewhere, some self-taught artists were able to enjoy considerable success. In Thailand,

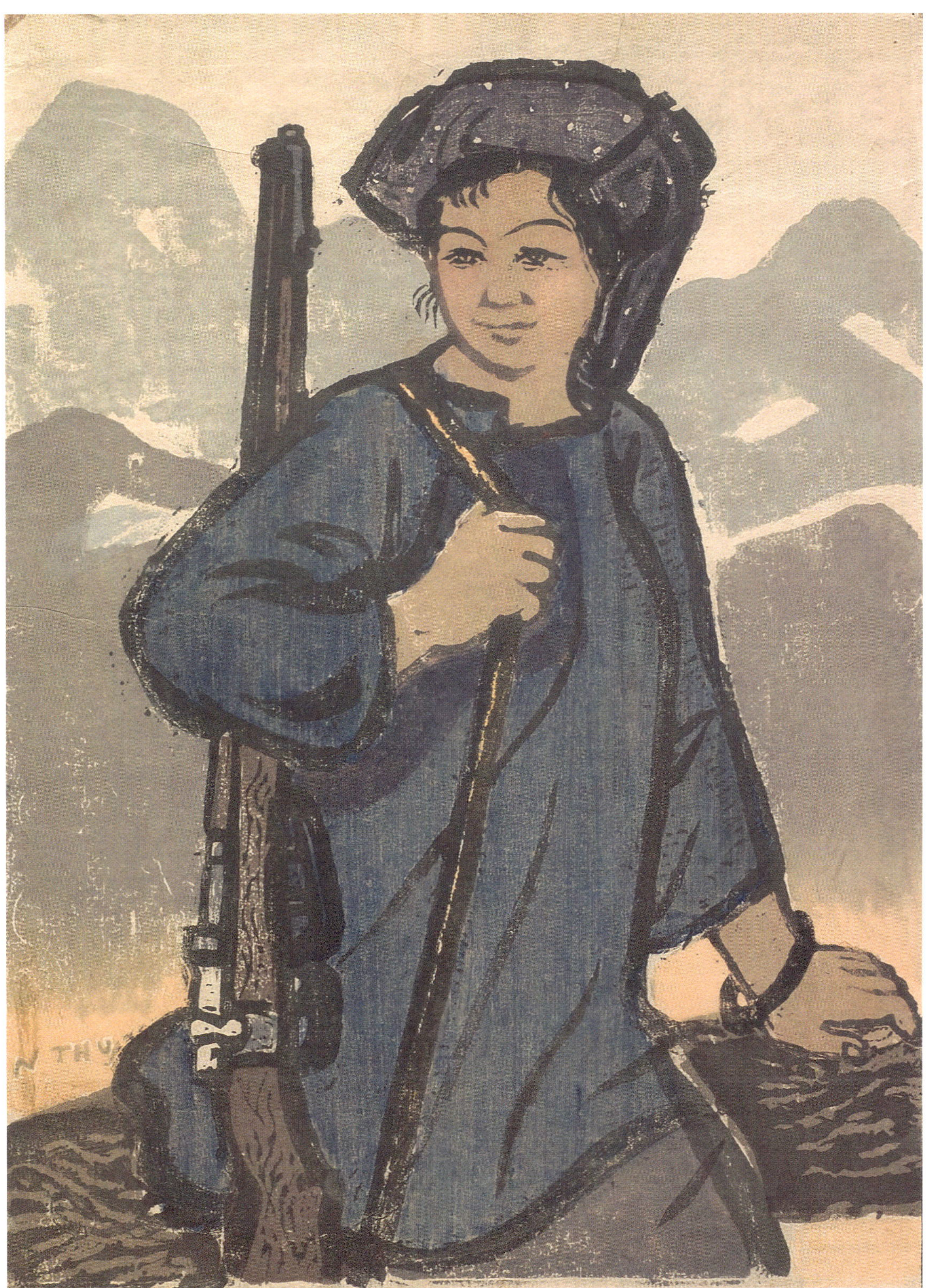

Nguyen Thu. *Militia Girl*. 1966. Woodblock print on paper, 52 x 38 cm. Collection of the Asian Civilisations Museum, Singapore.

Misiem Yipintsoi was awarded three gold medals at National Exhibitions between 1949 and 1951, and her paintings were widely exhibited and internationally toured, despite her lack of formal training. She was born into an elite merchant family, which (along with her skill and originality) likely gave Misiem greater mobility and opportunity than many of her peers.

Yet cases like Misiem's were the exception, rather than the norm. Photographs from Singapore since the 1940s, as well as from Cambodia during the 1960s—among many other examples—reveal that many female students were enrolled in art schools by then. Yet very few of them formally exhibited their artworks, or became known as artists.

As art historian Yvonne Low has argued, there has been no shortage of women making art in Southeast Asia; however, because of motherhood and other demands, many have remained "amateur" rather than "professional artists," and therefore have been often excluded from canonical accounts of art history. More research is needed to make such "amateur" <u>oeuvres</u> by both Southeast Asian as well as colonial women known, such as that of aristocrat and civil servant's wife Dorothea Aldworth, whose watercolour illustrations Low has recovered from obscurity.

The use of unconventional materials and techniques for art—as seen in the work of Paterno, Lluch, Kanitha, and many other artists—has been celebrated as one possible way to create new spaces for women in art. Such approaches have also been important in the development of <u>conceptual</u> and <u>contemporary</u> art practices: perhaps there is a symbiotic link between women and challenges to conventions of the modern.

Many feminist and other scholars have argued that it is not enough just to register that women have been excluded from the canon of art history or to try to raise the profile of artists who are women so that they are included in more exhibitions and histories; the very nature and structure of the canon works to authorise an idea of the artist as male. Women can only be admitted to the <u>canon</u> as "women artists," their status always secondary and exceptional. Affandi, or any other <u>artist</u> identified as male, would never be described as a "man artist."

Without studying art made by women, and without studying representations of women in art, we miss half the story. Our sense of <u>history</u>, of <u>Southeast Asia</u>, and of the <u>zeitgeist</u> or spirit of the times, will remain blinkered and misshapen.

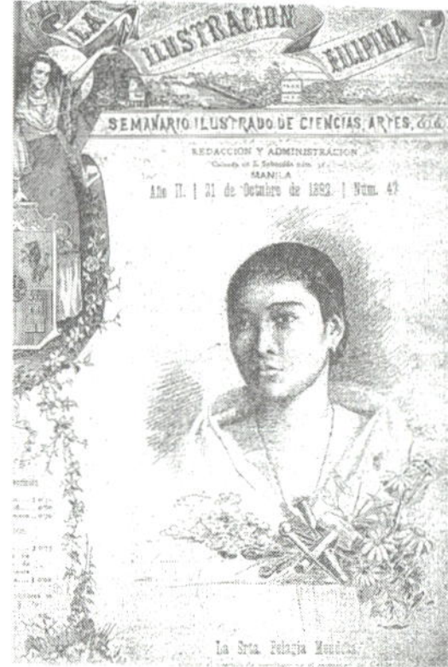

Pelagia Mendoza, depicted on the cover of *Ilustracion Filipina*, 21 October 1892.

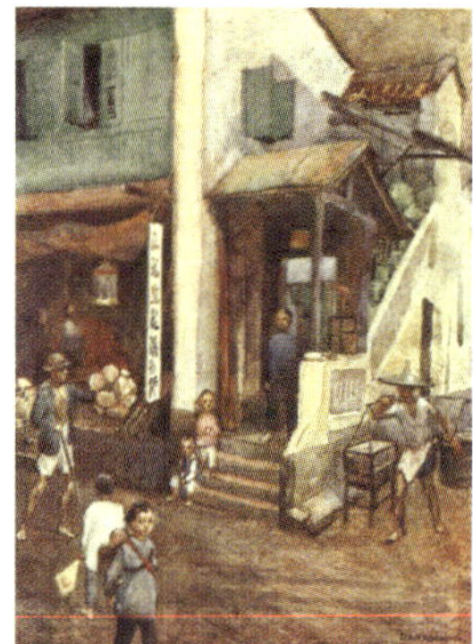

Dorothea Aldworth, *Untitled*, c. 1910. Watercolour, dimensions unknown.

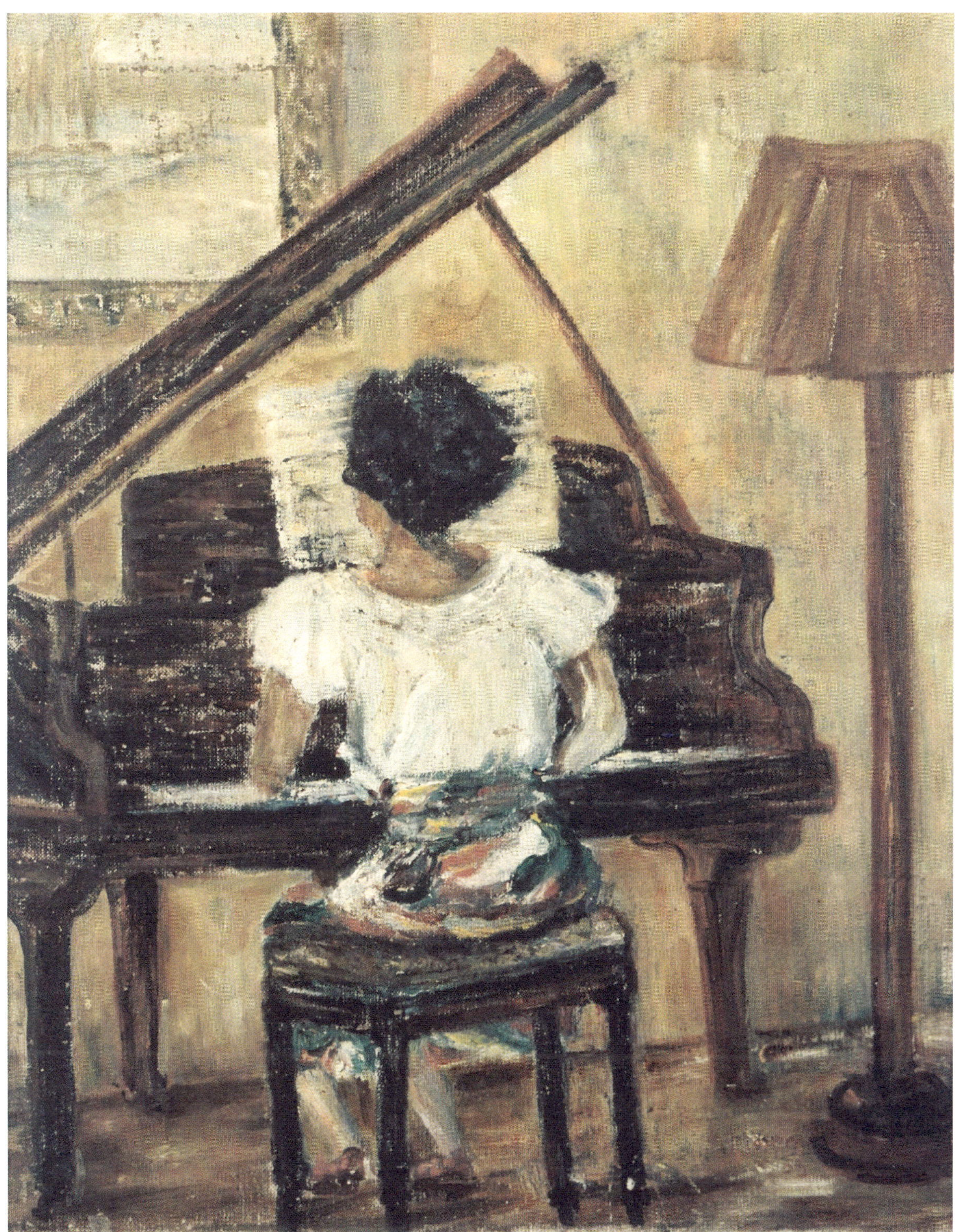

Misiem Yipintsoi. *Self-Portrait*. 1959. Oil on canvas, 51 x 64 cm. Collection of Misiem Yipintsoi.

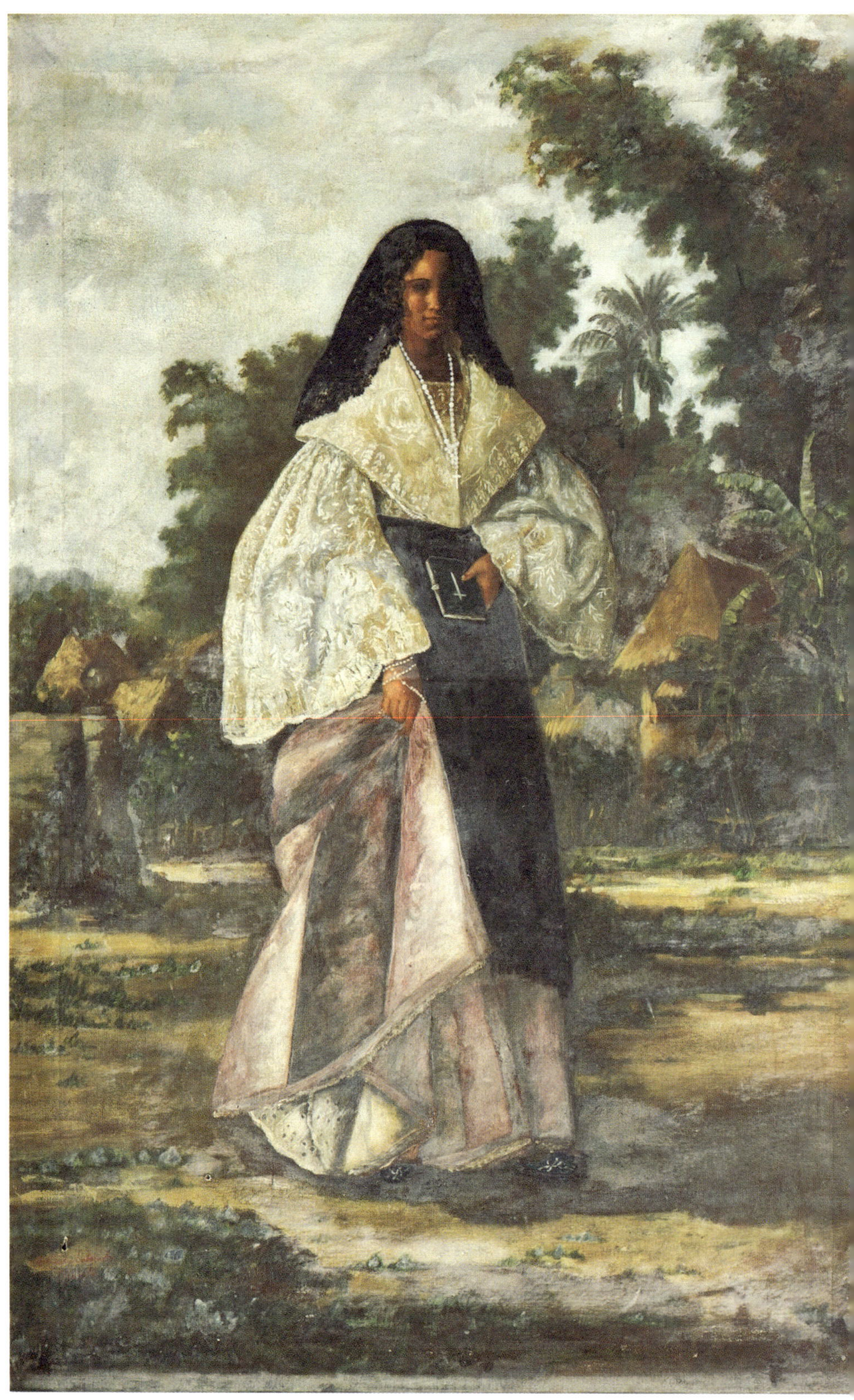

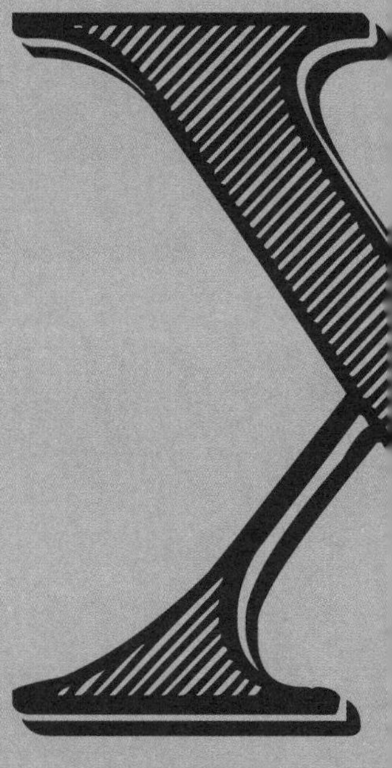

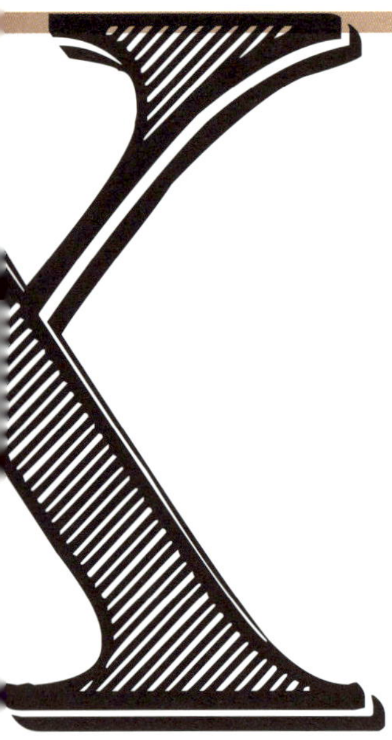

XENOPHILIA

The love of and attraction to all things unknown and for-eign—also called xenophilia—has been significant in the development of modern art in Southeast Asia. The allure of the unfamiliar and exotic is seen in the <u>oeuvre</u> and <u>biography</u> of many artists, often tempered by a deeply held interest in local <u>traditions</u>, and <u>vernacular</u> forms.

A pervasive and recurrent manifestation of xenophilia is seen in the tendency for modern artists to seek approval abroad, and especially in the West. This began during the 19th century, when artists from Southeast Asia first travelled to Europe, seeking <u>education</u> in modern art, as well as joining <u>exhibitions</u> and enjoying the <u>patronage</u> of European elites. The tendency continues in the 21st century, with joining international <u>biennials</u> becoming an increasingly important aspiration for many <u>contemporary</u> artists, and a key indicator of <u>value</u> which often trumps any recognition an artist might win closer to "home."

The <u>reception</u> of many of the best-known Southeast Asian artists from the 19th century, such as Raden Saleh, Juan Luna, and Felix Hidalgo, has focused on celebrating their successes in Europe, including being awarded prizes in competitions that pitted them against their European peers. Artists were celebrated for mastering European styles and techniques, and even adopting European manners, as seen in a portrait of Raden Saleh attributed to Friedrich Carl Albert Schreuel. Some of the few records of exhibiting artists who were <u>women</u> from this period indicate that they also won prizes, but these were local rather than international; for example, artworks by both Pelagia Mendoza and Carmen Zaragoza were discussed and reproduced in prominent Philippine periodicals, and both artists received awards in 1892. Yet perhaps because neither artist was able to travel to Europe to study or join competitions or exhibitions there, their names have since faded into obscurity, and most of their artworks are presumed lost or destroyed.

The xenophilic acclaim for artists who achieved recognition abroad continued in the 20th century. For example, in 1959 when Lai Foong Moi returned from study at one of Paris's most prestigious art schools, "all eyes were on her," as art historian Yvonne Low has noted. Lai was celebrated as the first Malaysian woman sent to study art in Paris, and who had exhibited in several important salon exhibitions. According to Low, "Her professional reputation was boosted by several successful exhibitions upon her return which showcased the oil paintings she completed in Paris and

Raden Saleh
b. circa 1811, Indonesia; d. 1880, Indonesia

Juan Luna
b. 1857, Philippines; d. 1899, Hong Kong

Felix Hidalgo
b. 1855, Philippines; d. 1913, Spain

Friedrich Carl Albert Schreuel
b. 1773, Netherlands; d. 1853, Germany

Pelagia Mendoza
b. 1867, Philippines; d. 1939, Philippines

Carmen Zaragoza
b. 1876, Philippines; d. 1943, Philippines

Lai Foong Moi
b. 1931, Malaysia; d. 1994. Singaporepines

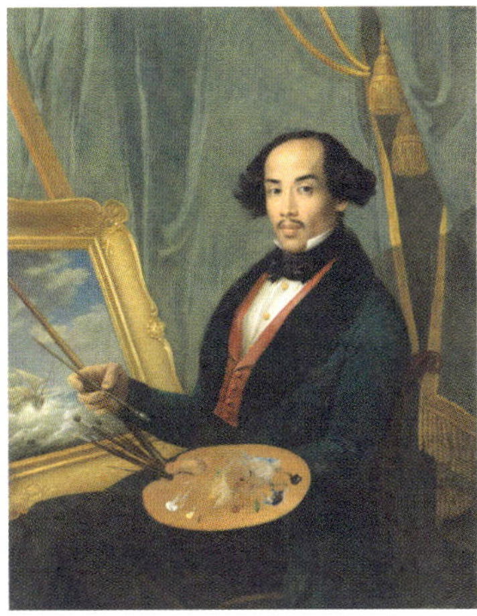

Attributed to Friedrich Carl Albert Schreuel. *Portrait of Raden Saleh Syarif Bustaman.* c. 1840. Oil on canvas, 107 x 85 cm. Collection of Rijksmuseum.

positioned her as an internationally recognized artist." Around the same time in Thailand, many artists began to embark on long odysseys abroad, seeking inspiration and forming new connections, but also proving their worth to local audiences upon their eventual return. Art historian David Teh offers numerous examples to argue that "international mobility has been an important currency in Thai modern art."

Xenophilia extends both ways. During the 19th century, many European and diaspora artists also demonstrated a kind of xenophilia in their fascination with aspects of life in Southeast Asia which they perceived as exotic. An example is a painting by Granada Cabezudo, depicting a mestiza Filipina woman who appears to be dressed for church. The artist has carefully captured details in the subject's fashions, as well as the tropical vegetation and vernacular housing in the background. Cabezudo was the daughter of a Spanish colonial military officer stationed in Manila since 1847, according to researcher Concha Diaz. She was also the only woman to join an 1887 exhibition in Madrid, according to art historian Eloisa Hernandez. During the 20th century, countless artists hailing from diverse locations were increasingly drawn to Bali as an especially fertile source of foreign charms. Miguel Covarrubias, for example, repeatedly expressed the appeal of human figures he saw in Bali, while Walter Spies rendered the lush foliage found on the island with a memorable and influential flourish.

While the beguiling appeal of the strange and unfamiliar has been a significant force shaping modern art, it is crucial to note that the foreign and unknown have not been uncritically accepted or reproduced without change. Rather, artists have actively selected and adapted foreign ideas and techniques, as part of the dynamic process of transfer.

EAGER, ALERT,
AS IF EVERY
NERVE IN MY
BEING WAS
STANDING
ON TIPTOE TO
STRETCH OUT
AND FEEL THE
BLOOD, BONE
AND SINEW OF
THE PLACE.

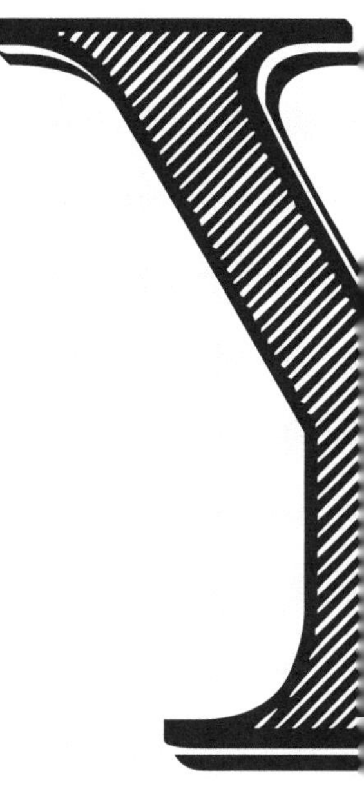

—Vicente Manansala

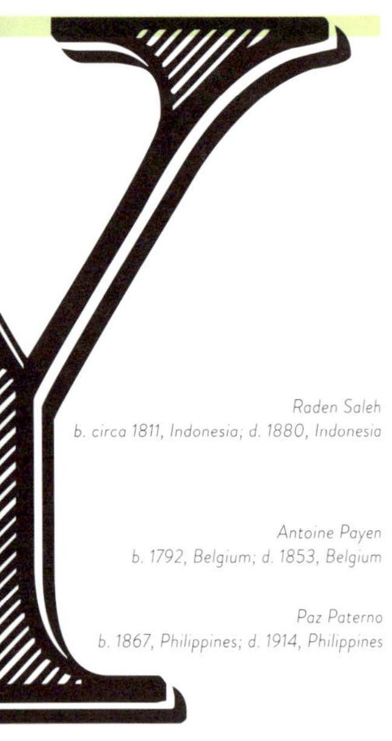

YOUTH

Qualities of wide-eyed enthusiasm and unpretentious appreciation are often associated with youth. These qualities abound in the modern art of Southeast Asia.

In part, this may have to do with the young age at which many artists began their education and started making artwork. The modern idea of the artist as a distinguished individual, with singular talent, has emerged partly from the repeated recognition of "genius" in artists while they were still very youthful. For example, Raden Saleh, who is celebrated for being the first Southeast Asian <u>artist</u> sent for <u>education</u> in Europe, was first entrusted to the tutelage of artist Antoine Payen in Java when he was only around eight years old. Similarly, <u>women</u> who were artists in the 19th century, such as Paz Paterno and Adelaida Paterno, also began practising while still in their teens. In the 20th century, it became increasingly common for the sons and daughters of artists to follow their parents, and also become artists. This continued and extended the tendency for artists to begin studying at a young age. Examples include Kartika Affandi, daughter of Affandi, who began painting with her father while still an infant, and Lim Yew Kuan, son of Lim Hak Tai, who studied under his father at Singapore's Nanyang Academy of Fine Arts (NAFA), graduated at age 22, taught at NAFA from age 24, and co-established the <u>social realist</u> Equator Art Society at age 28.

Youth has also frequently been taken up by artists as an evocative subject matter. The depiction of fresh faces, nubile and healthy bodies, and bright eyes is often imbued with the suggestion of allegory, as if the artist's models might also be emblems of the artist's curious mind, or even of the young <u>nation</u>. When the subject portrayed is female, this may also contribute to the common association of women with the land.

Vicente Manansala is acclaimed for his depiction of nude women. He seemed to pay little mind to the <u>taboo</u> of nudity, instead using the genre to demonstrate his mastery over both naturalistic <u>realism</u> and more <u>abstract</u> styles of composition, which recall cubism in their use of angular blocks and lines. Significantly, almost all the women Manansala portrayed in his nude drawings and paintings are palpably youthful. Writing of his time in Paris, where he lived and studied in 1950, Manansala described "that feeling of humility and open-mindedness [that] gave me a keen sense of wonder as I roamed the streets of Paris." He recalled the feeling of being "suddenly transplanted into a new world, a

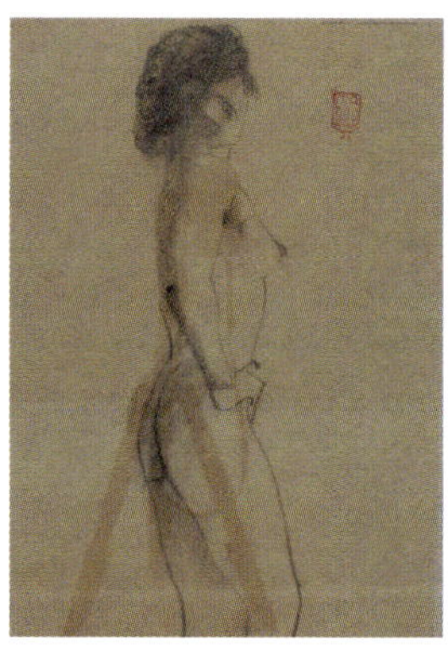

Vicente Manansala. *Not titled (Nude)*. c. 1950s. Ink on paper, 42 x 30 cm. Lito and Kim Camacho Collection.

different world, a world full of color, exuberance and sparkle like the city of Paris." Although he was 40 years old at the time, Manansala clearly experienced a youthful awakening while in Paris, and he conveyed this in his artworks and their depictions of young women. His drawings made at the time, and in the decades following, viscerally evoke this sensation of being "eager, alert, as if every nerve in my being was standing on tiptoe to stretch out and feel the blood, bone and sinew of the place."

Youth are also implicitly addressed by some artists as primary audiences for their work. For example, Lim Yew Kuan's *For the Future Generation II*, made when the artist was only 26 years old, indicates Lim's orientation to his youthful peers. Moreover, survivors of <u>war</u> and <u>genocide</u>, such as Svay Ken and Khamsouk Keomingmuang, also speak of being motivated to depict their past experiences in part by a desire to ensure that <u>history</u> is remembered by younger generations.

It is often said that modern art is chiefly oriented toward the future, and that artists visualise the feeling of <u>time</u> speeding up. The pervasive presence of youth perpetuates this, while also offering the promise of renewal, and the possibility of change.

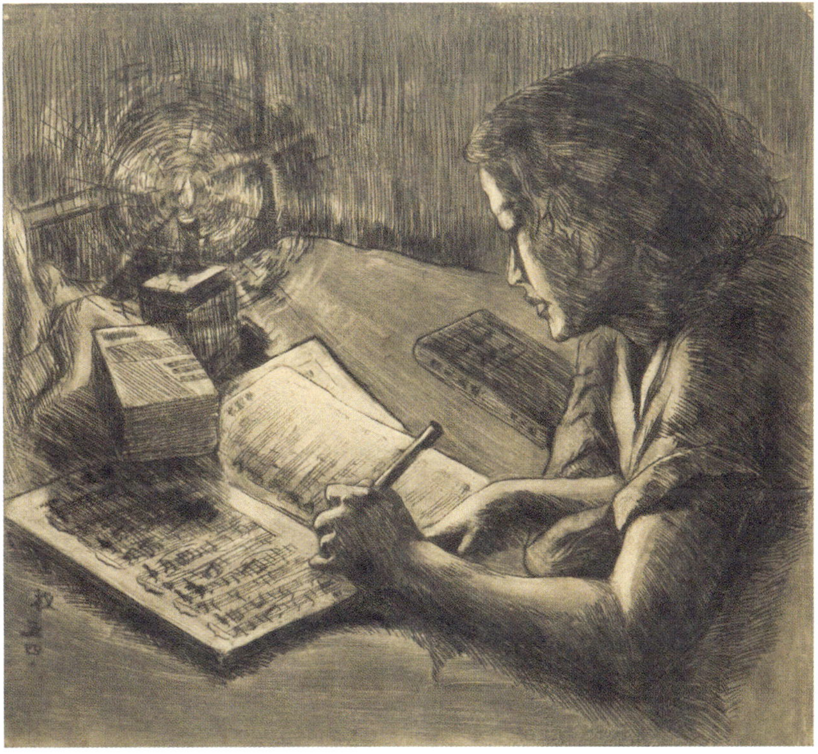

Lim Yew Kuan. *For the Future Generation II*. 1954. Etching, 20.5 x 18.5 cm. Gift of the artist. Collection of National Gallery Singapore.

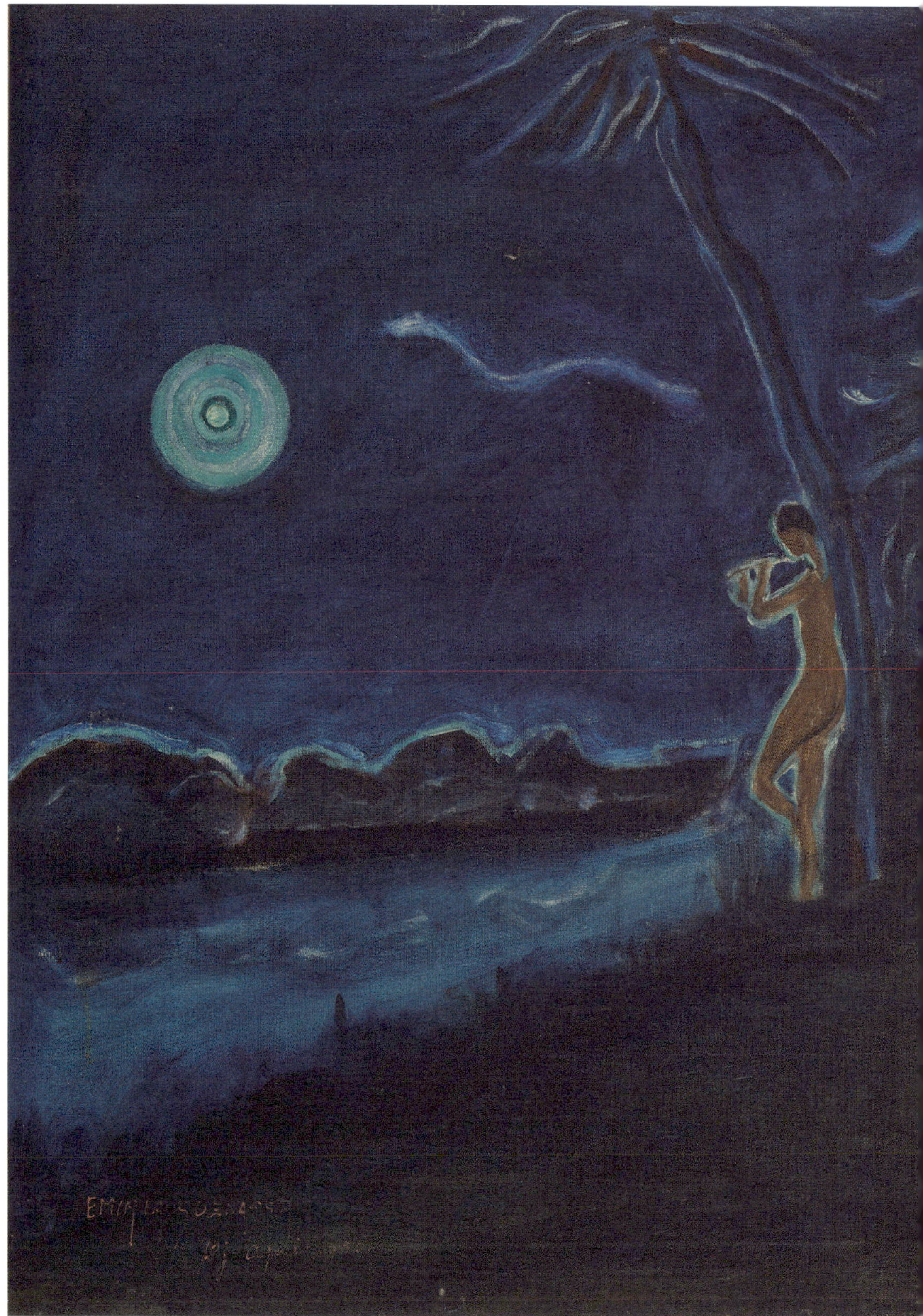

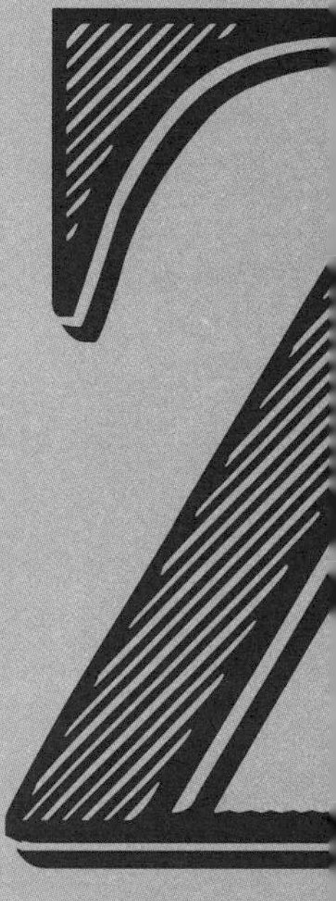

Emiria Sunassa. *Peniup Seruling dan Purnama* (Flute Blower and Full Moon). 1958. Oil on board, 80 x 60 cm. Collection of Iskandar Waworuntu.

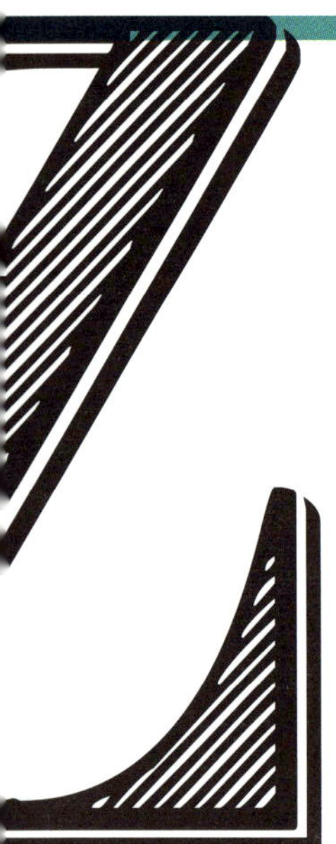

ZEITGEIST

"At every turn, we are surrounded by images on billboards, paintings, sculptures, drawings, illustrations, prints, cartoons, posters, murals, photographs, film, and computer graphics," writes art historian Alice Guillermo. A proliferation of art and visual culture, sometimes taking bewilderingly new forms, is indeed one of the defining features of <u>modern</u> life. Notwithstanding the occasionally dizzying effects of this ocular overload, art can nevertheless sometimes offer a sense of clarity.

Modern art is often said to capture the zeitgeist—that is, to express the defining spirit or mood of a moment in history, through its prevailing ideas. "Zeitgeist" is a term originally derived from German philosophy, but now widely used in cultural discourse. The zeitgeist is a concept that allows us to interpret art by seeing it in relation to ideas circulating in the world at a specific time. As Guillermo suggests, "Understanding art has to do with 'reading' the visual work as a re-presentation of the world." Art, she affirms, is a "signifying practice conveying a complex of ideas, feelings, values, attitudes, moods, and atmospheres that derive from world views and ideologies." That is, artworks reflect key ideas in the world in the moment when they are made. This is one reason why the study of modern art, for all its challenges, can be so deeply rewarding.

Po Po. *Painting for the Blind #3*. 1986 (reconstructed 2015). Nail, enamel, and oil on canvas, 78.5 x 78.5 x 3.5 cm. Collection of National Gallery Singapore.

One especially clear way in which art can be seen to express the zeitgeist, or spirit of the times, is when many artists choose to make artworks in a similar style, or about the same subject matter. Sometimes, artists working in far-flung locations may even share a common approach, without being aware of each other. In a surprisingly stark example of this unusual scenario, art historian Simon Soon recounts that none of the several left-leaning arts organisations he studied who were active in Indonesia, Malaysia, Singapore and Thailand between the 1950s and 1970s were in communication with any of the others. "In spite of this lack of evidence of direct contact," Soon remarks, the groups "shared many similar features." Another case is found in the early <u>oeuvre</u> of the artist Po Po who, during the 1980s in Myanmar, made artworks which have been described as <u>conceptual</u> and <u>contemporary</u>, despite having no <u>connections</u> with artists working in similar ways elsewhere. How did Po Po seize upon such similarly new ideas about art, all by himself? This is a mystery, but the notion of an artist having a special ability to intuit the zeitgeist offers one possible answer.

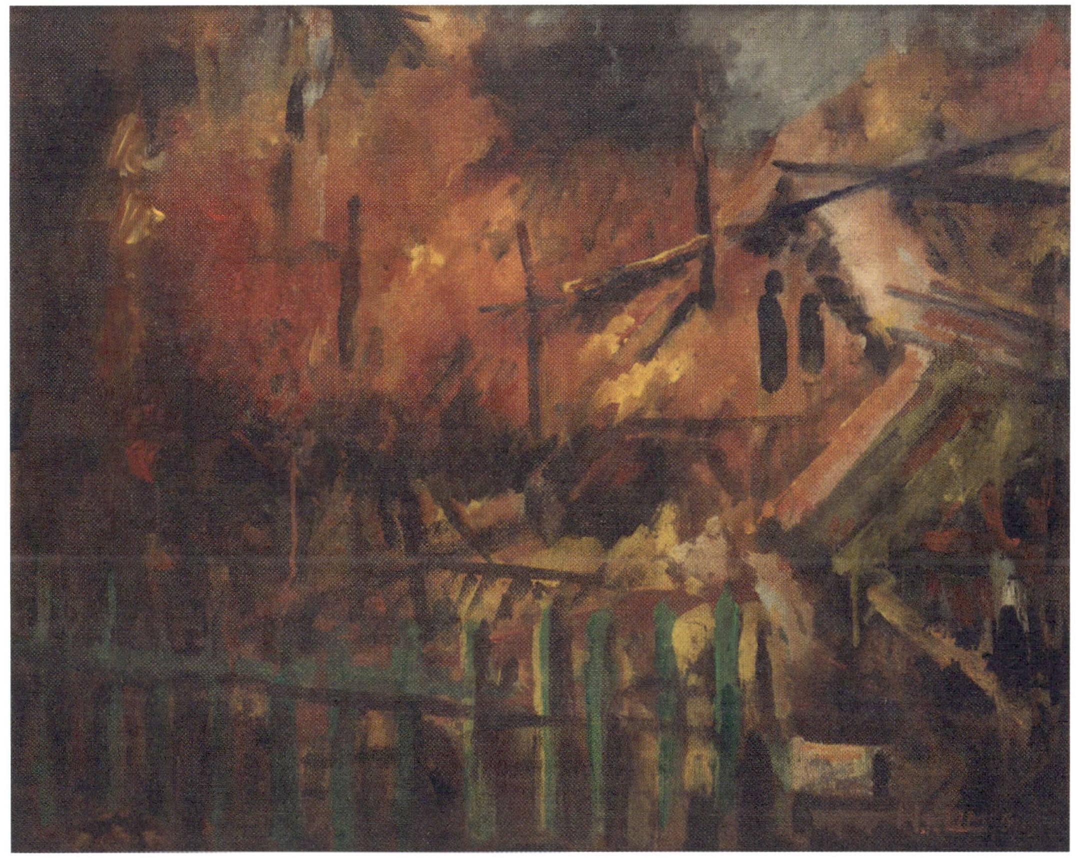

Lim Hak Tai. *Fire*. 1961. Acrylic on board, 59 x 75.5 cm. Gift of Lim Yew Kuan. Collection of National Gallery Singapore.

More commonly, artists choose to make works about a similar topic because of its prominence in public life at a given moment. An example of this is seen in the many art-works made in response to a catastrophic blaze in Singapore's Bukit Ho Swee neighbourhood in 1961, which left 16,000 people homeless and precipitated the construction of large-scale social housing, which now dominates the city. In Lim Hak Tai's *Fire*, the mercurial and formless qualities of fire and smoke are heightened by the jumble of not-quite-vertical lines, which appear to represent houses collapsing in the inferno. More than simply depicting the Bukit Ho Swee blaze, Lim's *Fire* evokes a larger sense of drama and upheaval —tinged with danger, but also possibility—which character-ises the post-World War II period; it captures the zeitgeist, common to Southeast Asia then, of the heated years of <u>debate</u>, <u>urbanisation</u>, and social change leading up to and following national <u>independence</u>.

Lim's *Fire* is one of many representations of the Bukit Ho Swee fire and its aftermath. The artist's son, Lim Yew Kuan, as well as Koeh Sia Yong, Tan Choo Kuan and Liu Kang, also made artworks about this event. There may have been others as well; for instance, it is unknown how many of the <u>women</u> who studied art at the time (but never became "professional" <u>artists</u>) might have addressed this topic. From the works that did emerge, however, we can see a variety of responses, each highlighting the different sentiments that existed then. Koeh's work, made five years after the fire, is a <u>social realist</u> woodblock print in which the suffering of those who lost their homes appears emblematic of the hardships endured by the mass of lower-income people. By contrast, Tan's de-pictions disregard the tragedy of the fire, instead optimisti-cally celebrating the rapid and ambitious development which followed, as part of a larger process of urban transforma-tion. Lim's *Fire* was made the same year the blaze took place, which suggests perhaps a prescient awareness of the historic importance of the event. Bukit Ho Swee's destruction fol-lowed several other kampong (village) fires across the island; rumours circulated that the fires may have been deliberately caused by the government, which heightened their pregnant power as symbols of the politically turbulent zeitgeist.

The example of kampong fires and subsequent urban transformations captures something of the public sphere during this historical moment, but the 1960s zeitgeist is also reflected in private settings, and through the realignment of interpersonal relations. In Patrick Ng's *Self-Portrait with Friends*, the spirit of the times is reflected in the <u>fashions</u>

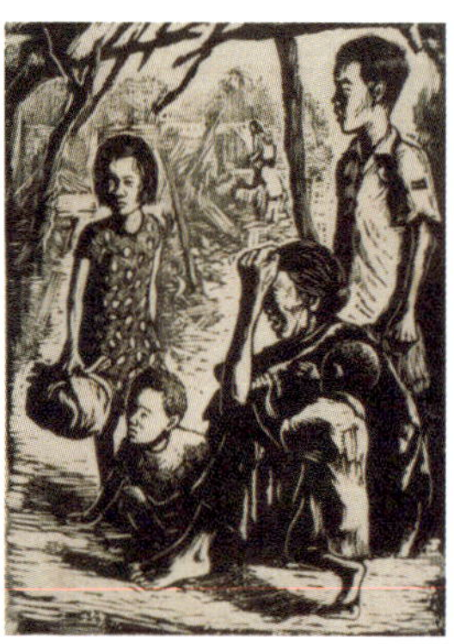

Koeh Sia Yong. *Scene of Bukit Ho Swee Fire*. Undated. Woodblock print on pa-per, 21 x 15 cm. Collection of National Museum of Singapore.

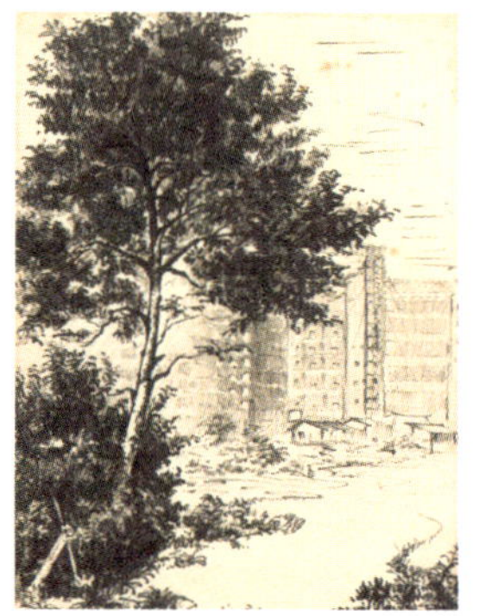

Tan Choo Kuan. *Rebuilding Bukit Ho Swee*. 1962. Ink on paper, 37.3 x 27.2 cm. Gift of Ms Tan Teng Teng. Collection of National Gallery Singapore.

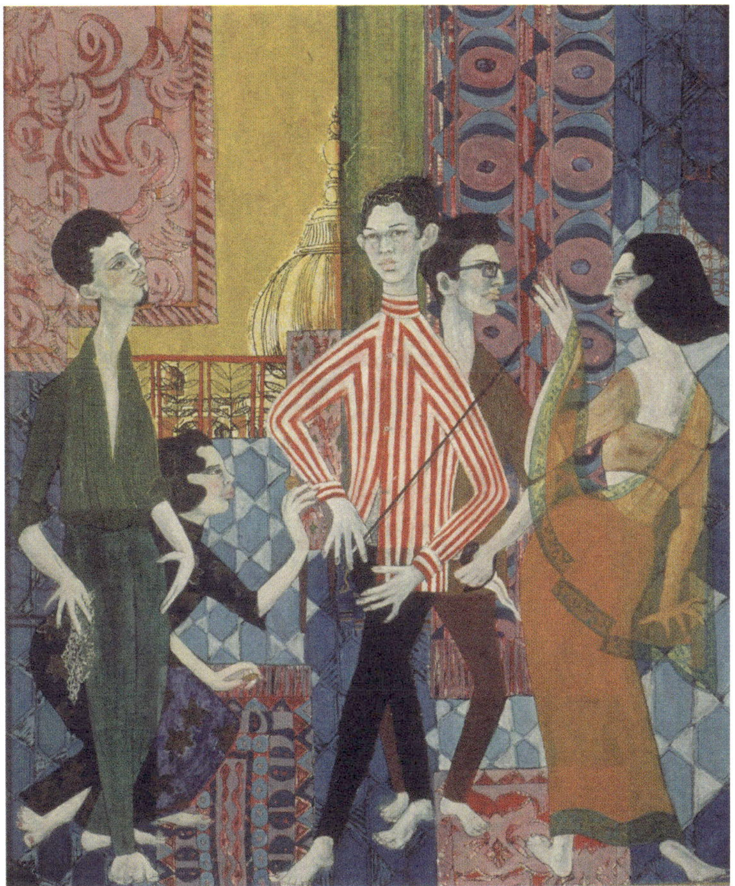

Patrick Ng. *Self-Portrait with Friends*. 1962. Oil on board, 69.7 x 59.5 cm. Collection of National Gallery Singapore.

depicted, as well as the charged atmosphere of poly-directional sensual intimacy implied between the figures, and the <u>craft</u>-inspired decor. Simon Soon observes that the work "brings the atmosphere of then contemporary Kuala Lumpur alive... No longer positioned as a backwater town in relation to Singapore, independence refashioned the artistic milieu of Kuala Lumpur as urbane and chic." Noting the culturally diverse soiree of artists depicted in the work, Soon sees Ng "capturing the electric pulse of the city as it... assume[d] increased importance."

These various examples, by Lim, Koeh, and Ng, all convey the zeitgeist not only in their subject matter, but also in the experimental and mostly effervescent styles which the artists have adopted.

A similarly novel style is seen in Emiria Sunassa's work from the time. Her compositions feature unusual framings of her chosen subjects, and she uses a limited palette of colours in most pictures, with the density of tones compounding the emotional force of each image. Yet whereas the examples cited above reflect aspects of mainstream ideas and issues, Emiria's work instead repeatedly focuses on marginal subjects far from the centre of political power, such as people from the eastern edges of Indonesia. Perhaps the air of solitude and mystery in *Peniup Seruling dan Purnama* (Flute Blower and Full Moon), for example, reflects the spirit of the times in Emiria's world; after all, the zeitgeist not only changes with time, but is always also a reflection of individual perspective.

If Emiria's work embodies her vision of the zeitgeist, it does so, at least in part, because it is so enigmatic. As Emiria's oeuvre makes thrillingly apparent, art can hold many ideas together in a single work. Contradictions and confusions are brought to light, and celebrated as sources of inspiration and insight.

A work of art can also speak to the spirit of multiple different <u>times</u>. An example is Erika Tan's series of artworks gathered under the title, *Halimah-The-Empire-Exhibition -Weaver-Who-Died-Whilst-Demonstrating-Her-Craft* (2015–2017). The works in this series together advance a semi-fictional account of a <u>historical</u> figure named Halimah Binti Abdullah. A woman about whom very little is known, Halimah is identified as an expert Malay weaver who, together with 19 others from the former colony of Malaya, was transported to London for the *1924 British Empire Exhibition*. Tan speculatively and provocatively asks whether we might retrospectively consider Halimah as an "artist," too.

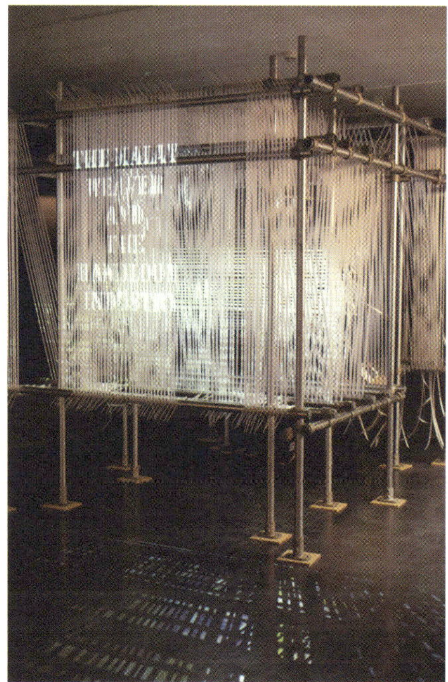

Erika Tan. *The "Forgotten" Weaver*. 2018. Video, 2 channels, sound, 10 min; metal structure; packaging strapping; dimensions variable. From the series *Halimah- The-Empire-Exhibition-Weaver-Who- Died-Whilst-Demonstrating-Her-Craft*. Installation view, NUA Norwich, 2018.

Tan's series conveys at once both the mood of the time in which it was made, as well as the zeitgeist of a specific moment in the past, which she takes up as the work's subject matter. The work's indictment of colonialism and its exploitation of people perceived as <u>exotic</u> casts in sharp relief the spirit of European imperialism in the early 20th century. But simultaneously, the artist's choice of <u>medium</u>, as well as her melding of fiction with history and humour with critique, captures the zeitgeist of the <u>contemporary</u> moment in which the work was made, and in which we view it today. An important part of this is the artist's challenge to the emerging <u>canon</u> of modern art history in Southeast Asia, including its new museums and other institutions.

Art may reflect the ideas of the past, but it also illuminates the present, and can engender new ideas for the future.

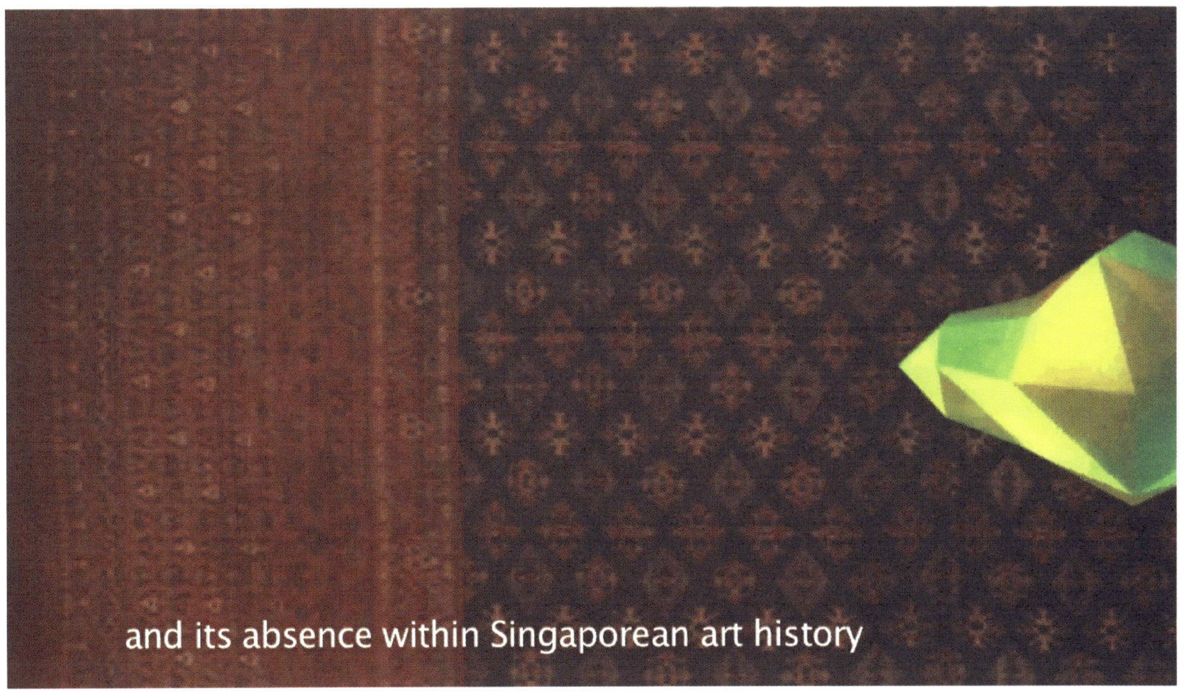

Erika Tan. Still from *A Presentation By Proxy*. 2013. Video, single channel, sound, 20 min 14 sec. From the series *Halimah-The-Empire-Exhibition-Weaver-Who-Died-Whilst-Demonstrating-Her-Craft*.

ACKNOWLEDGEMENTS

Writing this book has been a thrilling, but also daunting process. For his generous encouragement of my work, and for believing in the potential usefulness of the book for students and general readers, I am grateful to Simon Soon. His friendship, insights and suggestions on earlier draft sections have been invaluable. I also warmly thank Phoebe Scott for her patience and care in offering wise comments and astute corrections on an earlier complete draft. Thanks also to Liz Reed, Guo-Liang Tan, and Seng Yu Jin for their kind support and helpful suggestions on earlier drafts. Any remaining errors are, of course, my own.

For his role in bringing me to Singapore, and enriching my time here with his guidance, I am especially grateful to T.K. Sabapathy.

Work on this book began while I was a Postdoctoral Fellow at Nanyang Technological University, Singapore. I completed the writing after taking up the role of Curator at the National Gallery Singapore. I am grateful to both institutions for their support. I also thank the librarians at both institutions, and elsewhere.

My work has benefited from conversations with many colleagues and friends, too numerous to list here. I thank them all, including: David Chandler, Isabel Ching, Thanavi Chotpradit, John Clark, May Adadol Ingawanij, Brigitta Isabella, Patrick D. Flores, Gridthiya Gaweewong, Edwin Jurriens, Eileen Legaspi-Ramirez, Yvonne Low, Lewis Mayo, Ute Meta Bauer, Vera Mey, Nikos Papastergiadis, Siddharta Perez, Chairat Polmuk, Ashley Thompson, and Clare Veal. Also many others too numerous to name, especially colleagues at the National Gallery Singapore, and artists.

Some of these people share with me the pleasure of editing the journal, *Southeast of Now: Directions in Contemporary and Modern Art in Asia*, published by the National University of Singapore Press. I thank all those whose contribution make that publication possible.

This book includes over 250 illustrations, drawn from both public and private collections across Southeast Asia and beyond, including not only artworks found in exhibitions, catalogues, and other publications, but also archival materials, and images of works which are no longer extant. The inclusion of so many and such diverse illustrations would have been impossible without the generosity of many people, and the patience of Sara Siew, Renee Staal and others at the National Gallery Singapore. I thank all the many artists, as well as their families and estates, who kindly granted us permission to reproduce their work here. I also thank the following people for their kind assistance with securing images and permissions: Sarena Abdullah, Karen Adair, Aung Min, Eric Booth, Khamvone Boulyaphonh, Bonnie Brereton, Bui Thi Thanh Mai, Ringo Bunoan, Zoe Butt, Ca Le Thang, Kim Camacho, Siobhan Campbell, Melissa Carlson, Yvon Chalm, Kittima Chareeprasit, Clarissa Chikiamco, Thanavi Chotpradit, Kevin Chua, Matt Cox, Vandy Dim Nhek, Wulan Dirgantoro, Kathleen Ditzig, the Dogma Collection, Editions Didier Millet, Rene Anant Feddersen, Shona Findlay, Gallery Ver, Gilles de Flogny, Patrick D. Flores, Reinhart Frais, Harris Fried, Marc Gloede, Goh Sze Ying, Albert I. Goodman, Tada Hengsapkul, Misouda Heaungsoukkhoun, Eloisa May P. Hernandez, Doris Ho, Hoai Trai, Horikawa Lisa, Lucas Huang, Anders Jiras, Nathalie Johnston, Rahel Joseph, Yin Ker, Khin Mya Zin, Jean-Sien Kin, Le Thien Bao, Joleen Loh, Yvonne Low, Sharman Minus, Tarun Nagesh, Isabel Consuelo A. Nazareno, Bill Nguyen, Ngoc Nguyen, Nova Contemporary, Oei Hong Djien, Mary Pansanga, Pen Sereypagna, Siddharta Perez, Pakpoom Pholakorn, Tuksina Pipitkul, Phan Thao Nguyen, Chairat Polmuk, Quang Viet, Tyler Rollins Fine Art, Eksuda Singhalampong, the late Andrew Ranard, Phoebe Scott, Seng Yu Jin, Simon Soon, Renee Staal, Mikke Susanto, Svay Pisith, Adele Tan, Erika Tan, Wei Leng Tay, Nora A. Taylor, Ma Thanegi, Sarah Tiffin, Charmaine Toh, Trung Pham, Phiny Ung, Pierrette Van Cleve, Vuth Lyno, Farah Wardani, U Win Aung, Kerstin Winking, Julie Wolf, You Muoy, and many others.

It has been a great pleasure to work with Sara Siew at the National Gallery Singapore on this publication. I am grateful for her patience, guidance, and care, and for the support of many other colleagues, especially Ryan How.

My final thanks are to my family and friends, especially Edward and Pam; Danni and Chris; Anna, Dom, Brandon, and Geoff; Tada, Pagna, Mera, Veasna, Samnang, Dara, Meta, and Daniel; Sidd, Kate, Kat, and Lynda; and most of all Liz, Myrina, and Georgia.

<u>BIBLIOGRAPHY</u>

This bibliography offers a short list of suggested further reading, as well as a longer list of selected works which have been directly cited. General histories not specifically related to art and culture, as well as archival materials, have largely been omitted from these lists, but readers should be aware that these often offer a wealth of additional information and ideas.

SELECTED FURTHER READING

Arus, Hj Baharudin bin Hj Mohd. *Modern Artists of Brunei Darassalam*. Bandar Seri Begawan: Doktor Haji Baharudin bin Arus, 2013.

Chotpradit, Thanavi, J Pilapil Jacobo, Eileen Legaspi-Ramirez, Roger Nelson, Nguyen Nhu Huy, Chairat Polmuk, San Lin Tun, Phoebe Scott, Simon Soon, Jim Supangkat. "Terminologies of 'Modern' and 'Contemporary' 'Art' in Southeast Asia's Vernacular Languages: Indonesian, Javanese, Khmer, Lao, Malay, Myanmar/Burmese, Tagalog/Filipino, Thai and Vietnamese." *Southeast of Now: Directions in Contemporary and Modern Art in Asia 2*, No. 2 (October 2018): 65–195.

Clark, John, editor. *Modernity in Asian Art*. Sydney: Wild Peony, 1993.

Clark, John. *Modern Asian Art*. Sydney: Craftsman House, 1998.

Guillermo, Alice. *Image to Meaning: Essays on Philippine Art*. Manila: Ateneo de Manila University Press, 2001.

Holt, Claire. *Art in Indonesia: Continuities and Change*. Ithaca, NY: Cornell University Press, 1967.

Hsu, Marco C.F. *A Brief History of Malayan Art* [1963]. Translated by Lai Chee Kien. Singapore: Millennium Books, 1999.

Nur Hanim Khairuddin and Beverly Yong, with T.K. Sabapathy, editors. *Imagining Identities: Narratives in Malaysian Art Volume 1* and *Reactions: New Critical Strategies. Narratives in Malaysian Art Volume 2*. Kuala Lumpur: RogueArt, 2012 and 2013.

Low Sze Wee, editor. *Between Declarations and Dreams: Art of Southeast Asia Since the 19ᵗʰ Century*. Exhibition catalogue. Singapore: National Gallery Singapore, 2015.

Low Sze Wee, editor. *Siapa Nama Kamu? Art in Singapore Since the 19ᵗʰ Century*. Exhibition catalogue. Singapore: National Gallery Singapore, 2015.

Low Sze Wee and Patrick D. Flores, editors. *Charting Thoughts: Essays on Art in Southeast Asia*. Singapore: National Gallery Singapore, 2017.

Muan, Ingrid. "Citing Angkor: The 'Cambodian Arts' in the Age of Restoration 1918–2000." Unpublished PhD dissertation. Columbia University, New York, USA, 2001.

Poshyananda, Apinan. *Modern Art in Thailand: Nineteenth and Twentieth Centuries*. Singapore: Oxford University Press, 1992.

Quang Phong and Quang Viet. *My Thuat Thu Do Ha Noi The Ky 20 / The Fine Arts of the Capital Hanoi in the 20ᵗʰ Century*. Hanoi: Fine Arts Publishers, 2000.

Ranard, Andrew. *Burmese Painting: A Linear and Lateral History*. Chiang Mai: Silkworm, 2009.

Sabapathy, T.K. *Writing the Modern: Selected Texts on Art and Art History in Singapore, Malaysia and Southeast Asia 1973–2015*. Edited by Ahmad Mashadi, Susie Lingham, Peter Schoppert and Joyce Toh. Singapore: Singapore Art Museum, 2018.

Taylor, Nora A. *Painters in Hanoi: An Ethnography of Vietnamese Art*. Honolulu: University of Hawai'i Press, 2004.

Taylor, Nora A. and Boreth Ly, editors. *Modern and Contemporary Southeast Asian Art: An Anthology*. Ithaca: Cornell Southeast Asia Program Publications, 2013.

Whiteman, Stephen H., Sarena Abdullah, Yvonne Low, and Phoebe Scott, editors. *Ambitious Alignments: New Histories of Southeast Asian Art, 1945–1990*. Sydney and Singapore: Power Publications and National Gallery Singapore, 2018.

SELECTED LIST OF
WORKS CITED

Abdullah, Sarena. "Adaptation of the Post-Impressionist Style in Yong Mun Sen and Tay Hooi Keat's Art Works." In *Proceedings of the Art and Design International Conference (AnDIC 2016)*, edited by Rusmadiah Anwar, Muliyadi Mahamood, D'zul Haimi Md. Zain, Mohamad Kamal Abd Aziz, Oskar Hasdinor Hassan, and Shahriman Zainal Abidin, 51–62. Singapore: Springer, 2018.

Albano, Raymundo. *Raymundo Albano: Texts*. Edited by Patrick D. Flores. Manila: Vargas Museum and Philippine Contemporary Art Network, 2017.

Anderson, Benedict R. O'G. and Ruchira Mendiones, editors and translators. *In the Mirror: Literature and Politics in Siam in the American Era*. Bangkok: Editions Duang Kamol, 1985.

Arbuckle, Heidi. "Performing Emiria Sunassa: Reframing the Female Subject in Post/Colonial Indonesia." Unpublished PhD thesis, University of Melbourne, Australia, 2011.

Aungsoeillustrations.org. https://www.aungsoeillustrations.org/ [Accessed March 2019].

Bal, Mieke. *Quoting Caravaggio: Contemporary Art, Preposterous History*. Chicago and London: University of Chicago Press, 1999.

Berman, Marshall. *All That Is Solid Melts into Air: The Experience of Modernity*. London: Penguin, 1988.

Bhabha, Homi. *The Location of Culture*. London: Routledge, 1994.

Bianpoen, Carla, Farah Wardani, and Wulan Dirgantoro. *Indonesian Women Artists: The Curtain Opens*. Jakarta: Yayasan Senirupa Indonesia, 2007.

Ang Choulean. *People and Earth*. Exhibition catalogue. Phnom Penh: Reyum, 2000.

Bauman, Zygmunt. *Modernity and the Holocaust*. Ithaca, NY: Cornell University Press, 1995.

Berger, Hans Georg. *Monks and the Camera: Buddhist Photography in Laos*. New York and Luang Prabang: Anantha Publishing, 2016.

Bhinyoying, Suchit. *The Drawings: Thawan Duchanee*. 2nd edition. Translated by Ampassa Chanchalor. Bangkok: Thai Art Museum, 2016.

Brereton, Bonnie Pacala and Somroay Yencheuy. *Buddhist Murals of Northeast Thailand: Reflections of the Isan Homeland*. Chiang Mai: Mekong Press, 2010.

Buchanan, Sherry. *Mekong Diaries: Viet Cong Drawings and Stories, 1964–1975*. Chicago, IL: University of Chicago Press, 2008.

Campbell, Siobhan. "Women, Tradition and Art History in Bali." *Southeast of Now: Directions in Contemporary and Modern Art in Asia* 3, No. 1 (March 2019): 77–101.

Capistrano-Baker, Florina H. *Multiple Originals, Original Multiples: 19th Century Images of Philippine Costumes*. Manila: Ayala Foundation, 2004.

Capistrano-Baker, Florina H., with Pieter ter Keurs and Sandra B. Castro. *Embroidered Multiples: 18th–19th Century Philippine Costumes from the National Museum of Ethnology, Leiden, The Netherlands*. Exhibition catalogue. Manila: Royal Netherlands Embassy and Ayala Foundation, 2007.

Carino, Jose Maria A. *Jose Honorato Lozano: Filipinas 1847*. Manila: Ars Mundi, Philippinae, 2002.

Carlson, Melissa. "Painting Through the Cheroot Haze: Censorship of Female Artists in Socialist Burma, 1962-88." In *Ambitious Alignments: New Histories of Southeast Asian Art, 1945–1990*, 291–324. Sydney and Singapore: Power Publications and National Gallery Singapore, 2018.

Chapakdee, Thanom. "The Artist's Front of Thailand." In *Routledge Encyclopedia of Modernism*. Online. DOI: 10.4324/0123456789-REM1888-1. Published 26 April 2018.

Chatterjee, Partha. *Nationalist Thought and the Colonial World: A Derivative Discourse*. London: Zed Books, 1993.

Chikiamco, Clarissa, Russell Storer, and Adele Tan, editors. *A Fact Has No Appearance: Art Beyond the Object*. Exhibition catalogue. Singapore: National Gallery Singapore, 2016.

Ching, Isabel. "Tracing (Un)Certain Legacies: Conceptualism in Singapore and the Philippines." *Asia Art Archive* website, 1 July 2011. https://aaa.org.hk/en/ideas/ideas/tracing-uncertain-legacies-conceptualism-in-singapore-and-the-philippines [Accessed February 2019].

Chua, Kevin. "On Teaching Modern and Contemporary Southeast Asian Art." *Third Text* 25, No. 4 (July 2011): 467–73.

Chua, Kevin. "Courbet After Sudjojono." *Art History* 41, No. 2 (April 2018): 292–317.

Chua Mia Tee. "TributeSG – Chua Mia Tee." *Esplanade – Theatres on the Bay*, 2012. https://www.esplanade.com/tributesg/visual-arts/chua-mia-tee [Accessed July 2018].

Clark, John. *Asian Modernities: Chinese and Thai Art Compared, 1980 to 1999.* Sydney: Power Publications, 2010.

Clark, John. "Negotiating Change in Recent Southeast Asian Art." *Southeast of Now: Directions in Contemporary and Modern Art in Asia* 2, No. 1 (March 2018): 43–92.

Cox, Matt. "The Painting of Prostitutes in Modern Indonesian Art." *Southeast of Now: Directions in Contemporary and Modern Art in Asia* 1, No. 2 (October 2017): 41–63.

Des Photographes en Indochine: Tonkin, Annam, Cochinchine, Cambodge et Laos au XIXe Siecle [Photographers in Indochina: Tonkin, Annam, Cochin China, Cambodia and Laos in the 19th century]. Exhibition catalogue. Paris: Marval: Reunion des Musees Nationaux, 2001.

Diaz, Concha. *Cuaderno de Sofonisba*, 19 July 2018. http://cuadernodesofonisba.blogspot.com /2018/07/pintoras-en-el-prado-in-out-iv.html [Accessed February 2019].

Dirgantoro, Wulan. *Feminisms and Contemporary Art in Indonesia: Defining Experiences.* Amsterdam: Amsterdam University Press, 2017.

Dobbs, Stephen. *The Singapore River: A Social History, 1819–2002.* Singapore: Singapore University Press, 2003.

Dove, Michael. *The Banana Tree at the Gate: A History of Marginal Peoples and Global Markets in Borneo.* Singapore: NUS Press, 2012.

Duong Dinh Chau, editor. *The Art of Diem Phung Thi.* Ho Chi Minh City: Ca Le Thang and Fine Arts Association of Ho Chi Minh City, 2000.

Edwards, Penny. *Cambodge: The Cultivation of a Nation, 1860–1945.* Chiang Mai: Silkworm, 2007.

Eisenstadt, Nicholas N., Jens Riedel and Dominic Sachsenmaier. "The Context of the Multiple Modernities Paradigm." In *Reflections on Multiple Modernities: European, Chinese and Other Interpretations*, edited by Dominic Sachsenmaier and Jens Riedel with Nicholas N. Eisenstadt, 1–23. Leiden, Boston and Köln: Brill, 2002.

Esa, Sulaiman and Redza Piyadasa. "Towards a Mystical Reality" (1974). Reprinted in *Why Are We 'Artists'? 100 World Art Manifestoes*, edited by Jessica Lack, 203–32. UK: Penguin Classics, 2017.

Evans, Grant. *The Politics of Ritual and Remembrance: Laos Since 1975.* Chiang Mai: Silkworm Books, 1998.

Farquhar, William, John Sturgus Bastin, Kwa Chong Guan, Hassan Ibrahim, and Morten Strange. *Natural History Drawings: The Complete William Farquhar Collection: Malay Peninsula, 1803–1818.* Singapore: Editions Didier Millet and National Museum Singapore, 2015.

Flores, Patrick D. *Painting History: Revisions in Philippine Colonial Art.* Quezon City and Manila: Office of Research Coordination, University of the Philippines and National Commission for Culture and the Arts, 1998.

Flores, Patrick D. "Style in Southeast Asia: A Political History." In *Realism in Asia, Volume One*, edited by Yeo Wei Wei, 30–37. Exhibition catalogue. Singapore: The National Art Gallery, Singapore, 2010.

Flores, Patrick D. "Social Realism: The Turns of a Term in the Philippines." *Afterall* 34 (Autumn/Winter 2013): 63–73.

Flores, Patrick D. "First Person Plural: Manifestoes of the 1970s in Southeast Asia." In *Global Studies: Mapping Contemporary Art and Culture*, edited by Hans Belting, Jacob Birken, Andrea Buddensieg and Peter Weibel, 224–71. Ostfildern: Hatje Cantz, 2011.

Flores, Patrick D., editor. *The Life and Art of Botong Francisco*. Quezon City: Vibal Foundation, 2010.

Gerakan Seni Rupa Baru (The Indonesian New Arts Movement). "Manifesto of the Indonesian New Arts Movement" (1975). Reprinted in *Why Are We 'Artists'? 100 World Art Manifestoes*, edited by Jessica Lack, 242–44. UK: Penguin Classics, 2017.

Gleeson, Erin. "Exhibition Histories of Cambodia: Indigenous-Foreign Simultaneity in Tang Tok." Unpublished MA thesis. SOAS, University of London, UK, 2018.

Grabowsky, Volker, Hans Georg Berger, in collaboration with Bounleuth Sengsoulin and Khamvone Boulyaphonh, editors. *The Lao Sangha and Modernity: Research at the Buddhist Archives of Luang Prabang, 2005-2015*. Luang Prabang and New York: Anantha Publishing, 2015.

Greenberg, Clement. "Modernist Painting" (1960–1965). Reprinted in *Art in Theory 1900–1990: An Anthology of Changing Ideas*, edited by Charles Harrison and Paul Wood, 754–59. Oxford, UK and Cambridge, MA: Blackwell, 1999.

Groslier, George. *Cambodian Dancers Ancient and Modern*. Edited by Kent Davis, translated by Pedro Rodríguez. Holmes Beach, FL: DatASIA, 2011.

Groys, Boris. "The Topology of Contemporary Art." In *Antinomies of Art and Culture: Modernity, Postmodernity, Contemporaneity*, edited by Terry Smith, Okwui Enwezor and Nancy Condee, 71–82. Durham: Duke University Press, 2008.

Guillermo, Alice. *Social Realism in the Philippines*. Manila: Asphodel, 1987.

Guise, Lucien de, editor. *Seni Halus Fabrik The Fine Art of Fabrics*. Exhibition catalogue. Kuala Lumpur: Bank Negara Malaysia Museum and Art Gallery, 2014.

Hanh Thi Pham. "Personal Statement." *Lesbian Photography on the U.S. West Coast 1972-1997*. https://www.cla.purdue.edu/waaw/corinne/Pham.htm [Accessed December 2018].

Herbelin, Caroline. "Deux conceptions de l'histoire de l'art en situation coloniale: George Groslier (1887–1945) et Victor Tardieu (1870–1937)." *Siksacakr: The Journal of Cambodia Research* 12-13 (2011): 206–18.

Hererra, Ma. Victoria, Clarissa Chikiamco, Cid Reyes, and Rod Paras-Perez. *The Life and Art of Lee Aguinaldo*. Quezon City: Vibal Foundation, 2011.

Hererra, Ma. Victoria and Clarissa Chikiamco. *Lee Aguinaldo: In Retrospect*. Exhibition catalogue. Quezon City: Ateneo Art Gallery, 2010.

Huynh-Beattie, Boitran. "Saigonese Art During the War: Modernity Versus Ideology." In *Cultures at War: The Cold War and Cultural Expression in Southeast Asia*, edited by Tony Day and Maya H.T. Liem, 81–102. Ithaca, NY: Cornell Southeast Asia Program Publications, 2010.

Ingawanij, May Adadol. "Introduction: Dialectics of Independence." In *Glimpses of Freedom: Independent Cinema in Southeast Asia*, edited by May Adadol Ingawanij and Benjamin McKay, 1-14. Ithaca, NY: Cornell Southeast Asia Program Publications, 2012.

Ingawanij, May Adadol. "Itinerant Cinema Practices in and Around Thailand during the Cold War." *Southeast of Now: Directions in Contemporary and Modern Art in Asia* 2, No. 1 (March 2018): 9-41.

Islamic Arts Magazine. "Photo Exhibition 'The Chulia in Penang.'" *Islamic Arts Magazine* (January-March 2016). http://islamicartsmagazine.com/magazine/view/the_chulia_in_penang/ [Accessed September 2018].

Joseph, Rahel, Nur Hanim Khairuddin, and Flo Simpson, editors. *Love Me in My Batik: Modern Batik Art from Malaysia and Beyond*. Exhibition catalogue. Kuala Lumpur: Ilham, 2016.

Kapur, Geeta. *When Was Modernism. Essays on Contemporary Cultural Practice in India*. New Delhi: Tulika Books, 2007 [2000].

Ker, Yin. "A Short Story of Bagyi Aung Soe in Five Images." *Asia Art Archive* website, 1 December 2013. https://aaa.org.hk/en/ideas/ideas/a-short-story-of-bagyi-aung-soe-in-five-images/type/essays [Accessed October 2018].

Khairuddin, Nur Hanim. "Anak Alam: Behind the Scenes." In *Reactions: New Critical Strategies. Narratives in Malaysian Art Volume 2*, edited by Nur Hanim Khairuddin and Beverly Yong, with T.K. Sabapathy, 24–30. Kuala Lumpur: RogueArt, 2013.

Kiernan, Ben. *Blood and Soil: A World History of Genocide and Extermination from Sparta to Darfur*. New Haven and London: Yale University Press, 2007.

Kraus, Werner. "Raden Saleh's Interpretation of the *Arrest of Diponegro*: An Example of Indonesian 'Proto-nationalist' Modernism." *Archipel* 69 (2005): 259–94.

Kraus, Werner. *Raden Saleh: The Beginning of Modern Indonesian Painting*. Exhibition catalogue. Jakarta: Goethe-Institut Indonesien, 2012.

Kwa Chong Guan. "The 19th-Century 'Origins' of Singapore Art." In *Charting Thoughts: Essays on Art in Southeast Asia*, edited by Low Sze Wee and Patrick D. Flores, 34–43. Singapore: National Gallery Singapore, 2017.

Legaspi-Ramirez, Eileen. "Art on the Back Burner: Gender as the Elephant in the Room of Southeast Asian Art Histories." *Southeast of Now: Directions in Contemporary and Modern Art in Asia* 3, No. 1 (March 2019): 25–48.

Lico, Gerard and Lorelei D.C. de Viana. *Regulating Colonial Spaces (1565–1944): A Collection of Laws, Decrees, Proclamations, Ordinances, Orders and Directives on Architecture and the Built Environment During the Colonial Eras in the Philippines*. Manila: National Commission for Culture and the Arts, 2017.

Liu Kang and Ho Ho Ying. *Re-Connecting. Selected Writings on Singapore Art and Art Criticism*. Edited by T.K. Sabapathy and Cheo Chai-Hiang. Translated by Cheo Chai-Hiang. Singapore: Institute of Contemporary Arts Singapore, 2005.

Loh, Joleen. "Relocating Kim Lim: A Cosmopolitan Perspective." *Southeast of Now: Directions in Contemporary and Modern Art in Asia* 2, no. 2 (October 2018): 33–62.

Loh Kah Seng. *Squatters into Citizens: The 1961 Bukit Ho Swee Fire and the Making of Modern Singapore*. Singapore: Asian Studies Association of Australia, NUS Press and NIAS Press, 2013.

Low Sze Wee, editor. *Chua Ek Kay: After the Rain*. Singapore: National Gallery Singapore, 2015.

Low, Yvonne. "Becoming Professionals: Women Artists in Singapore, Malaya and Indonesia." Unpublished PhD thesis. University of Sydney, Australia, 2015.

Magsaysay-Ho, Anita. *An Artist's Memoirs*. Singapore: Editions Didier Millet, 2000.

"Manifesto Generation Anak Alam" (1974). Translated by Wong Hoy Cheong. In *Reactions: New Critical Strategies. Narratives in Malaysian Art Volume 2*, edited by Nur Hanim Khairuddin and Beverly Yong, with T.K. Sabapathy, 22–23. Kuala Lumpur: RogueArt, 2013.

Masahiro Ushiroshoji and Rawanchaikul Toshiko, editors. *The Birth of Modern Art in Southeast Asia: Artists and Movements*. Exhibition catalogue. Fukuoka: Fukuoka Art Museum, 1997.

Meyer, Richard. *What Was Contemporary Art?* Cambridge, MA and London: MIT Press, 2013.

Myat Kyaw. "Burmese Women, Make Art!" *Pangyi* [Art/Painting] (November 1959): 42–43. Unpublished translation by Htoo Lwin Myo, commissioned by Roger Nelson for "Site and Space in Southeast Asia."

Nakao Tomomichi, Tomiyama Megumi, Kokatsu Reiko, Hara Maiko, editors. *Women In-Between: Asian Women Artists 1984–2012*. Fukuoka, Okinawa, Tochigi and Mie: Fukuoka Asian Art Museum, Okinawa Prefectural Museum & Art Museum, Tochigi Prefectural Museum of Fine Arts, and Mie Prefectural Art Museum Assistance Foundation, 2012.

Nelson, Roger. "Modernity and Contemporaneity in 'Cambodian Arts' After Independence." Unpublished PhD thesis. University of Melbourne, Australia, 2017.

Nelson, Roger. "'The Work the Nation Depends On': Landscapes and Women in the Paintings of Nhek Dim.'" In *Ambitious Alignments*, 19–48.

Norindr, Panivong. *Phantasmatic Indochina: French Colonial Ideology in Architecture, Film, and Literature.* Durham and London: Duke University Press, 1996.

Oei Hong Djien and Edi Sunaryo. *Celebrating Indonesian Portraiture.* Exhibition catalogue. Translated by Hellen Lewis. Magelang, Indonesia: OHD Museum, 2018.

Okeke-Agulu, Chika. *Postcolonial Modernism: Art and Decolonization in Twentieth-Century Nigeria.* Durham and London: Duke University Press, 2015.

Osborne, Peter. *Anywhere or Not at All: Philosophy of Contemporary Art.* London and New York: Verso, 2013.

Paras-Perez, Rod. *Manansala Nudes.* Manila: Eugenio Lopez Foundation, 1990.

Pham Thanh Tam. *Drawing Under Fire: War Diary of a Young Vietnamese Artist.* Edited by Sherry Buchanan. Translated by Nguyen Van Ha. London: Asia Ink, 2005.

Pollock, Griselda. *Differencing the Canon: Feminist Desire and the Writing of Art's Histories.* London and New York: Routledge, 1999.

Pollock, Griselda. *Vision and Difference: Feminism, Femininity and the Histories of Art.* London and New York: Routledge, 2003 [1988].

Rabinow, Paul. *French Modern: Norms and Forms of the Social Environment.* Chicago and London: University of Chicago Press, 1995 [1989].

Rhodes, Colin. *Outsider Art: Spontaneous Alternatives.* London: Thames & Hudson, 2000.

Rizal, Jose. *Noli Me Tangere.* Translated by Harold Augenbraum. New York: Penguin Books, 2006 [1887].

Ross, Helen Grant and Darryl Leon Collins. *Building Cambodia: 'New Khmer Architecture' 1953–1970.* Bangkok: Key Publisher, 2006.

Sabapathy, T.K. "Intersecting Histories: Thoughts on Contemporary Art and History in Southeast Asia." In *Intersecting Histories: Contemporary Turns in Southeast Asian Art*, edited by T.K. Sabapathy, 36–82. Exhibition catalogue. Singapore: School of Art, Design and Media, Nanyang Technological University, 2012.

Sabapathy, T.K., editor. *Semsar Siahaan: Art, Liberation.* Exhibition catalogue. Singapore: Gajah Gallery, 2017.

Sabapathy, T.K. and Cecily Briggs. *Cheo Chai-Hiang: The Thirty-Six Strategies.* Exhibition catalogue. Casula, Australia: Casula Powerhouse Arts Centre, 2000.

Santiago, Luciano P.R. *The Life, Art, and Times of Damian Domingo.* Quezon City: Vibal Foundation, 2010.

Scalliet, Marie Odette, Koos van Brakel, David van Duuren, and Jeannette ten Kate. *Pictures from the Tropics: Paintings by Western Artists During the Dutch Colonial Period in Indonesia.* Translated by Karin Beks. Exhibition catalogue. Wijk en Aalburg and Amsterdam: Pictures Publishers and Royal Tropical Institute, 1999.

Scott, Phoebe. "Forming and Reforming the Artist: Modernity, Agency, and the Discourse of Art in North Vietnam, 1925–1954." Unpublished PhD thesis. University of Sydney, Australia, 2012.

Seng Yu Jin. "Embracing the Everyday." In *Cheong Soo Pieng: Visions of Southeast Asia*, edited by Yeo Wei Wei, 52–75. Exhibition catalogue. Singapore: The National Art Gallery, 2010.

Seng Yu Jin. "The Primacy of Painting: Institutional Structures in the Singapore Art World, 1935–1972." Unpublished MA thesis. National University of Singapore, Singapore, 2006.

Seng Yu Jin. "The Age of Art Manifestos: The Inter-discursive Struggle Between the 'New' & the 'Real.'" Paper presented at "Intersections of the Literary and Artistic Worlds in Myanmar and the Region in the 20th Century." Symposium convened by Yin Ker. School of Art, Design and Media, Nanyang Technological University, Singapore, 17 November 2017.

Shabbir Hussain Mustafa. "Pago Pago, Conversations with Latiff Mohidin." In *Latiff Mohidin: Pago Pago (1960–1969)*, edited by Shabbir Hussain Mustafa and Catherine David, 14–63. Exhibition catalogue. Singapore: National Gallery Singapore, 2018.

Siburapha. *Behind the Painting and Other Stories*. Translated by David Smyth. Chiang Mai: Silkworm Books, 2000.

Sidharta, Amir. "Indonesian Views of Raden Saleh." In *Between Worlds: Raden Saleh and Juan Luna*, edited by Russell Storer, 54–65. Exhibition catalogue. Singapore: National Gallery Singapore, 2017.

Singhalampong, Eksuda. "Picturing Femininity: Portraits of the Early Modern Siamese Women." *Southeast of Now: Directions in Contemporary and Modern Art in Asia* 3, No. 1 (March 2019): 49–75.

Siregar, Aminudin T.H. "Sentencing and Capturing: Appropriation and Parody in the Paintings of Heri Dono and Semsar Siahaan." In *Intersecting Histories: Contemporary Turns in Southeast Asian Art*, edited by T.K. Sabapathy, 130–43. Exhibition catalogue. Singapore: School of Art, Design and Media, Nanyang Technological University, 2012.

Smith, Terry. *What Is Contemporary Art?* Chicago: University of Chicago Press, 2009.

Smith, Terry. "The State of Art History: Contemporary Art." *Art Bulletin* 92, no. 4 (December 2010): 366–83.

Soon, Simon. "Fabric and the Fabrication of a Queer Narrative: The Batik Paintings of Patrick Ng Kah Onn." *Intersections: Gender and Sexuality in Asia and the Pacific* 38 (August 2015). http://intersections.anu.edu.au/issue38/soon.html [Accessed June 2018].

Soon, Simon. "What is Left of Art? The Spatio-Visual Practice of Political Art in Indonesia, Singapore, Thailand, and the Philippines, 1950s–1970s." Unpublished PhD thesis. University of Sydney, 2015.

Sriwanichpoom, Manit. *Rediscovering Forgotten Thai Masters of Photography*. Translated by Ing K. and Pinida Kongsiri. Bangkok: Kathmandu Photo Gallery, 2015.

Suon Sorin. *A New Sun Rises Over the Old Land: A Novel of Sihanouk's Cambodia*. Translated by Roger Nelson. Introduction by Roger Nelson. Singapore: NUS Press, 2019. Forthcoming.

Tajudeen, Imran bin. "Mosques and Minarets: Transregional Connections in Eighteenth-Century Southeast Asia." *Journal18*, No. 4 (Fall 2017). http://www.journal18.org/2056 [Accessed January 2019].

Tang Chang: Abstract Paintings – Concrete Poetry. Exhibition catalogue. Bangkok: g23 Srinahkarinwirot University, 2013.

Taylor, Nora A. "Framing the National Spirit: Viewing and Reviewing Painting under the Revolution." In *Country of Memory: Remaking the Past in Late Socialist Vietnam*, edited by Hue-Tam Ho Tai, 109–34. Berkeley and Los Angeles, CA and London: University of California Press, 2001.

Taylor, Nora A. "Introduction: Who Speaks for Southeast Asian Art?" In *Modern and Contemporary Southeast Asian Art: An Anthology*, edited by Nora A. Taylor and Boreth Ly, 1–13. Ithaca, NY: Cornell Southeast Asia Program Publications, 2012.

Taylor, Nora A. *Post-War Vietnamese Art. Albert I. Goodman Collection*. Exhibition catalogue. Chicago: John David Mooney Foundation, 2016.

Tazzi, Pier Luigi. *Trance-Formations: Nim Kruasaeng*. Exhibition catalogue. Bangkok: Ver Gallery, 2007.

Teh, David, editor. *"Misfits": Pages from a Loose-leaf Modernity. Rox Lee, Tang Chang and Bagyi Aung Soe*. Exhibition catalogue. Berlin: Haus der Kulturen der Welt, 2017.

Teh, David. *Thai Art: Currencies of the Contemporary*. Singapore: NUS Press, 2017.

Thangchalok, Ithipol. "An Analysis of the Paintings of Ithipol." Translated by R. Michael Crabtree. In *Abstract: The Truth of Art*, exhibition catalogue, edited by Bangkok Art and Culture Centre and Toeingam Guptabutra, 128–34. Bangkok: Bangkok Art and Culture Centre Foundation, 2015.

Thangchalok, Ithipol. "The Evolution of a Primal Spirit." Translated by Den Wasikiri. In *Abstract: The Truth of Art*, 143–57.

The Artists' Front of Thailand. "Manifesto of the Artists' Front of Thailand" (1975). Translated by Kritsana Canilao. Reprinted in *Why Are We "Artists"? 100 World Art Manifestoes*, edited by Jessica Lack, 239–41. UK: Penguin Classics, 2017.

Thompson, Ashley. *Engendering the Buddhist State: Territory, Sovereignty and Sexual Difference in the Inventions of Angkor*. London and New York: Routledge, 2016.

Thun, Theara. "*Bangsāvatār*: The Evolution of Historiographical Genres in Colonial Cambodia." Unpublished PhD thesis, National University of Singapore, 2017.

Tiffin, Sarah. *Southeast Asia in Ruins: Art and Empire in the Early 19th Century*. Singapore: NUS Press, 2016.

Toer, Pramoedya Ananta. *This Earth of Mankind: A Novel*. Translated by Max Lane. Ringwood, Vic: Harmondsworth: Penguin, 1982.

Tse, Nicole and Robyn Sloggett. "Southeast Asian Oil Paintings: Supports and Preparatory Layers." In *Preparation for Painting: The Artist's Choice and its Consequence*, 161–70. London: Archetype Books, 2008.

Vann Nath. *A Cambodian Prison Portrait: One Year in the Khmer Rouge's S-21*. Translated by Moeun Chhean Nariddh. Bangkok: White Lotus, 1998.

Veal, Clare. "Thainess Framed: Photography and Thai Identity, 1946–2010." Unpublished PhD thesis. University of Sydney, Australia, 2016.

Vickers, Adrian. *Balinese Art: Paintings and Drawings of Bali, 1800–2010*. Tokyo, Rutland, VT, and Singapore: Tuttle, 2011.

Wanlayangkun, Wat (Wirawat). "Before Reaching the Stars" [1975]. In *In the Mirror: Literature and Politics in Siam in the American Era*. Edited and translated by Benedict R. O'G. Anderson and Ruchira Mendiones, 155–66. Bangkok: Editions Duang Kamol, 1985.

Williams, Raymond. *Keywords: A Vocabulary of Culture and Society*. London: Fontana, 1988 [1976].

Winking, Kerstin. "Fighting Colonial Claims to Power: Agus Djaya and Otto Djaya in Amsterdam 1947-1950." Part of the exhibition, *The Djaya Brothers: Revolusi in the Stedelijk*, 9 June to 2 September 2018. Amsterdam: Stedelijk Museum. https://www.stedelijk.nl/en/digdeeper/fighting-colonial-claims-power#slideshow-42926 [Accessed January 2019].

Woodhouse, Leslie. "Concubines with Cameras: Royal Siamese Consorts Picturing Femininity and Ethnic Difference in Early 20th Century Siam." *Trans Asia Photography Review* 2, No. 2 (Spring 2012). http://hdl.handle.net/2027/spo.7977573.0002.202 [Accessed February 2019].

Wright, Astri. *Soul, Spirit, and Mountain: Preoccupations of Contemporary Indonesian Painters*. Kuala Lumpur: Oxford University Press, 1994.

Wright, Astri. "Self-Taught Against the Grain: Three Artists and a Writer." In *Women Imaging Women: Home, Body, Memory. Papers from the Conference on Artists from Indonesia, Philippines, Thailand and Vietnam*, edited by Flaudette May V. Datuin and Patrick D. Flores, 118–54. Manila: Ford Foundation, Art Studies Foundation, Cultural Center of the Philippines, 1999.

Wright, Astri. "Lucia Hartini, Javanese Painter: Against the Grain, Towards Herself." In *Studies in Southeast Asian Art: Essays in Honor of Stanley J. O'Connor*, edited by Nora A. Taylor, 93–121. Ithaca, NY: Cornell Southeast Asia Program, 2000.

Yap, Arthur. *The Collected Poems of Arthur Yap*. Singapore: NUS Press, 2013.

Yeo Wei Wei. "Editor's Note." In *Realism in Asia, Volume One*, 6–9.

Yoon, Prabda. *The Sad Part Was*. Translated by Mui Poopoksakul. London: Tilted Axis Press, 2017.

Zain, Ismail. "Towards an Utopian Paradigm: A Matter of Contingencies and Displacement." Originally published 1989. In *Reactions: New Critical Strategies. Narratives in Malaysian Art Volume 2*, edited by Nur Hanim Khairuddin and Beverly Yong, with T.K. Sabapathy, 136–45. Kuala Lumpur: RogueArt, 2013.

In this book, the author and editor have tried to strike a balance between ease of readability and respect for established norms. To assist the reader, places are referred to by their present-day names. This includes references to places of birth and death in the biographical data provided for each artist mentioned in the text.

Artists' and others' names are given using the most commonly used roman spellings. In the case where multiple spellings of a name exist, the most current and prevalent spelling is used. This means, for example, that some Indonesian names are spelled using the older, Dutch-derived Van Ophuijsen spelling system, while others are spelled using the more recent Republican spelling system.

The presentation of surnames and given names also follows the usual convention in each language. For example, artists with Cambodian and Thai names are referred to by their given names, while those with Chinese and Philippine names are referred to using their family names. Subsequent references also follow the norm for each case. Throughout, accents and diacritical marks have been omitted, in words and names, from both Asian and European languages.

<u>**IMAGE CREDITS**</u>   Page

8	© Thip Sae-tang.
10	© Asian Civilisations Museum.
11, top	© Fukuoka Asian Art Museum.
11, bottom	Courtesy of ILHAM Gallery.
13	Courtesy of National Heritage Board.
14, bottom	© Tow Eng.
16	Photo by Lee Chee Kheong, Heritage Conservation Centre.
17	© Affandi Foundation.
32	*Shumawa* Vol. 27, No. 321. BAS1853, from aungsoeillustrations.org, used under CC BY-NC-ND 4.0.
33, top	Courtesy of Penang State Art Gallery.
36, left	© Estate of Roberto Chabet; photo by Natasha Harth, QAGOMA.
43	Courtesy of the artist; photo by Lincoln Mulcahy.
44, top	Courtesy of the artist and Gallery Ver.
45, bottom	Courtesy of the artist, photo by Paul Litherland.
50, top	© Nguyen Thi Nguyet Tu.
55	© 2010 Christie's Image Limited.
72	Courtesy of Quang Viet.
78	Courtesy of the Bureau of the Royal Household, Kingdom of Thailand, 2003–2015.
83	Courtesy of Ateneo Art Gallery; photo by Cocoy Sarmenta.
91, bottom	© Phiny Ung and family.
92	Courtesy of the National Archives of Malaysia, 2001/0025919.
96	Photo by San Phalla, 2005.
101, bottom	Photo from https://www.flickr.com/photos/bjacques/110656271/in/album-72057594082747296/, used under CC BY-NC-SA 2.0.
107, middle	Photo by Frederic C. Benson (detail), 1969.
107, bottom	© Moongift Films; courtesy of Moongift Films.
110	© Asia Ink 2005.
115	Photo (TM-60019291) from https://hdl.handle.net/20.500.11840/24843, used under CC BY-SA 4.0.
120, top	Photo from https://commons.wikimedia.org/wiki/File:Bas-reliefs_du_Bayon_(Angkor)_(6912582597).jpg, used under CC BY 2.0.
122, top	Courtesy of Singapore Art Museum.
122, bottom	© Abdullah Ariff Family, Kuala Lumpur.
126, top to bottom	Courtesy of Para Site, Hong Kong; photo by Eddie Lam, Image Art Studio.
134, left	Courtesy of family of Ho Kian-Ngiap.
134, right	© Asian Civilisations Museum.
157, bottom	Courtesy of the artist and Tyler Rollins Fine Art, New York.
160	Photo (TM-A-5752) from https://hdl.handle.net/20.500.11840/193289, used under CC BY-SA 4.0.
166	© The Trustees of the British Museum.
167	© The Trustees of the British Museum.
176	© Bonnie Brereton.
177, top	© Roger Nelson, 2017.
177, bottom	Courtesy of the late Andrew Ranard.
182	© S. Sudjojono Center.
183, top left	Courtesy of the Division of Anthropology, American Museum of Natural History, 70.3/4189.
188	© British Library Board WD 957 f.1 (82).

189, bottom   © S. Sudjojono Center.

192   © Lee Boon Wang.

196, second from top   Courtesy of the Dogma Collection.

206   © S. Sudjojono Center.

207   Courtesy of the Estate of Kim Lim.

209, top   Courtesy of the Frick Collection/Frick Art References Library Archives, photo by Edouard Fiorillo.

209, middle   Courtesy of Professor Ambeth Ocampo.

210   Courtesy of the artist and Tyler Rollins Fine Art, New York.

213, right   Photo from https://digitalcollections.universiteitleiden.nl/view/item/230808, used under CC BY 4.0.

215, bottom   © Vuth Lyno and family. Photo from *Free World* (United States: United States Information Service, 1961).

216, top   © MNAAG, Paris, Dist. RMN-Grand Palais/image musée Guimet.

218, left   © Lim Chwen.

229, middle   © Wu Peng Seng family.

231, top   © Anida Yoeu Ali.

231, bottom   Courtesy of Sharman Minus.

238   © Wei Leng Tay, 2018.

247   Photo by Anders Jiras.

249   © Asian Civilisations Museum.

250, bottom   Photo from Philip C. Coote, *Peeps at Many Lands: The Malay States* (London: A&C Black Publishers, 1923), used with permission from Bloomsbury Publishing Plc.

252   © Photographic Archive Museo Nacional del Prado.

265   © Family of Patrick Ng.

266   © Jeanette Bolton-Martin, 2018.

267   © Erika Tan, 2017.

Published 2019

Please direct all enquiries to the publisher at:
National Gallery Singapore
1 St Andrew's Road, #01-01
Singapore 178957

Author: Roger Nelson
Editorial Advisors: Phoebe Scott, Seng Yu Jin
Managing Editor: Elaine Ee
Project Editors: Sara Siew, Ryan How
Designers: Theseus Chan (WORK Pte Ltd), Seet Ming Li (WORK Pte Ltd)

With kind assistance from: Renee Staal, Genevieve Ng

National Library Board, Singapore Cataloguing in Publication Data
Name: Nelson, Roger Edward, 1982-
Title: Modern art of Southeast Asia : introductions from A to Z / by Roger Nelson.
Description: Singapore : National Gallery Singapore, [2019] | Includes bibliographical references.
Identifier(s): OCN 1104150031 | ISBN 978-981-11-4725-8 (paperback)
Subject(s): LCSH: Art, Southeast Asian. | Art, Modern--20th century. | Art--Southeast Asia.
Classification: DDC 709.59--dc23